Thanks for picking up volume 32! The final act
has begun. The series has gone on for longer
than I anticipated. To that point, I'm trying to
make the final act good enough that people
think, "I'm glad I stuck it out and kept reading."
I mean, here's hoping!

KOHEI HORIKOSHI

MY HERO ACADEMIA

32

SHONEN JUMP Edition

STORY & ART **KOHEI HORIKOSHI**

TRANSLATION & ENGLISH ADAPTATION **Caleb Cook**
TOUCH-UP ART & LETTERING **John Hunt**
DESIGNER **Julian [JR] Robinson**
SHONEN JUMP SERIES EDITOR **Rae First**
GRAPHIC NOVEL EDITOR **Mike Montesa**

Printed in the U.S.A.

Published by VIZ Media, LLC
P.O. Box 77010
San Francisco, CA 94107

10 9 8 7 6 5 4 3 2 1
First printing, October 2022

PARENTAL ADVISORY
MY HERO ACADEMIA is rated T for Teen
and is recommended for ages 13 and up.
This volume contains fantasy violence.

MY HERO ACADEMIA vol.32

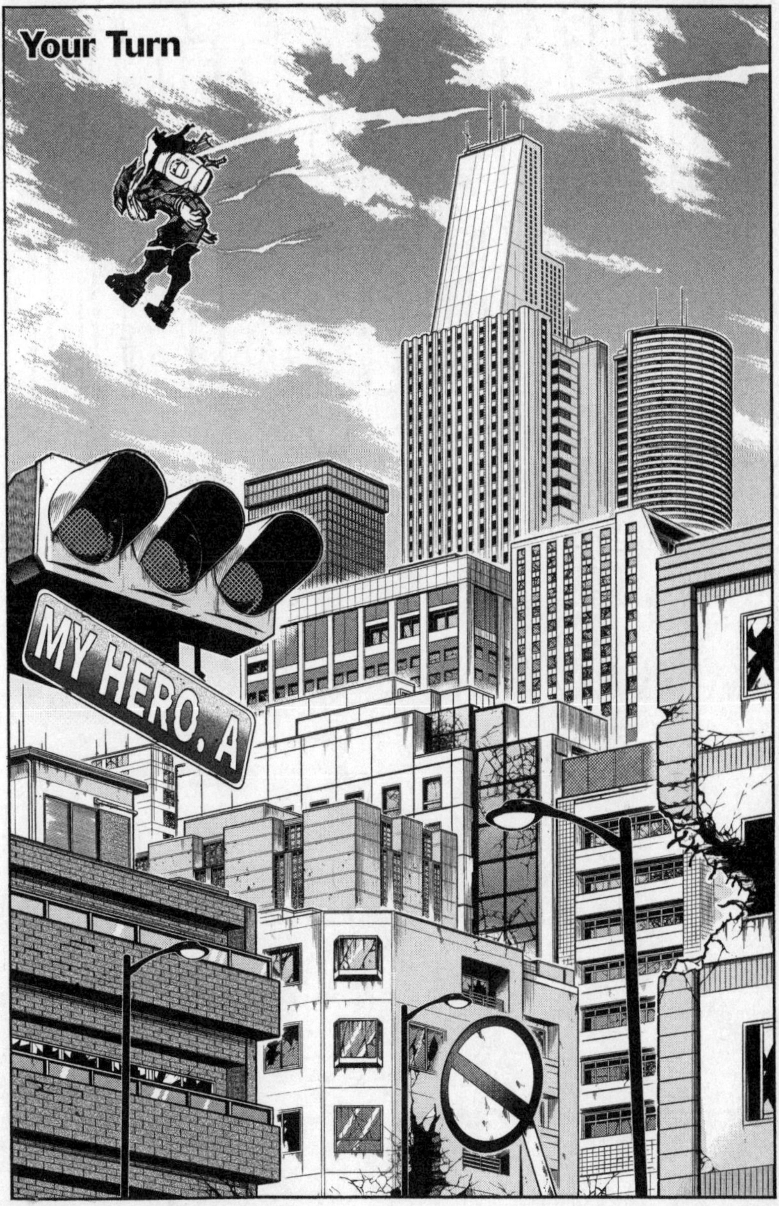
Your Turn
MY HERO. A

KOHEI HORIKOSHI

CHARACTERS

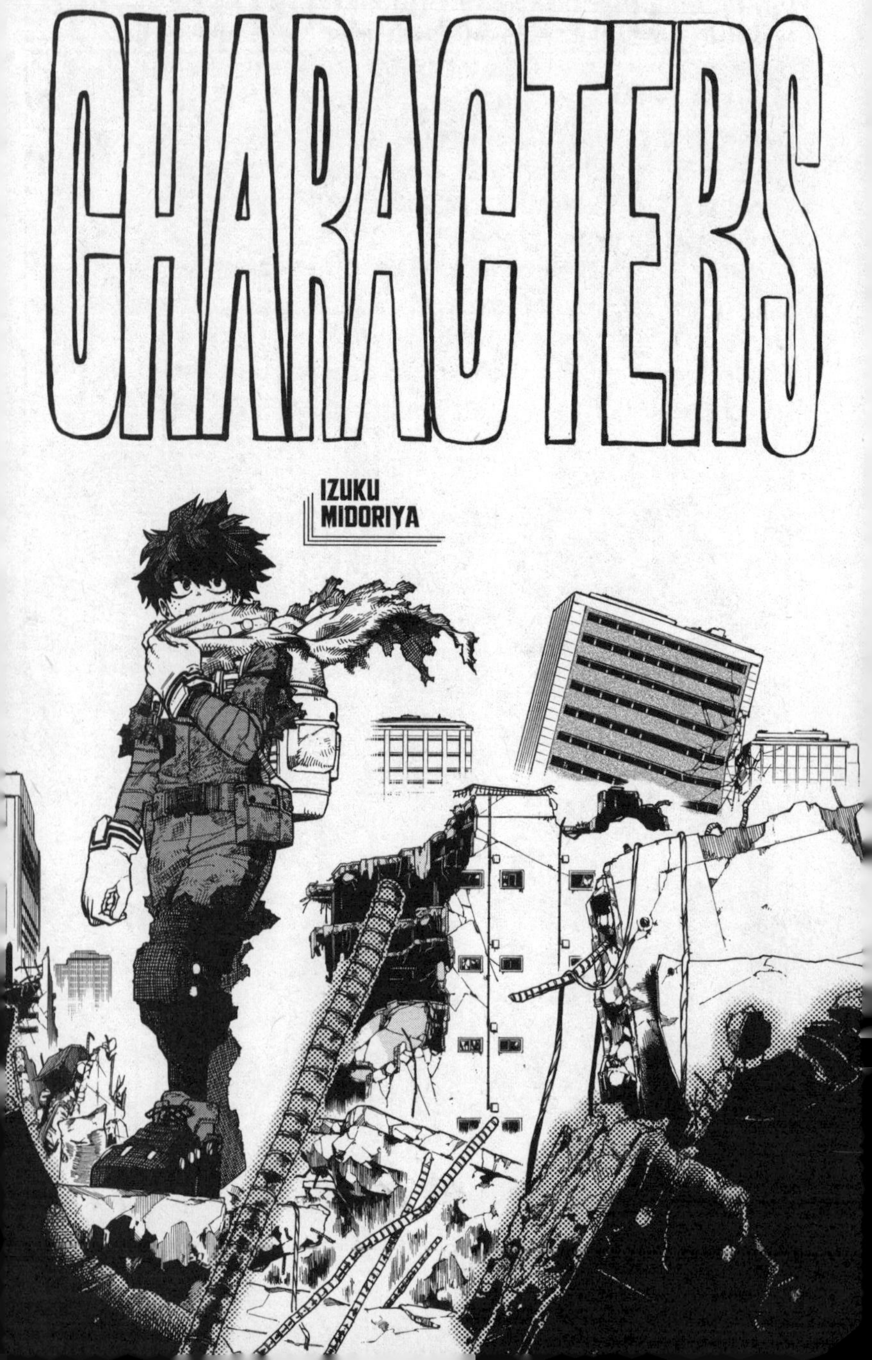
IZUKU MIDORIYA

One day, people began manifesting special abilities that came to be known as "Quirks," and before long, the world was full of superpowered humans. But with the advent of these exceptional individuals came an increase in crime, and governments alone were unable to deal with the situation. At the same time, others emerged to oppose the spread of evil! As if straight from the comic books, these heroes keep the peace and are even officially authorized to fight crime. Our story begins when a certain Quirkless boy and lifelong hero fan meets the world's number one hero, starting him on his path to becoming the greatest hero ever!

STORY

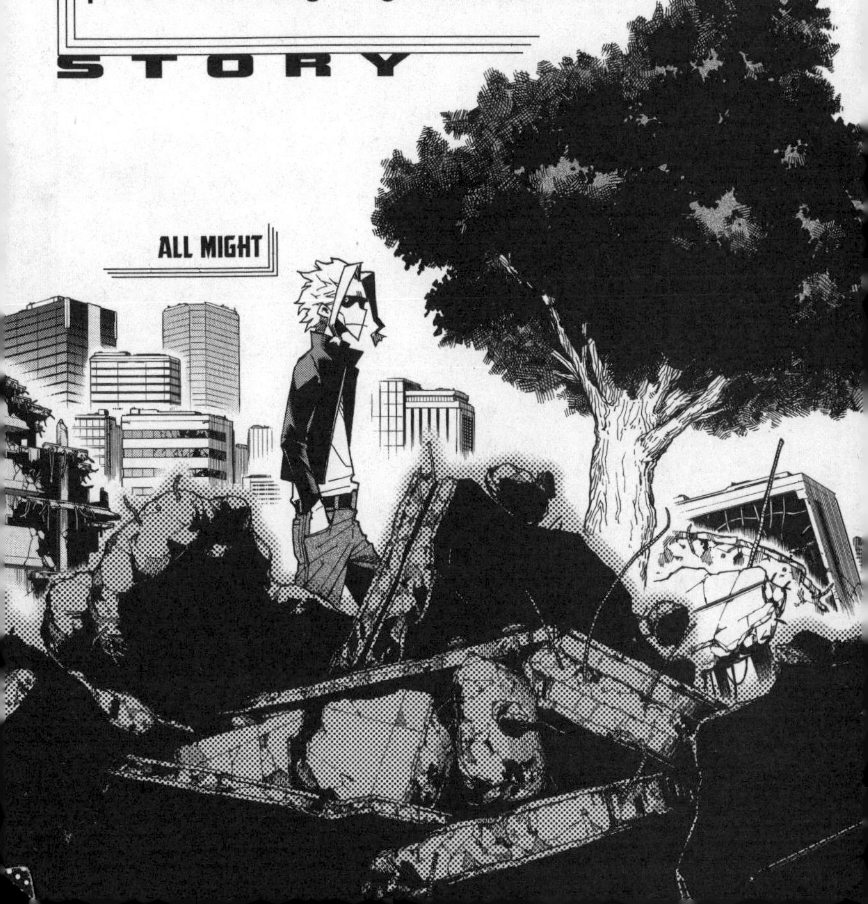
ALL MIGHT

Vol. 32
Your Turn

MY HERO ACADEMIA

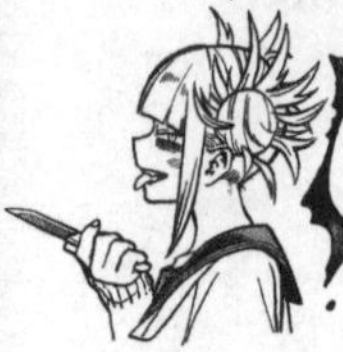

CONTENTS

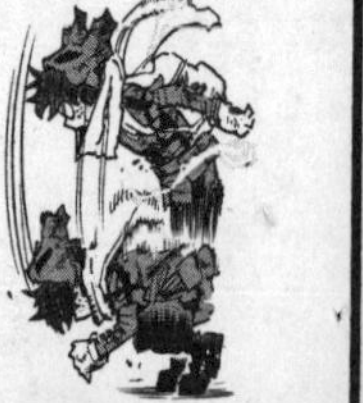

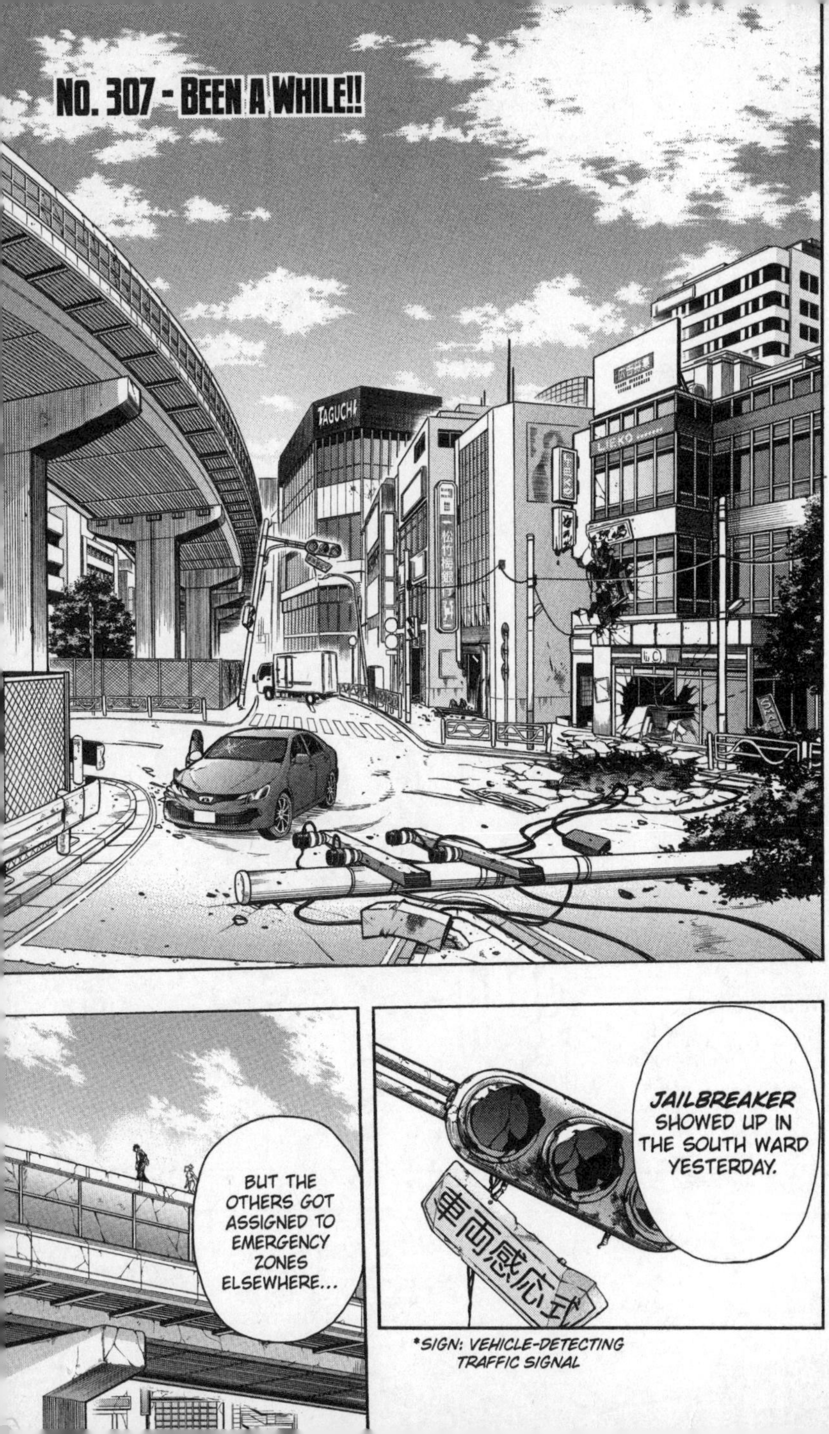
NO. 307 - BEEN A WHILE!!
TAGUCHI
JAILBREAKER SHOWED UP IN THE SOUTH WARD YESTERDAY.
車両感応式
BUT THE OTHERS GOT ASSIGNED TO EMERGENCY ZONES ELSEWHERE...

*SIGN: VEHICLE-DETECTING TRAFFIC SIGNAL

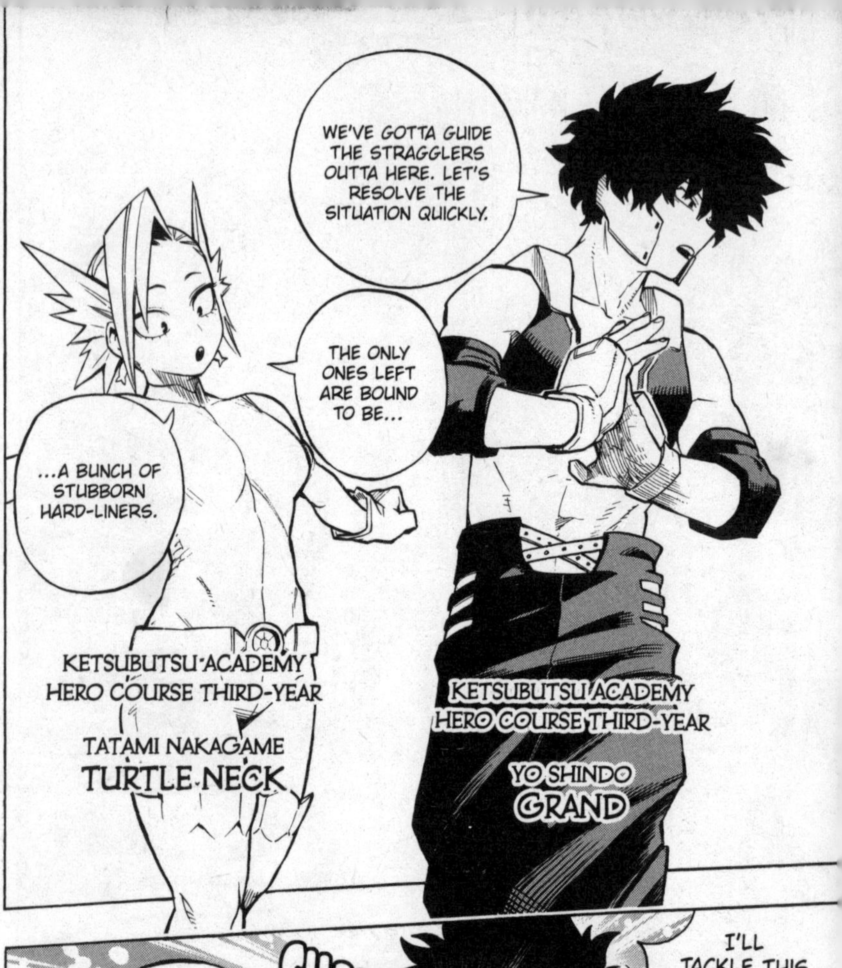
WE'VE GOTTA GUIDE THE STRAGGLERS OUTTA HERE. LET'S RESOLVE THE SITUATION QUICKLY.
THE ONLY ONES LEFT ARE BOUND TO BE...
...A BUNCH OF STUBBORN HARD-LINERS.
KETSUBUTSU ACADEMY HERO COURSE THIRD-YEAR
YO SHINDO
GRAND
KETSUBUTSU ACADEMY HERO COURSE THIRD-YEAR
TATAMI NAKAGAME
TURTLE NECK
I'LL TACKLE THIS NEGOTIATION WITH A CHARMING SMILE, JUST LIKE JOKE SENSEI WOULD!
SHAH
THIS IS... GONNA SUCK.

*THESE TWO DEBUTED IN VOLUME 12! BAKUGO REFUSED TO SHAKE YO'S HAND.

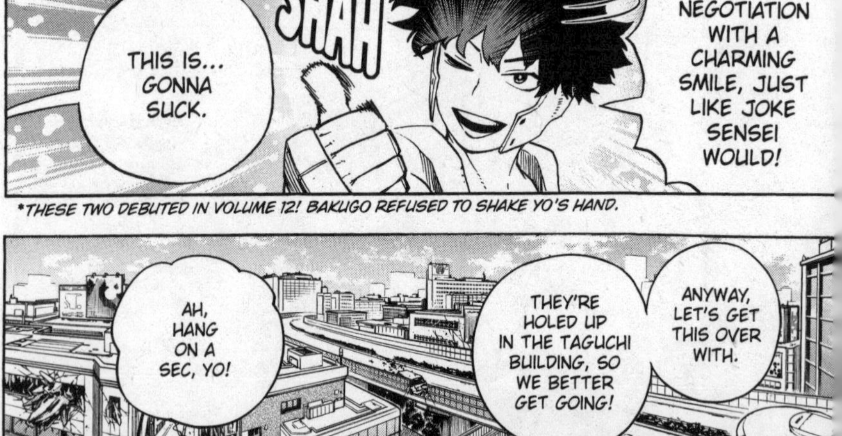
ANYWAY, LET'S GET THIS OVER WITH.
THEY'RE HOLED UP IN THE TAGUCHI BUILDING, SO WE BETTER GET GOING!
AH, HANG ON A SEC, YO!

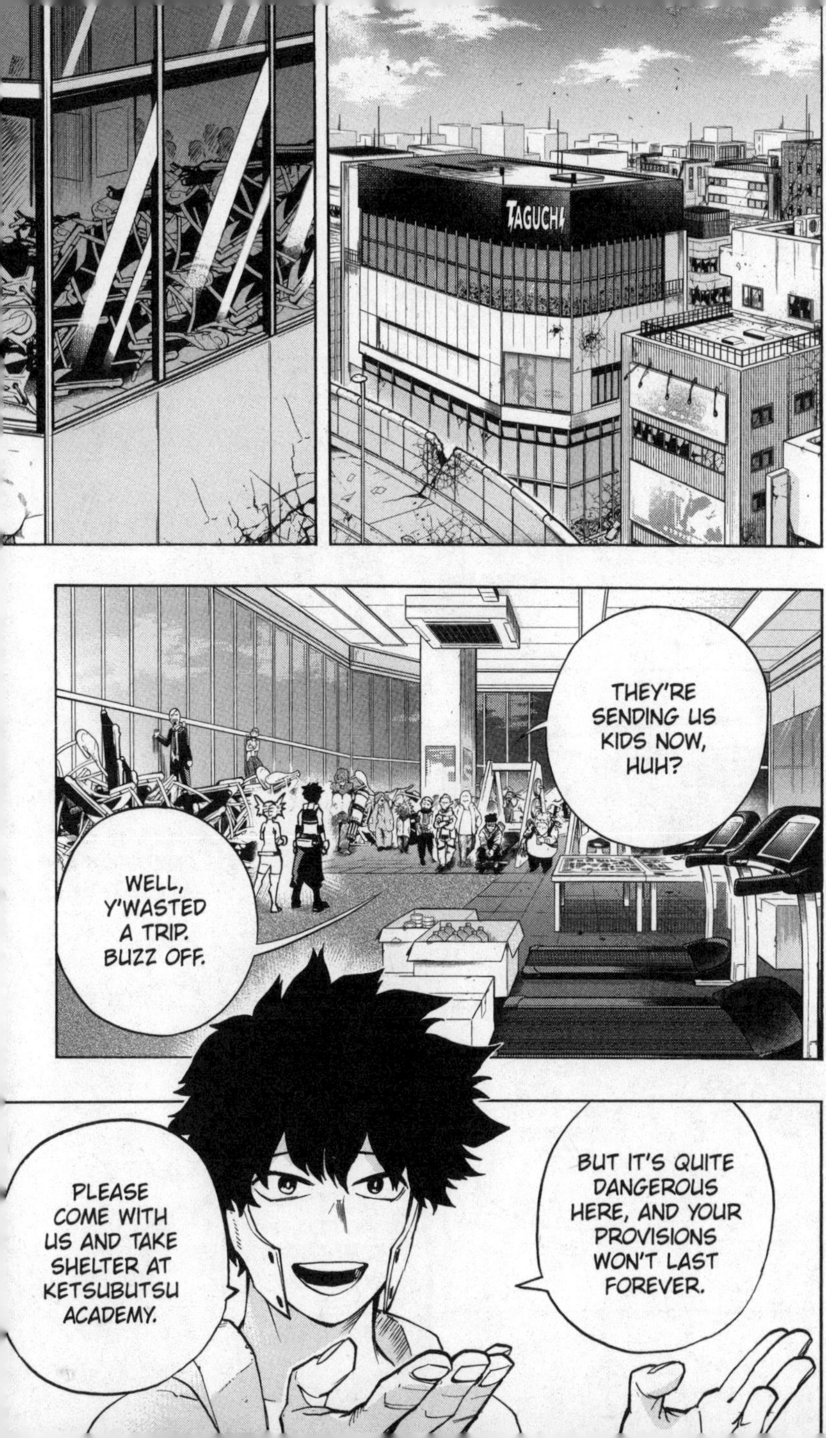
TAGUCHI
THEY'RE SENDING US KIDS NOW, HUH?
WELL, Y'WASTED A TRIP. BUZZ OFF.
BUT IT'S QUITE DANGEROUS HERE, AND YOUR PROVISIONS WON'T LAST FOREVER.
PLEASE COME WITH US AND TAKE SHELTER AT KETSUBUTSU ACADEMY.

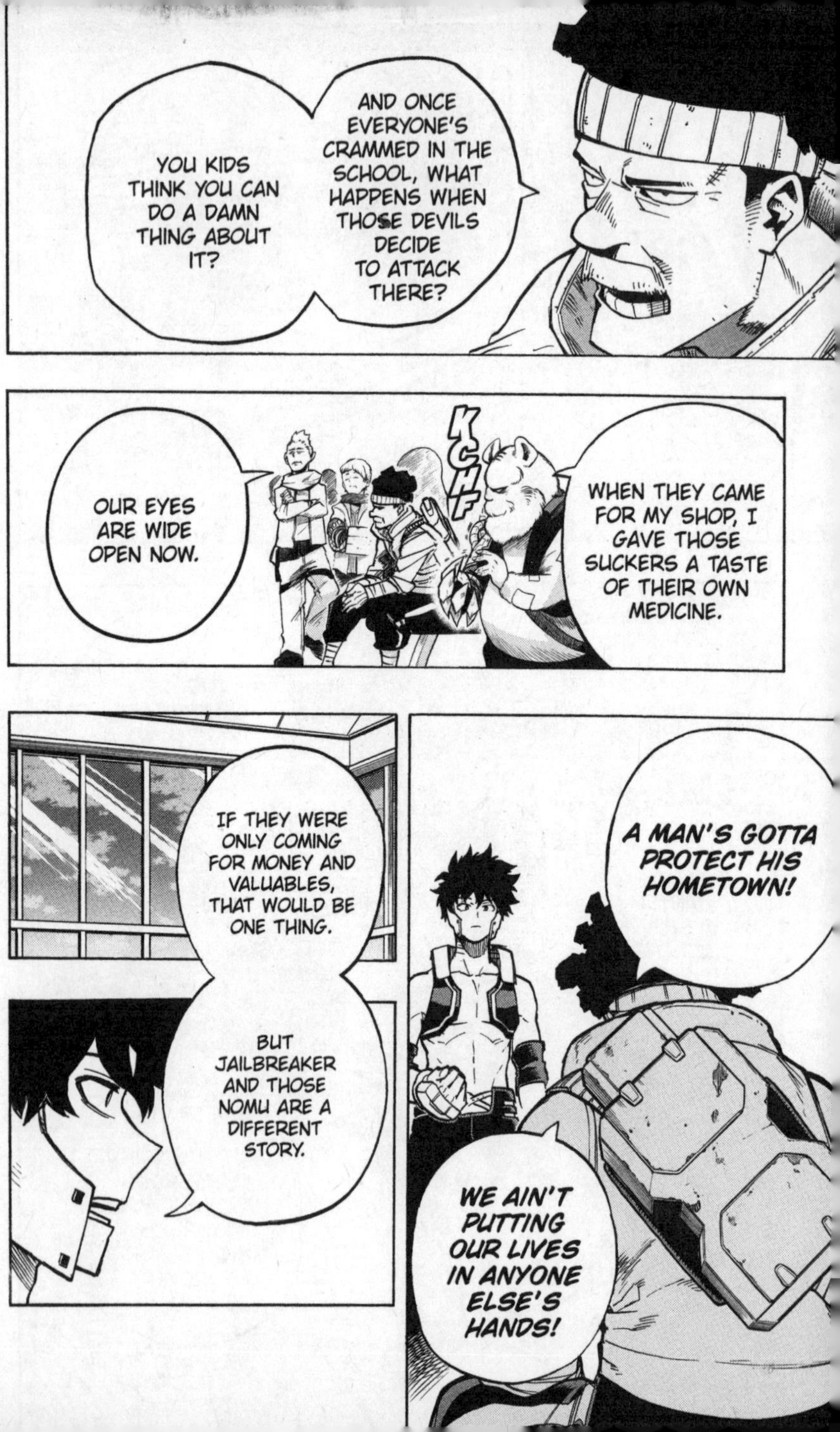
AND ONCE EVERYONE'S CRAMMED IN THE SCHOOL, WHAT HAPPENS WHEN THOSE DEVILS DECIDE TO ATTACK THERE?
YOU KIDS THINK YOU CAN DO A DAMN THING ABOUT IT?
KCHF
WHEN THEY CAME FOR MY SHOP, I GAVE THOSE SUCKERS A TASTE OF THEIR OWN MEDICINE.
OUR EYES ARE WIDE OPEN NOW.
A MAN'S GOTTA PROTECT HIS HOMETOWN!
WE AIN'T PUTTING OUR LIVES IN ANYONE ELSE'S HANDS!
IF THEY WERE ONLY COMING FOR MONEY AND VALUABLES, THAT WOULD BE ONE THING.
BUT JAILBREAKER AND THOSE NOMU ARE A DIFFERENT STORY.

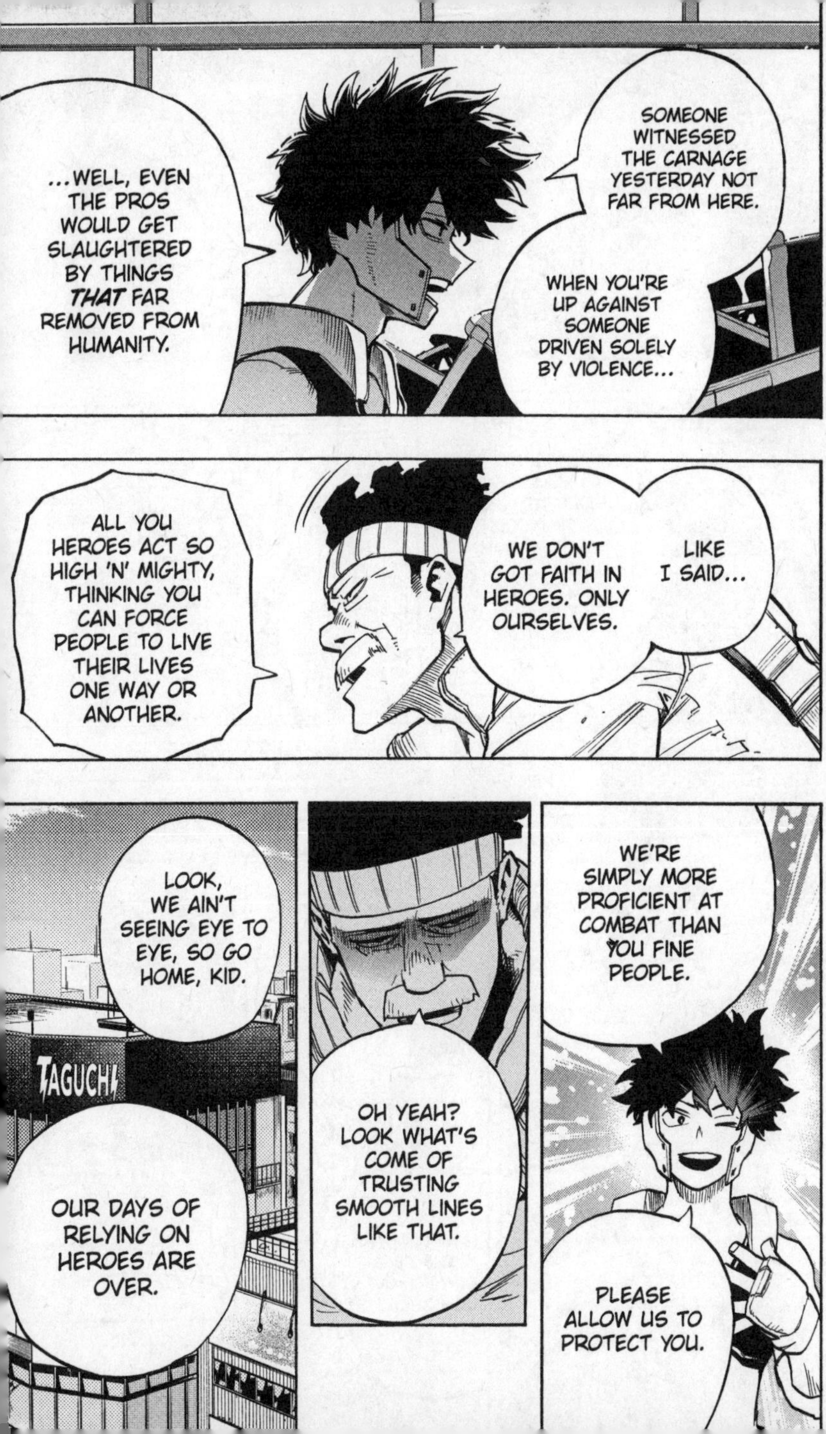
SOMEONE WITNESSED THE CARNAGE YESTERDAY NOT FAR FROM HERE.
WHEN YOU'RE UP AGAINST SOMEONE DRIVEN SOLELY BY VIOLENCE...
...WELL, EVEN THE PROS WOULD GET SLAUGHTERED BY THINGS *THAT* FAR REMOVED FROM HUMANITY.
LIKE I SAID...
WE DON'T GOT FAITH IN HEROES. ONLY OURSELVES.
ALL YOU HEROES ACT SO HIGH 'N' MIGHTY, THINKING YOU CAN FORCE PEOPLE TO LIVE THEIR LIVES ONE WAY OR ANOTHER.
WE'RE SIMPLY MORE PROFICIENT AT COMBAT THAN YOU FINE PEOPLE.
PLEASE ALLOW US TO PROTECT YOU.
OH YEAH? LOOK WHAT'S COME OF TRUSTING SMOOTH LINES LIKE THAT.
LOOK, WE AIN'T SEEING EYE TO EYE, SO GO HOME, KID.
TAGUCHI
OUR DAYS OF RELYING ON HEROES ARE OVER.

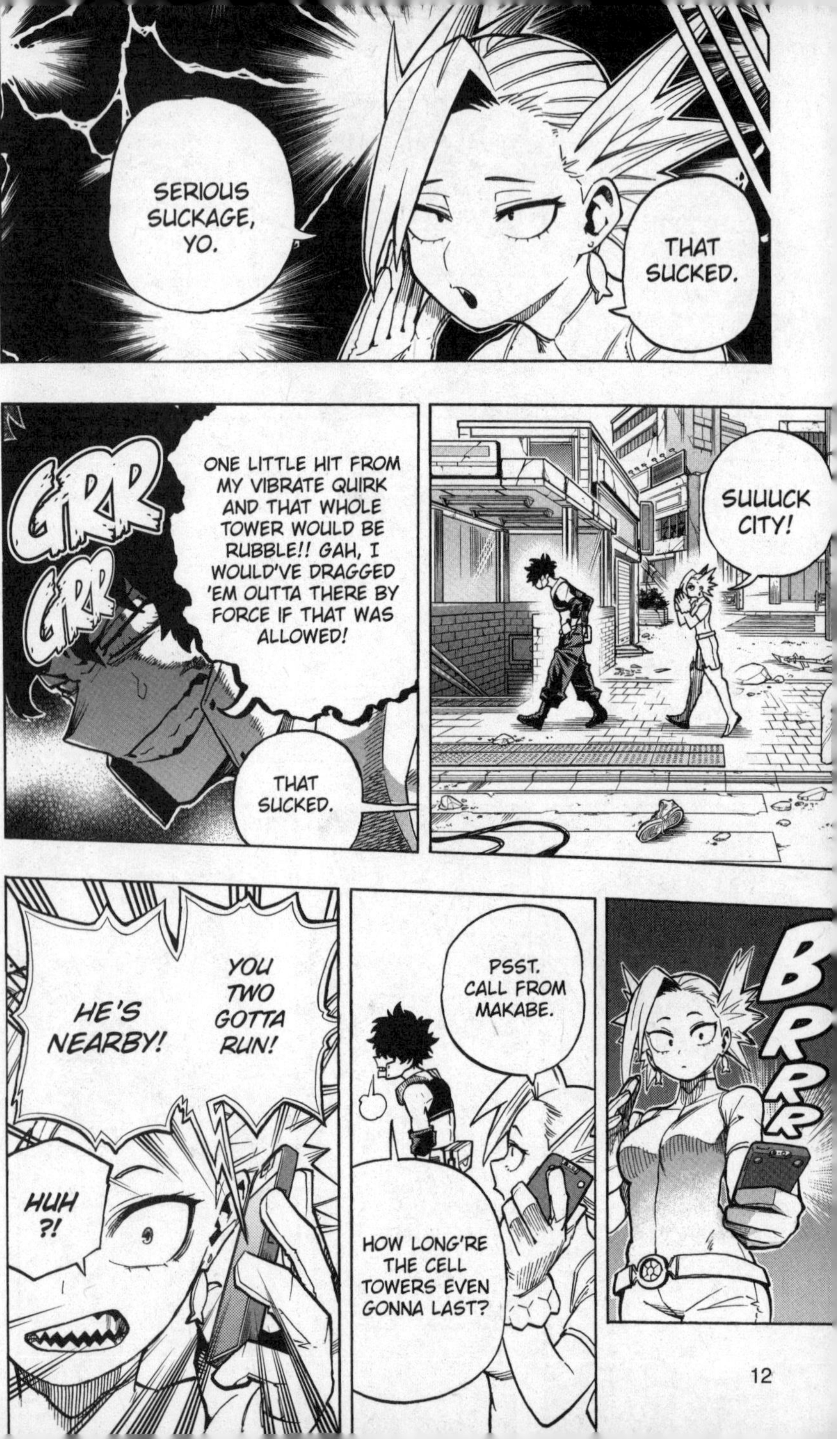
THAT SUCKED.
SERIOUS SUCKAGE, YO.
SUUUCK CITY!
ONE LITTLE HIT FROM MY VIBRATE QUIRK AND THAT WHOLE TOWER WOULD BE RUBBLE!! GAH, I WOULD'VE DRAGGED 'EM OUTTA THERE BY FORCE IF THAT WAS ALLOWED!
GRR GRR
THAT SUCKED.
BRRR
PSST. CALL FROM MAKABE.
HOW LONG'RE THE CELL TOWERS EVEN GONNA LAST?
YOU TWO GOTTA RUN!
HE'S NEARBY!
HUH ?!

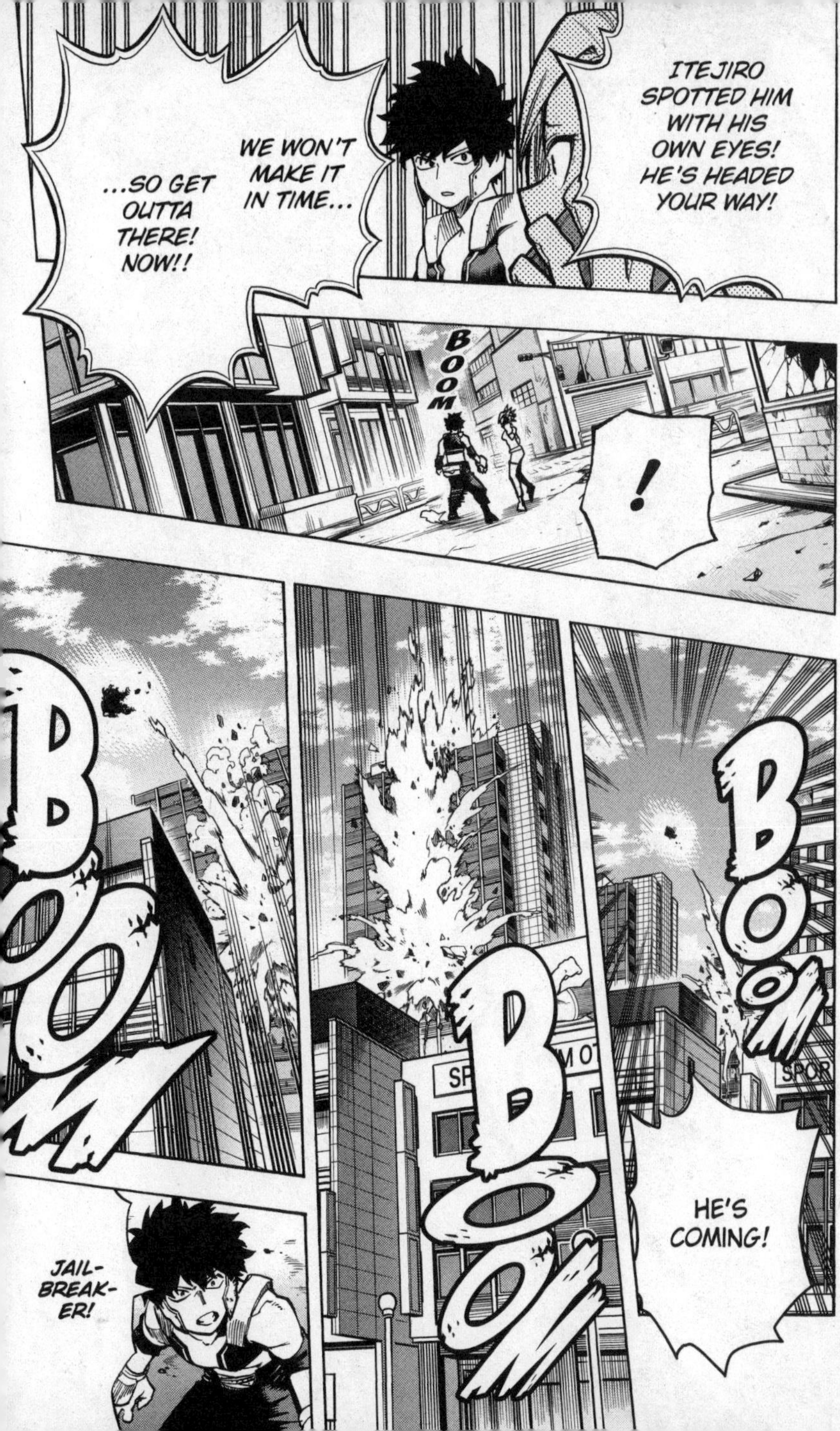

ITEJIRO SPOTTED HIM WITH HIS OWN EYES! HE'S HEADED YOUR WAY!
WE WON'T MAKE IT IN TIME...
...SO GET OUTTA THERE! NOW!!
BOOM
!
BOOM
SPOR
HE'S COMING!
BOOM
SP
MOT
BOOM
JAIL-BREAK-ER!

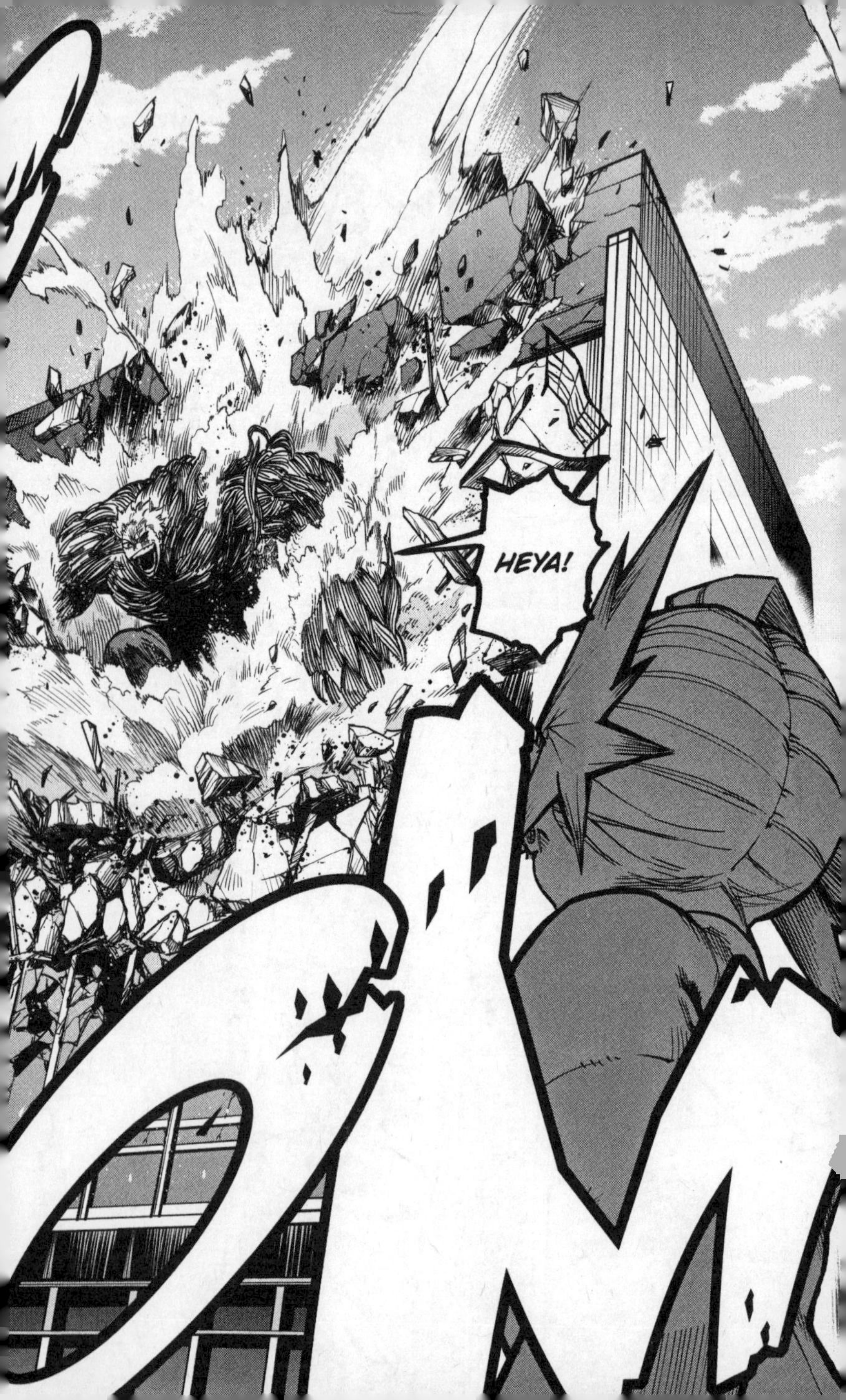
HEYA!

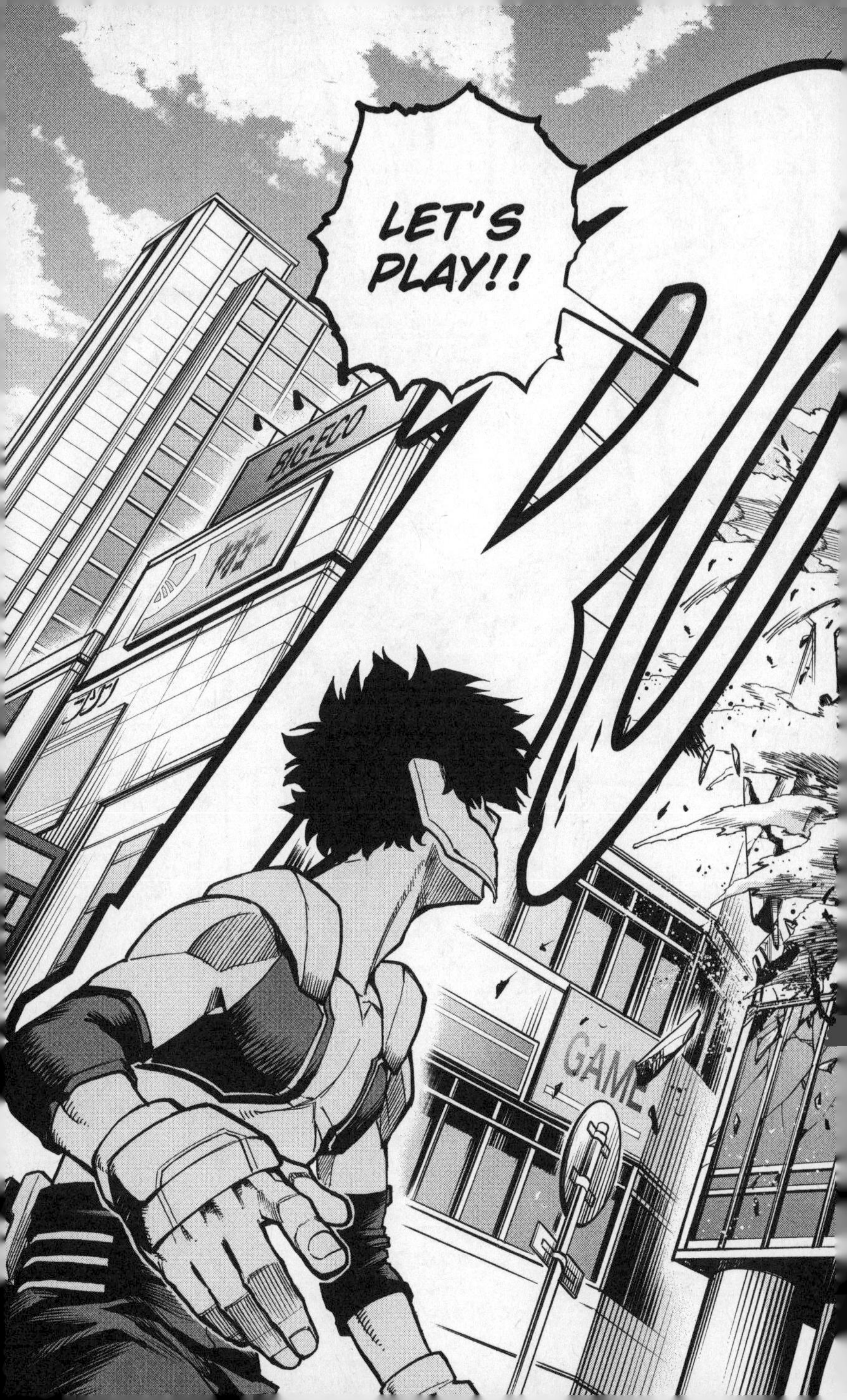
LET'S PLAY!!
BIG ECO
GAME

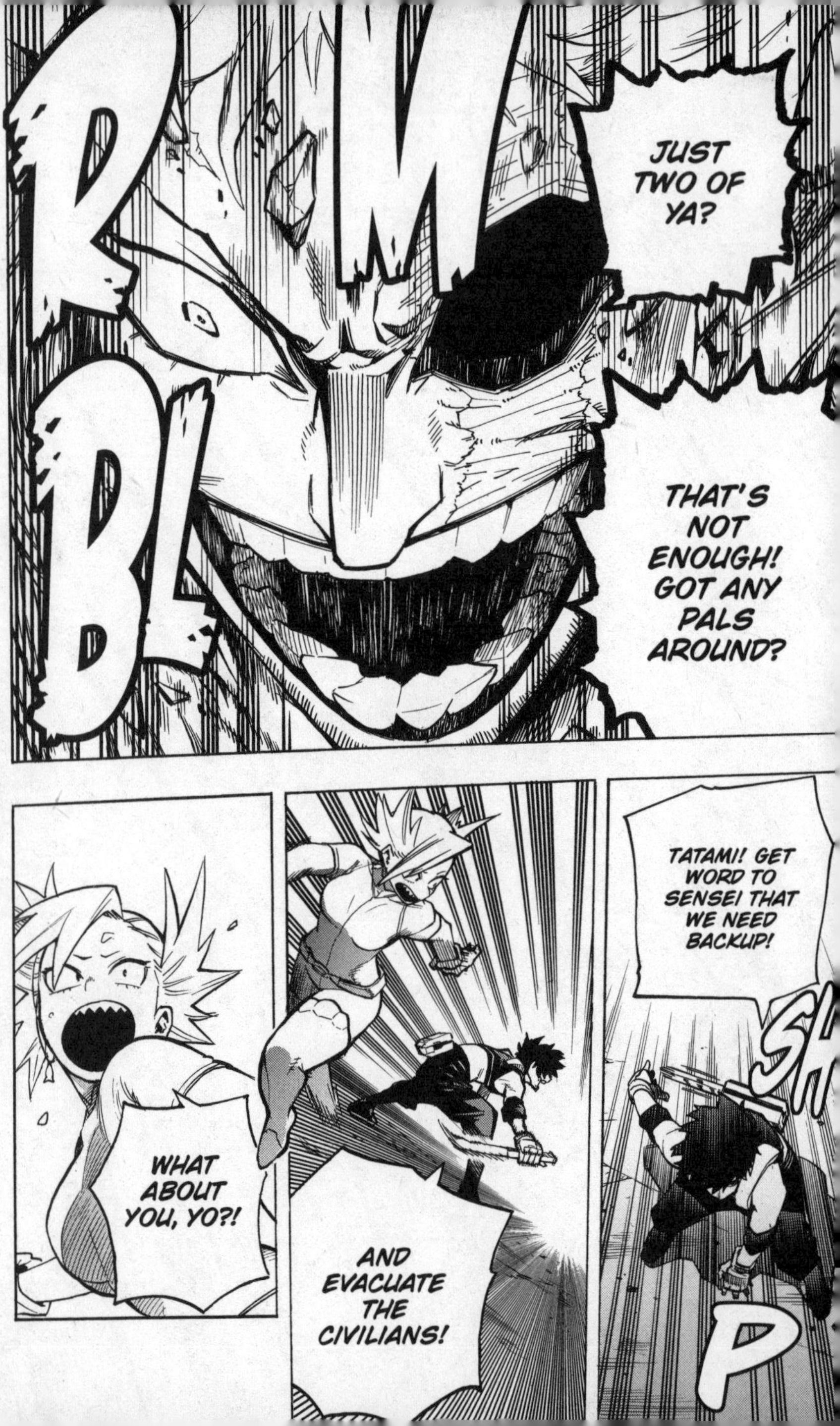
JUST TWO OF YA?
THAT'S NOT ENOUGH! GOT ANY PALS AROUND?
TATAMI! GET WORD TO SENSEI THAT WE NEED BACKUP!
AND EVACUATE THE CIVILIANS!
WHAT ABOUT YOU, YO?!

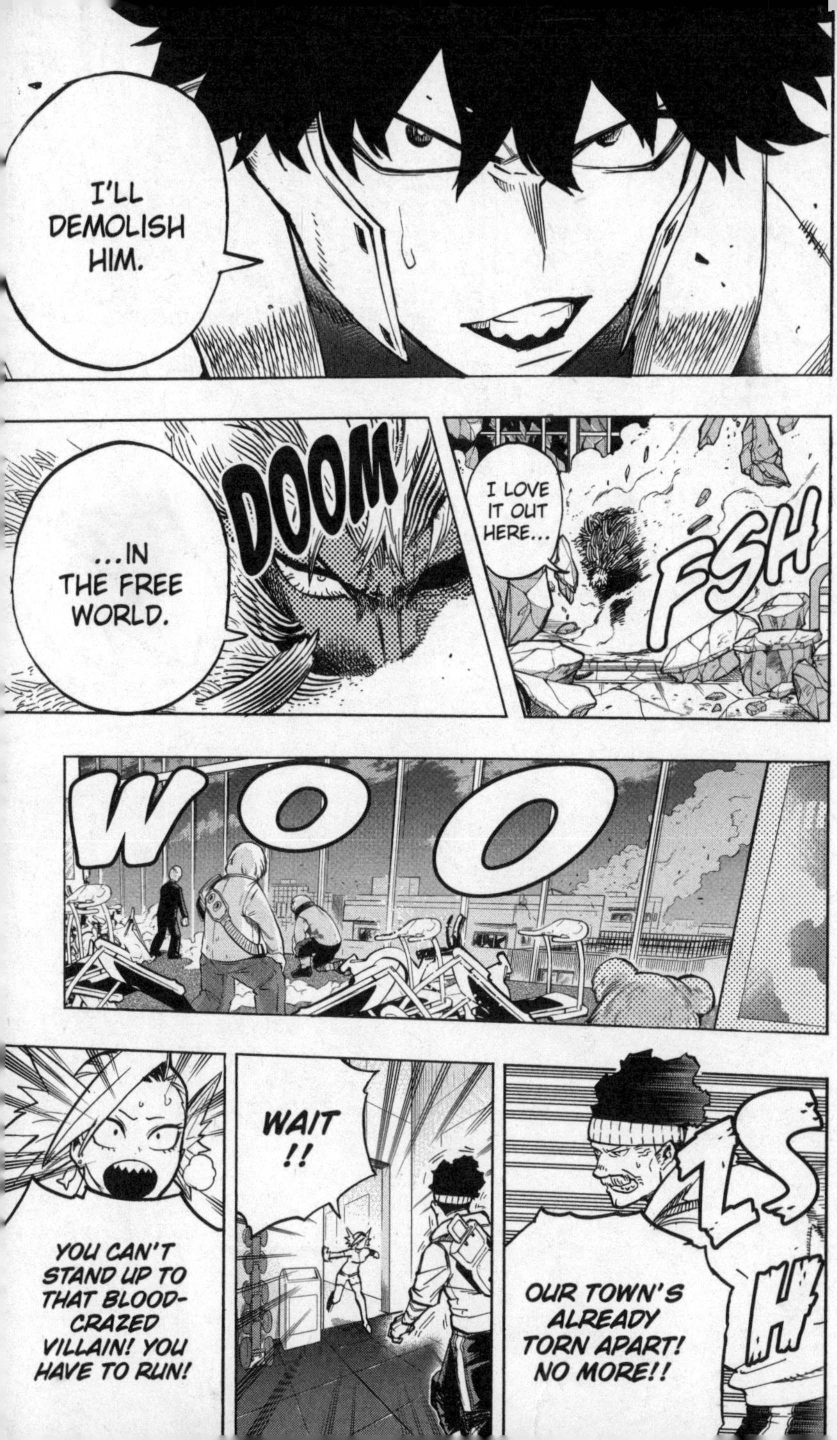
I'LL DEMOLISH HIM.
I LOVE IT OUT HERE...
FSH
DOOM
...IN THE FREE WORLD.
WOO
OUR TOWN'S ALREADY TORN APART! NO MORE!!
WAIT !!
YOU CAN'T STAND UP TO THAT BLOOD-CRAZED VILLAIN! YOU HAVE TO RUN!

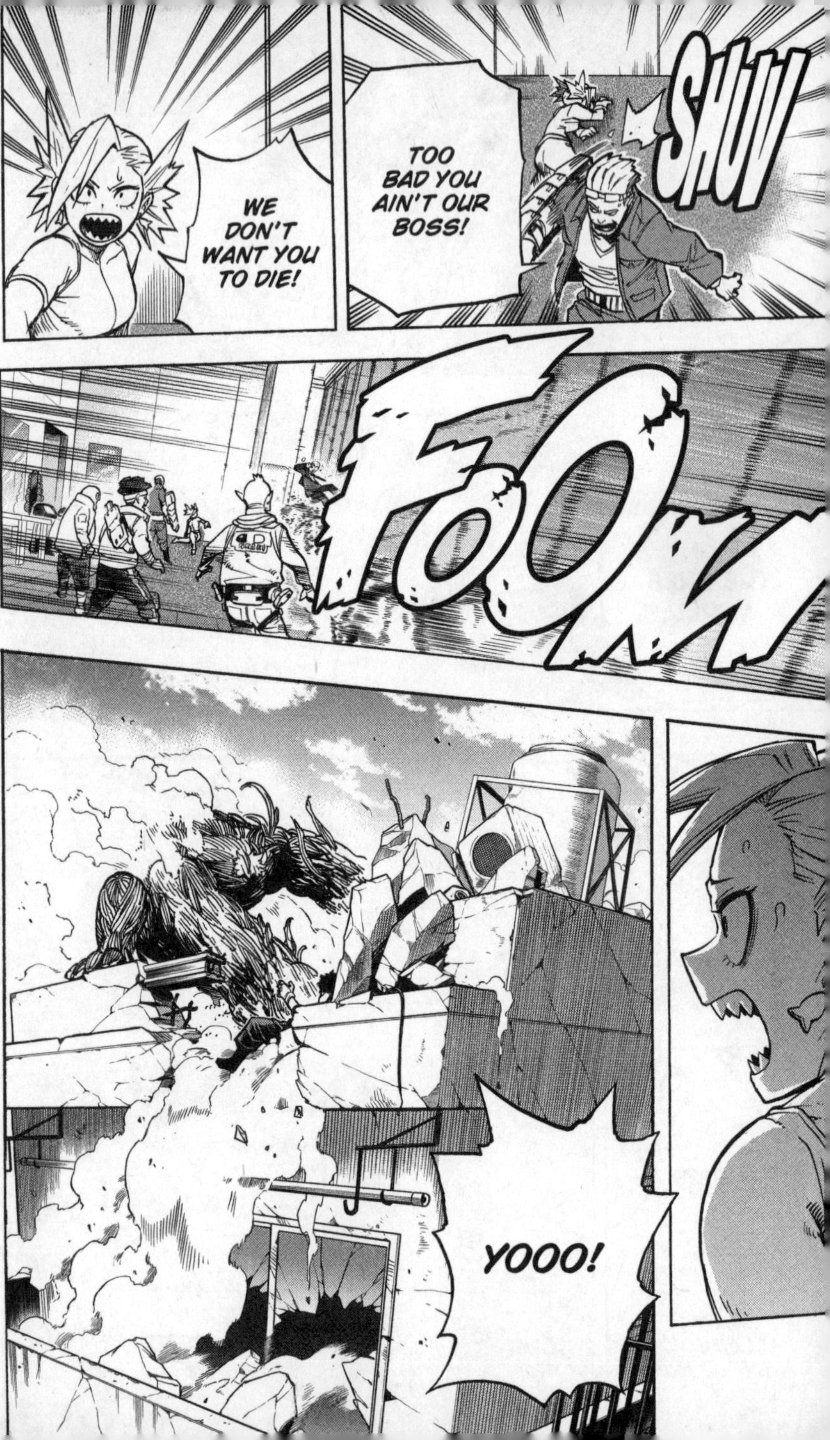
SHUV
TOO BAD YOU AIN'T OUR BOSS!
WE DON'T WANT YOU TO DIE!
FOOM
YOOO!

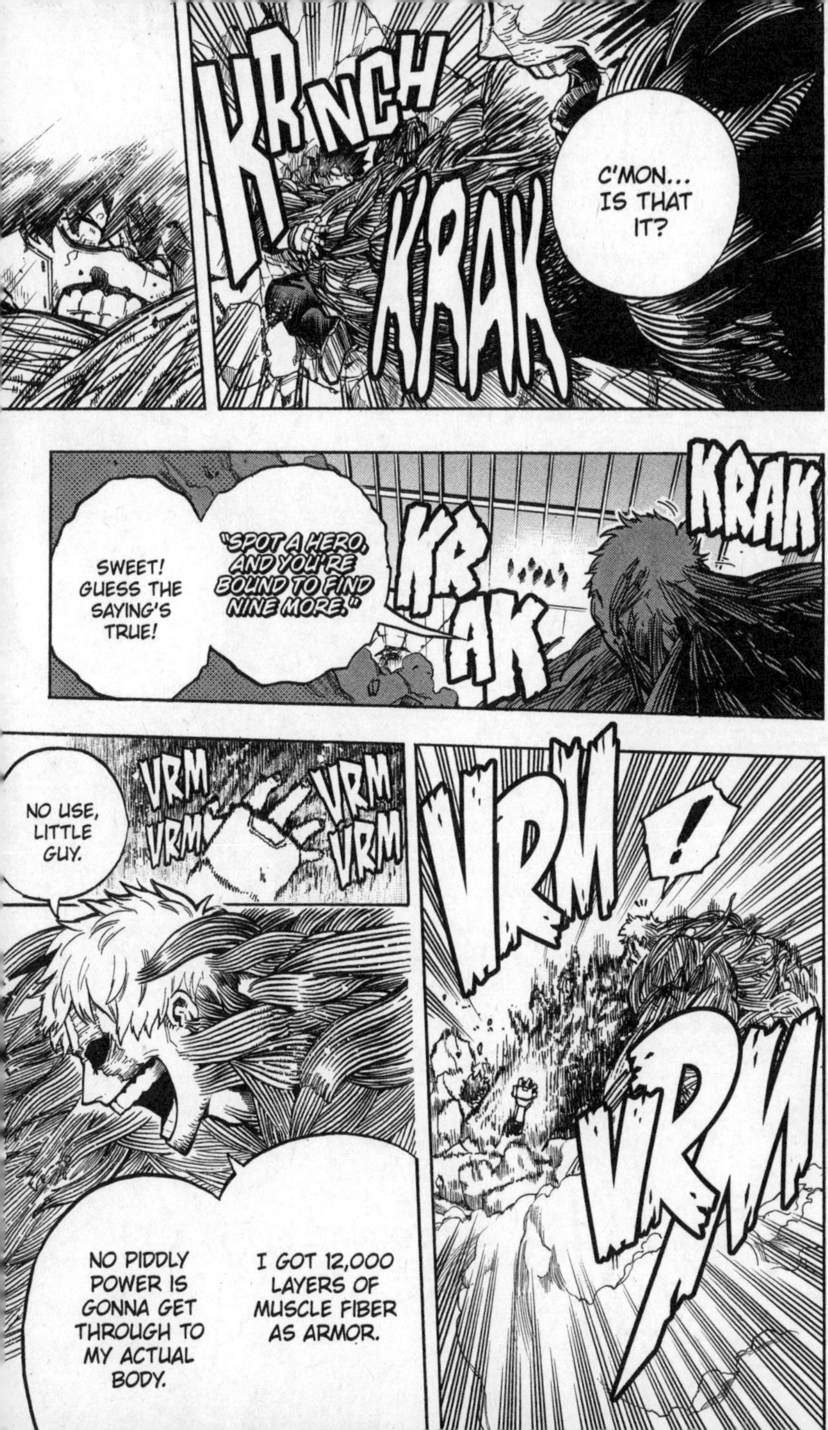

C'MON… IS THAT IT?
KRNCH
KRAK
KRAK
KR
AK
SWEET! GUESS THE SAYING'S TRUE!
"SPOT A HERO, AND YOU'RE BOUND TO FIND NINE MORE."
VRM
!
VRM
VRM
VRM
VRM
VRM
NO USE, LITTLE GUY.
NO PIDDLY POWER IS GONNA GET THROUGH TO MY ACTUAL BODY.
I GOT 12,000 LAYERS OF MUSCLE FIBER AS ARMOR.

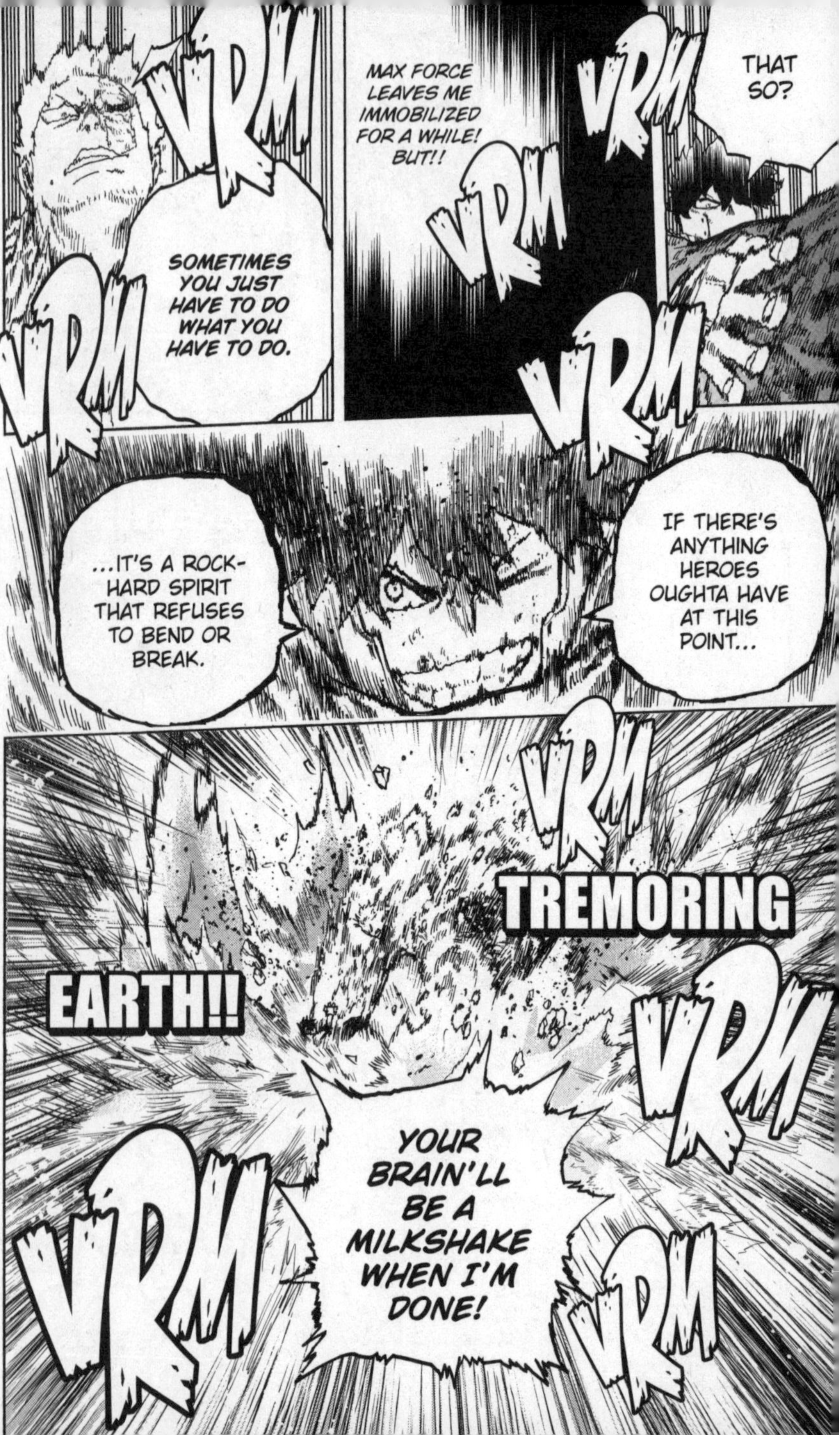
THAT SO?
VRM
VRM
MAX FORCE LEAVES ME IMMOBILIZED FOR A WHILE! BUT!!
VRM
VRM
VRM
SOMETIMES YOU JUST HAVE TO DO WHAT YOU HAVE TO DO.
VRM
IF THERE'S ANYTHING HEROES OUGHTA HAVE AT THIS POINT...
...IT'S A ROCK-HARD SPIRIT THAT REFUSES TO BEND OR BREAK.
VRM
TREMORING
EARTH!!
VRM
YOUR BRAIN'LL BE A MILKSHAKE WHEN I'M DONE!
VRM
VRM

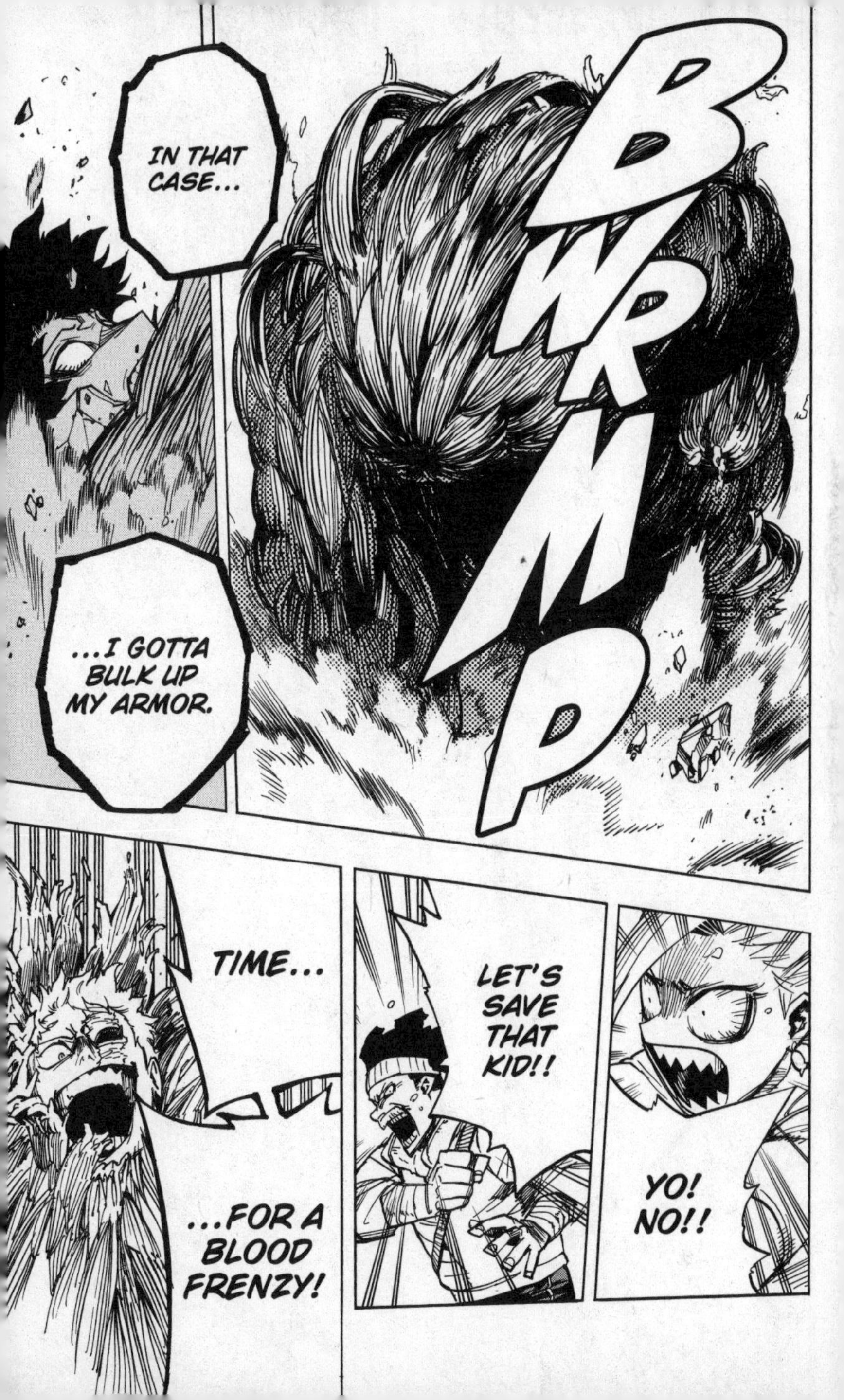
BWRMP
IN THAT CASE...
...I GOTTA BULK UP MY ARMOR.
YO! NO!!
LET'S SAVE THAT KID!!
TIME...
...FOR A BLOOD FRENZY!

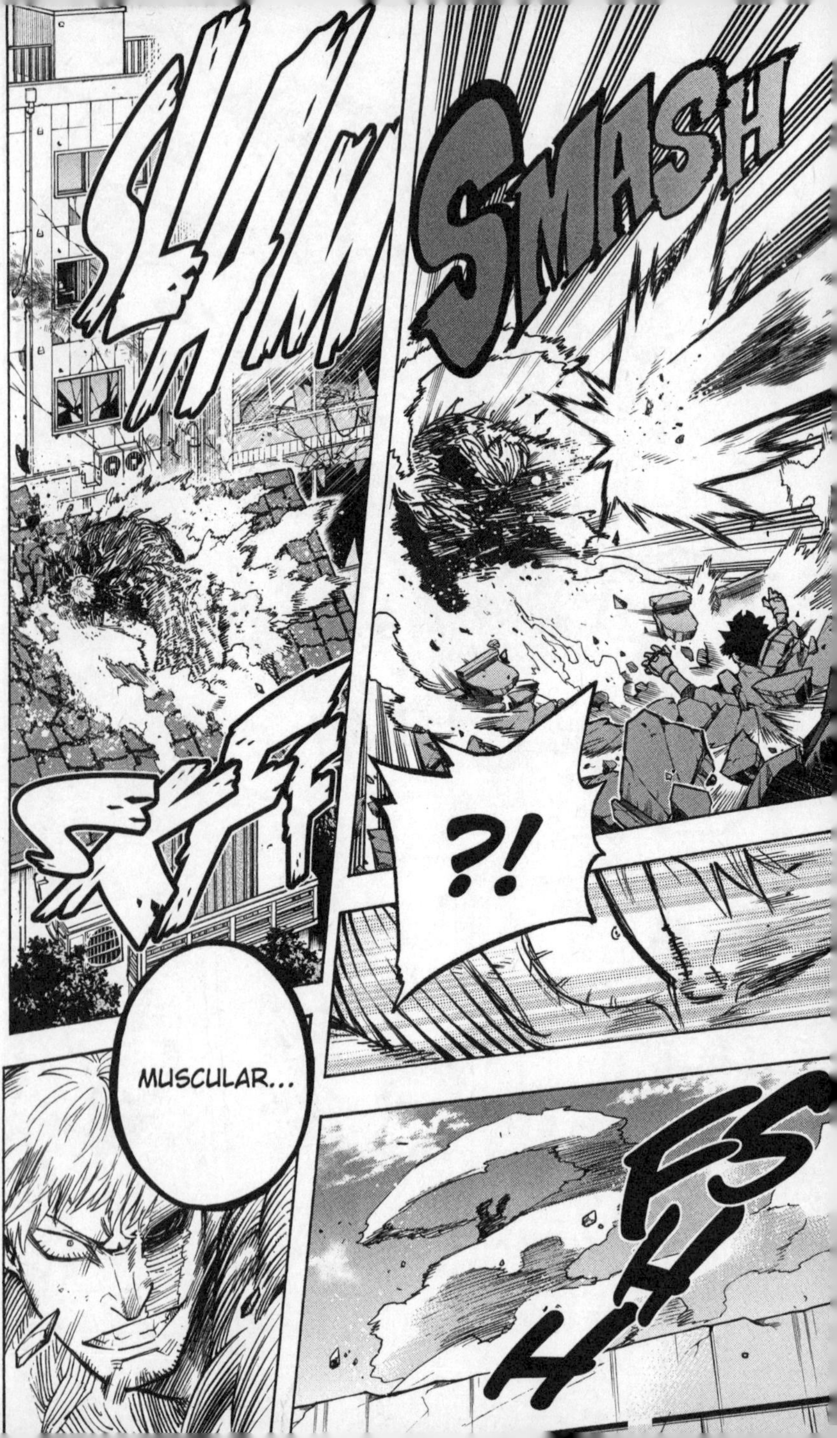
SMASH
?!
MUSCULAR...

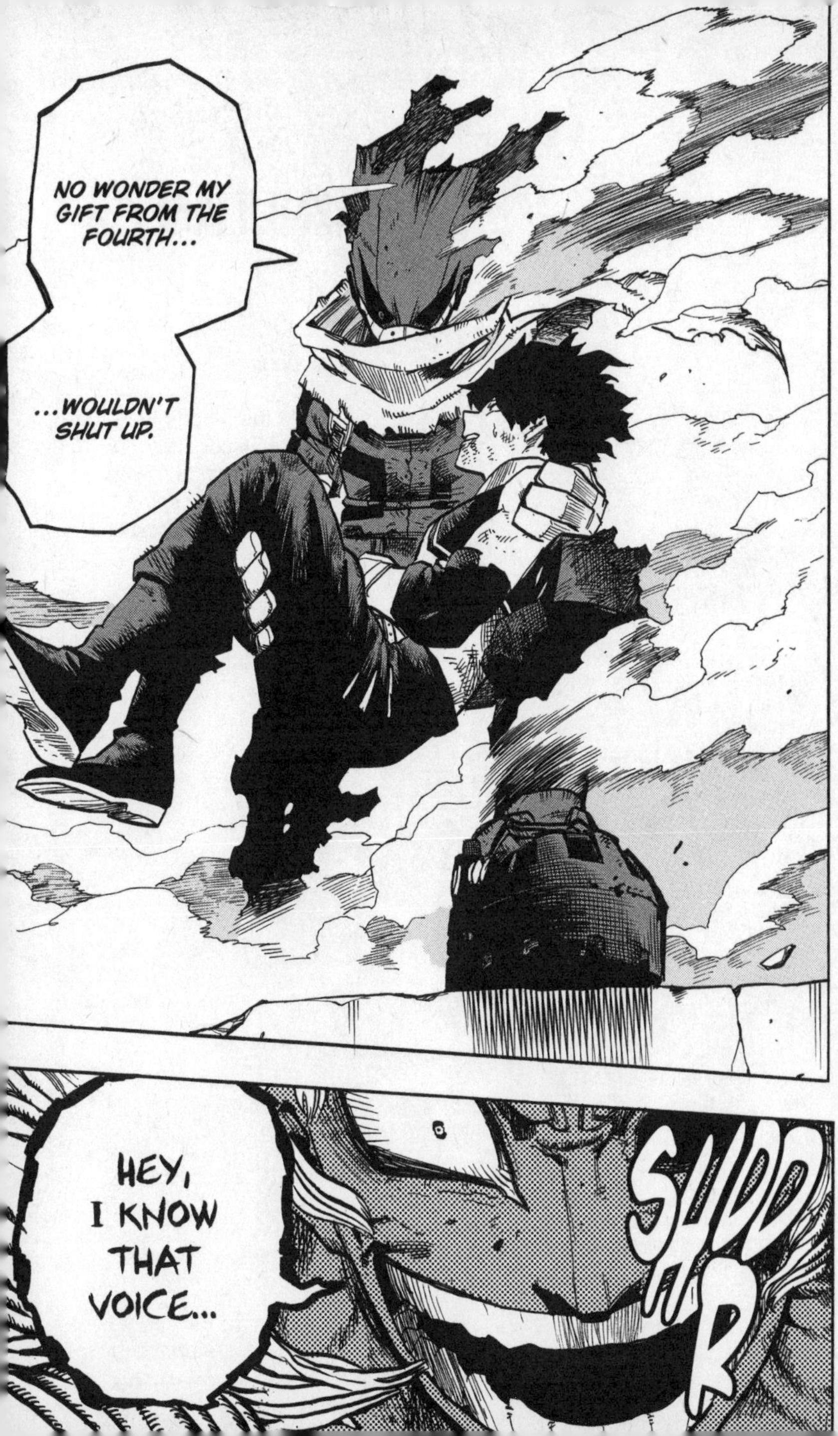
NO WONDER MY GIFT FROM THE FOURTH...
...WOULDN'T SHUT UP.
HEY, I KNOW THAT VOICE...

GOTO IMASUJI (AGE 26)

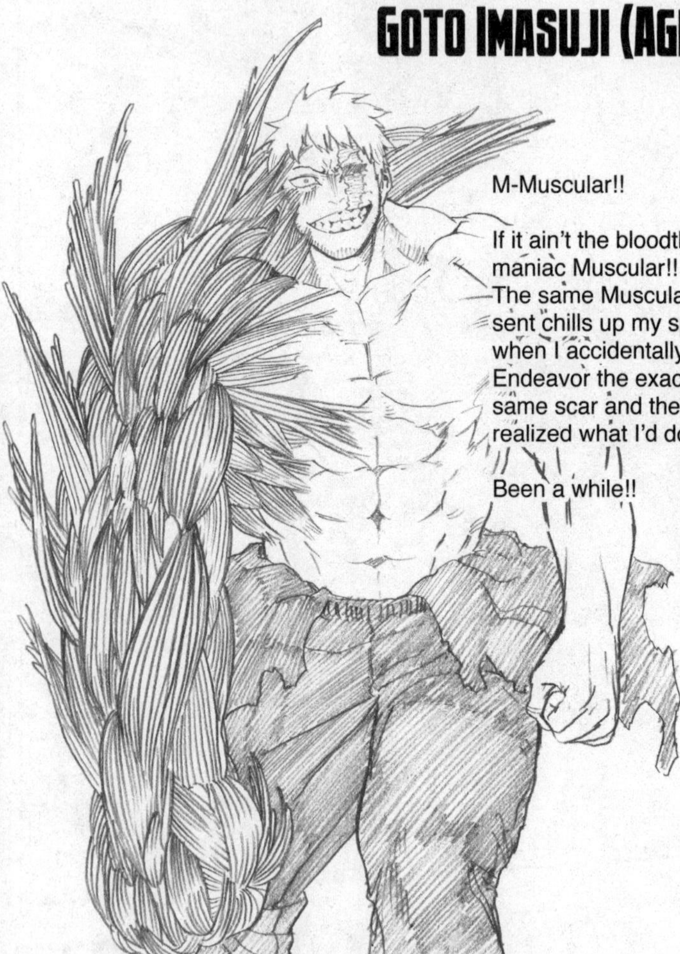

M-Muscular!!

If it ain't the bloodthirsty maniac Muscular!! The same Muscular who sent chills up my spine when I accidentally gave Endeavor the exact same scar and then realized what I'd done!!

Been a while!!

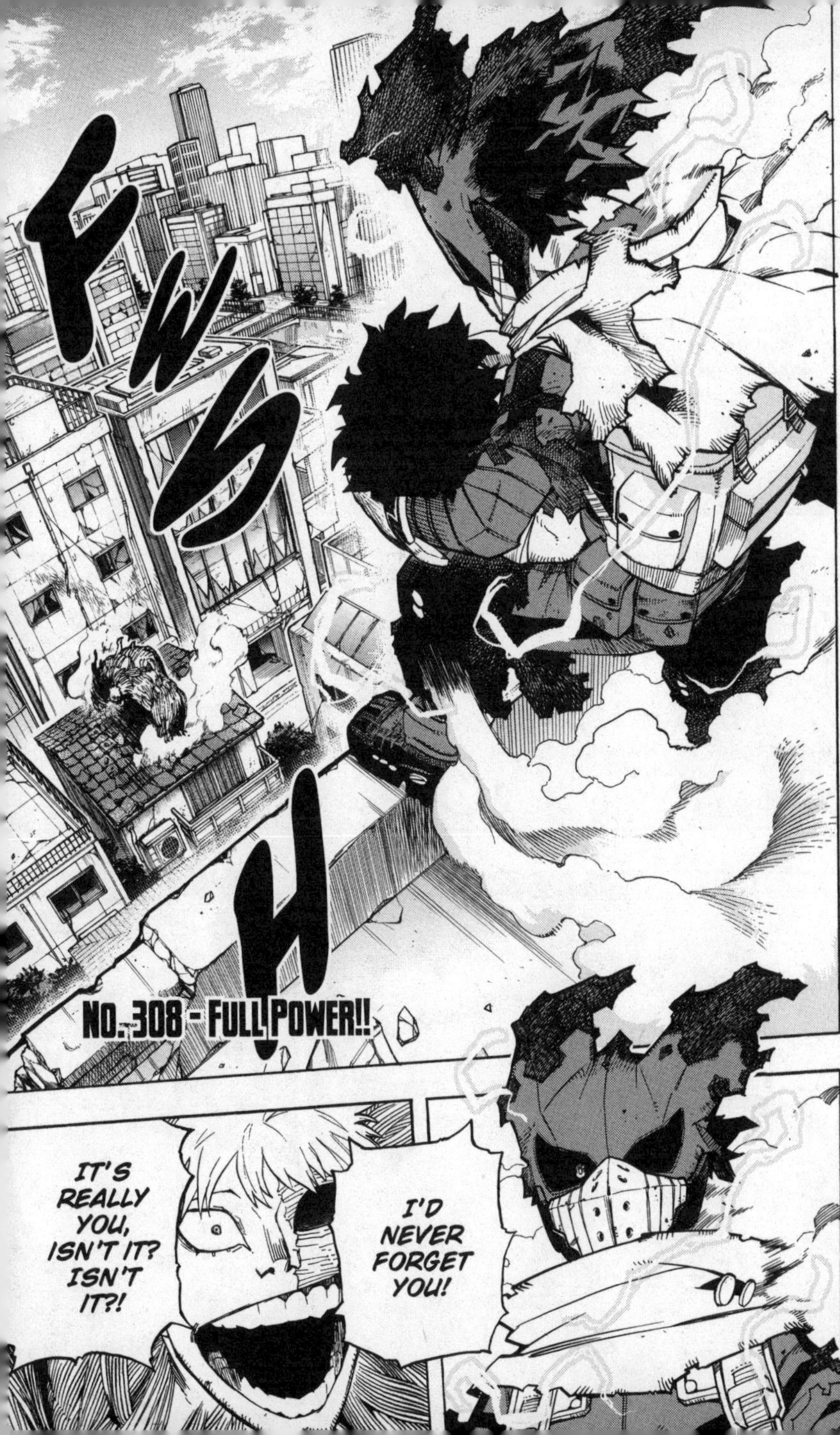
NO. 308 - FULL POWER!!
I'D NEVER FORGET YOU!
IT'S REALLY YOU, ISN'T IT? ISN'T IT?!

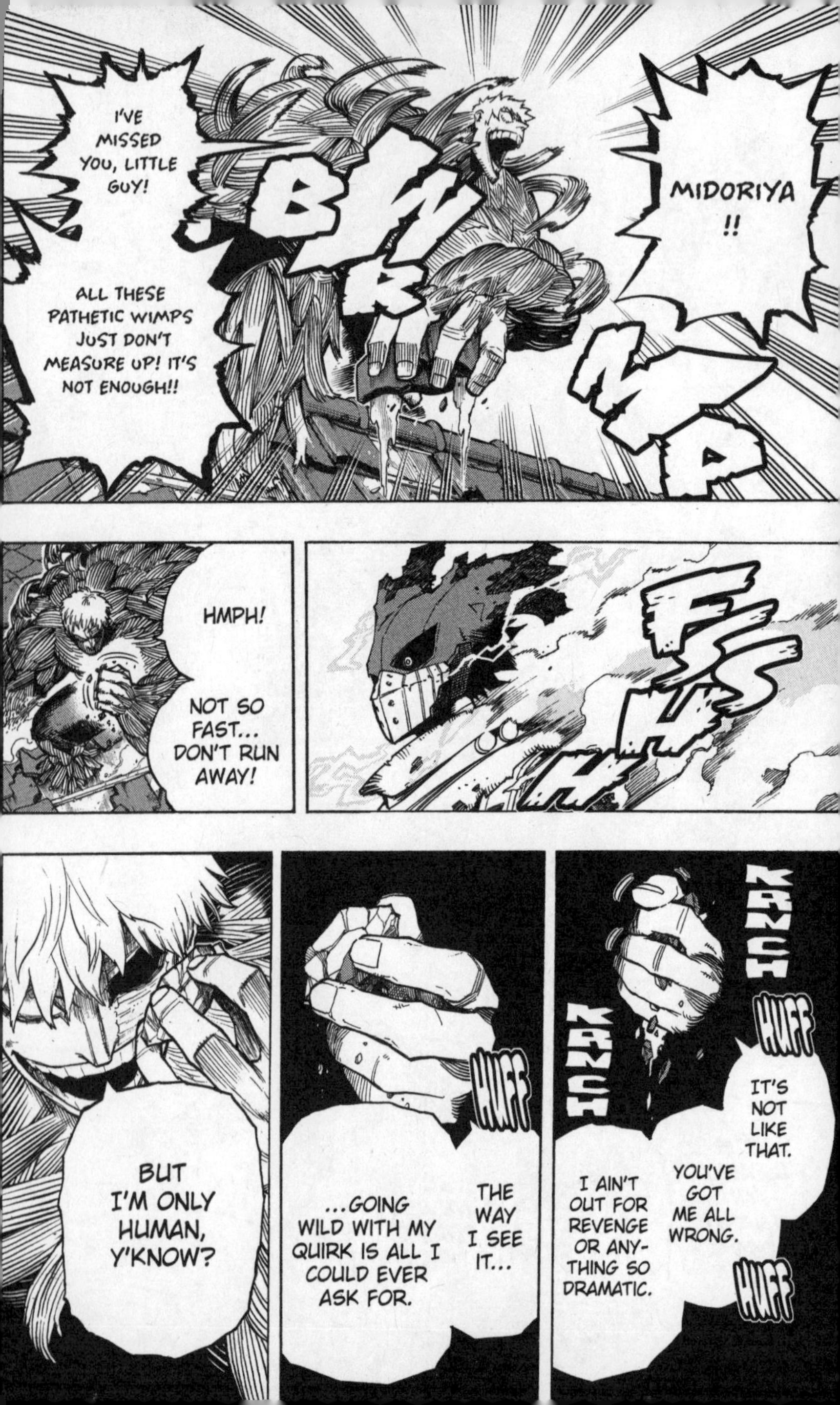
MIDORIYA !!
I'VE MISSED YOU, LITTLE GUY!
ALL THESE PATHETIC WIMPS JUST DON'T MEASURE UP! IT'S NOT ENOUGH!!
HMPH!
NOT SO FAST... DON'T RUN AWAY!
KRNCH
HUFF
IT'S NOT LIKE THAT.
YOU'VE GOT ME ALL WRONG.
I AIN'T OUT FOR REVENGE OR ANY-THING SO DRAMATIC.
KRNCH
HUFF
HUFF
THE WAY I SEE IT...
...GOING WILD WITH MY QUIRK IS ALL I COULD EVER ASK FOR.
BUT I'M ONLY HUMAN, Y'KNOW?

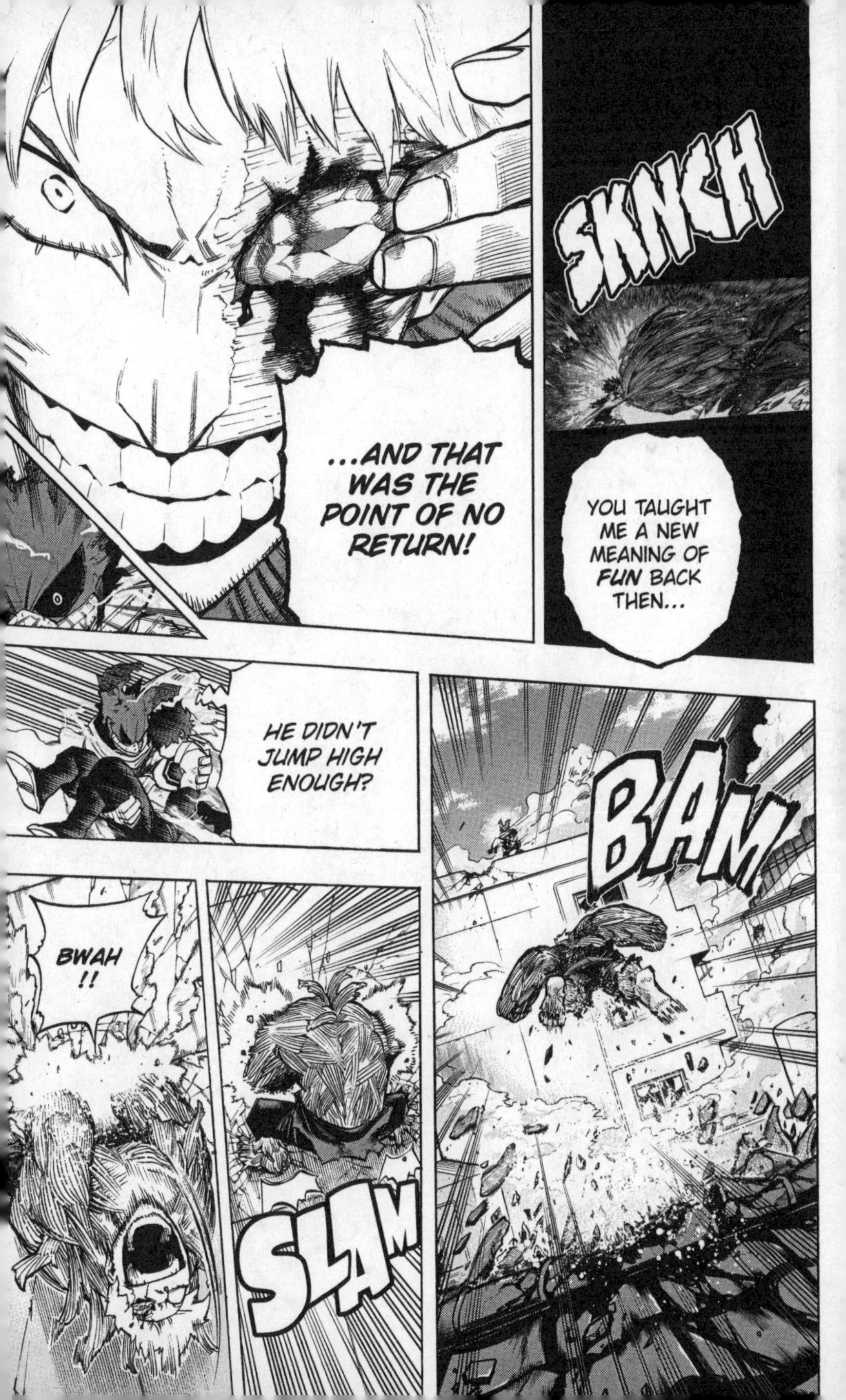
SKNCH
YOU TAUGHT ME A NEW MEANING OF *FUN* BACK THEN...
...AND THAT WAS THE POINT OF NO RETURN!
BAM
HE DIDN'T JUMP HIGH ENOUGH?
SLAM
BWAH !!

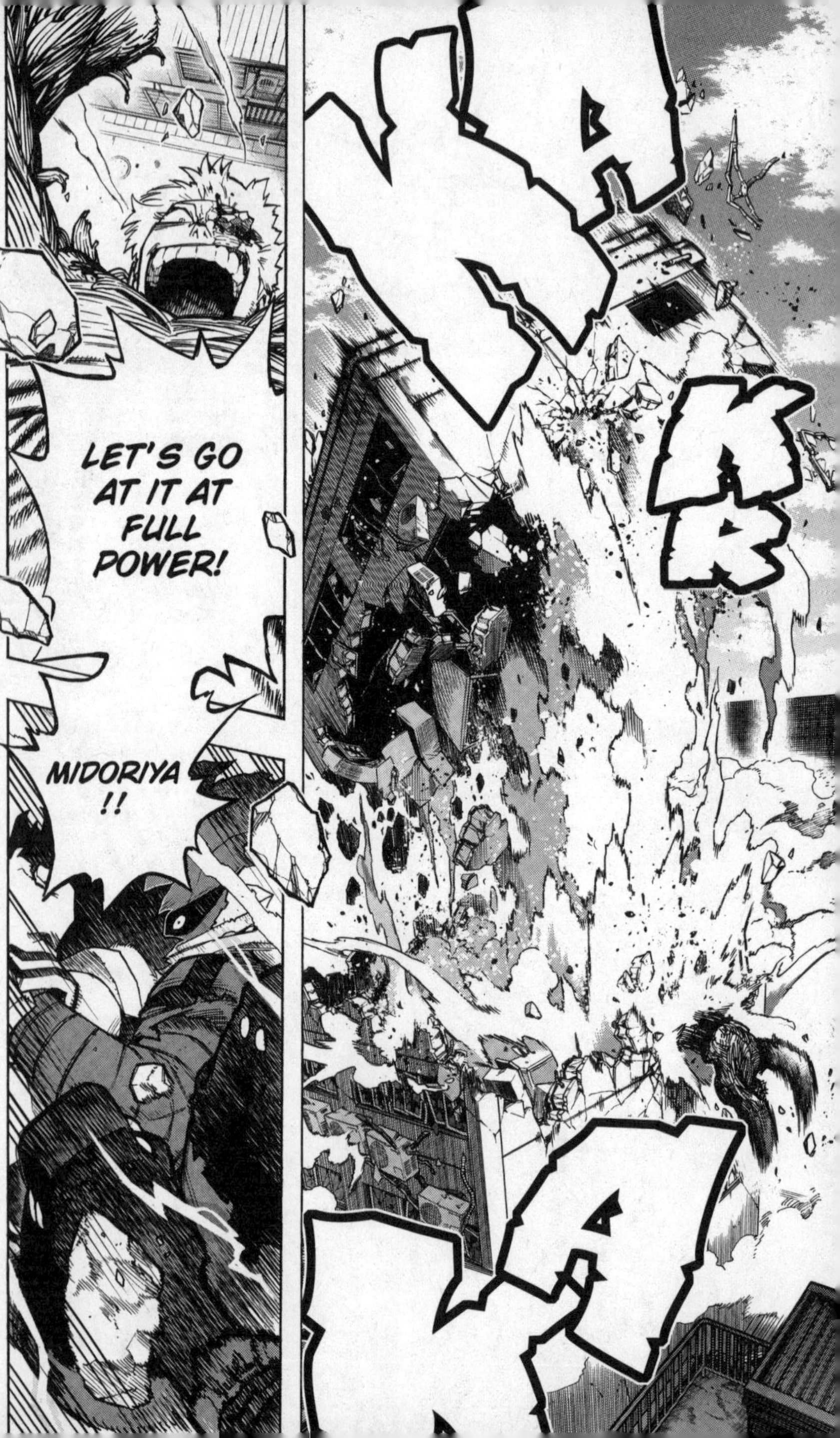
LET'S GO AT IT AT FULL POWER!
MIDORIYA !!

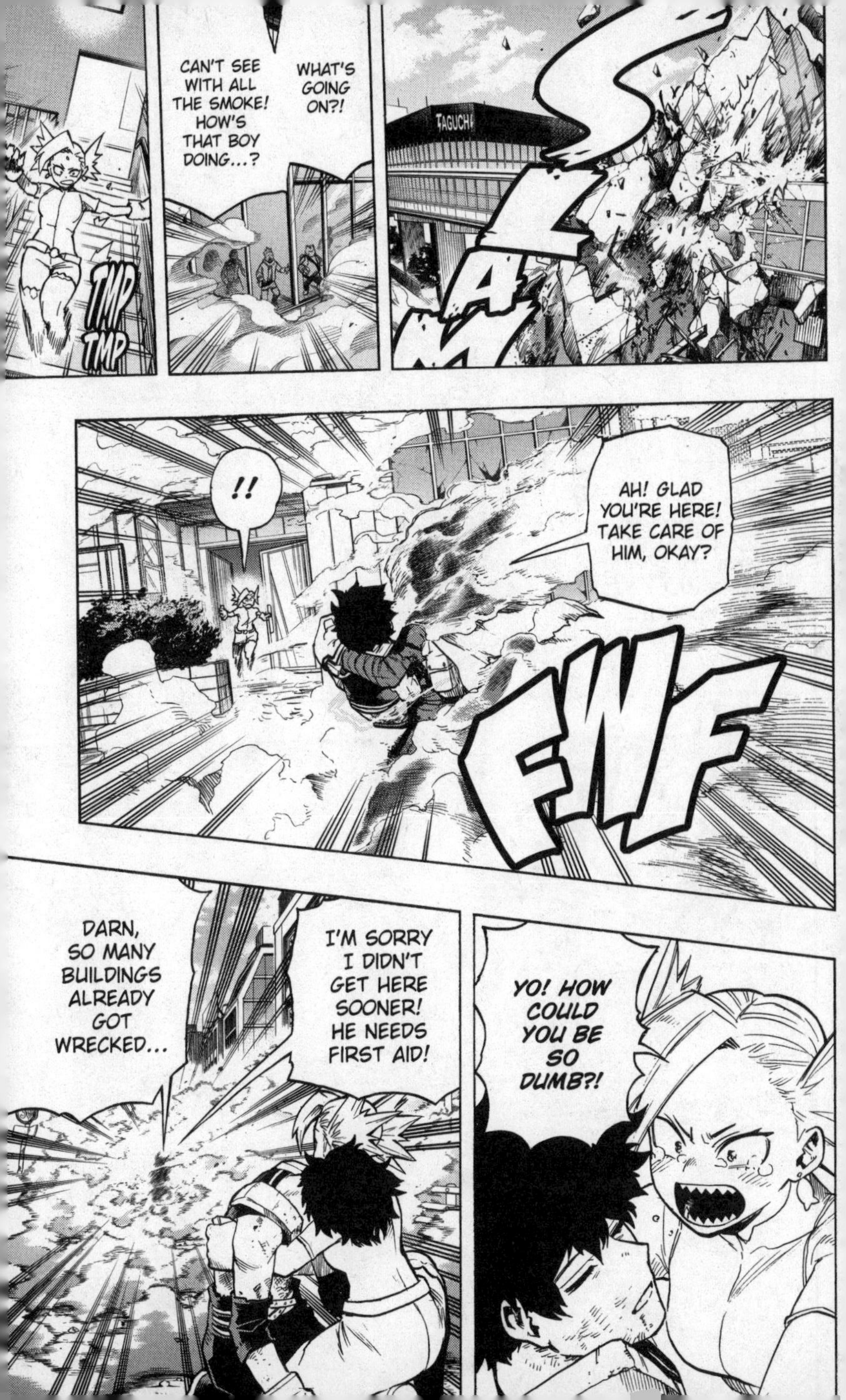
TAGUCHI
SLAM
WHAT'S GOING ON?!
CAN'T SEE WITH ALL THE SMOKE! HOW'S THAT BOY DOING...?
TMP TMP
AH! GLAD YOU'RE HERE! TAKE CARE OF HIM, OKAY?
!!
FWF
YO! HOW COULD YOU BE SO DUMB?!
I'M SORRY I DIDN'T GET HERE SOONER! HE NEEDS FIRST AID!
DARN, SO MANY BUILDINGS ALREADY GOT WRECKED...

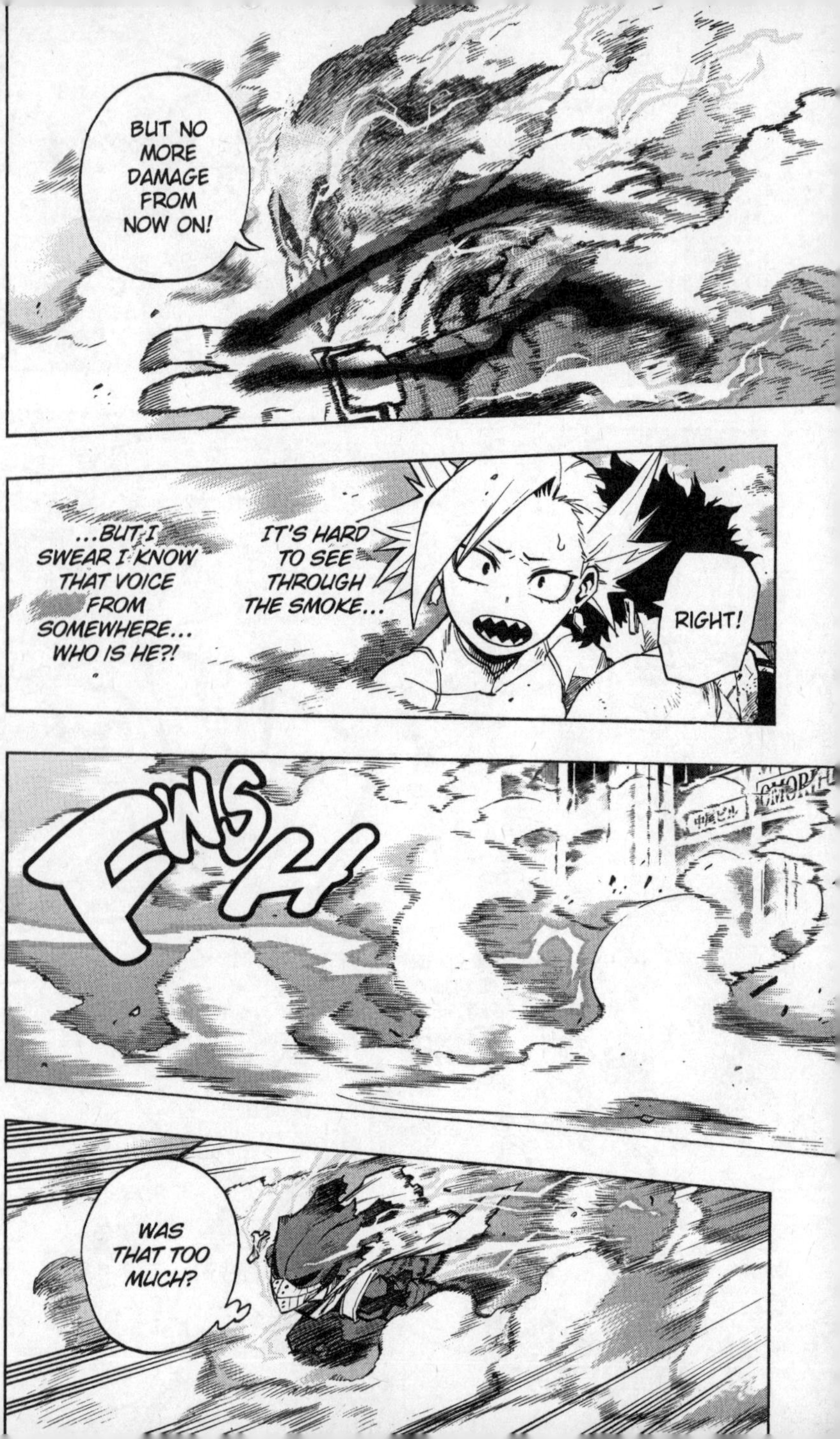
BUT NO MORE DAMAGE FROM NOW ON!
RIGHT!
IT'S HARD TO SEE THROUGH THE SMOKE...
...BUT I SWEAR I KNOW THAT VOICE FROM SOMEWHERE... WHO IS HE?!
WAS THAT TOO MUCH?

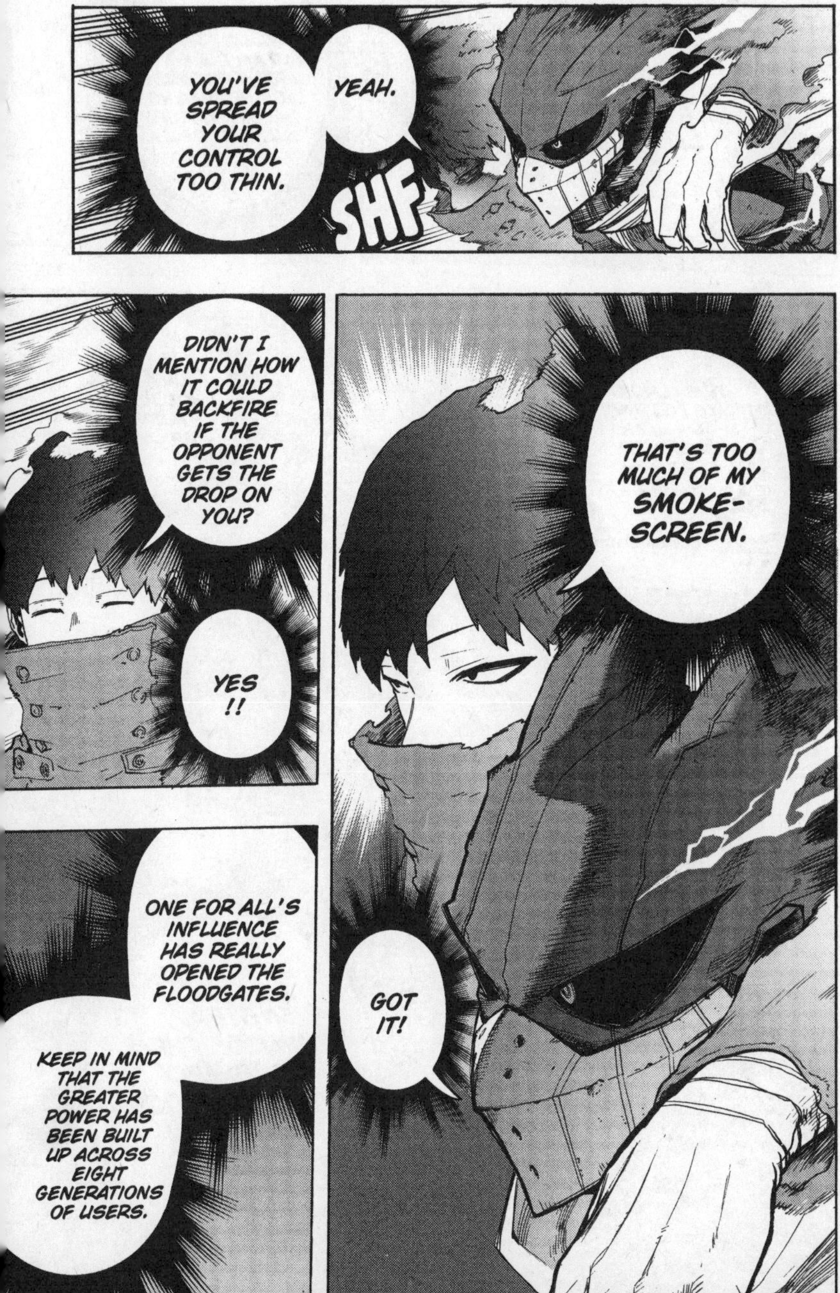
YEAH.
YOU'VE SPREAD YOUR CONTROL TOO THIN.
SHF
THAT'S TOO MUCH OF MY SMOKE-SCREEN.
GOT IT!
DIDN'T I MENTION HOW IT COULD BACKFIRE IF THE OPPONENT GETS THE DROP ON YOU?
YES !!
ONE FOR ALL'S INFLUENCE HAS REALLY OPENED THE FLOODGATES.
KEEP IN MIND THAT THE GREATER POWER HAS BEEN BUILT UP ACROSS EIGHT GENERATIONS OF USERS.

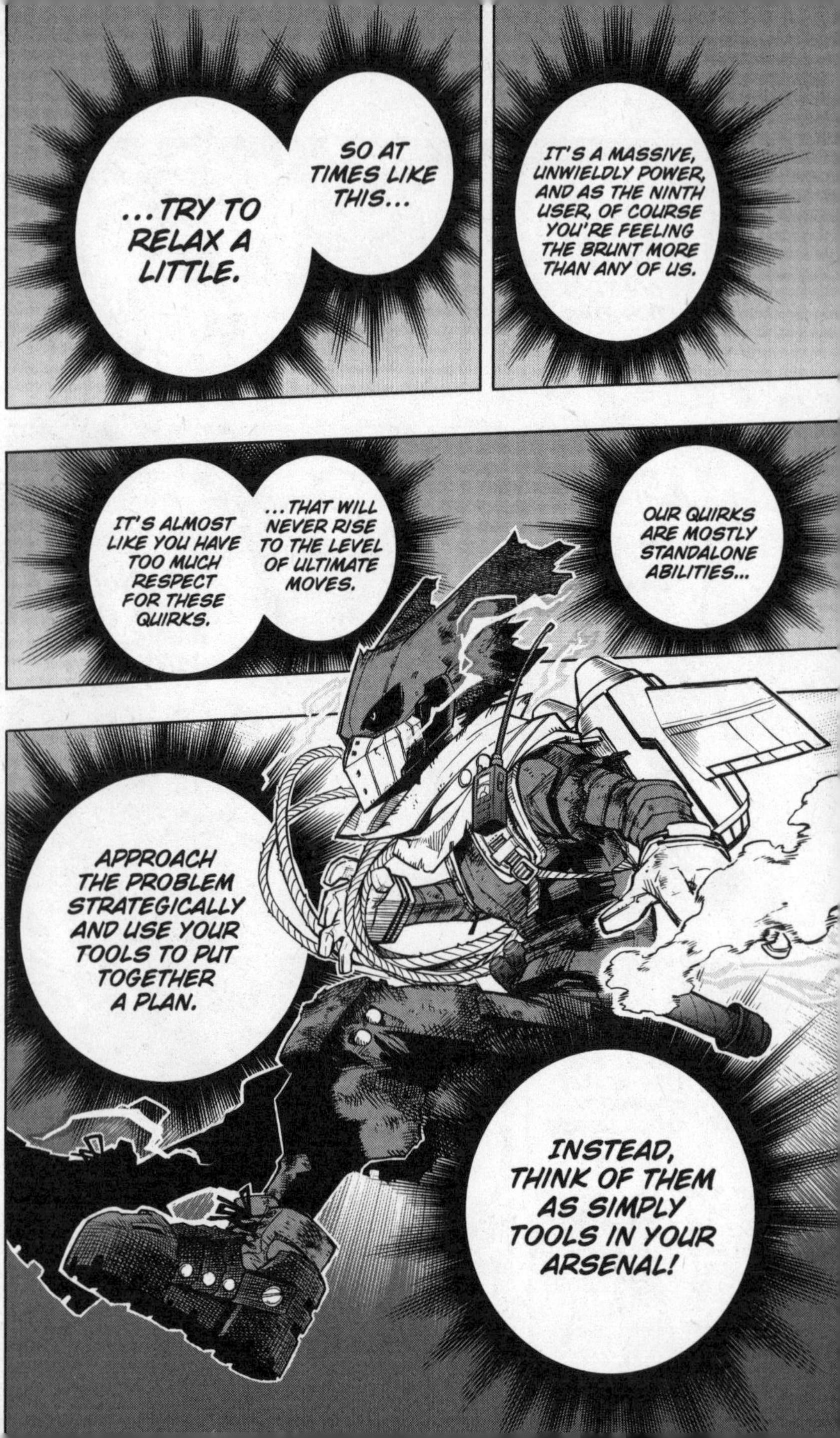
IT'S A MASSIVE, UNWIELDLY POWER, AND AS THE NINTH USER, OF COURSE YOU'RE FEELING THE BRUNT MORE THAN ANY OF US.
SO AT TIMES LIKE THIS...
...TRY TO RELAX A LITTLE.
OUR QUIRKS ARE MOSTLY STANDALONE ABILITIES...
...THAT WILL NEVER RISE TO THE LEVEL OF ULTIMATE MOVES.
IT'S ALMOST LIKE YOU HAVE TOO MUCH RESPECT FOR THESE QUIRKS.
INSTEAD, THINK OF THEM AS SIMPLY TOOLS IN YOUR ARSENAL!
APPROACH THE PROBLEM STRATEGICALLY AND USE YOUR TOOLS TO PUT TOGETHER A PLAN.

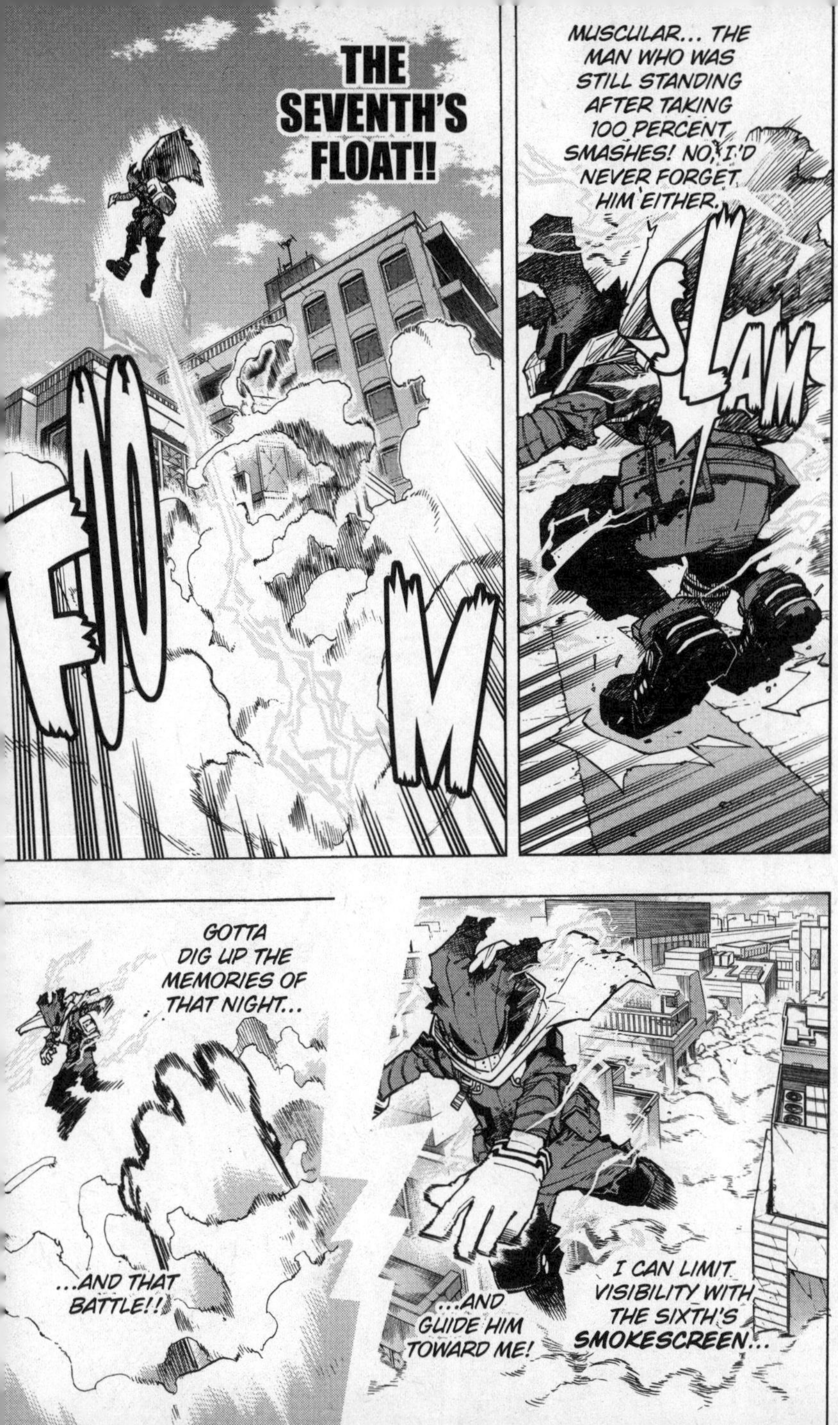
MUSCULAR... THE MAN WHO WAS STILL STANDING AFTER TAKING 100 PERCENT SMASHES! NO, I'D NEVER FORGET HIM EITHER.
SLAM
THE SEVENTH'S FLOAT!!
FOOM
I CAN LIMIT VISIBILITY WITH THE SIXTH'S SMOKESCREEN...
...AND GUIDE HIM TOWARD ME!
GOTTA DIG UP THE MEMORIES OF THAT NIGHT...
...AND THAT BATTLE!!

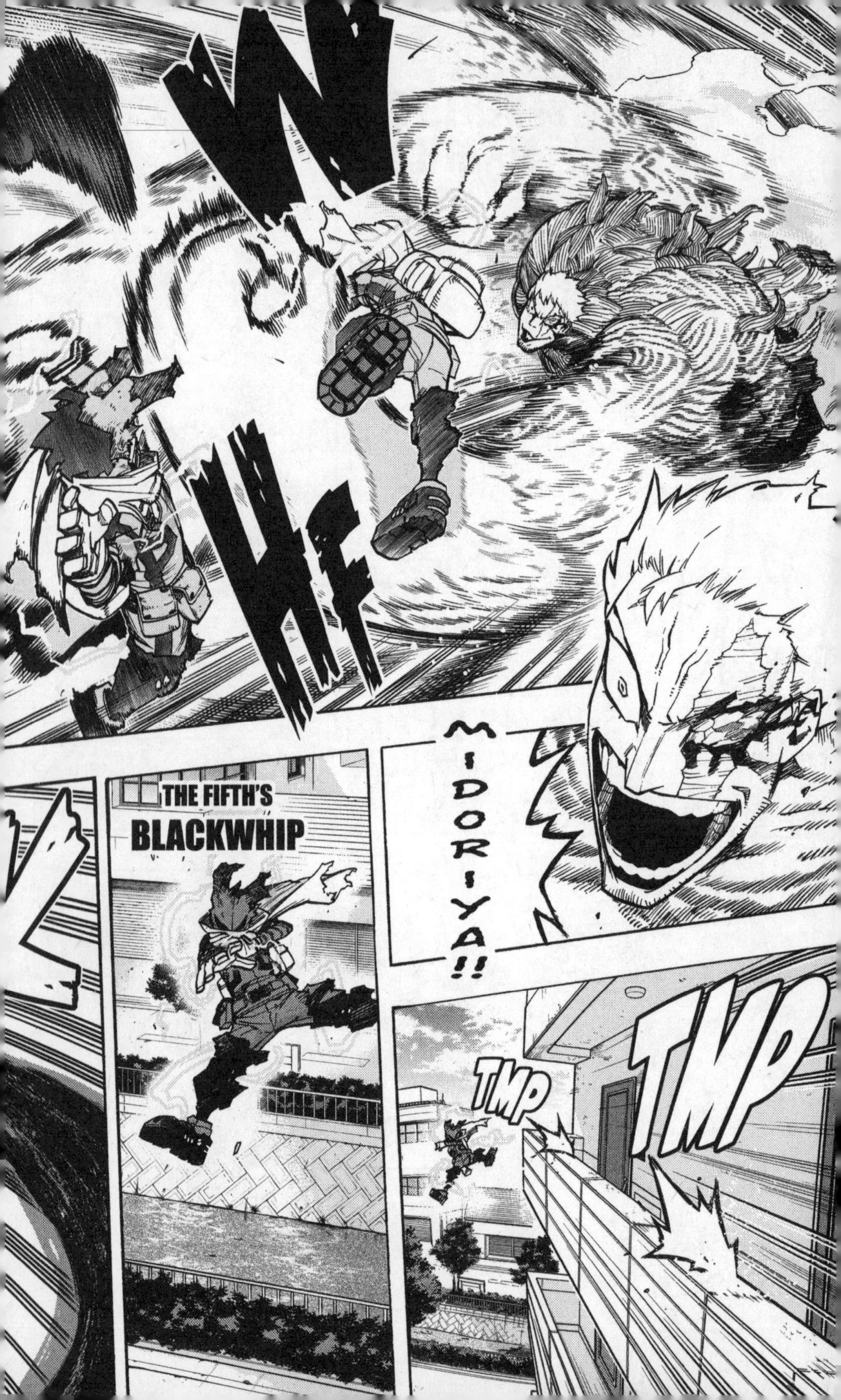

WHF
MIDORIYA!!
THE FIFTH'S
BLACKWHIP
TMP
TMP

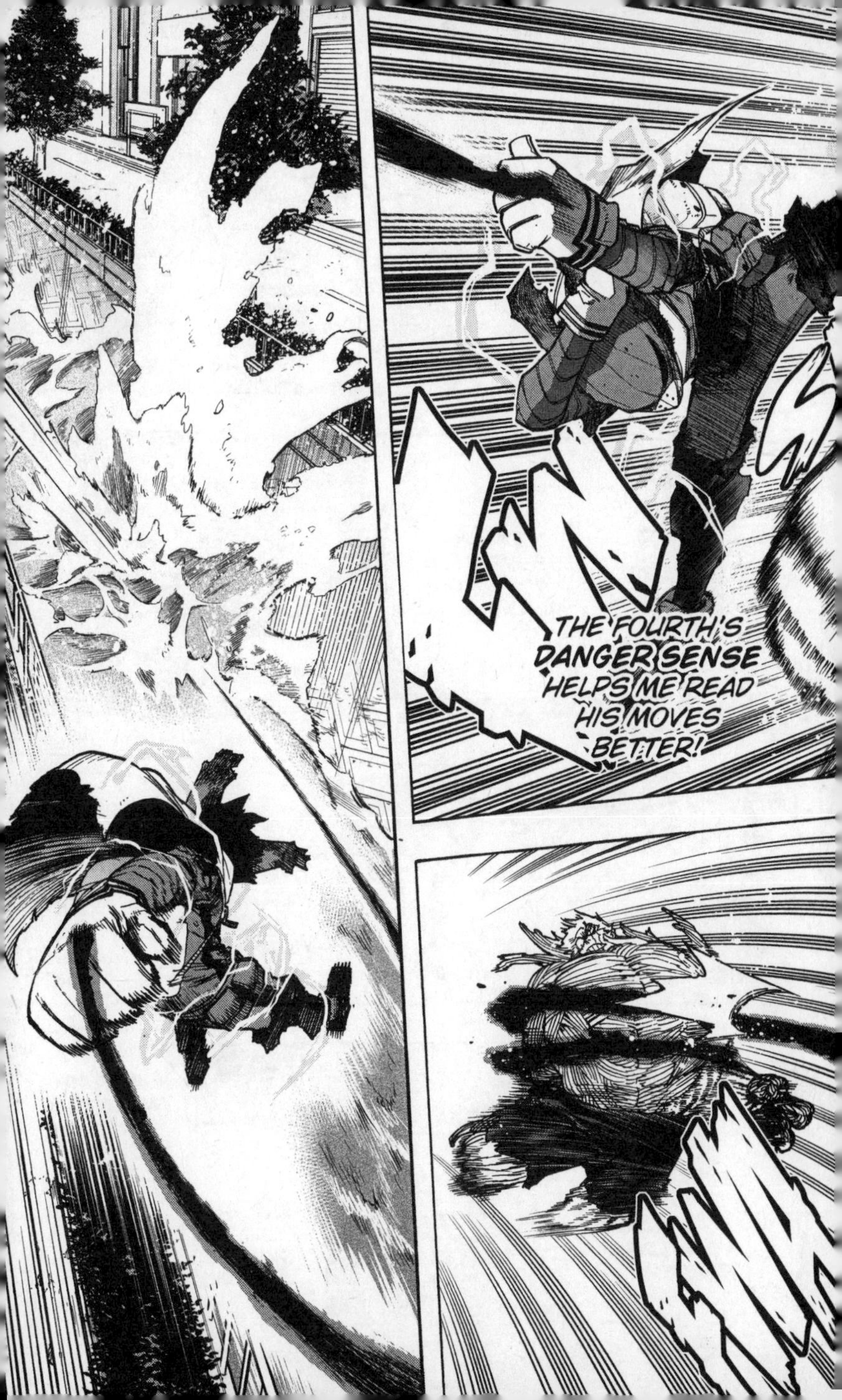
THE FOURTH'S DANGER SENSE HELPS ME READ HIS MOVES BETTER!

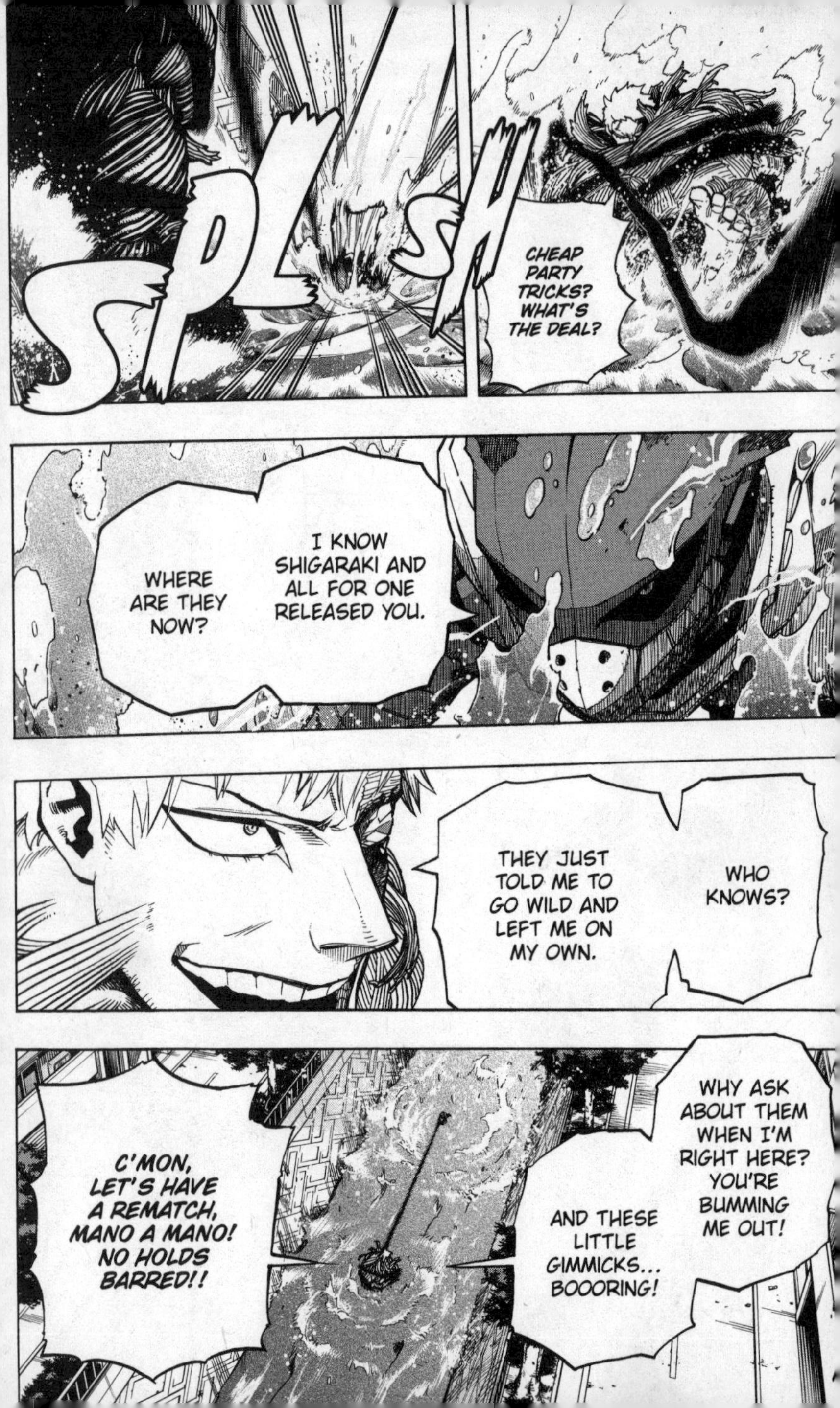
CHEAP PARTY TRICKS? WHAT'S THE DEAL?
SPLSH
I KNOW SHIGARAKI AND ALL FOR ONE RELEASED YOU.
WHERE ARE THEY NOW?
WHO KNOWS?
THEY JUST TOLD ME TO GO WILD AND LEFT ME ON MY OWN.
WHY ASK ABOUT THEM WHEN I'M RIGHT HERE? YOU'RE BUMMING ME OUT!
AND THESE LITTLE GIMMICKS... BOOORING!
C'MON, LET'S HAVE A REMATCH, MANO A MANO! NO HOLDS BARRED!!

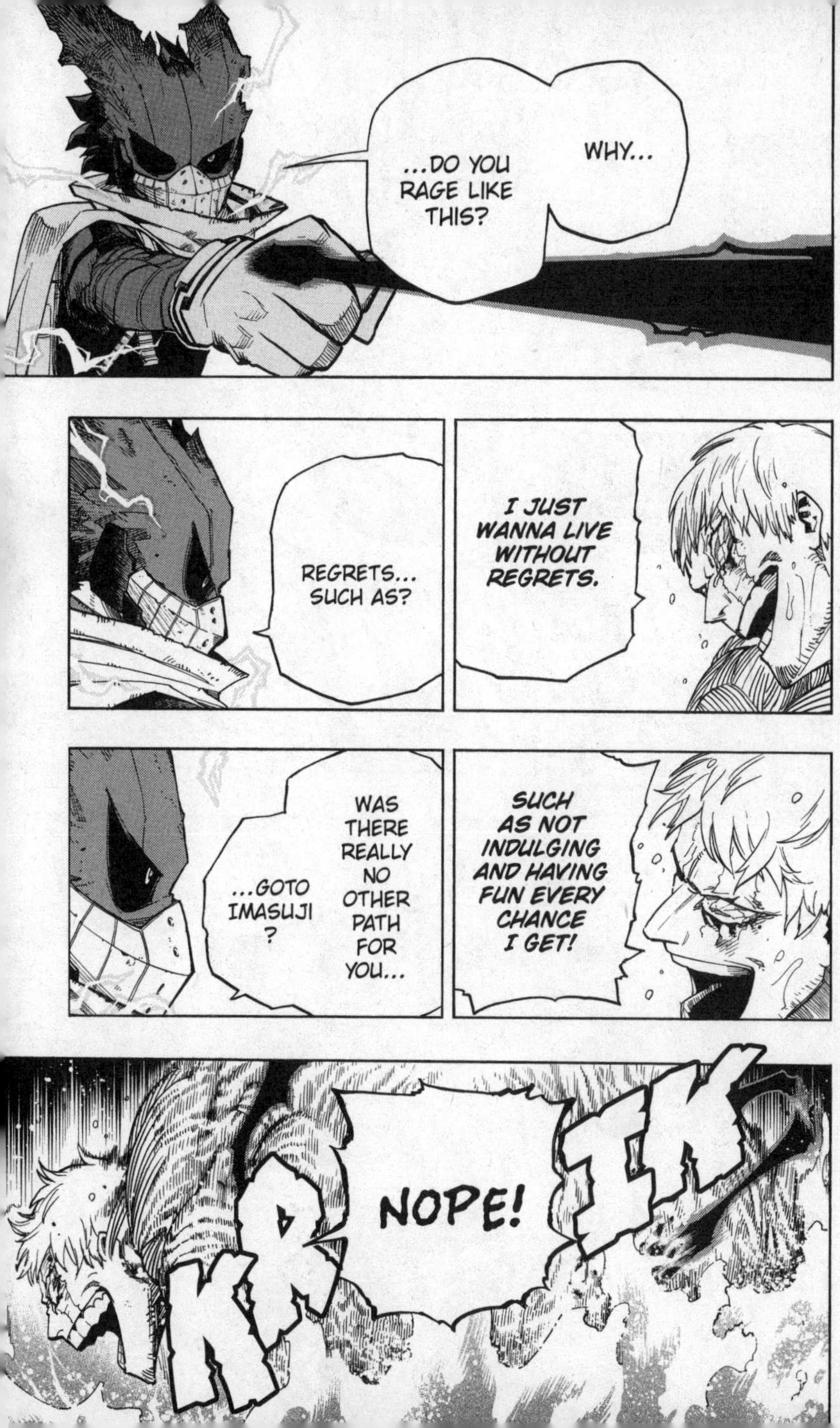
WHY...
...DO YOU RAGE LIKE THIS?
I JUST WANNA LIVE WITHOUT REGRETS.
REGRETS... SUCH AS?
SUCH AS NOT INDULGING AND HAVING FUN EVERY CHANCE I GET!
WAS THERE REALLY NO OTHER PATH FOR YOU...
...GOTO IMASUJI?
KRIK
NOPE!

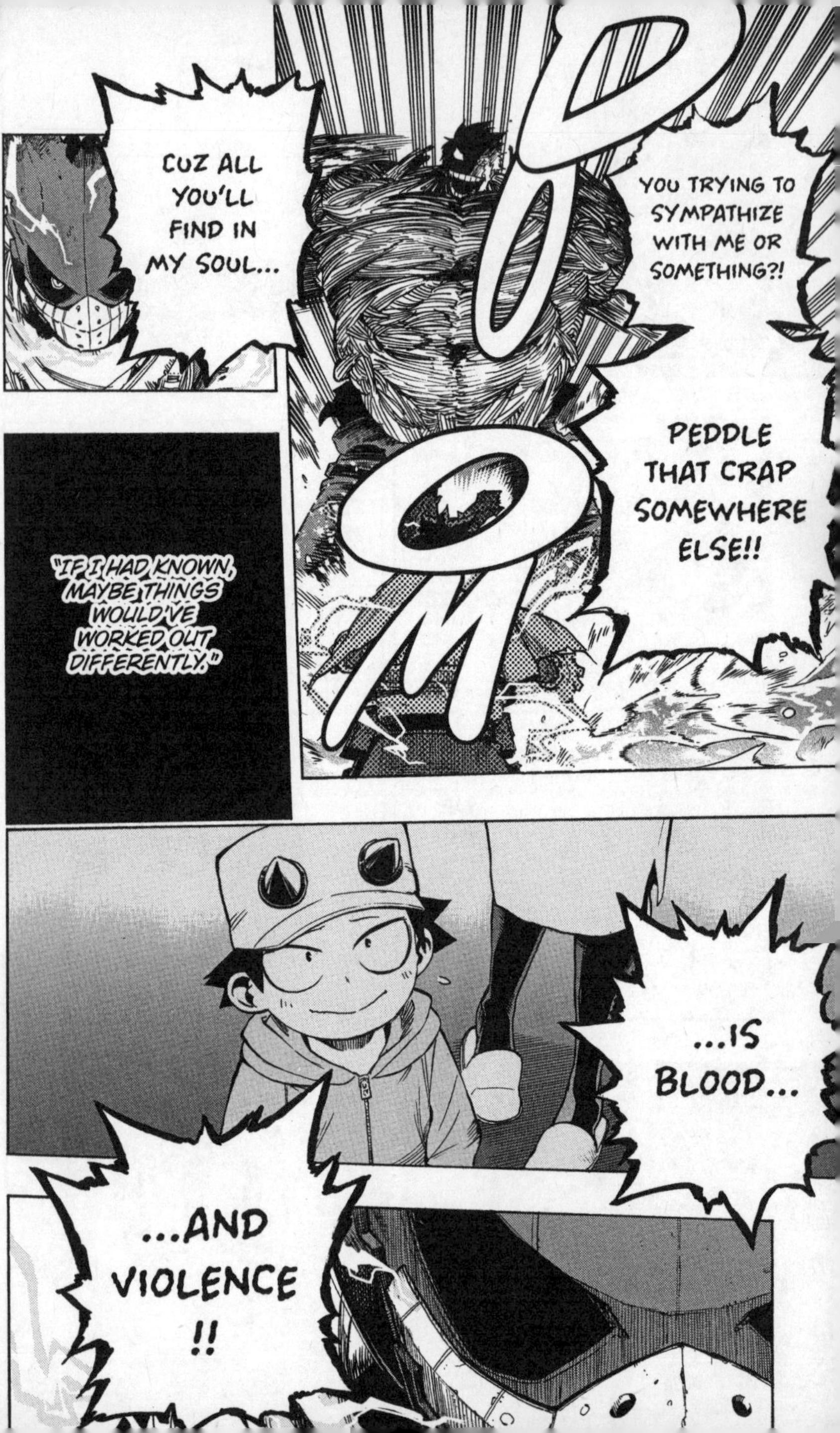
YOU TRYING TO SYMPATHIZE WITH ME OR SOMETHING?!
DOOM
PEDDLE THAT CRAP SOMEWHERE ELSE!!
CUZ ALL YOU'LL FIND IN MY SOUL...
"IF I HAD KNOWN, MAYBE THINGS WOULD'VE WORKED OUT DIFFERENTLY."
...IS BLOOD...
...AND VIOLENCE !!

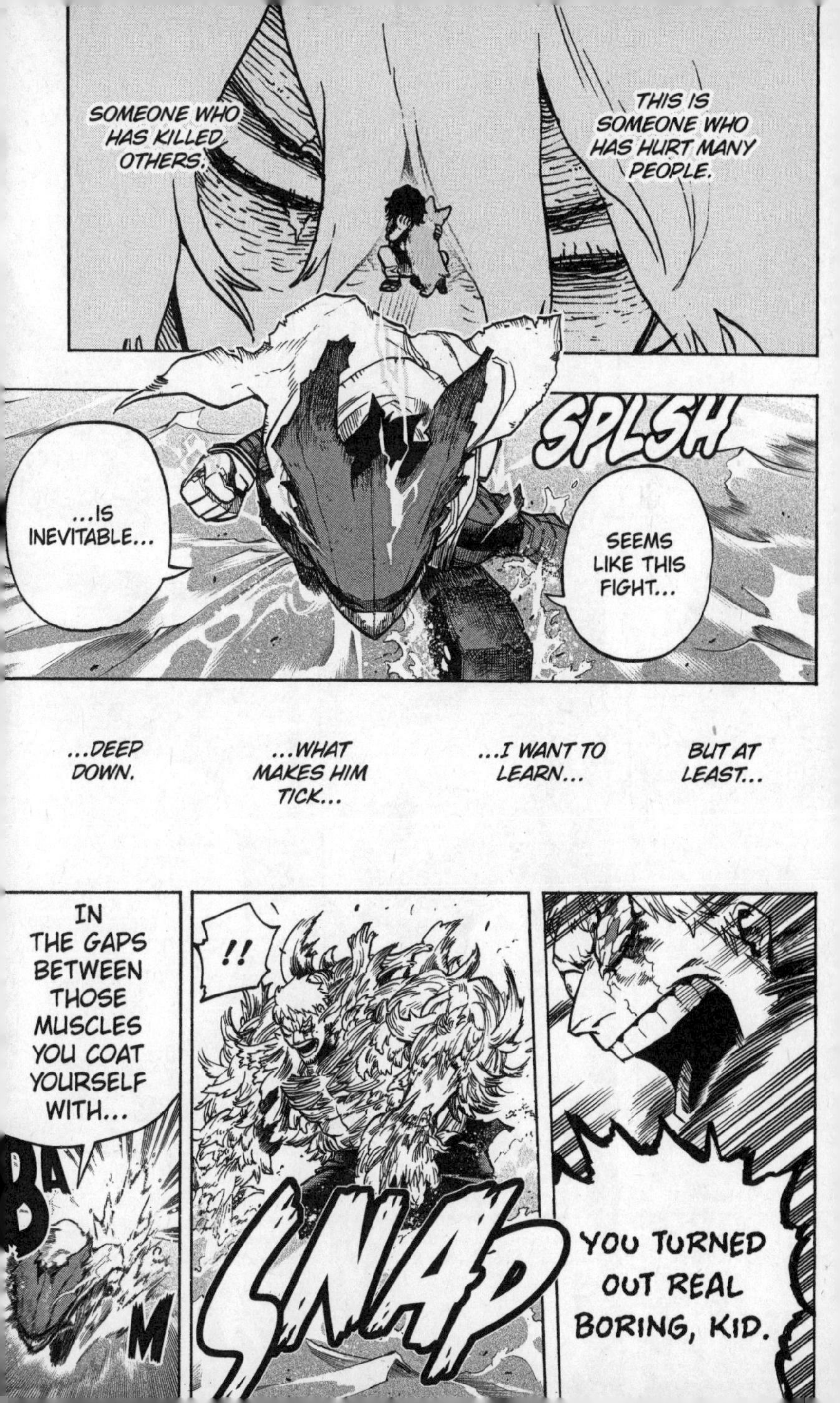
THIS IS SOMEONE WHO HAS HURT MANY PEOPLE.
SOMEONE WHO HAS KILLED OTHERS.
SPLSH
SEEMS LIKE THIS FIGHT...
...IS INEVITABLE...
BUT AT LEAST...
...I WANT TO LEARN...
...WHAT MAKES HIM TICK...
...DEEP DOWN.
YOU TURNED OUT REAL BORING, KID.
!!
SNAP
IN THE GAPS BETWEEN THOSE MUSCLES YOU COAT YOURSELF WITH...
BAM

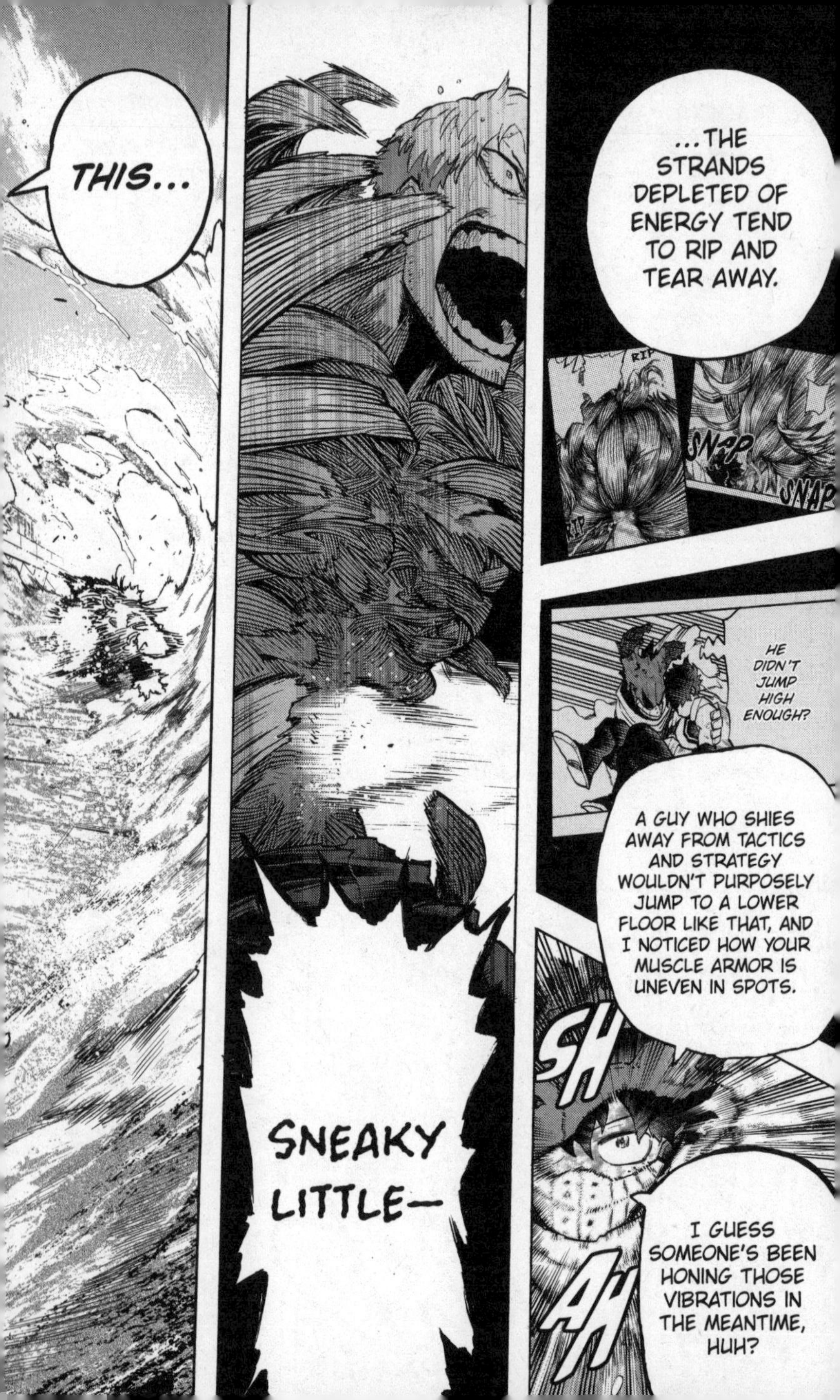
...THE STRANDS DEPLETED OF ENERGY TEND TO RIP AND TEAR AWAY.
SNAP
SNAP
RIP
RIP
HE DIDN'T JUMP HIGH ENOUGH?
A GUY WHO SHIES AWAY FROM TACTICS AND STRATEGY WOULDN'T PURPOSELY JUMP TO A LOWER FLOOR LIKE THAT, AND I NOTICED HOW YOUR MUSCLE ARMOR IS UNEVEN IN SPOTS.
SHAAH
I GUESS SOMEONE'S BEEN HONING THOSE VIBRATIONS IN THE MEANTIME, HUH?
SNEAKY LITTLE—
THIS...

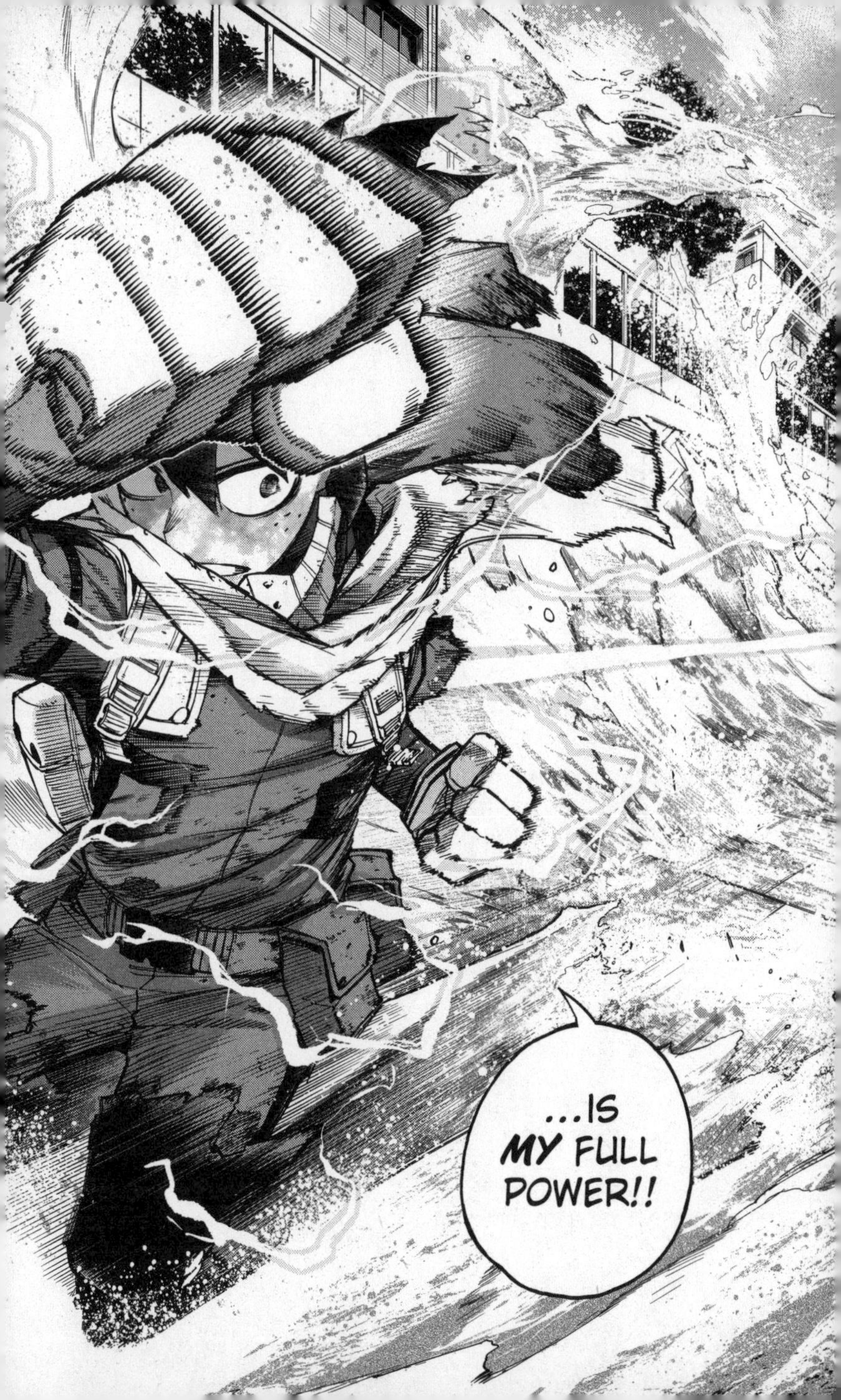
...IS MY FULL POWER!!

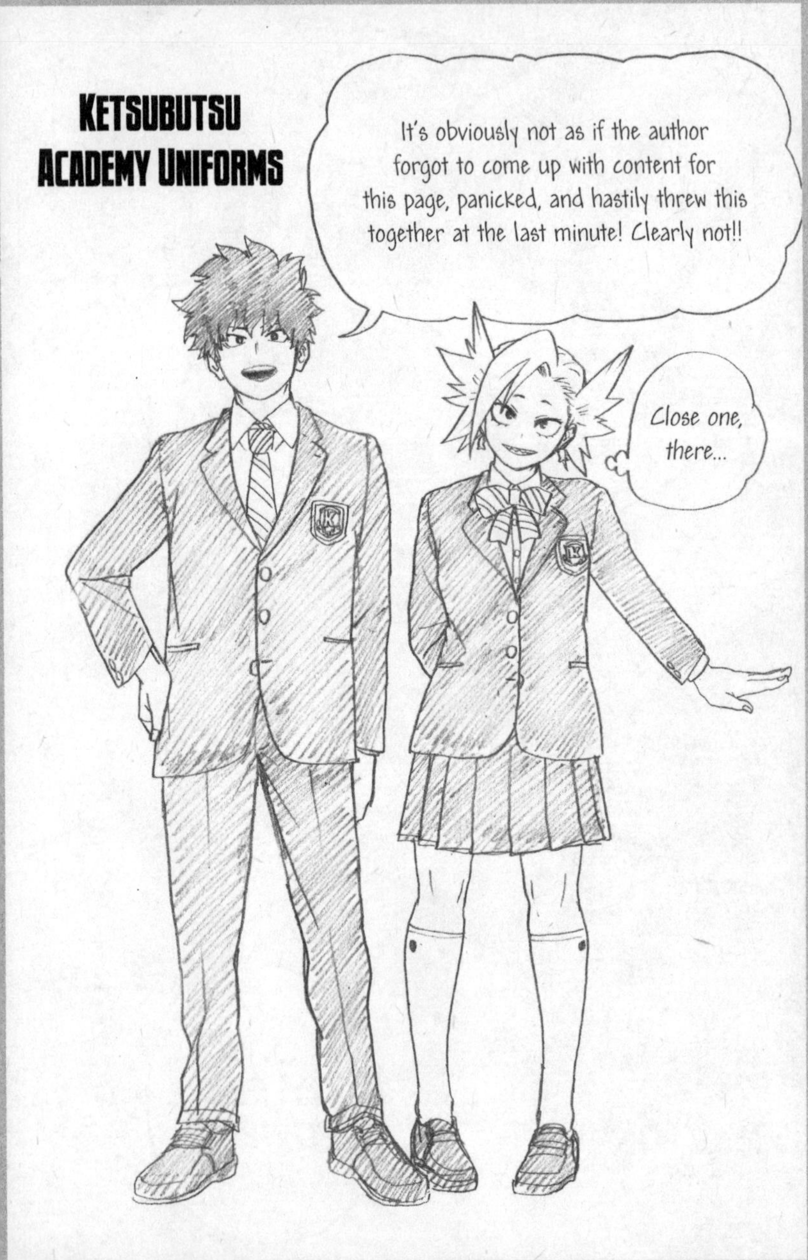
KETSUBUTSU ACADEMY UNIFORMS
It's obviously not as if the author forgot to come up with content for this page, panicked, and hastily threw this together at the last minute! Clearly not!!
Close one, there...

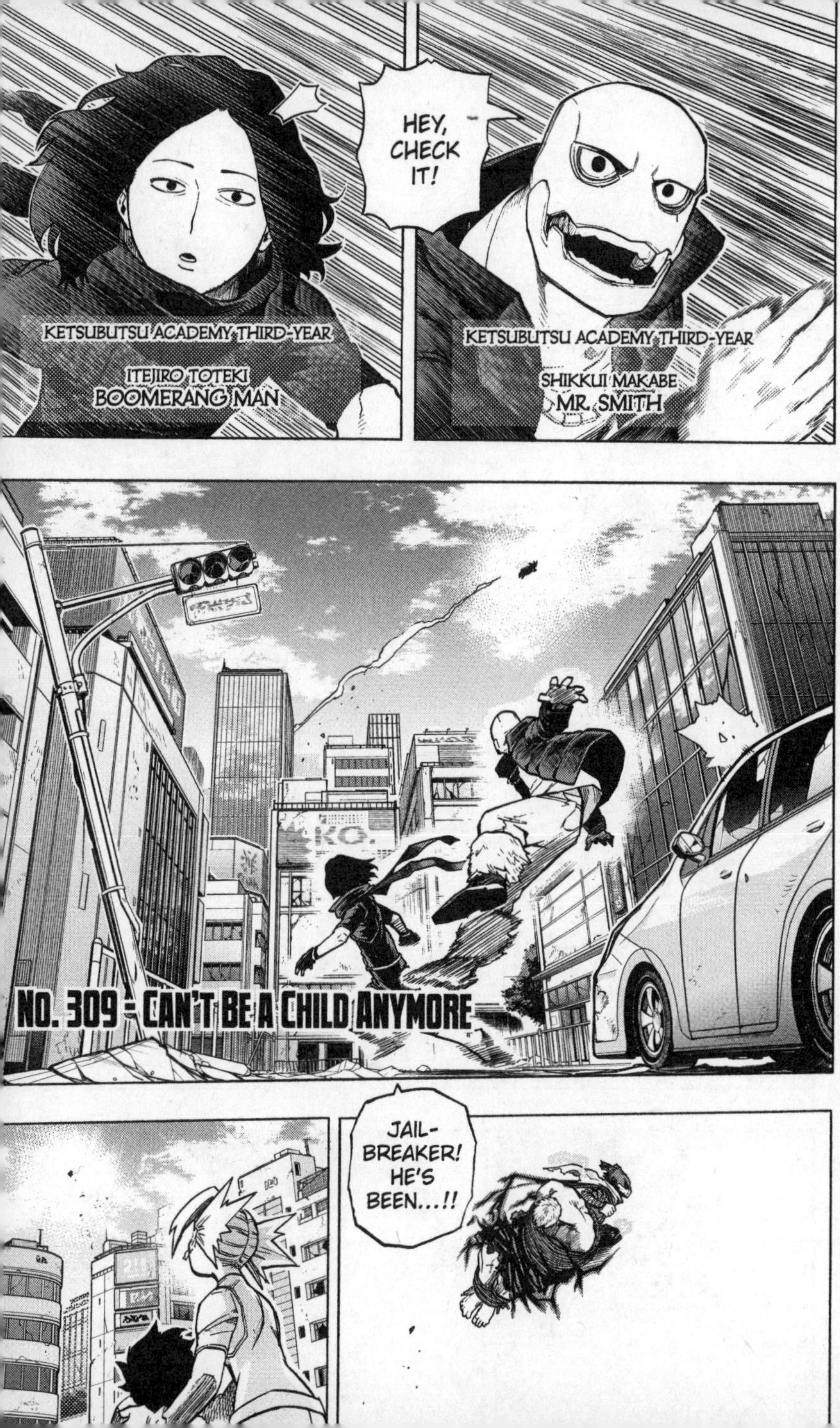
HEY, CHECK IT!
KETSUBUTSU ACADEMY THIRD-YEAR
SHIKKUI MAKABE
MR. SMITH
KETSUBUTSU ACADEMY THIRD-YEAR
ITEJIRO TOTEKI
BOOMERANG MAN
NO. 309 - CAN'T BE A CHILD ANYMORE
JAIL-BREAKER! HE'S BEEN...!!

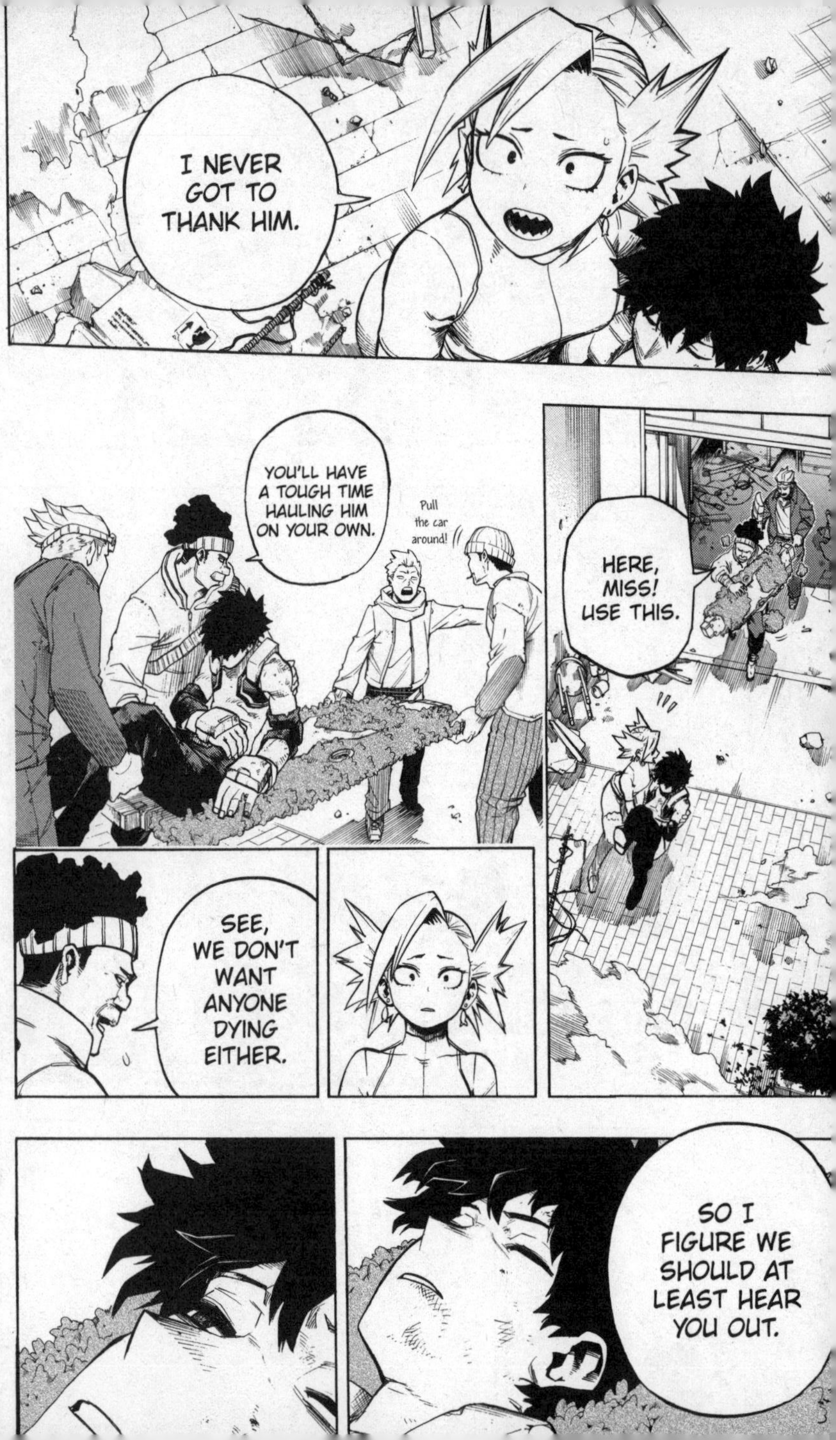
I NEVER GOT TO THANK HIM.
HERE, MISS! USE THIS.
YOU'LL HAVE A TOUGH TIME HAULING HIM ON YOUR OWN.
Pull the car around!
SEE, WE DON'T WANT ANYONE DYING EITHER.
SO I FIGURE WE SHOULD AT LEAST HEAR YOU OUT.

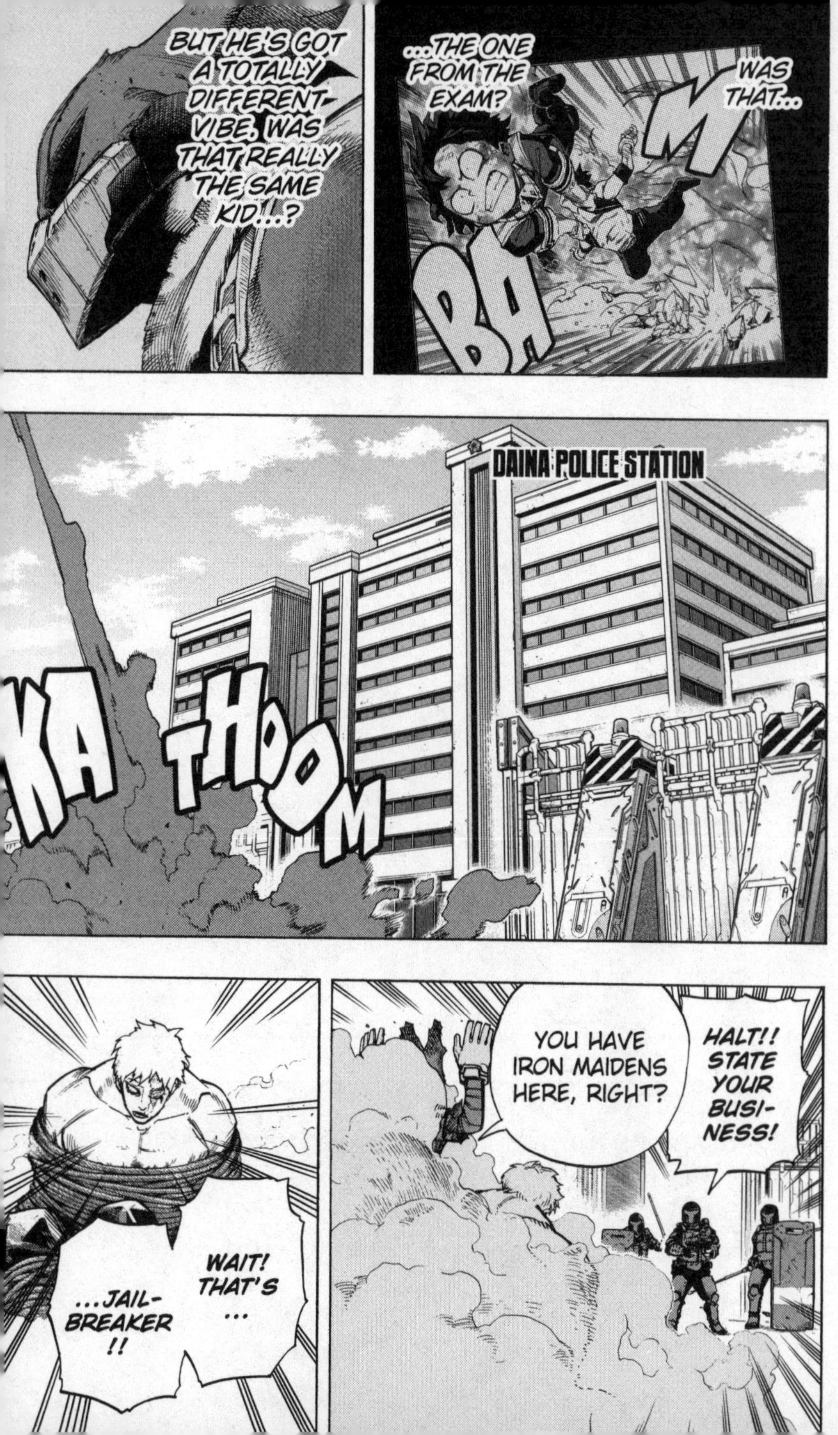
WAS THAT...
...THE ONE FROM THE EXAM?
BAM
BUT HE'S GOT A TOTALLY DIFFERENT VIBE. WAS THAT REALLY THE SAME KID...?
DAINA POLICE STATION
KATHOOM
HALT!! STATE YOUR BUSI-NESS!
YOU HAVE IRON MAIDENS HERE, RIGHT?
WAIT! THAT'S ...
...JAIL-BREAKER!!

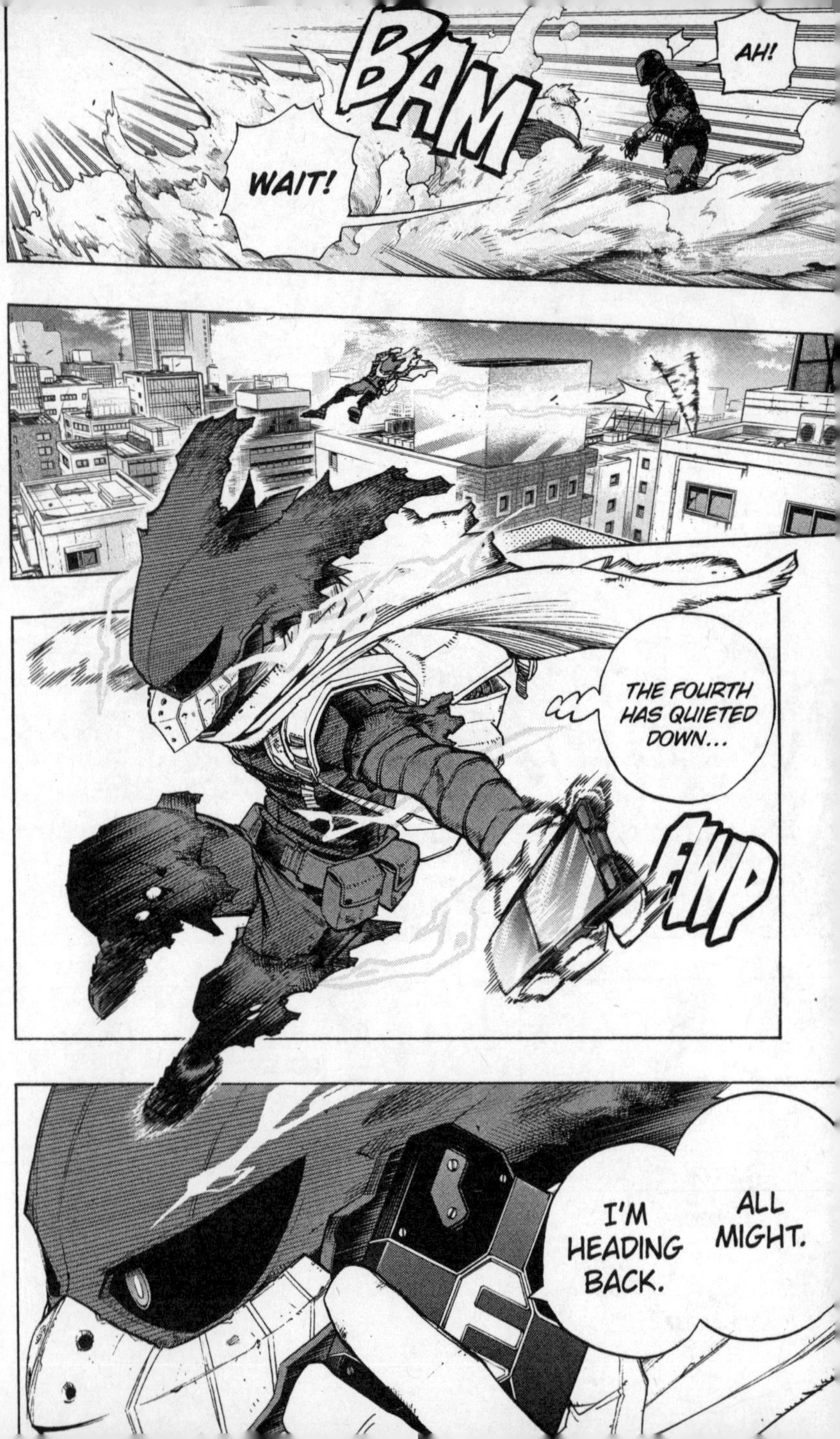
AH!
BAM
WAIT!
THE FOURTH HAS QUIETED DOWN...
FWP
ALL MIGHT.
I'M HEADING BACK.

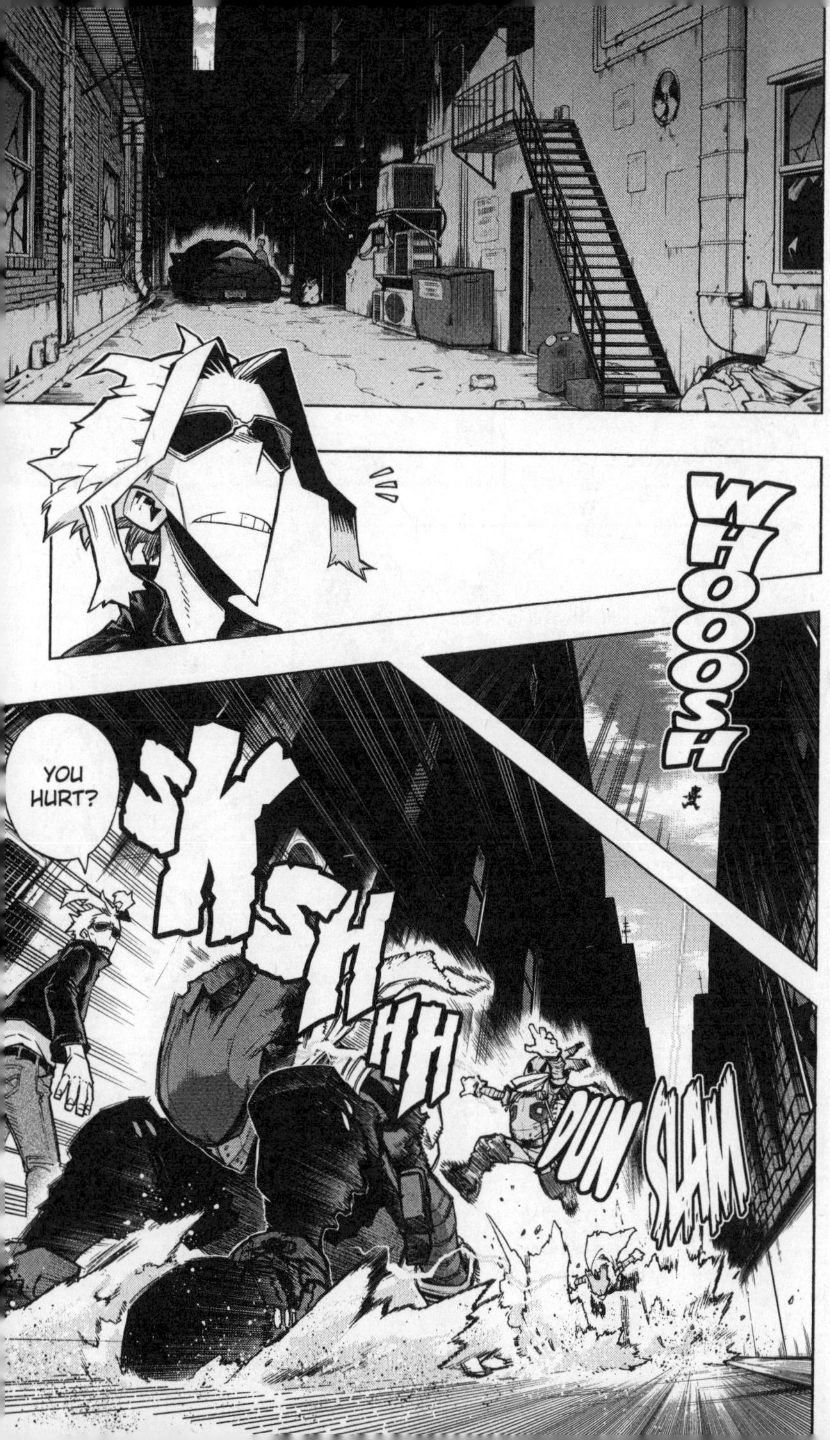
WHOOOOSH
SLAM
DUN
SHHHH
YOU HURT?

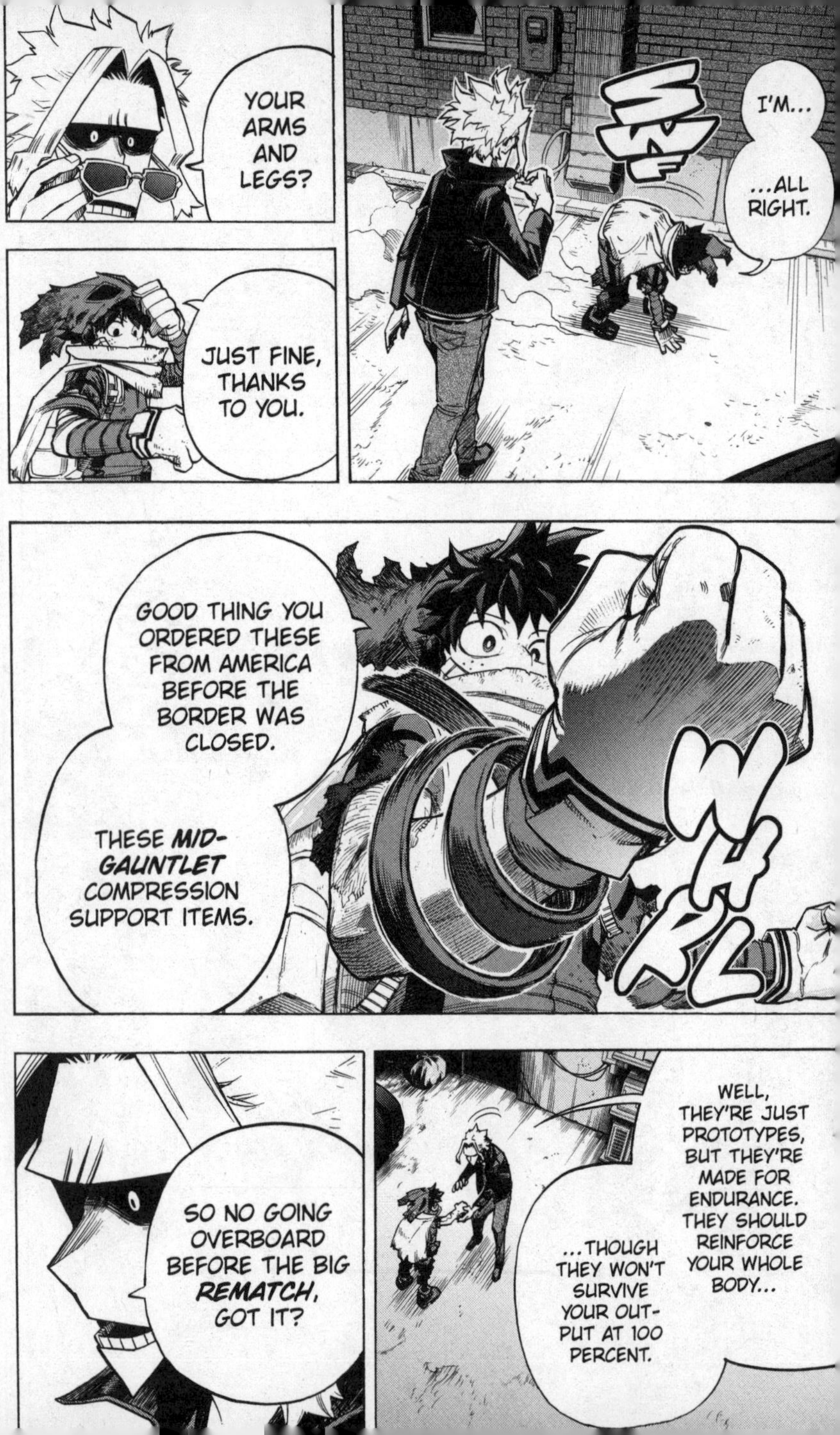
I'M...
...ALL RIGHT.
YOUR ARMS AND LEGS?
JUST FINE, THANKS TO YOU.
GOOD THING YOU ORDERED THESE FROM AMERICA BEFORE THE BORDER WAS CLOSED.
THESE *MID-GAUNTLET* COMPRESSION SUPPORT ITEMS.
WELL, THEY'RE JUST PROTOTYPES, BUT THEY'RE MADE FOR ENDURANCE. THEY SHOULD REINFORCE YOUR WHOLE BODY...
...THOUGH THEY WON'T SURVIVE YOUR OUT-PUT AT 100 PERCENT.
SO NO GOING OVERBOARD BEFORE THE BIG *REMATCH*, GOT IT?

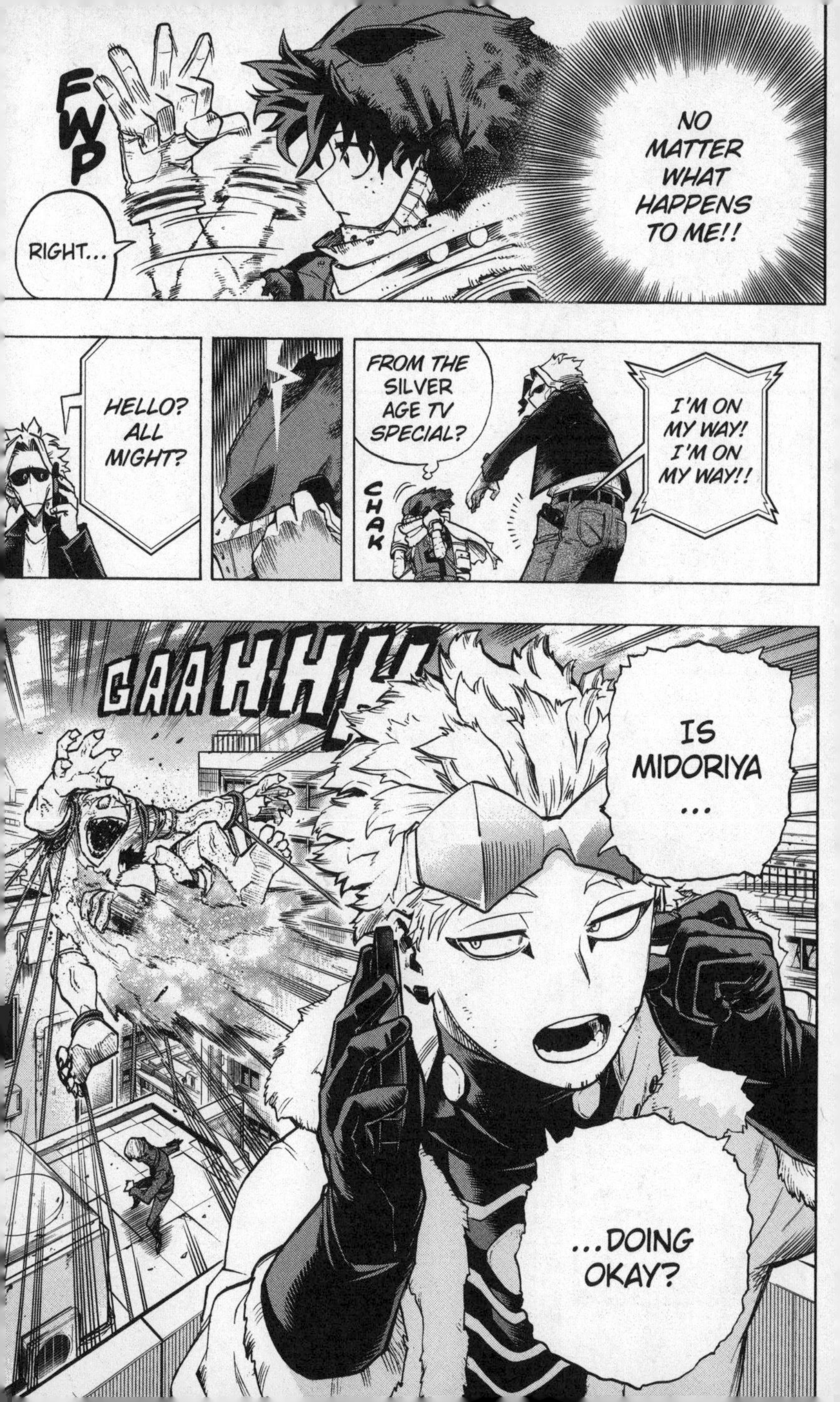
NO MATTER WHAT HAPPENS TO ME!!
FWP
RIGHT...
I'M ON MY WAY! I'M ON MY WAY!!
FROM THE SILVER AGE TV SPECIAL?
CHAK
HELLO? ALL MIGHT?
IS MIDORIYA ...
GAAHHH
...DOING OKAY?

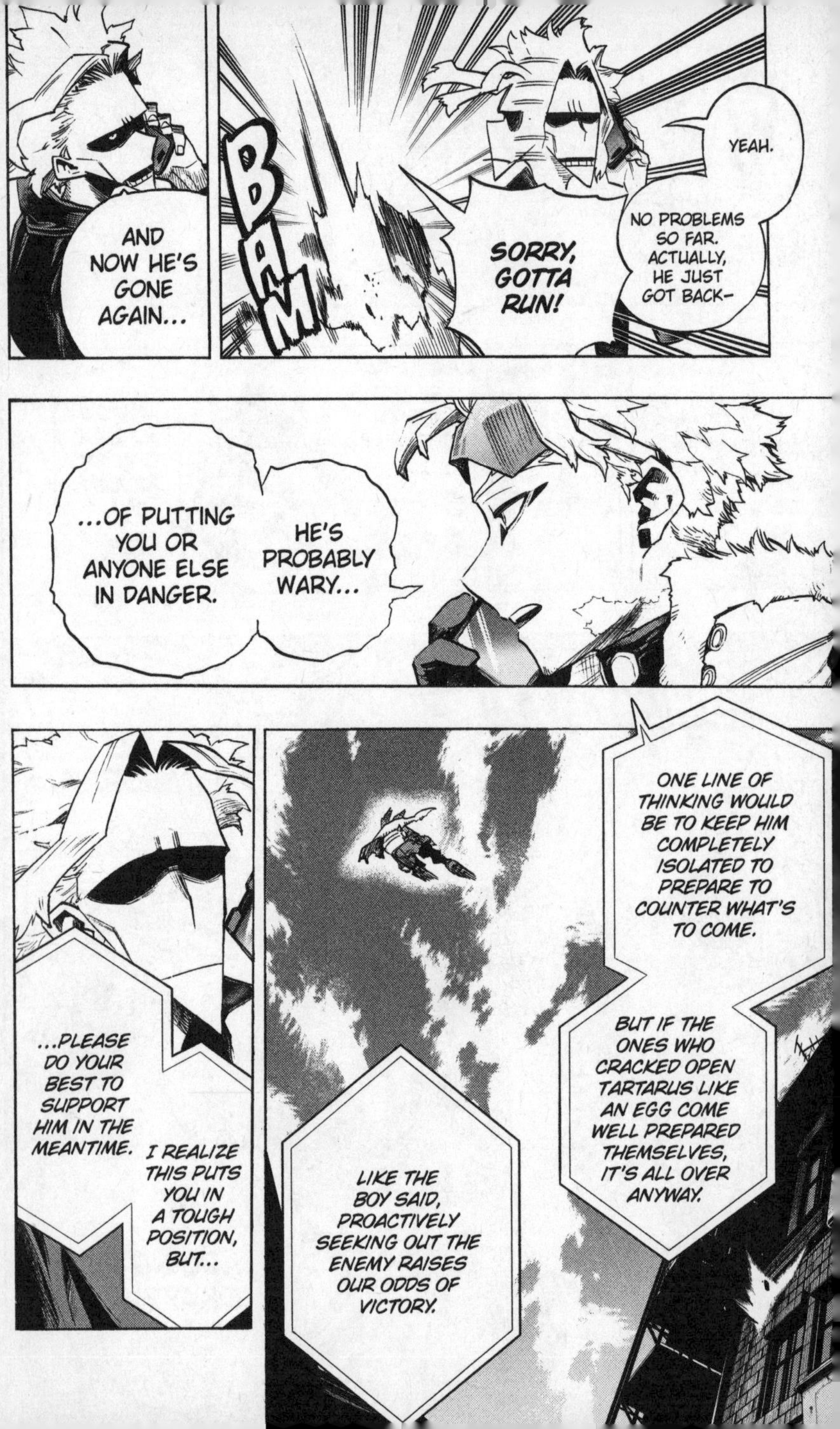
YEAH.
NO PROBLEMS SO FAR. ACTUALLY, HE JUST GOT BACK–
SORRY, GOTTA RUN!
BAM
AND NOW HE'S GONE AGAIN...
HE'S PROBABLY WARY...
...OF PUTTING YOU OR ANYONE ELSE IN DANGER.
ONE LINE OF THINKING WOULD BE TO KEEP HIM COMPLETELY ISOLATED TO PREPARE TO COUNTER WHAT'S TO COME.
BUT IF THE ONES WHO CRACKED OPEN TARTARUS LIKE AN EGG COME WELL PREPARED THEMSELVES, IT'S ALL OVER ANYWAY.
LIKE THE BOY SAID, PROACTIVELY SEEKING OUT THE ENEMY RAISES OUR ODDS OF VICTORY.
I REALIZE THIS PUTS YOU IN A TOUGH POSITION, BUT...
...PLEASE DO YOUR BEST TO SUPPORT HIM IN THE MEANTIME.

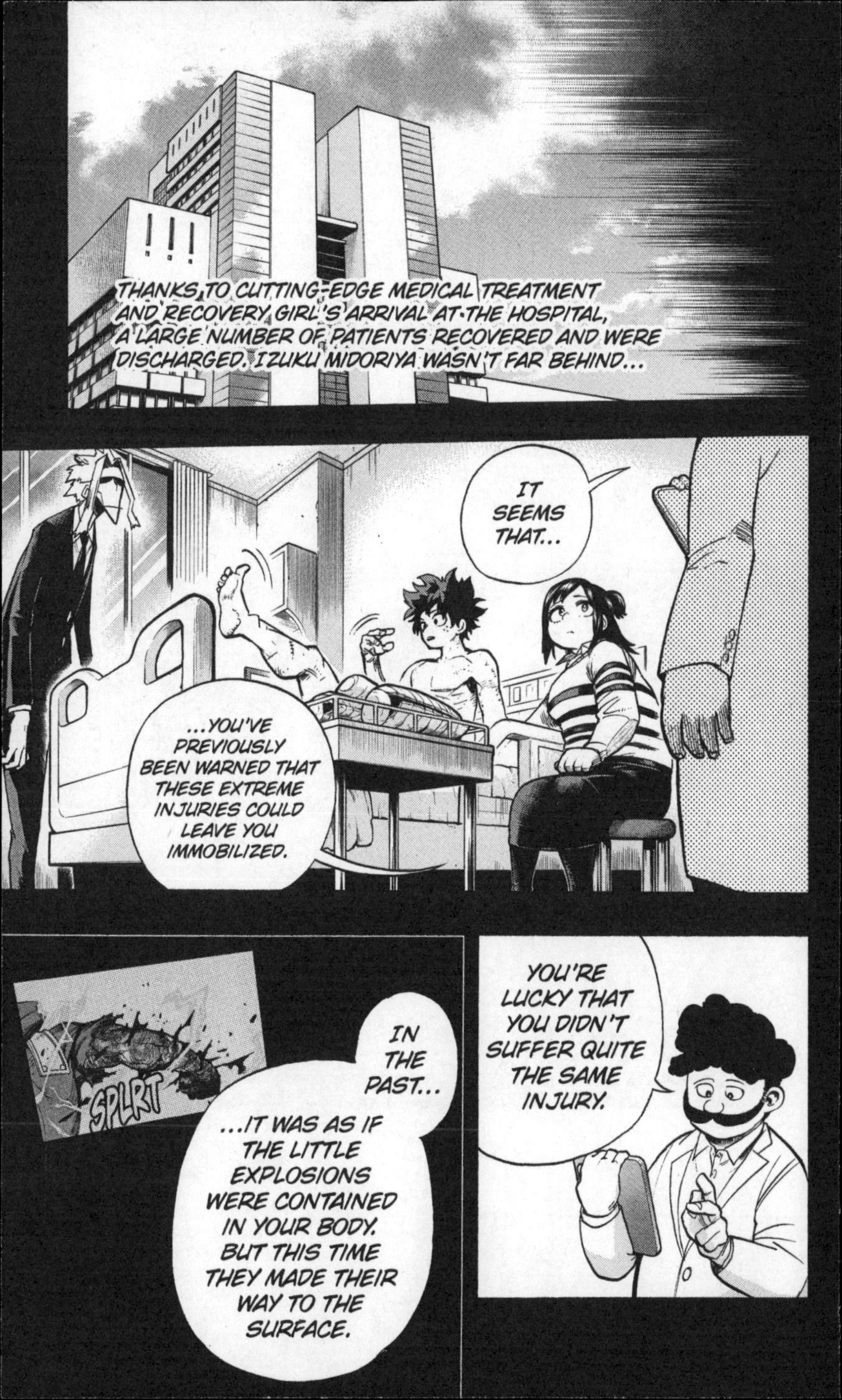

!!!
THANKS TO CUTTING-EDGE MEDICAL TREATMENT AND RECOVERY GIRL'S ARRIVAL AT THE HOSPITAL, A LARGE NUMBER OF PATIENTS RECOVERED AND WERE DISCHARGED. IZUKU MIDORIYA WASN'T FAR BEHIND...
IT SEEMS THAT...
...YOU'VE PREVIOUSLY BEEN WARNED THAT THESE EXTREME INJURIES COULD LEAVE YOU IMMOBILIZED.
YOU'RE LUCKY THAT YOU DIDN'T SUFFER QUITE THE SAME INJURY.
IN THE PAST...
...IT WAS AS IF THE LITTLE EXPLOSIONS WERE CONTAINED IN YOUR BODY. BUT THIS TIME THEY MADE THEIR WAY TO THE SURFACE.
SPLRT

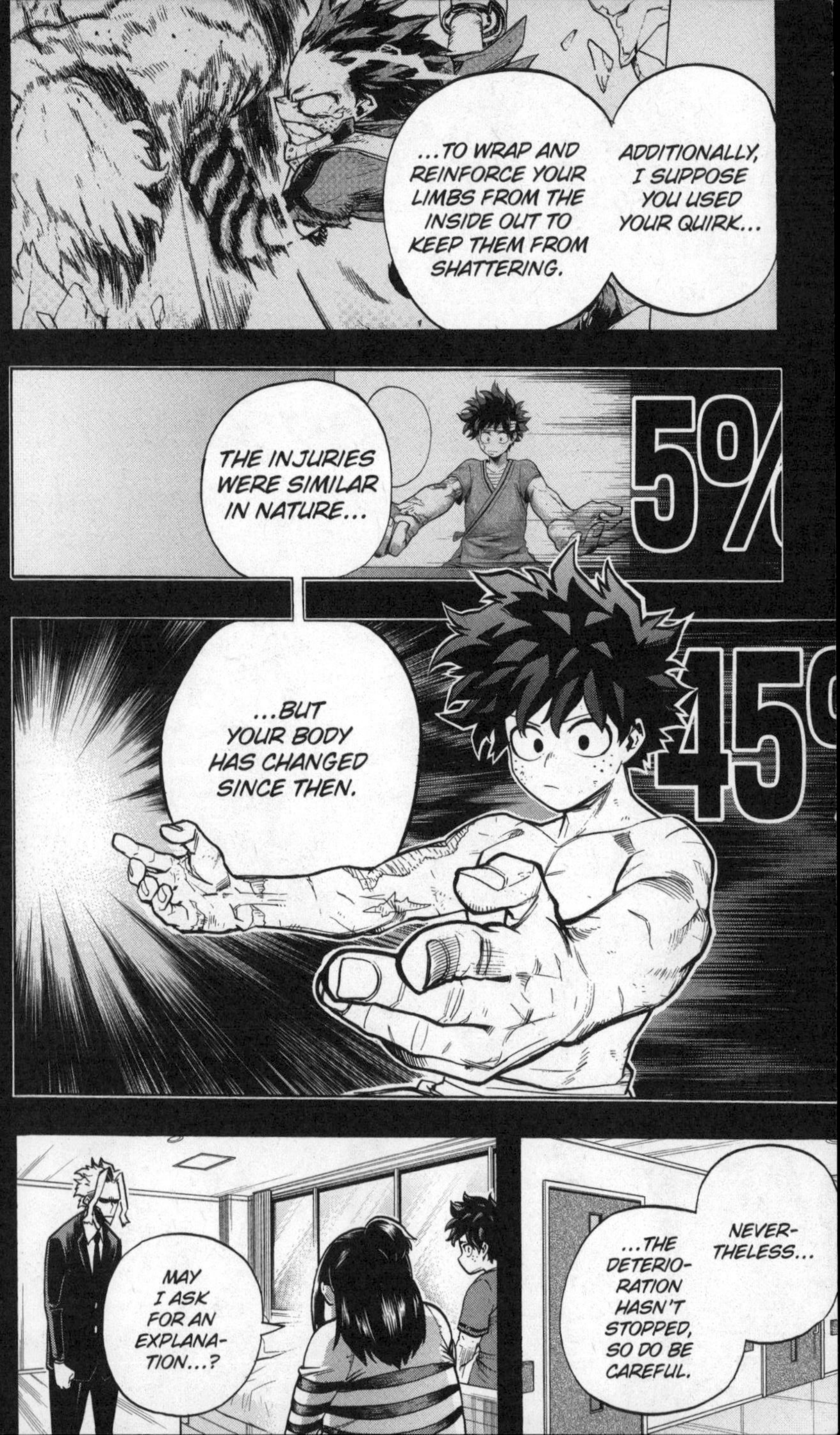
ADDITIONALLY, I SUPPOSE YOU USED YOUR QUIRK...
...TO WRAP AND REINFORCE YOUR LIMBS FROM THE INSIDE OUT TO KEEP THEM FROM SHATTERING.
5%
THE INJURIES WERE SIMILAR IN NATURE...
45
...BUT YOUR BODY HAS CHANGED SINCE THEN.
NEVER-THELESS...
...THE DETERIO-RATION HASN'T STOPPED, SO DO BE CAREFUL.
MAY I ASK FOR AN EXPLANA-TION...?

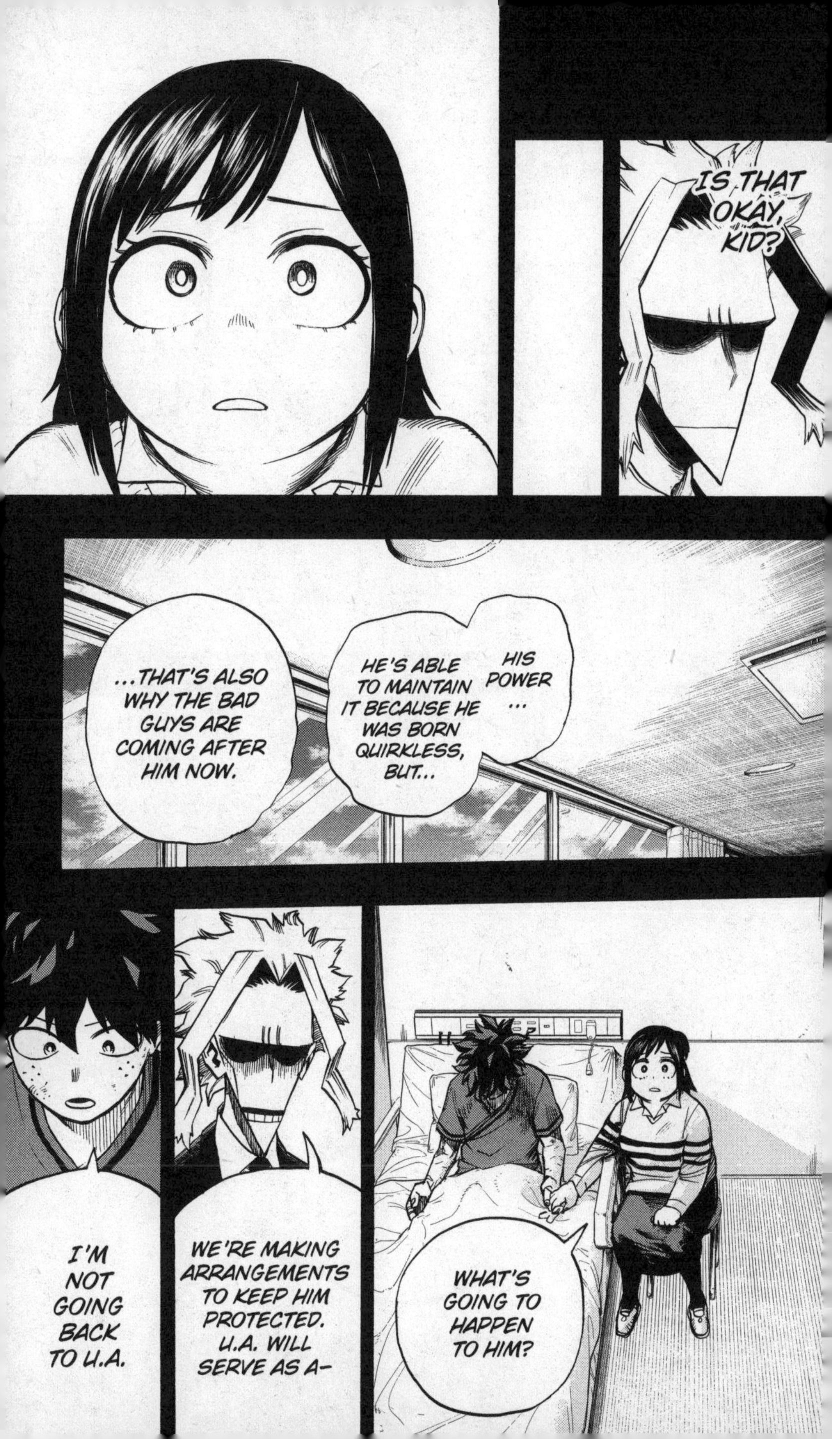
IS THAT OKAY, KID?
HIS POWER ...
HE'S ABLE TO MAINTAIN IT BECAUSE HE WAS BORN QUIRKLESS, BUT...
...THAT'S ALSO WHY THE BAD GUYS ARE COMING AFTER HIM NOW.
WHAT'S GOING TO HAPPEN TO HIM?
WE'RE MAKING ARRANGEMENTS TO KEEP HIM PROTECTED. U.A. WILL SERVE AS A-
I'M NOT GOING BACK TO U.A.

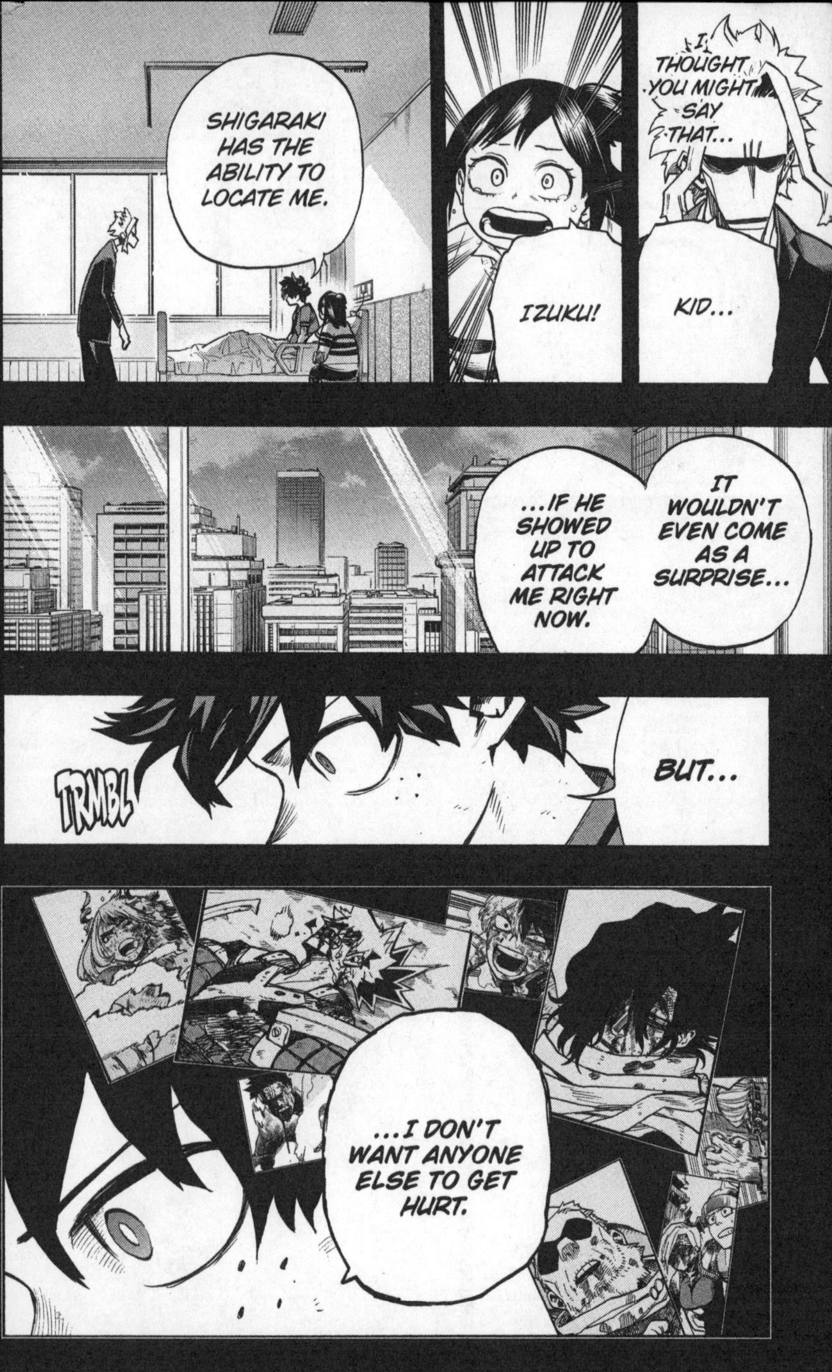
I THOUGHT YOU MIGHT SAY THAT...
KID...
IZUKU!
SHIGARAKI HAS THE ABILITY TO LOCATE ME.
IT WOULDN'T EVEN COME AS A SURPRISE...
...IF HE SHOWED UP TO ATTACK ME RIGHT NOW.
BUT...
TRMBL
...I DON'T WANT ANYONE ELSE TO GET HURT.

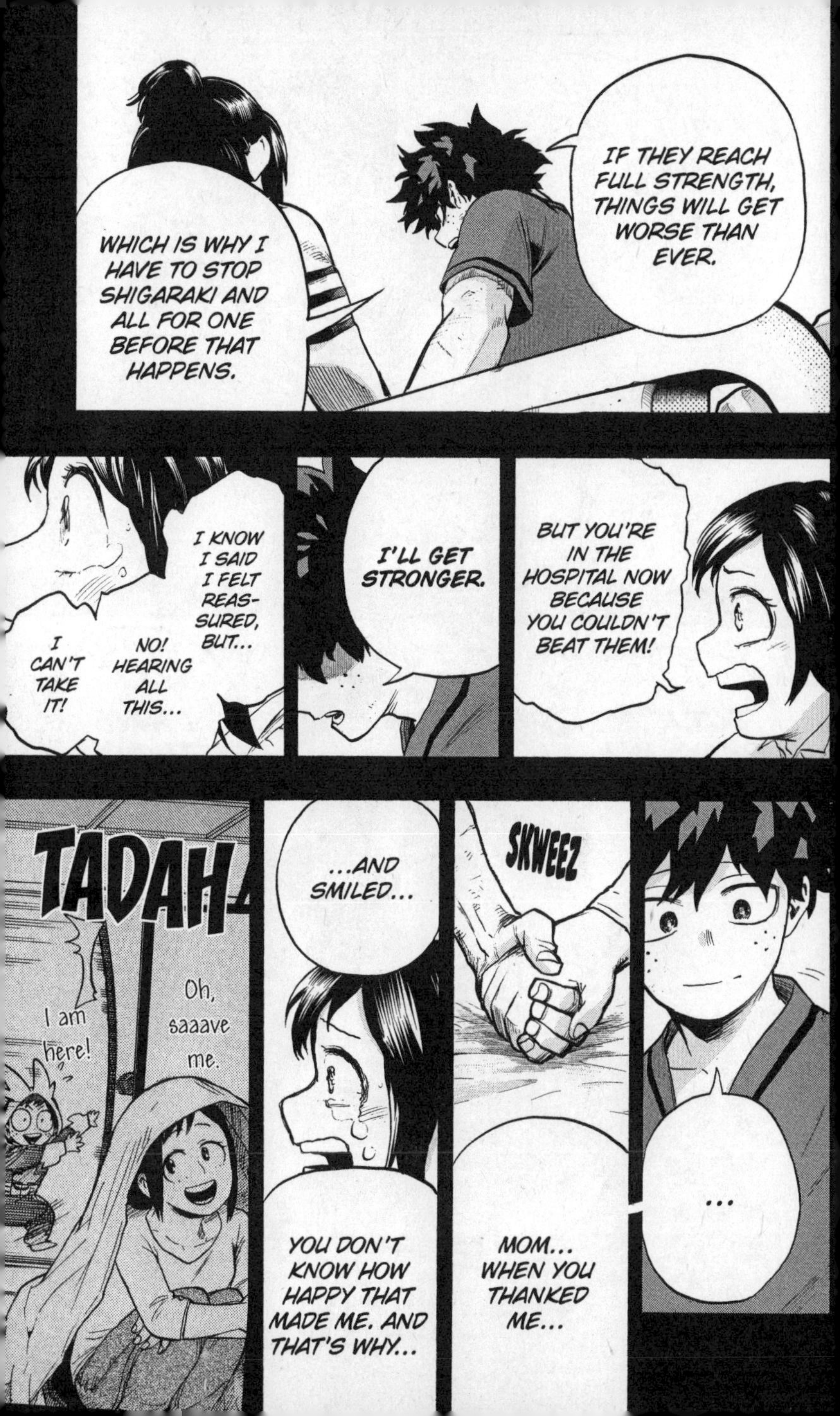
IF THEY REACH FULL STRENGTH, THINGS WILL GET WORSE THAN EVER.
WHICH IS WHY I HAVE TO STOP SHIGARAKI AND ALL FOR ONE BEFORE THAT HAPPENS.
BUT YOU'RE IN THE HOSPITAL NOW BECAUSE YOU COULDN'T BEAT THEM!
I'LL GET STRONGER.
I KNOW I SAID I FELT REAS-SURED, BUT...
NO! HEARING ALL THIS...
I CAN'T TAKE IT!
...
MOM... WHEN YOU THANKED ME...
SKWEEZ
...AND SMILED...
YOU DON'T KNOW HOW HAPPY THAT MADE ME. AND THAT'S WHY...
TADAH
Oh, saaave me.
I am here!

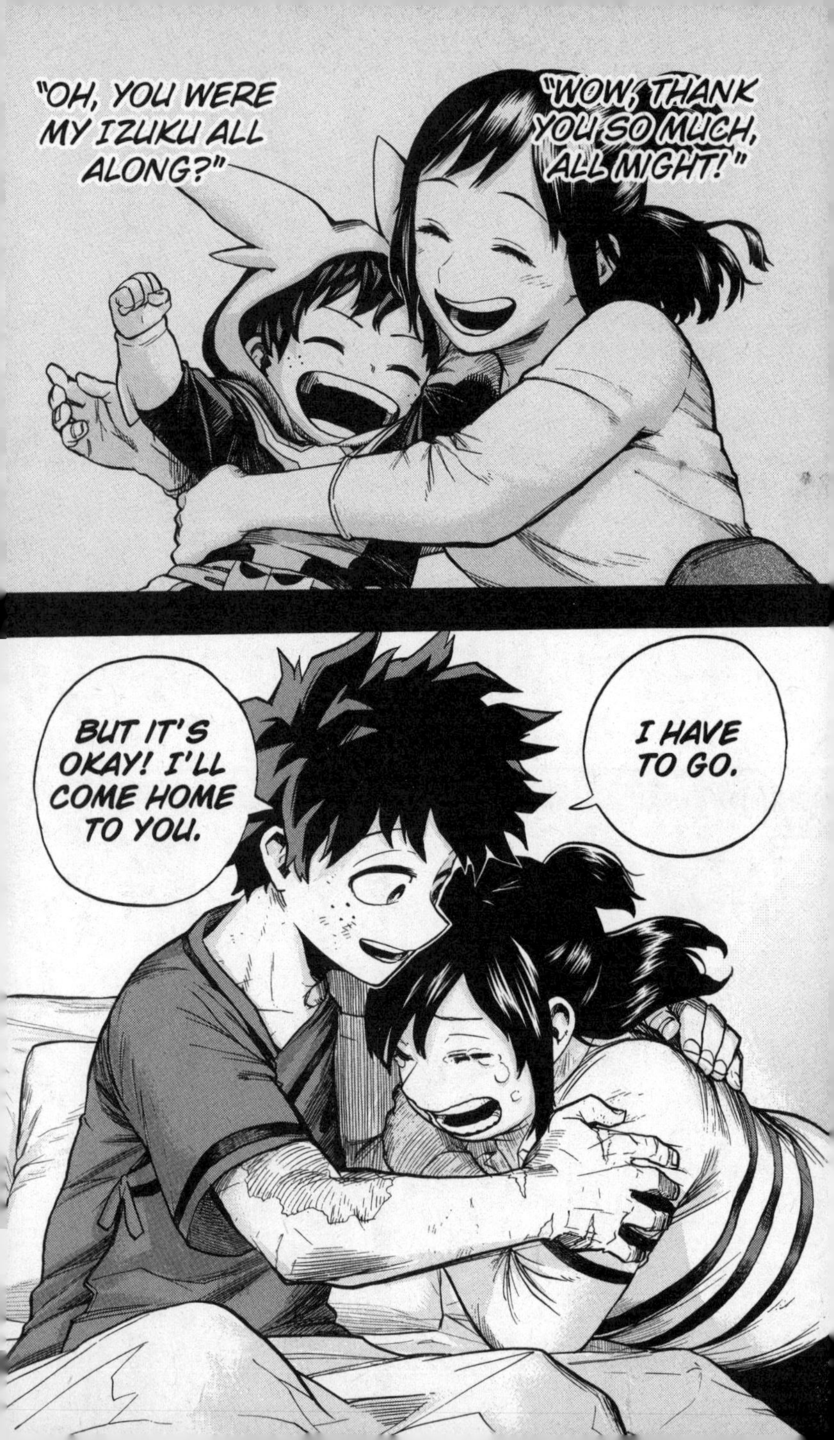
"WOW, THANK YOU SO MUCH, ALL MIGHT!"
"OH, YOU WERE MY IZUKU ALL ALONG?"
I HAVE TO GO.
BUT IT'S OKAY! I'LL COME HOME TO YOU.

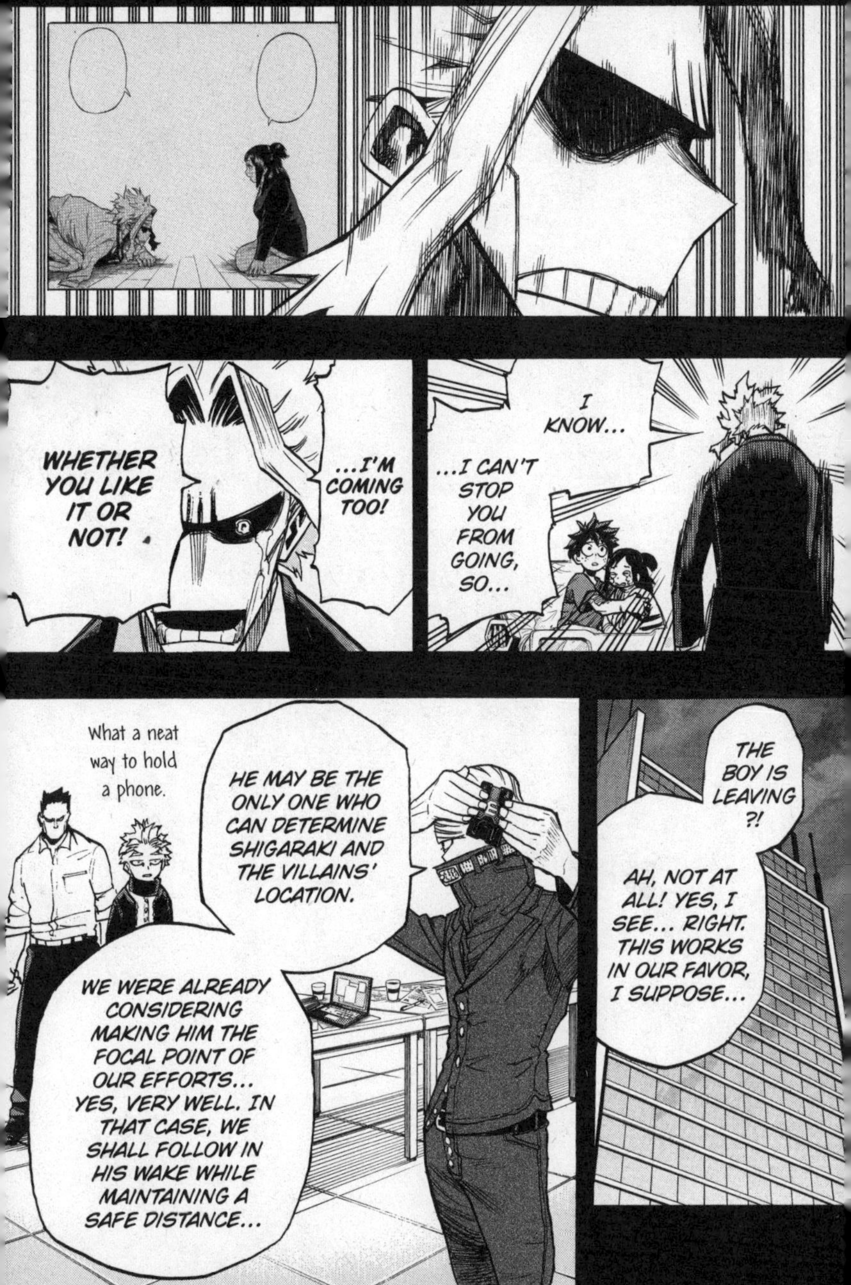
I KNOW...
...I CAN'T STOP YOU FROM GOING, SO...
...I'M COMING TOO!
WHETHER YOU LIKE IT OR NOT!
THE BOY IS LEAVING?!
AH, NOT AT ALL! YES, I SEE... RIGHT. THIS WORKS IN OUR FAVOR, I SUPPOSE...
HE MAY BE THE ONLY ONE WHO CAN DETERMINE SHIGARAKI AND THE VILLAINS' LOCATION.
What a neat way to hold a phone.
WE WERE ALREADY CONSIDERING MAKING HIM THE FOCAL POINT OF OUR EFFORTS... YES, VERY WELL. IN THAT CASE, WE SHALL FOLLOW IN HIS WAKE WHILE MAINTAINING A SAFE DISTANCE...

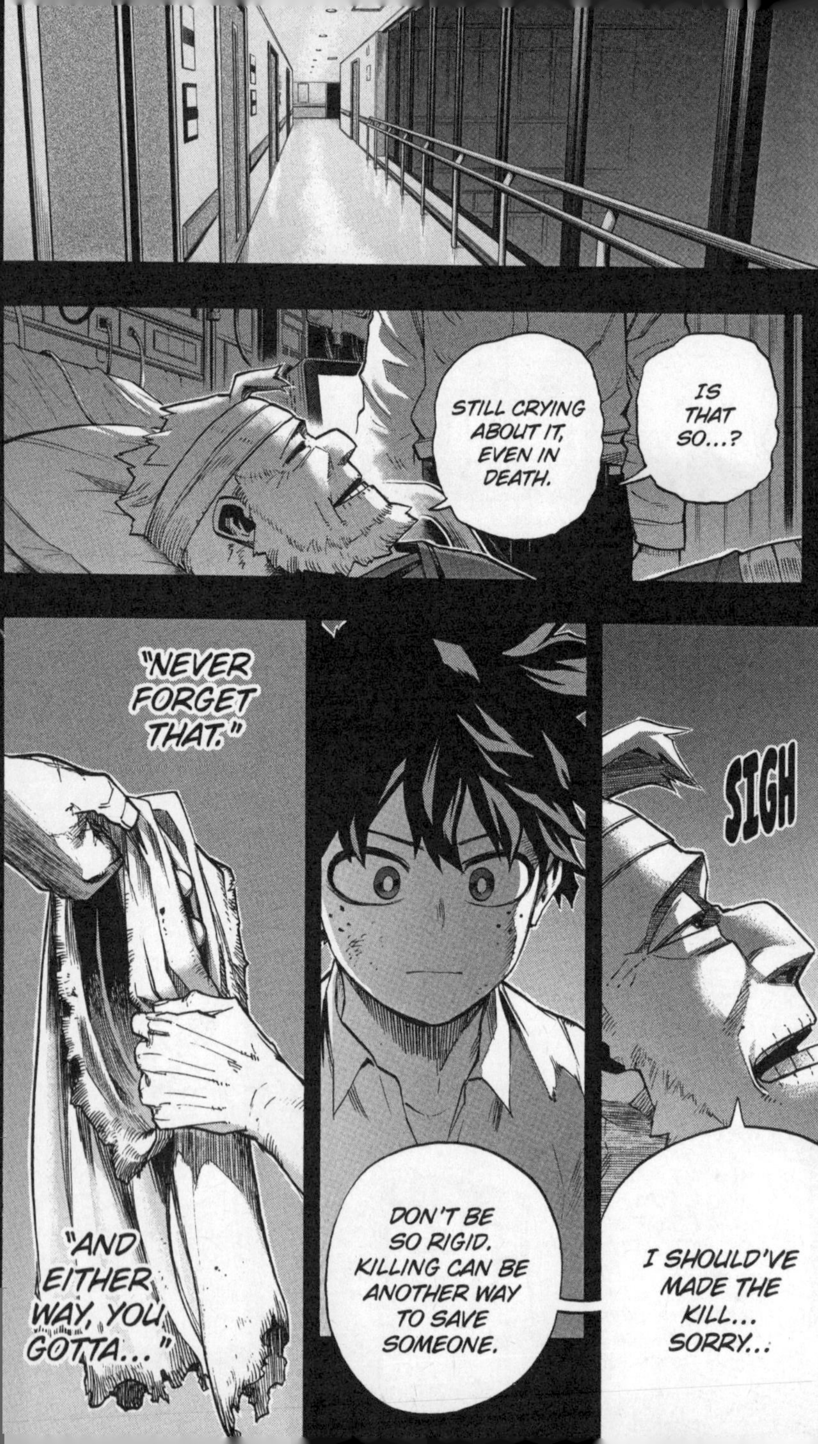
IS THAT SO...?
STILL CRYING ABOUT IT, EVEN IN DEATH.
SIGH
I SHOULD'VE MADE THE KILL... SORRY...
DON'T BE SO RIGID. KILLING CAN BE ANOTHER WAY TO SAVE SOMEONE.
"NEVER FORGET THAT."
"AND EITHER WAY, YOU GOTTA..."

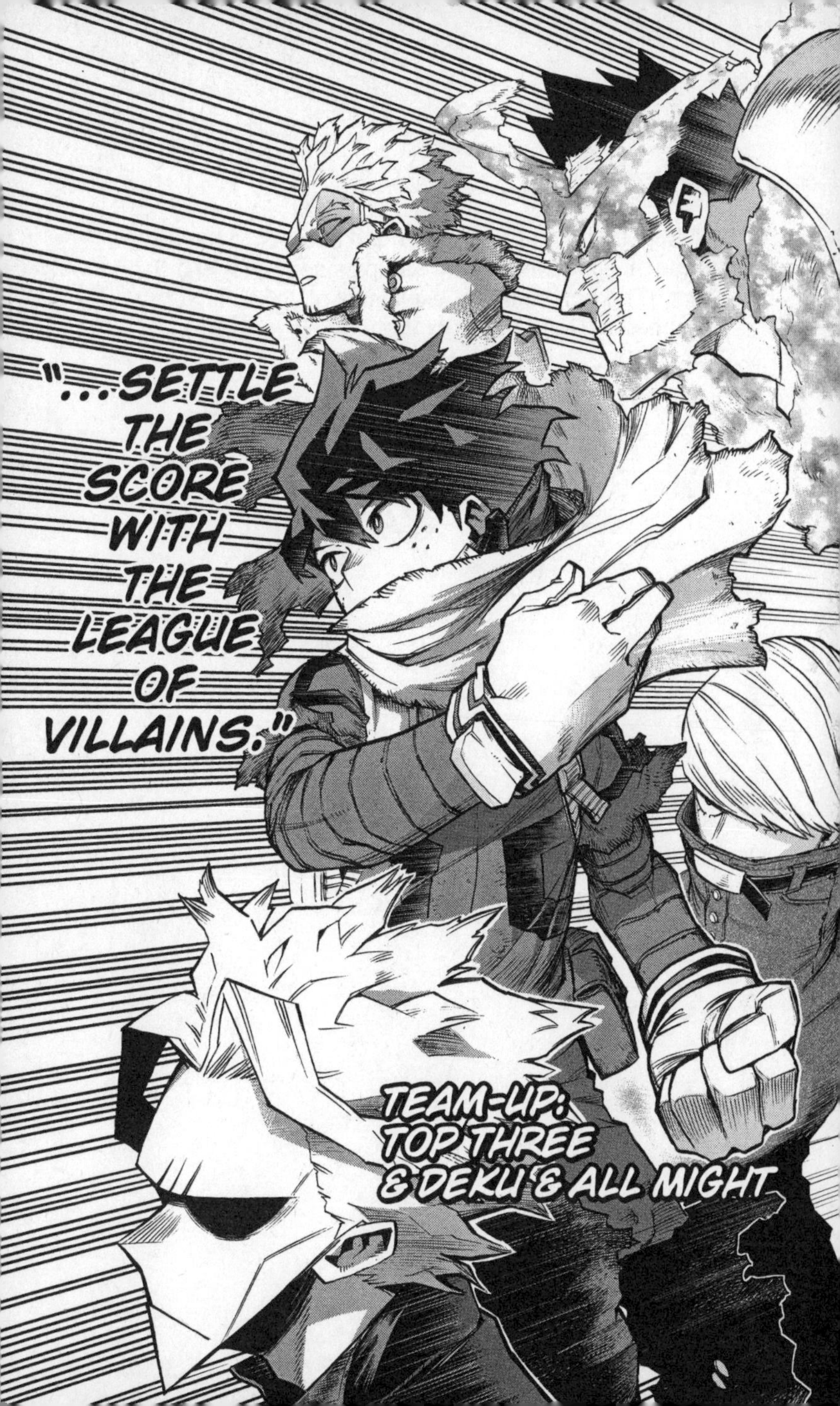
"...SETTLE THE SCORE WITH THE LEAGUE OF VILLAINS."
TEAM-UP: TOP THREE & DEKU & ALL MIGHT

MID-GAUNTLETS

All Might threw his weight around in order to have these still-in-development samples sent over in a hurry. The only four that exist in all of Japan are attached to Deku (he's got them on his legs too).

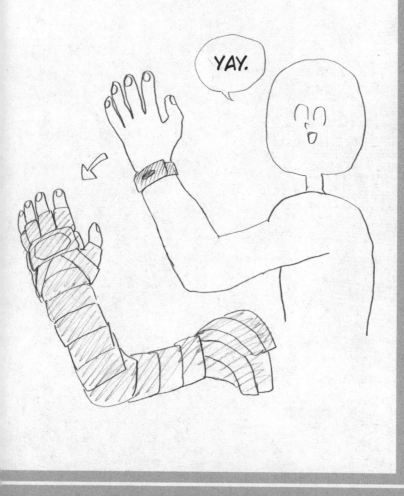

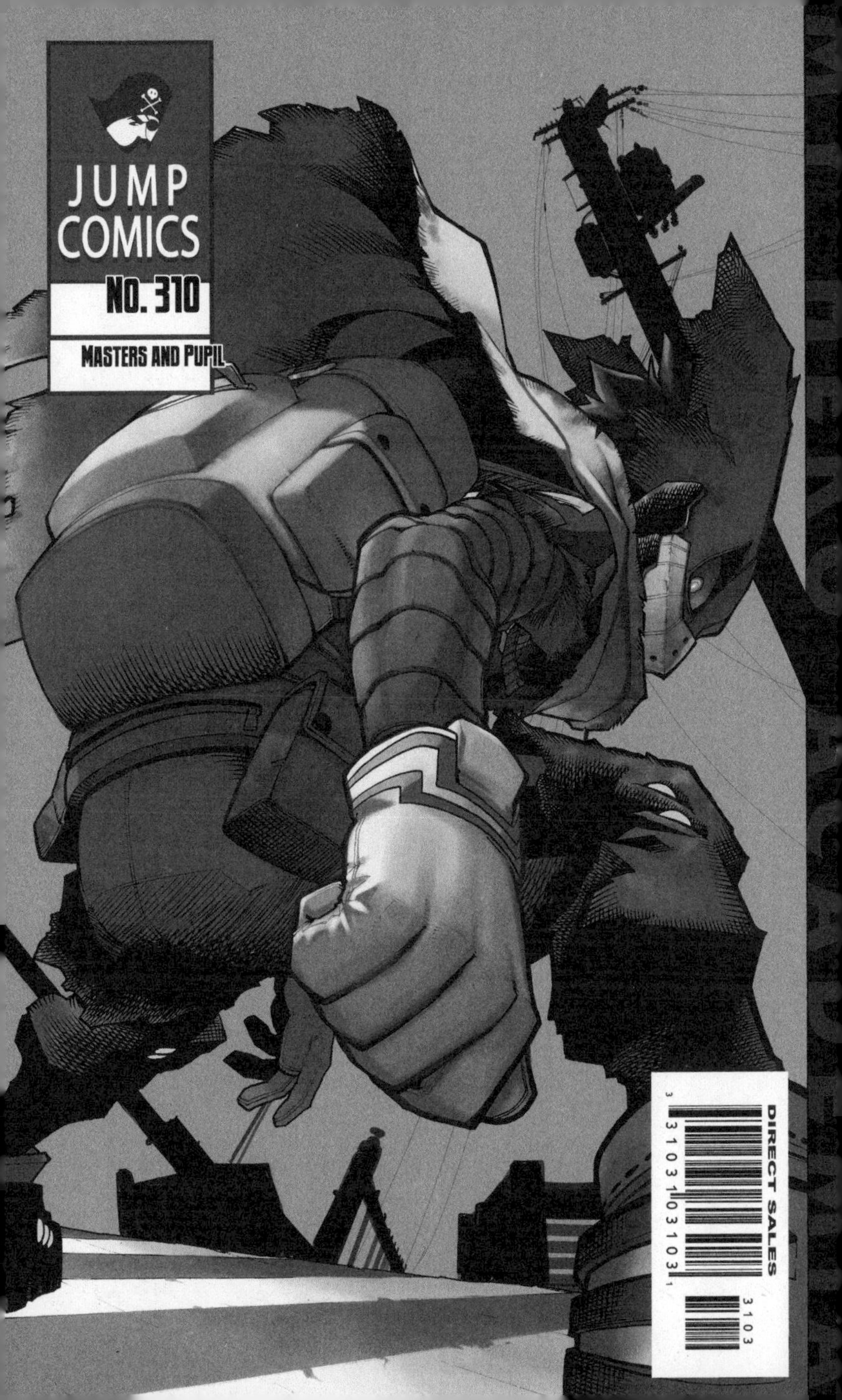
JUMP COMICS
NO. 310
MASTERS AND PUPIL
DIRECT SALES

MY HERO ACADEMIA

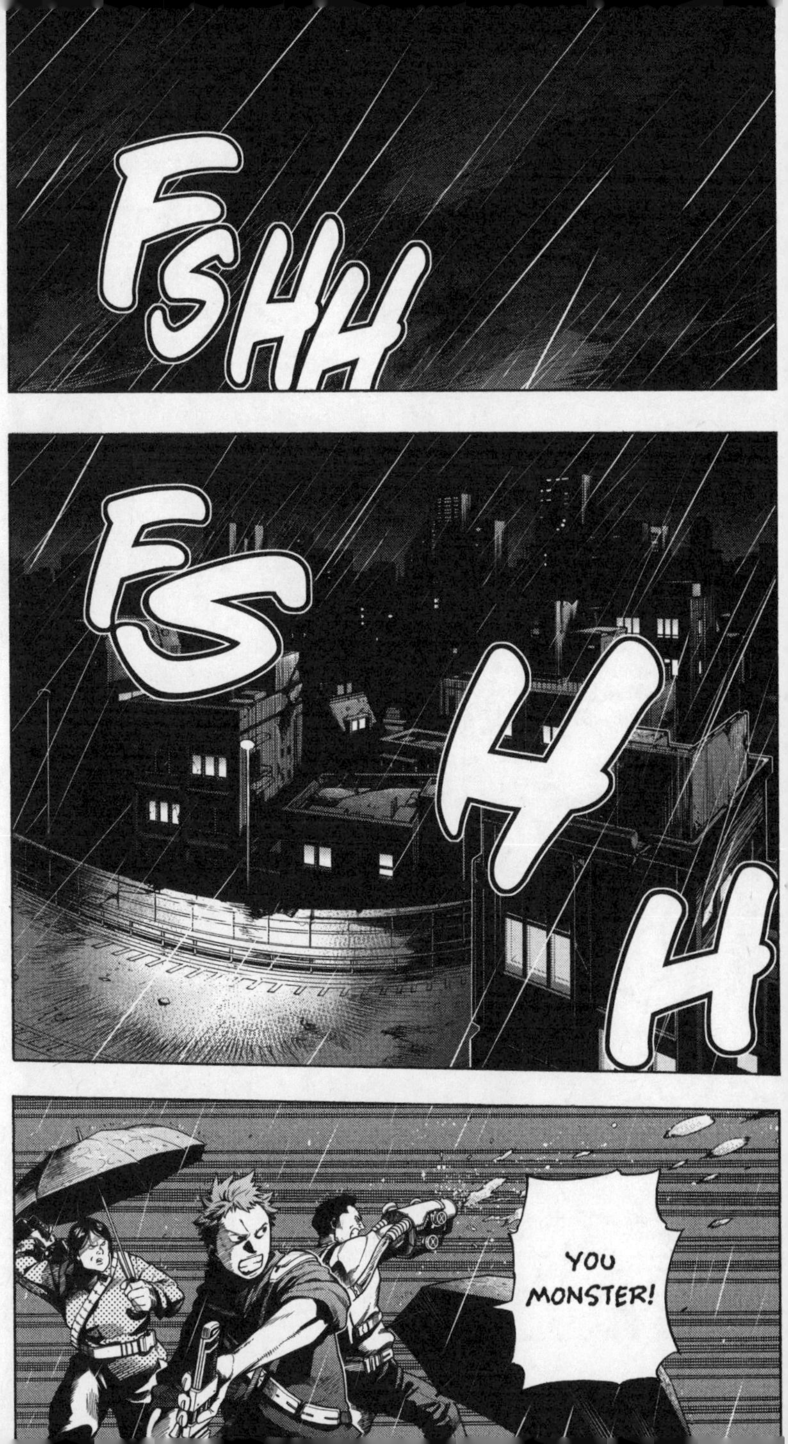
FSHH
FSHH
YOU MONSTER!

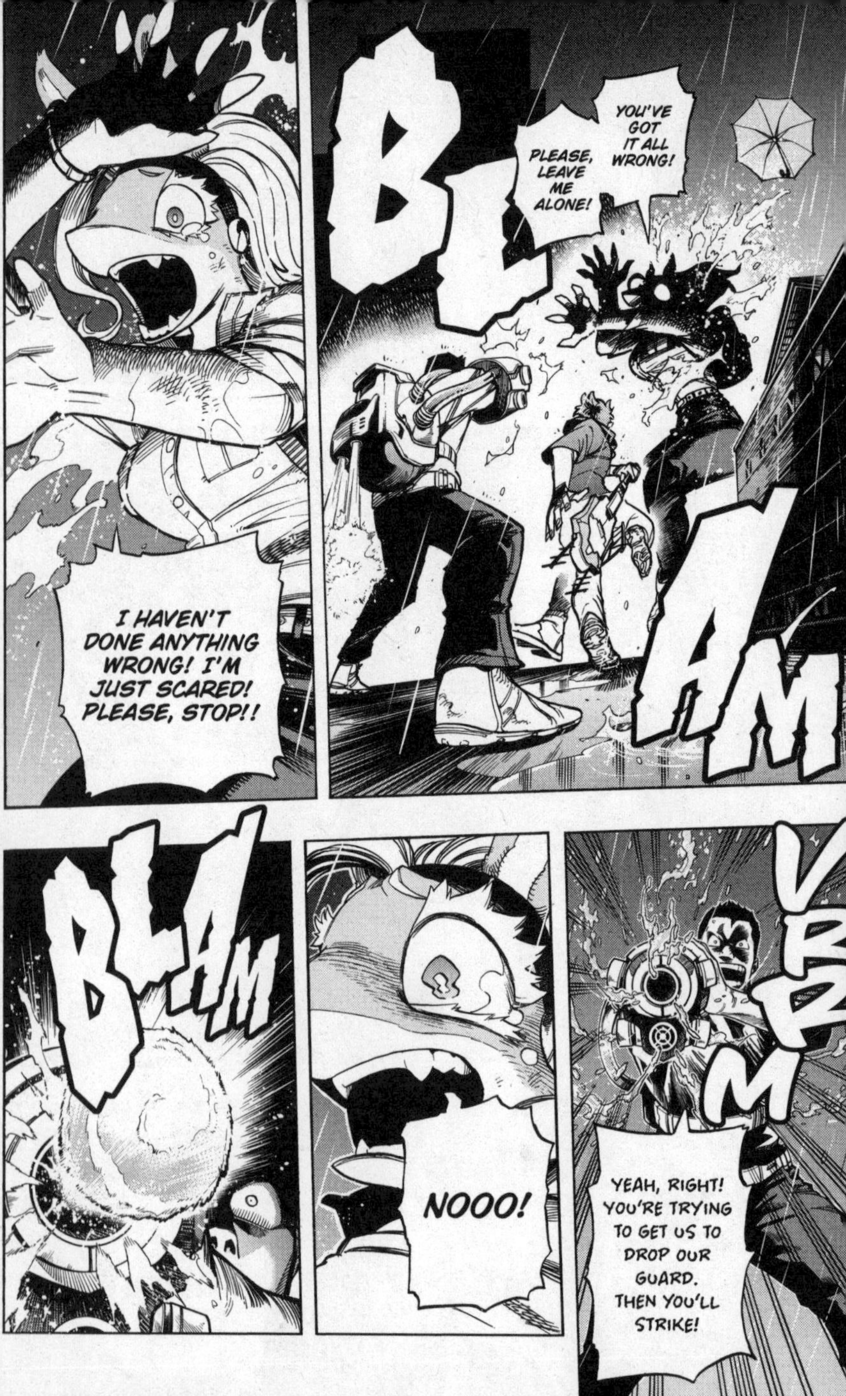
YOU'VE GOT IT ALL WRONG!
PLEASE, LEAVE ME ALONE!
BLAM
I HAVEN'T DONE ANYTHING WRONG! I'M JUST SCARED! PLEASE, STOP!!
VRRM
YEAH, RIGHT! YOU'RE TRYING TO GET US TO DROP OUR GUARD. THEN YOU'LL STRIKE!
NOOO!
BLAM

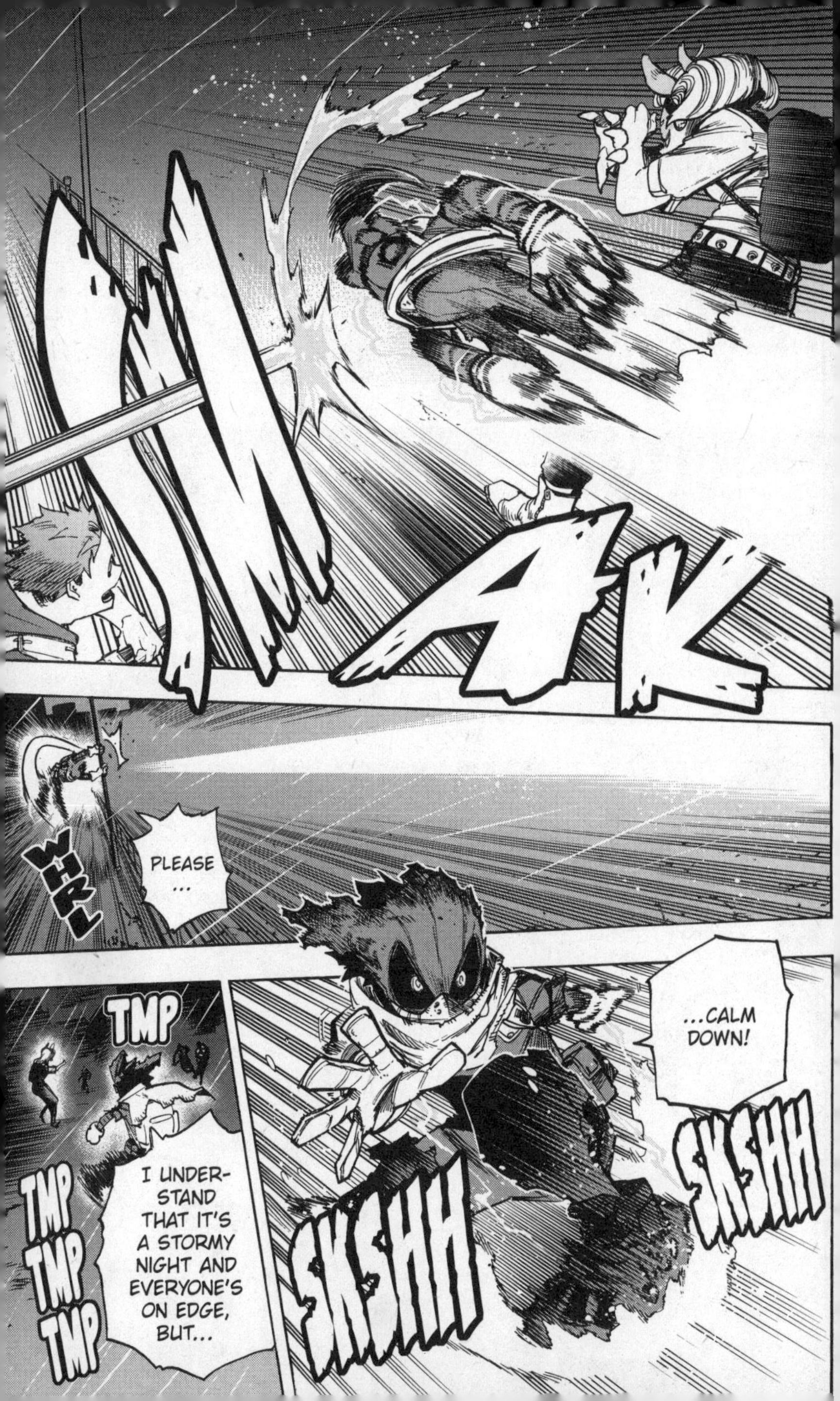
WHAK
WHRL
PLEASE ...
...CALM DOWN!
SKSHH
SKSHH
TMP
I UNDER-STAND THAT IT'S A STORMY NIGHT AND EVERYONE'S ON EDGE, BUT...
TMP TMP TMP

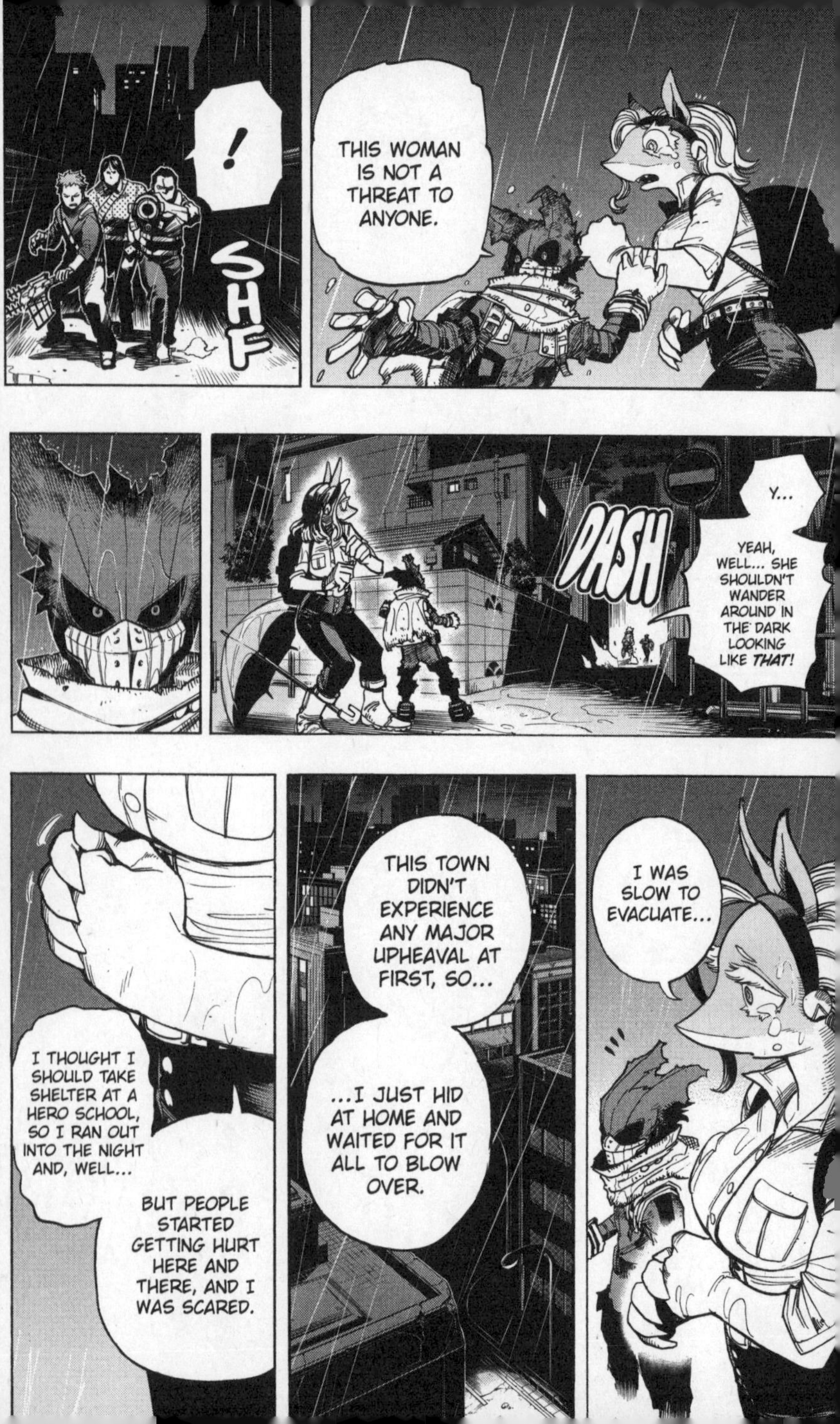
THIS WOMAN IS NOT A THREAT TO ANYONE.
!
SHF
Y...
YEAH, WELL... SHE SHOULDN'T WANDER AROUND IN THE DARK LOOKING LIKE *THAT*!
DASH
I WAS SLOW TO EVACUATE...
THIS TOWN DIDN'T EXPERIENCE ANY MAJOR UPHEAVAL AT FIRST, SO...
...I JUST HID AT HOME AND WAITED FOR IT ALL TO BLOW OVER.
I THOUGHT I SHOULD TAKE SHELTER AT A HERO SCHOOL, SO I RAN OUT INTO THE NIGHT AND, WELL...
BUT PEOPLE STARTED GETTING HURT HERE AND THERE, AND I WAS SCARED.

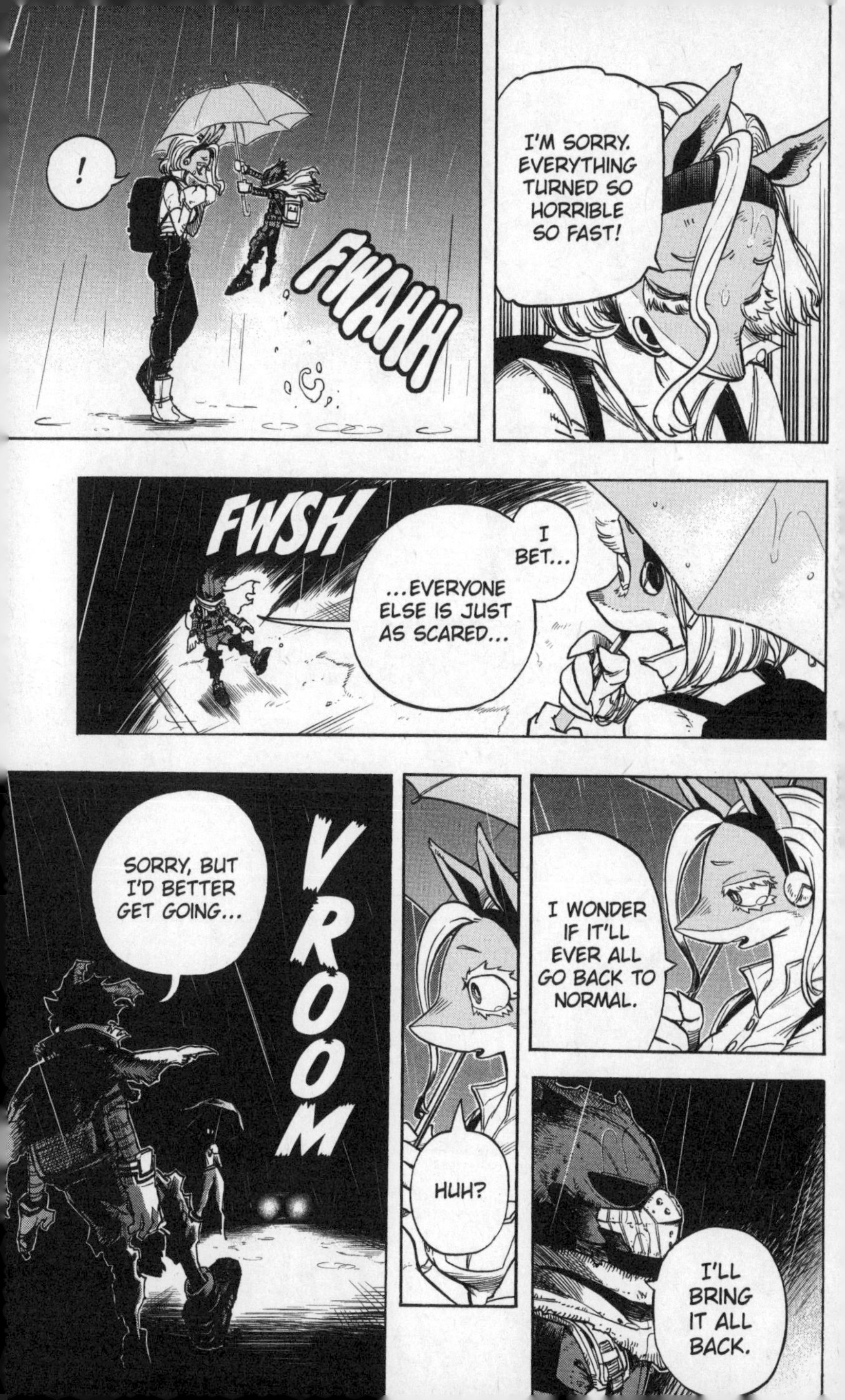
I'M SORRY. EVERYTHING TURNED SO HORRIBLE SO FAST!
!
FWAHH
FWSH
I BET...
...EVERYONE ELSE IS JUST AS SCARED...
I WONDER IF IT'LL EVER ALL GO BACK TO NORMAL.
I'LL BRING IT ALL BACK.
HUH?
SORRY, BUT I'D BETTER GET GOING...
VROOM

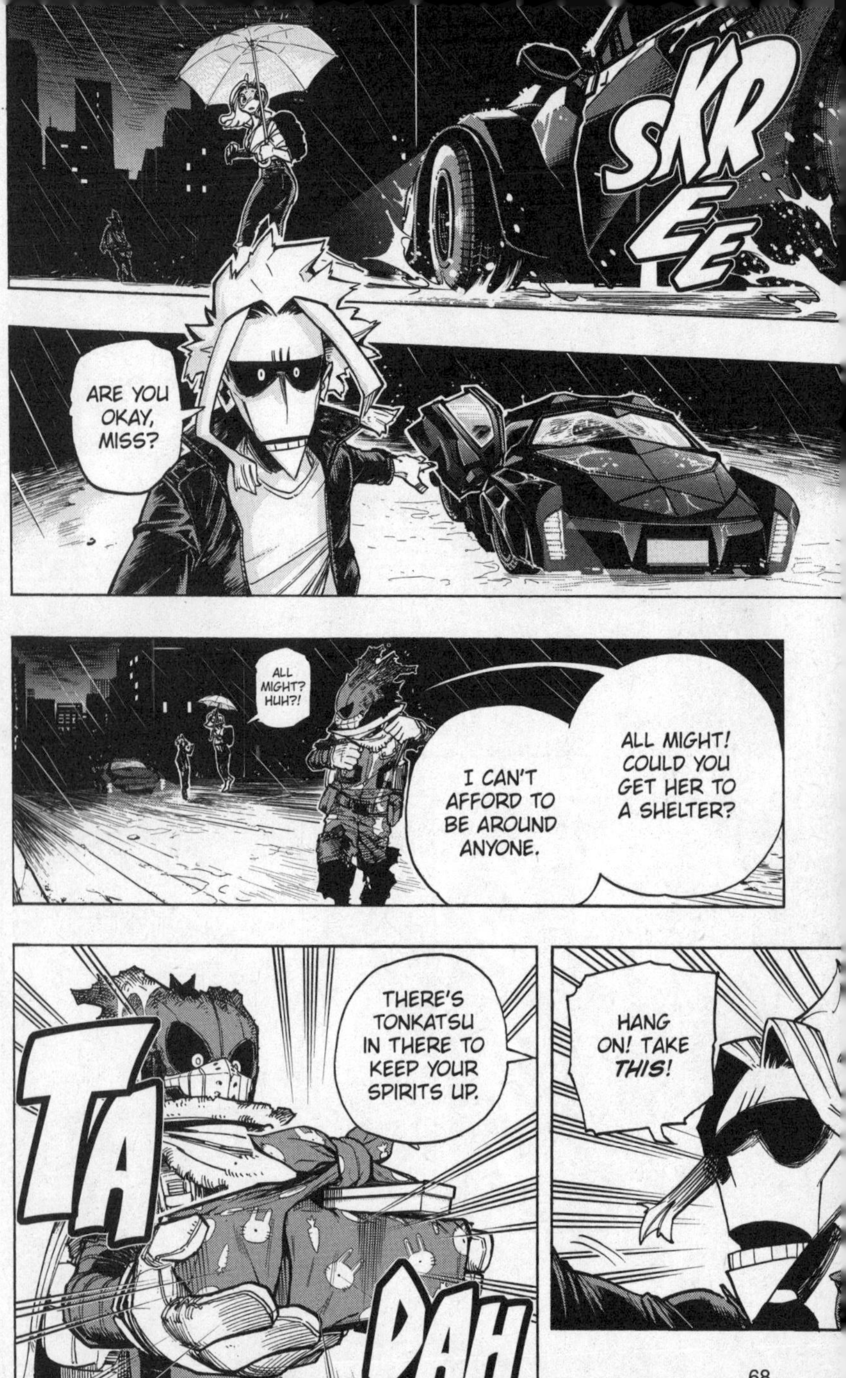
SKREE
ARE YOU OKAY, MISS?
ALL MIGHT! COULD YOU GET HER TO A SHELTER?
I CAN'T AFFORD TO BE AROUND ANYONE.
ALL MIGHT? HUH?!
HANG ON! TAKE *THIS*!
THERE'S TONKATSU IN THERE TO KEEP YOUR SPIRITS UP.
TA
DAH

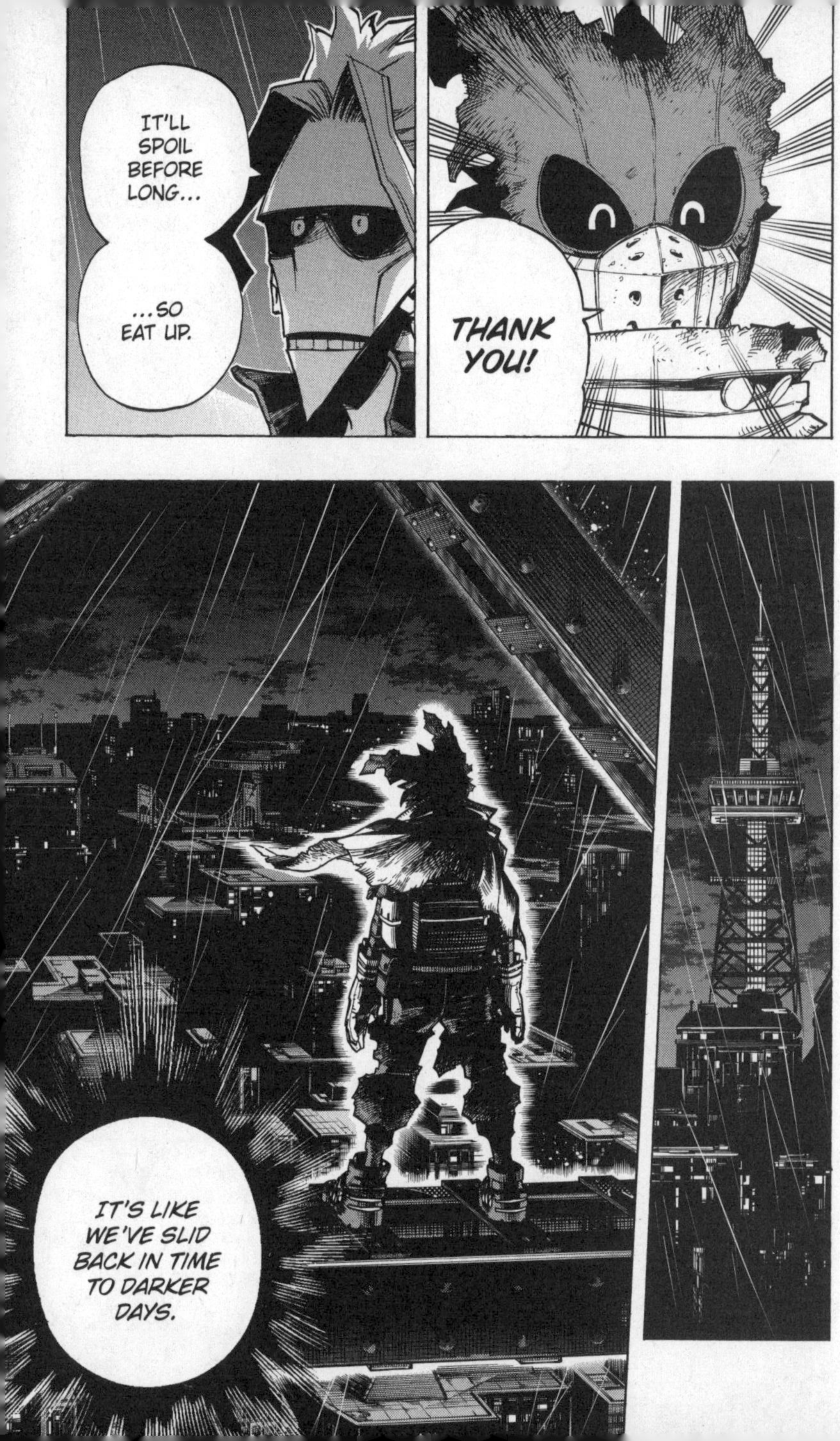
THANK YOU!
IT'LL SPOIL BEFORE LONG...
...SO EAT UP.
IT'S LIKE WE'VE SLID BACK IN TIME TO DARKER DAYS.

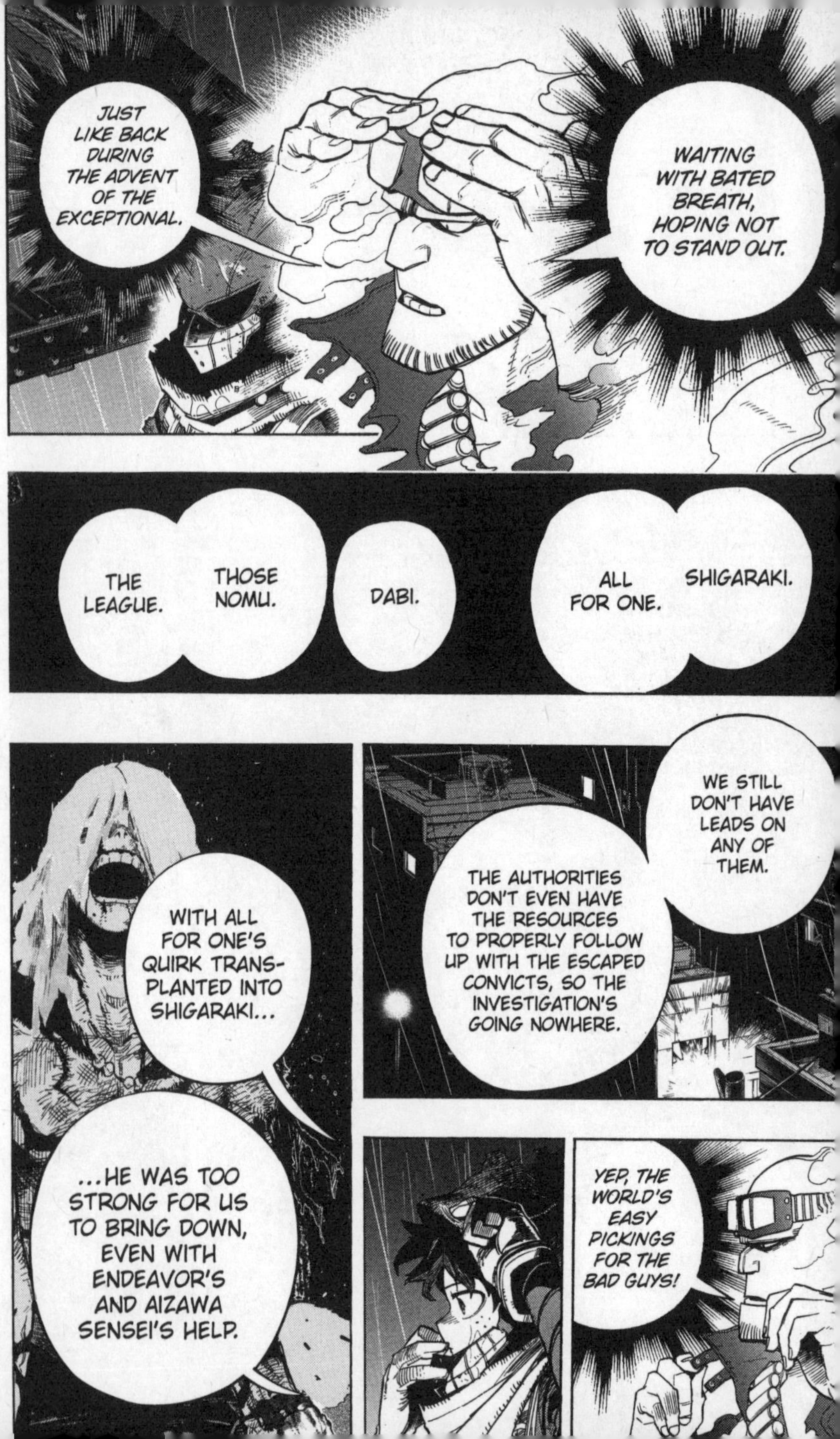
WAITING WITH BATED BREATH, HOPING NOT TO STAND OUT.
JUST LIKE BACK DURING THE ADVENT OF THE EXCEPTIONAL.
SHIGARAKI.
ALL FOR ONE.
DABI.
THOSE NOMU.
THE LEAGUE.
WE STILL DON'T HAVE LEADS ON ANY OF THEM.
THE AUTHORITIES DON'T EVEN HAVE THE RESOURCES TO PROPERLY FOLLOW UP WITH THE ESCAPED CONVICTS, SO THE INVESTIGATION'S GOING NOWHERE.
YEP, THE WORLD'S EASY PICKINGS FOR THE BAD GUYS!
WITH ALL FOR ONE'S QUIRK TRANS-PLANTED INTO SHIGARAKI...
...HE WAS TOO STRONG FOR US TO BRING DOWN, EVEN WITH ENDEAVOR'S AND AIZAWA SENSEI'S HELP.

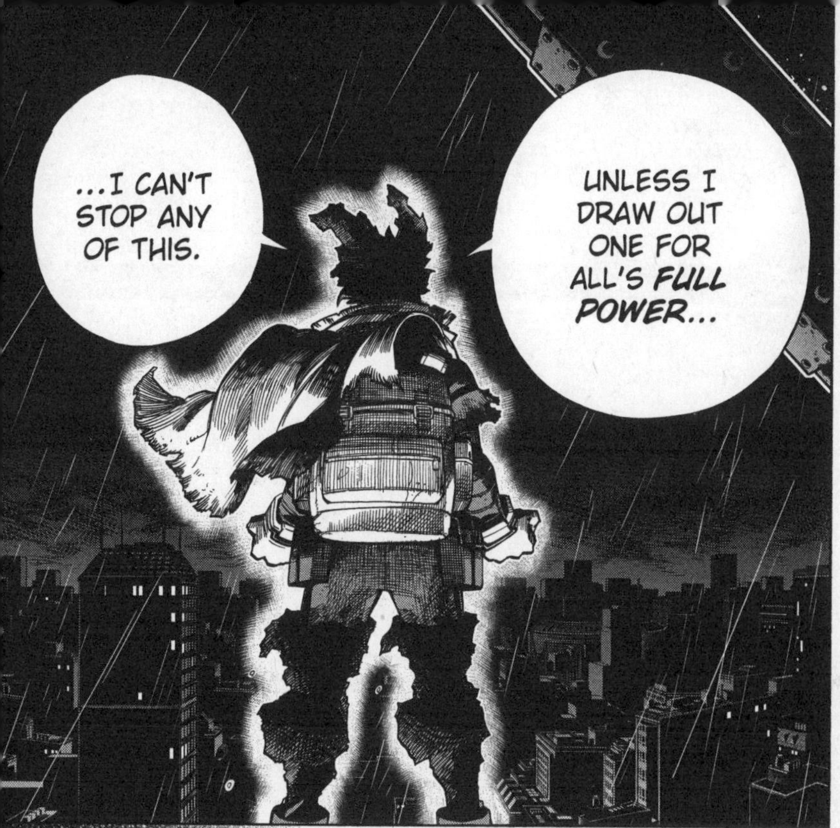
UNLESS I DRAW OUT ONE FOR ALL'S **FULL POWER...**
...I CAN'T STOP ANY OF THIS.

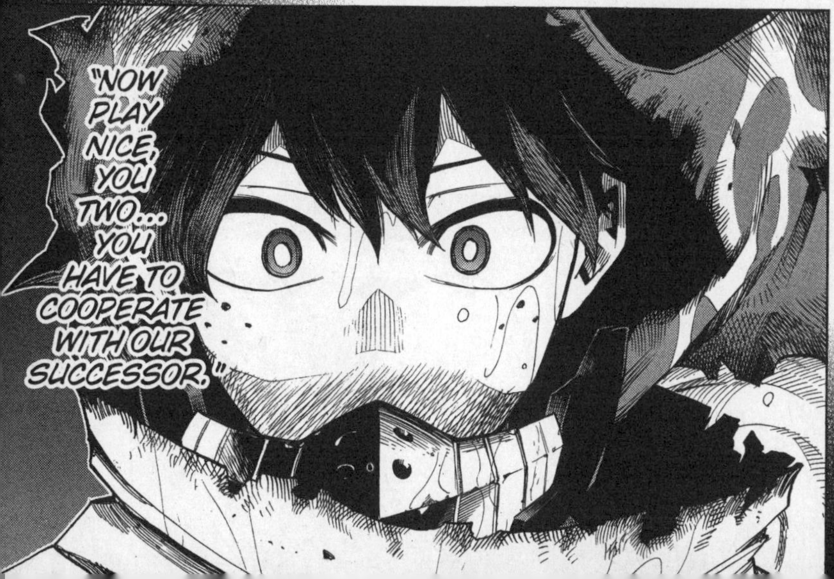
"NOW PLAY NICE, YOU TWO... YOU HAVE TO COOPERATE WITH OUR SUCCESSOR."

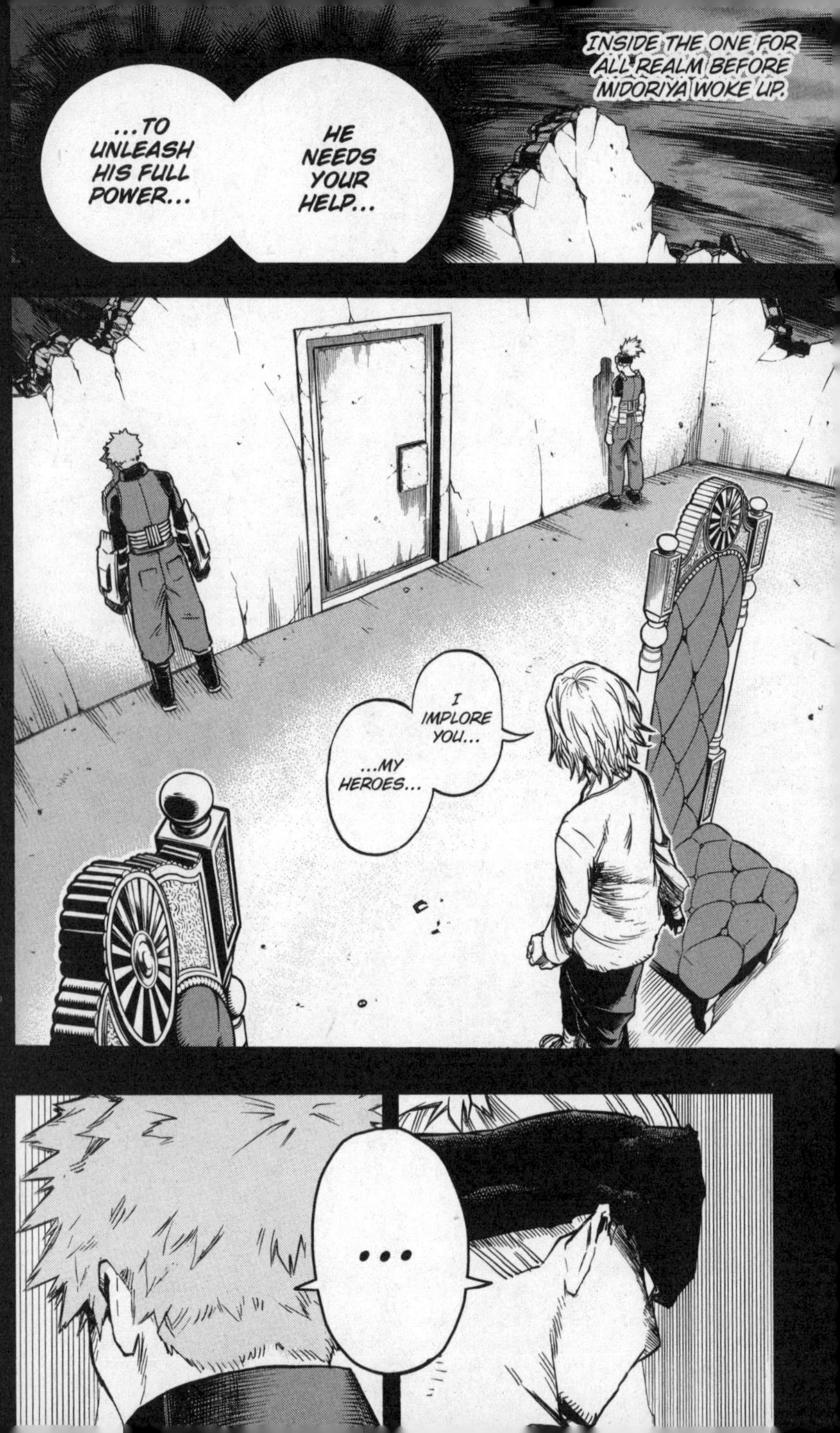
INSIDE THE ONE FOR ALL REALM BEFORE MIDORIYA WOKE UP.
HE NEEDS YOUR HELP...
...TO UNLEASH HIS FULL POWER...
I IMPLORE YOU...
...MY HEROES...
...

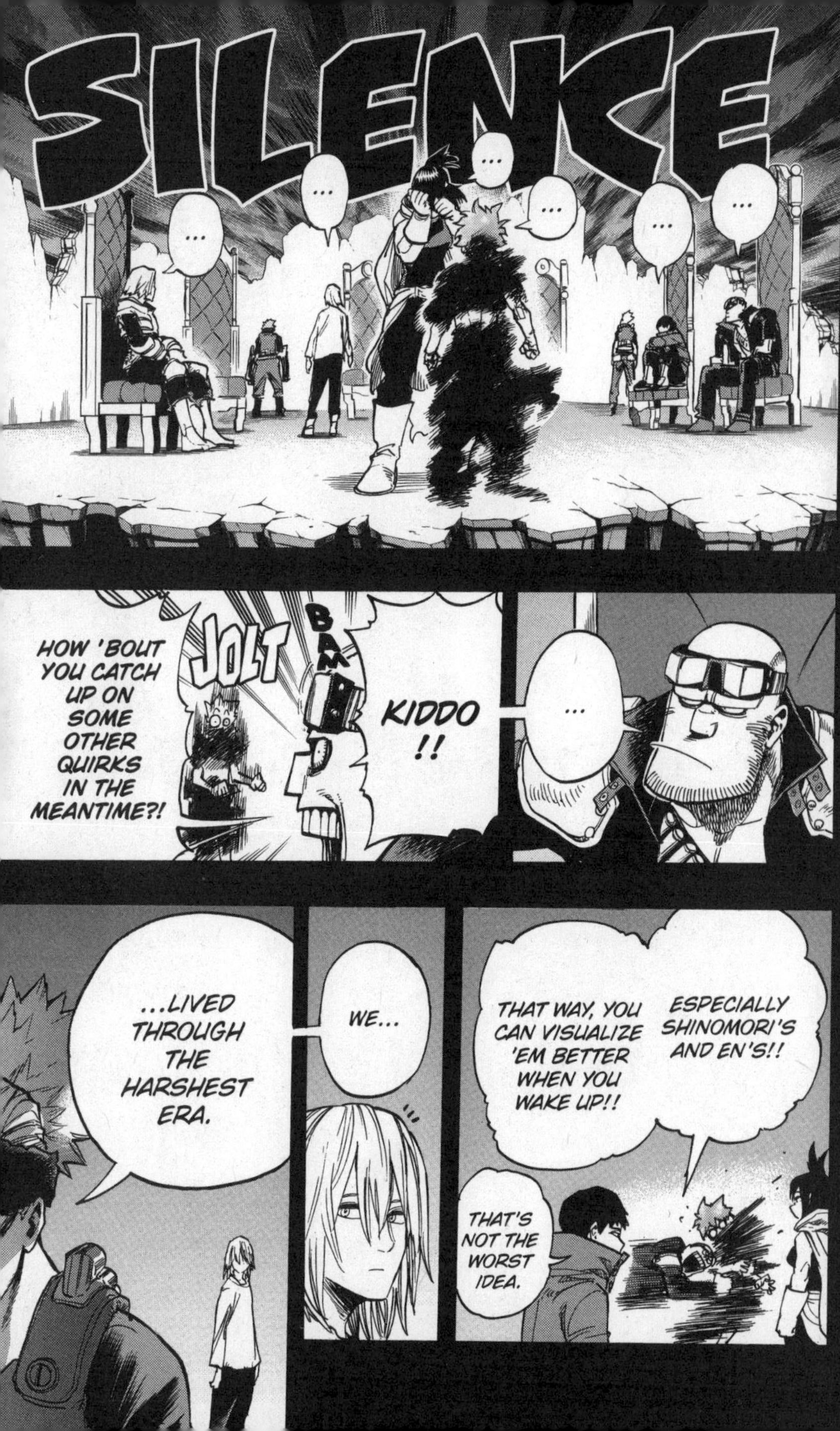
SILENCE
...
...
...
...
...
...
...
...
HOW 'BOUT YOU CATCH UP ON SOME OTHER QUIRKS IN THE MEANTIME?!
KIDDO!!
BAM
JOLT
ESPECIALLY SHINOMORI'S AND EN'S!!
THAT WAY, YOU CAN VISUALIZE 'EM BETTER WHEN YOU WAKE UP!!
THAT'S NOT THE WORST IDEA.
WE...
...LIVED THROUGH THE HARSHEST ERA.

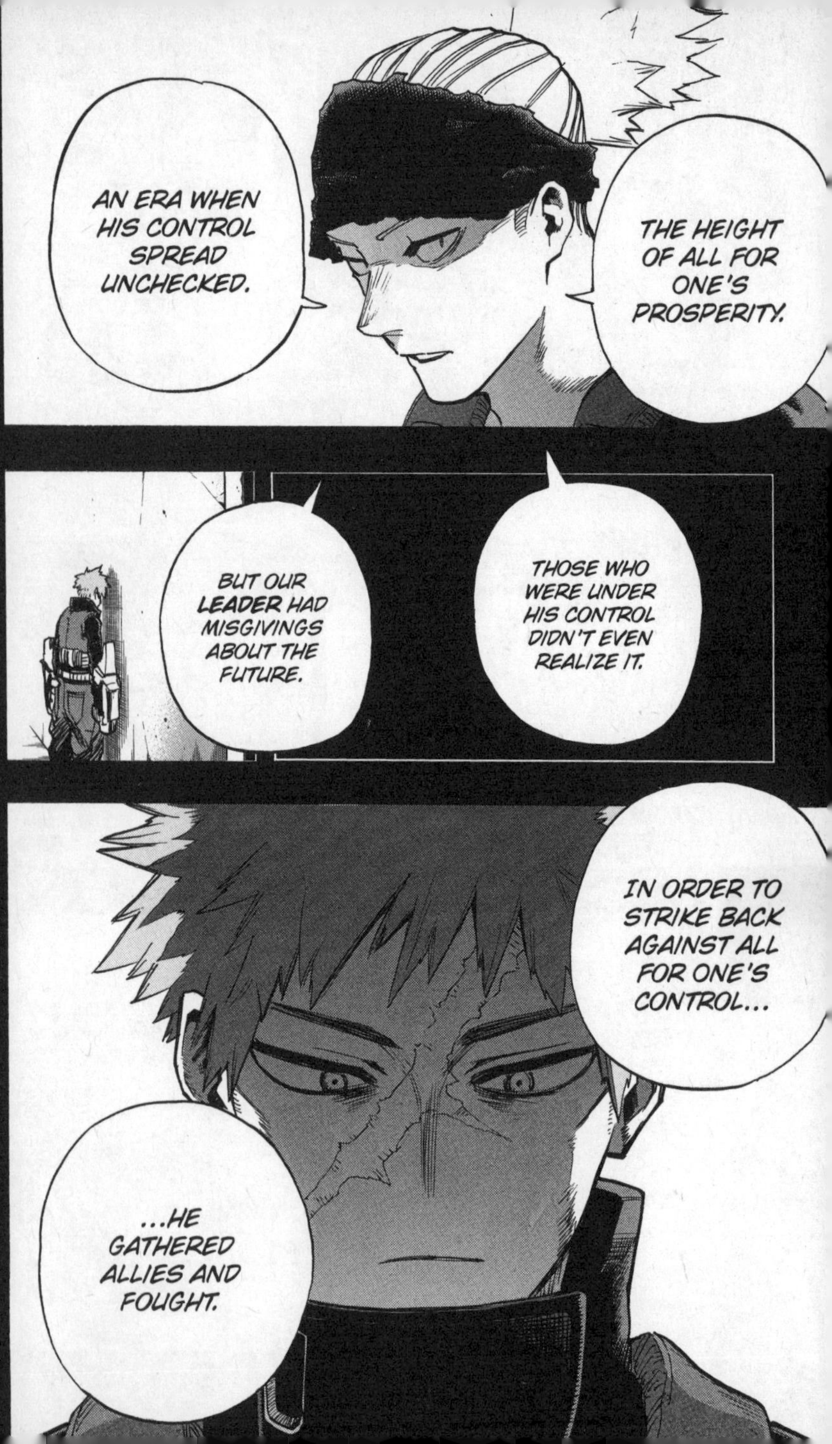
THE HEIGHT OF ALL FOR ONE'S PROSPERITY.
AN ERA WHEN HIS CONTROL SPREAD UNCHECKED.
THOSE WHO WERE UNDER HIS CONTROL DIDN'T EVEN REALIZE IT.
BUT OUR LEADER HAD MISGIVINGS ABOUT THE FUTURE.
IN ORDER TO STRIKE BACK AGAINST ALL FOR ONE'S CONTROL...
...HE GATHERED ALLIES AND FOUGHT.

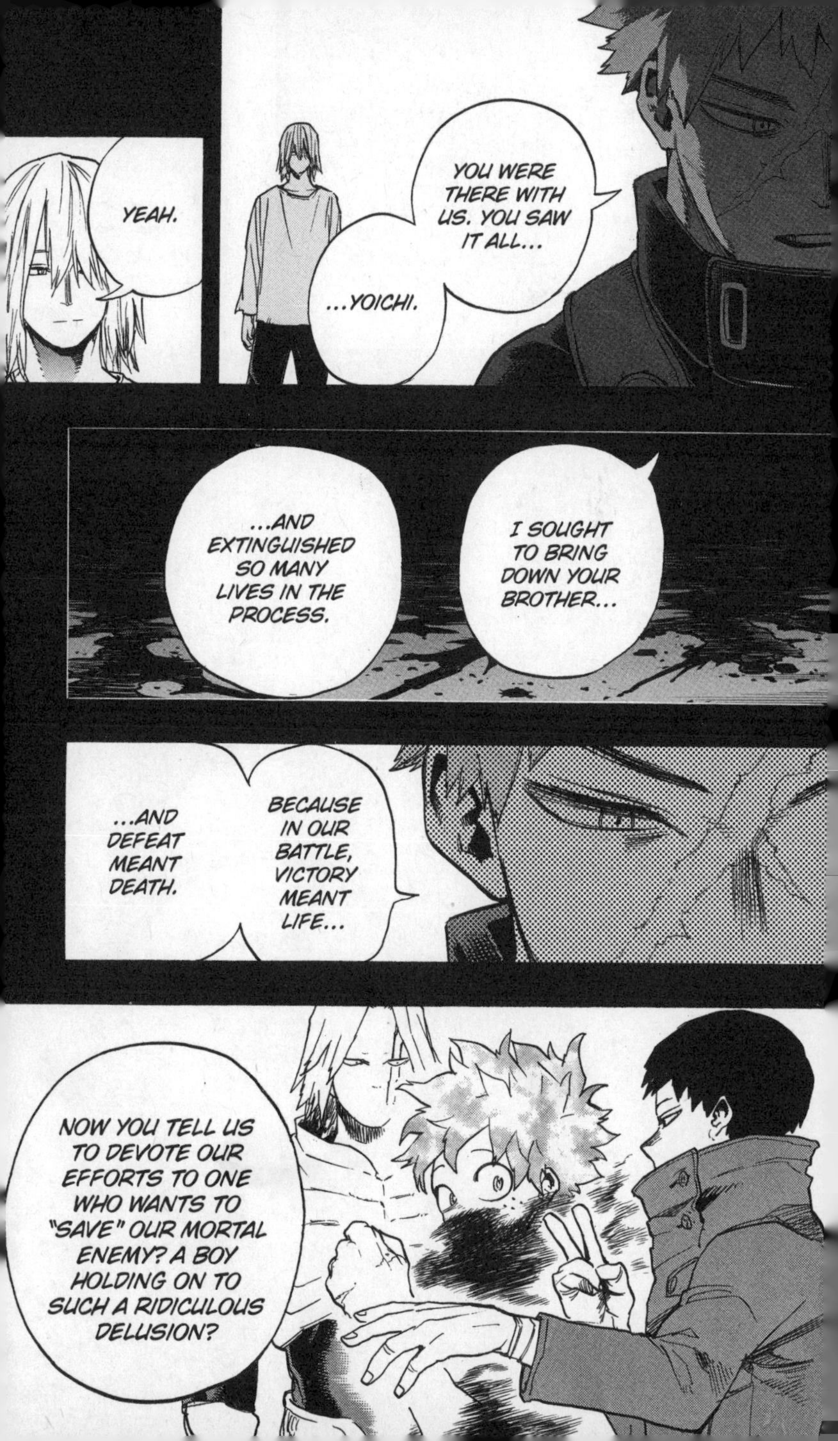
YOU WERE THERE WITH US. YOU SAW IT ALL...
...YOICHI.
YEAH.
I SOUGHT TO BRING DOWN YOUR BROTHER...
...AND EXTINGUISHED SO MANY LIVES IN THE PROCESS.
BECAUSE IN OUR BATTLE, VICTORY MEANT LIFE...
...AND DEFEAT MEANT DEATH.
NOW YOU TELL US TO DEVOTE OUR EFFORTS TO ONE WHO WANTS TO "SAVE" OUR MORTAL ENEMY? A BOY HOLDING ON TO SUCH A RIDICULOUS DELUSION?

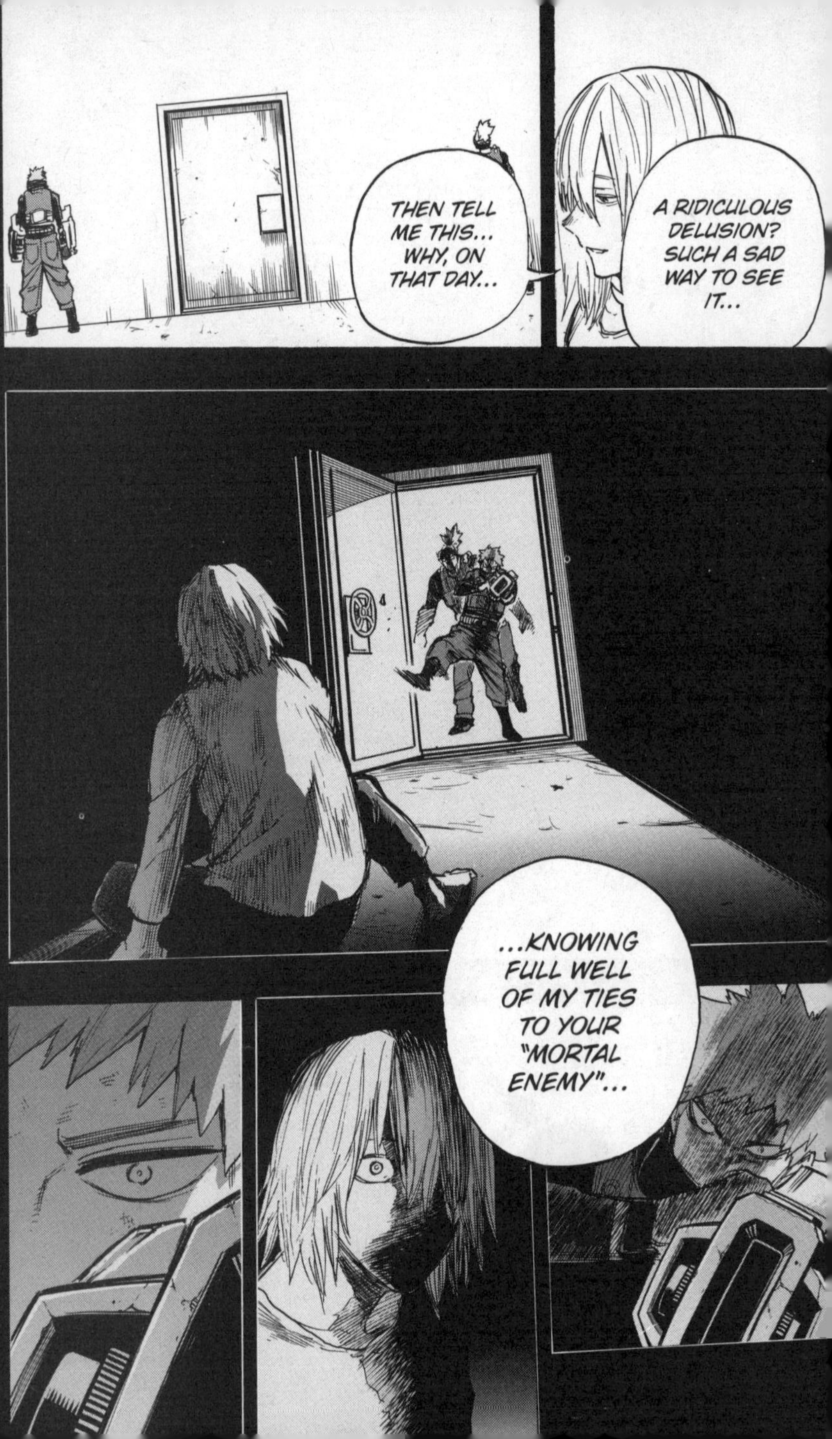
A RIDICULOUS DELUSION? SUCH A SAD WAY TO SEE IT...
THEN TELL ME THIS... WHY, ON THAT DAY...
...KNOWING FULL WELL OF MY TIES TO YOUR "MORTAL ENEMY"...

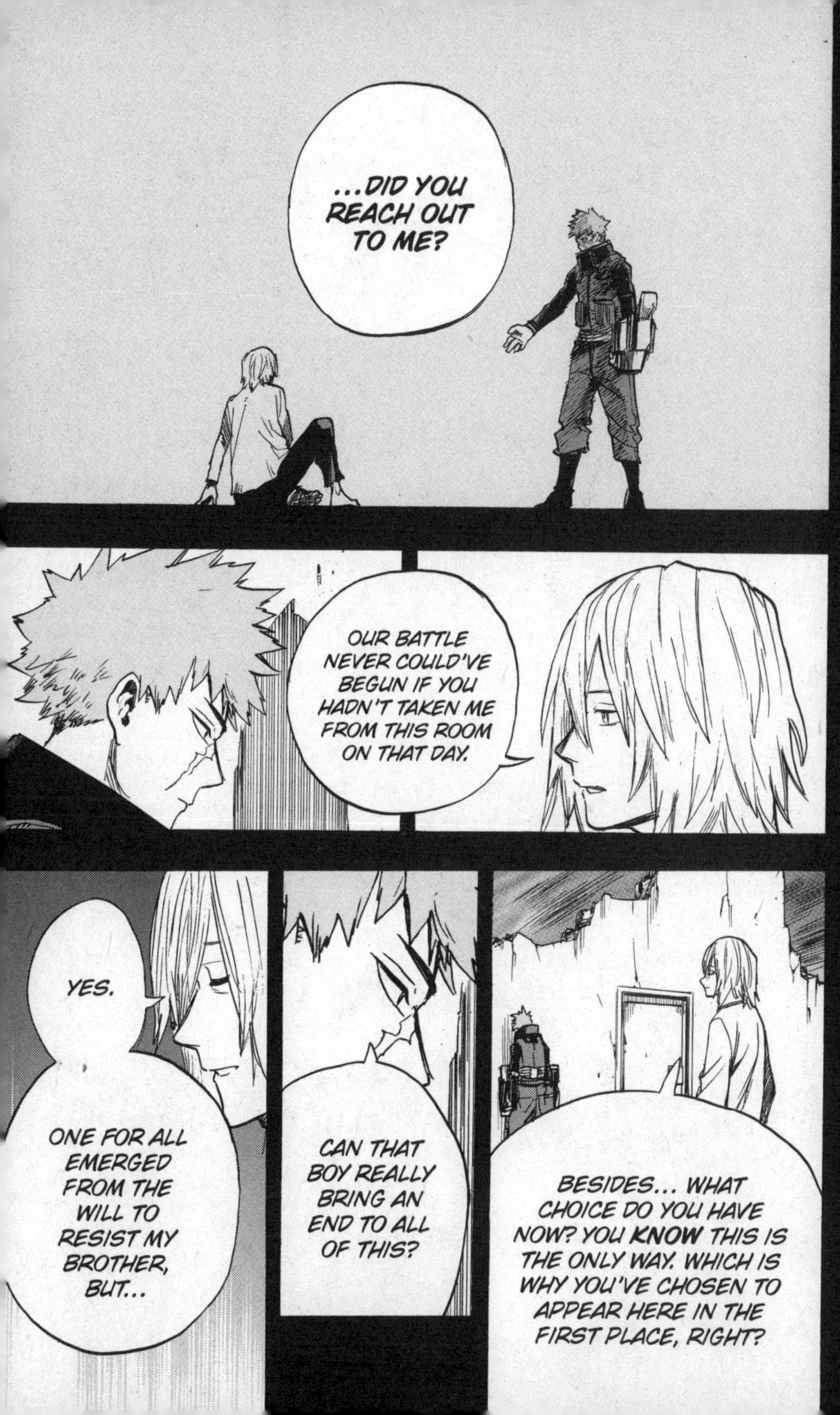
...DID YOU REACH OUT TO ME?
OUR BATTLE NEVER COULD'VE BEGUN IF YOU HADN'T TAKEN ME FROM THIS ROOM ON THAT DAY.
BESIDES... WHAT CHOICE DO YOU HAVE NOW? YOU **KNOW** THIS IS THE ONLY WAY. WHICH IS WHY YOU'VE CHOSEN TO APPEAR HERE IN THE FIRST PLACE, RIGHT?
CAN THAT BOY REALLY BRING AN END TO ALL OF THIS?
YES.
ONE FOR ALL EMERGED FROM THE WILL TO RESIST MY BROTHER, BUT...

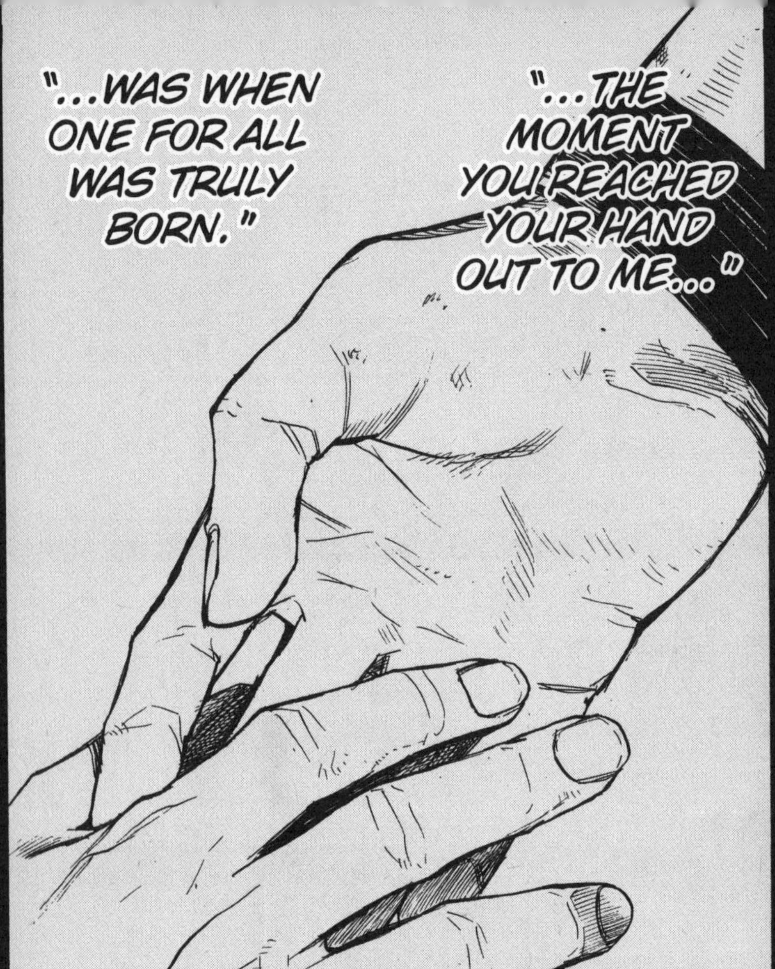
"...THE MOMENT YOU REACHED YOUR HAND OUT TO ME..."
"...WAS WHEN ONE FOR ALL WAS TRULY BORN."
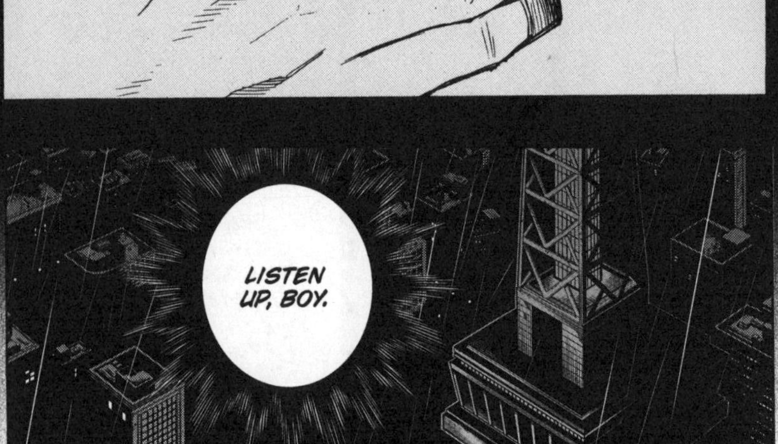
LISTEN UP, BOY.

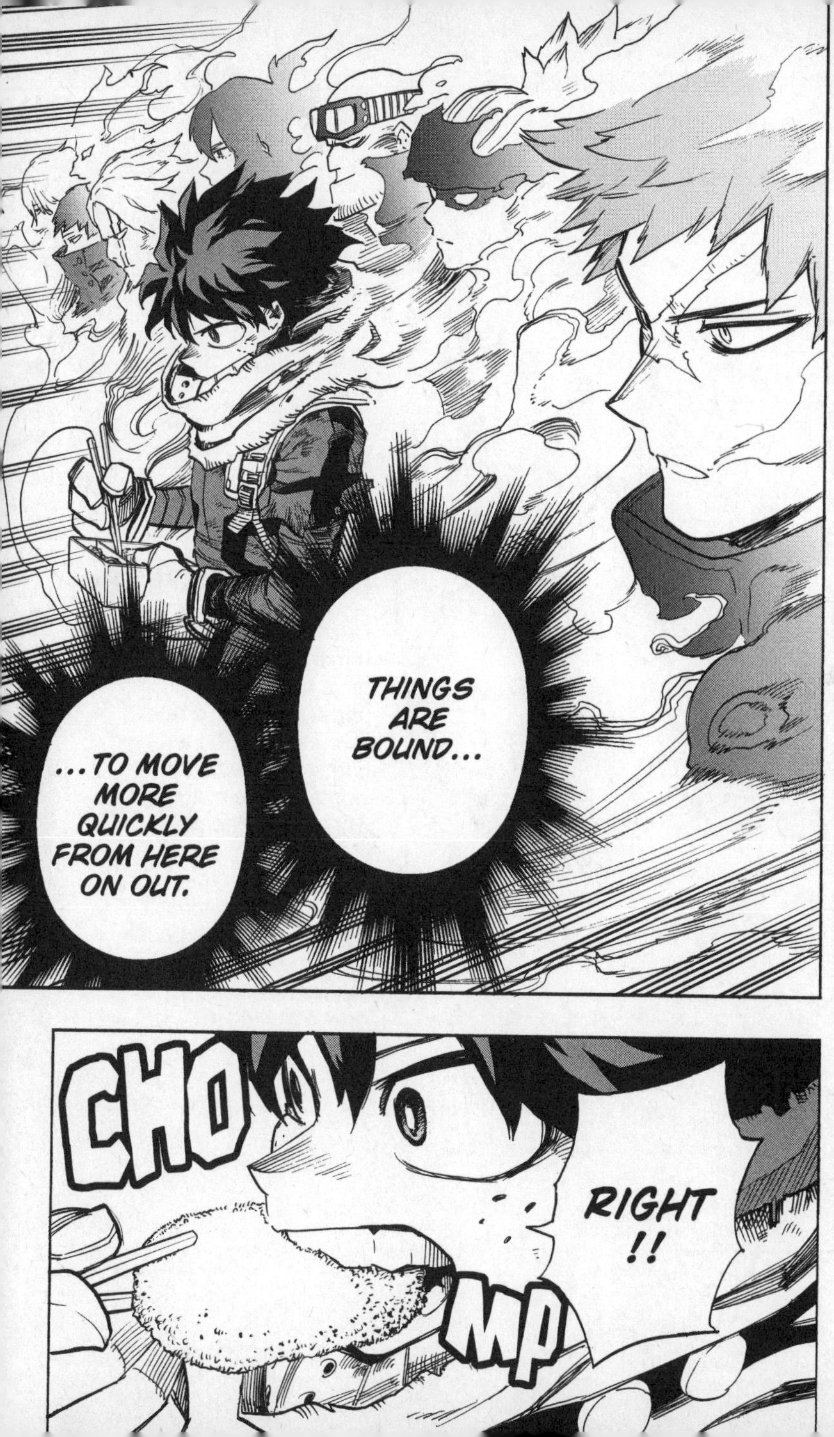
THINGS ARE BOUND...
...TO MOVE MORE QUICKLY FROM HERE ON OUT.
CHOMP
RIGHT !!

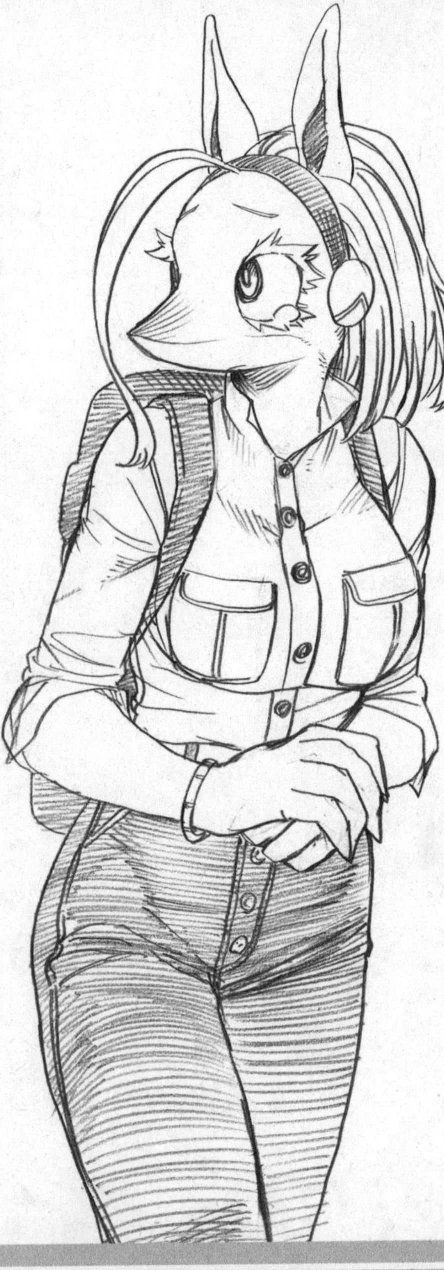

ORDINARY WOMAN

I wanted readers to remember this one, so I gave her a pretty striking appearance. As a result, I wound up with the cutest darn ordinary woman in the history of *My Hero Academia*.

An ordinary woman whose height varies depending on the panel, ranging from 2.6 to 3 meters? That's how it worked in *Evangelion* too.

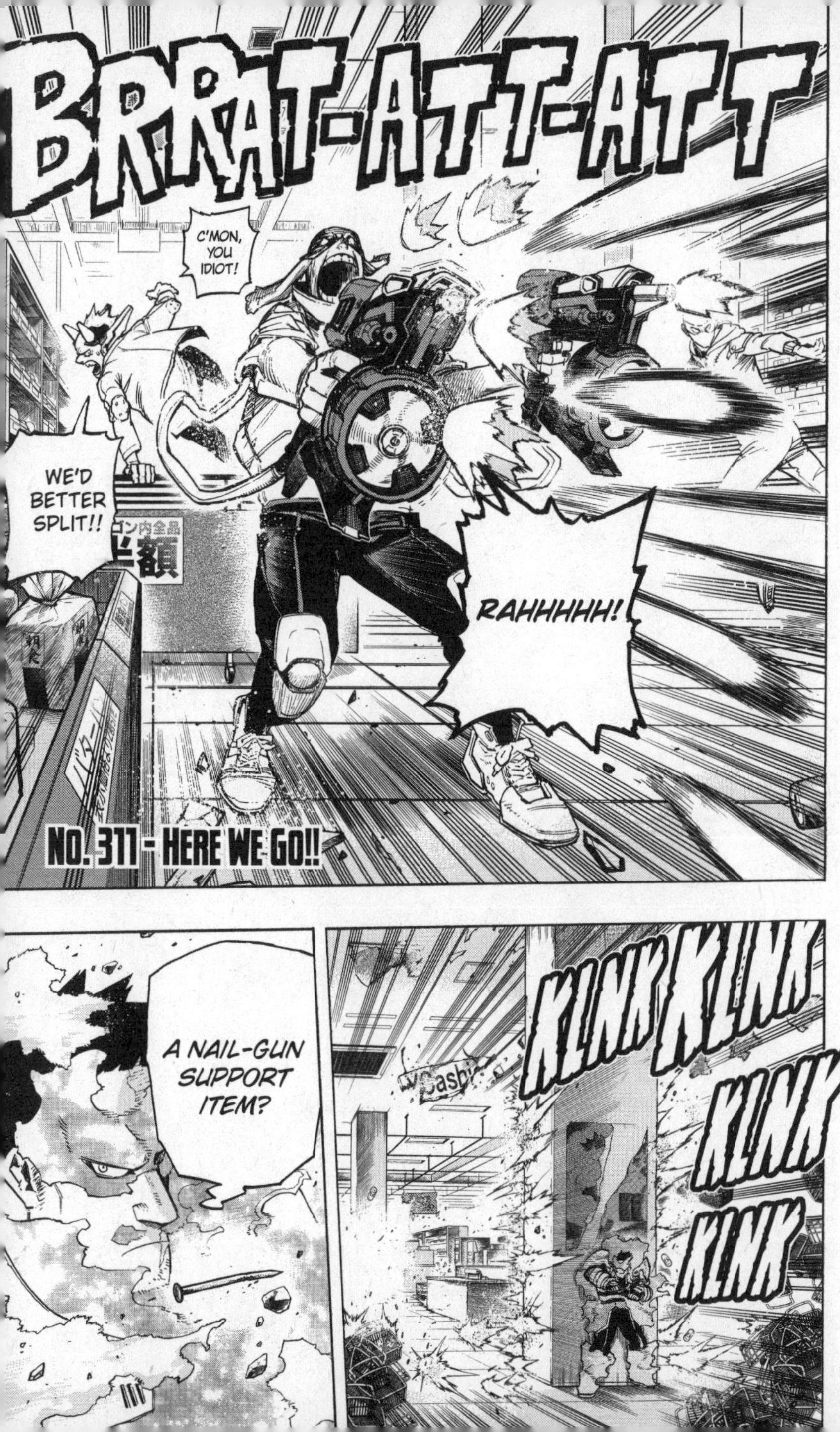
BRRAT-AT-T-AT-T
C'MON, YOU IDIOT!
RAHHHHH!
WE'D BETTER SPLIT!!
NO. 311 - HERE WE GO!!
KLINK KLINK KLINK KLINK
A NAIL-GUN SUPPORT ITEM?

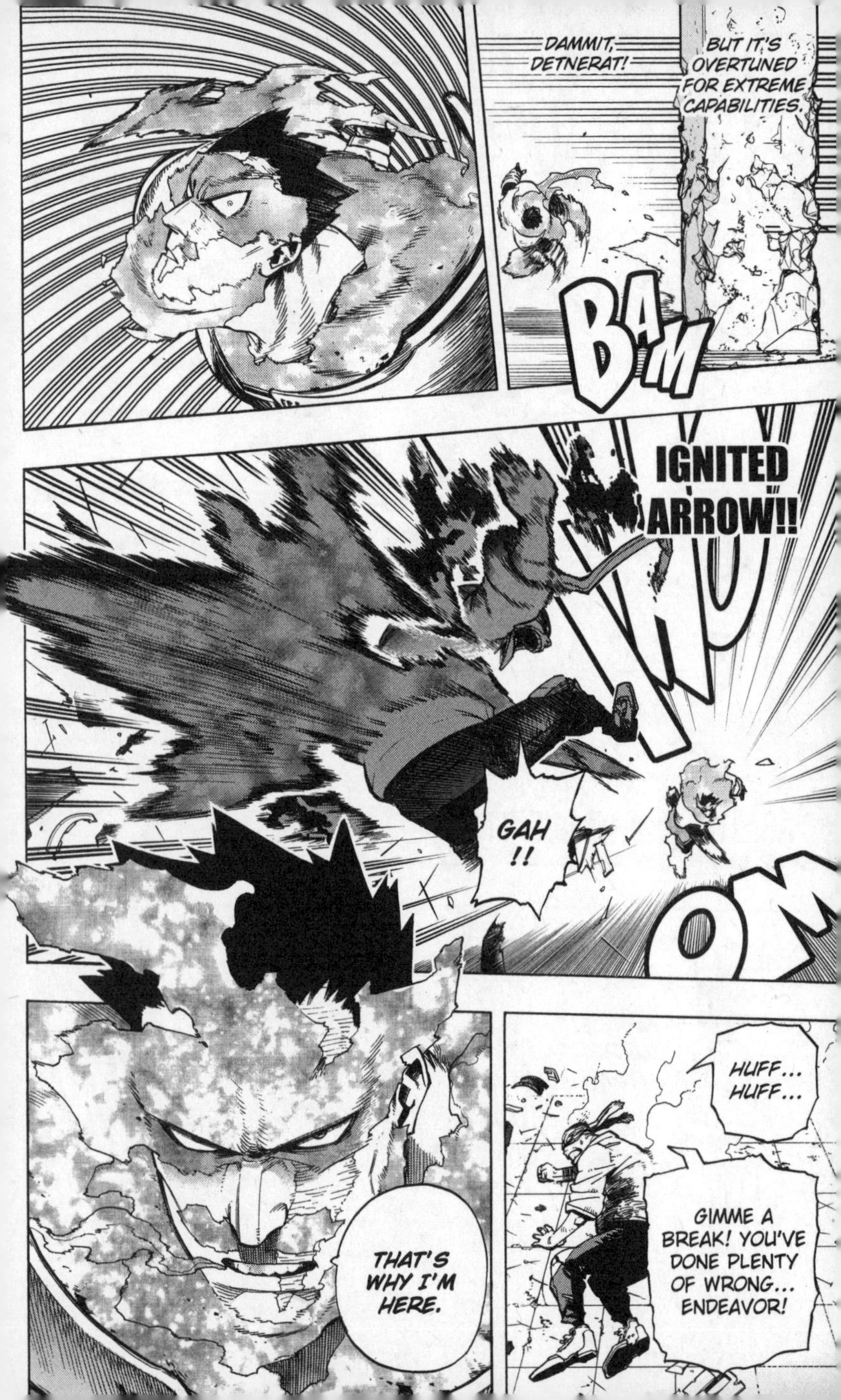
BUT IT'S OVERTUNED FOR EXTREME CAPABILITIES.
DAMMIT, DETNERAT!
BAM
IGNITED ARROW!!
GAH !!
HUFF... HUFF...
GIMME A BREAK! YOU'VE DONE PLENTY OF WRONG... ENDEAVOR!
THAT'S WHY I'M HERE.

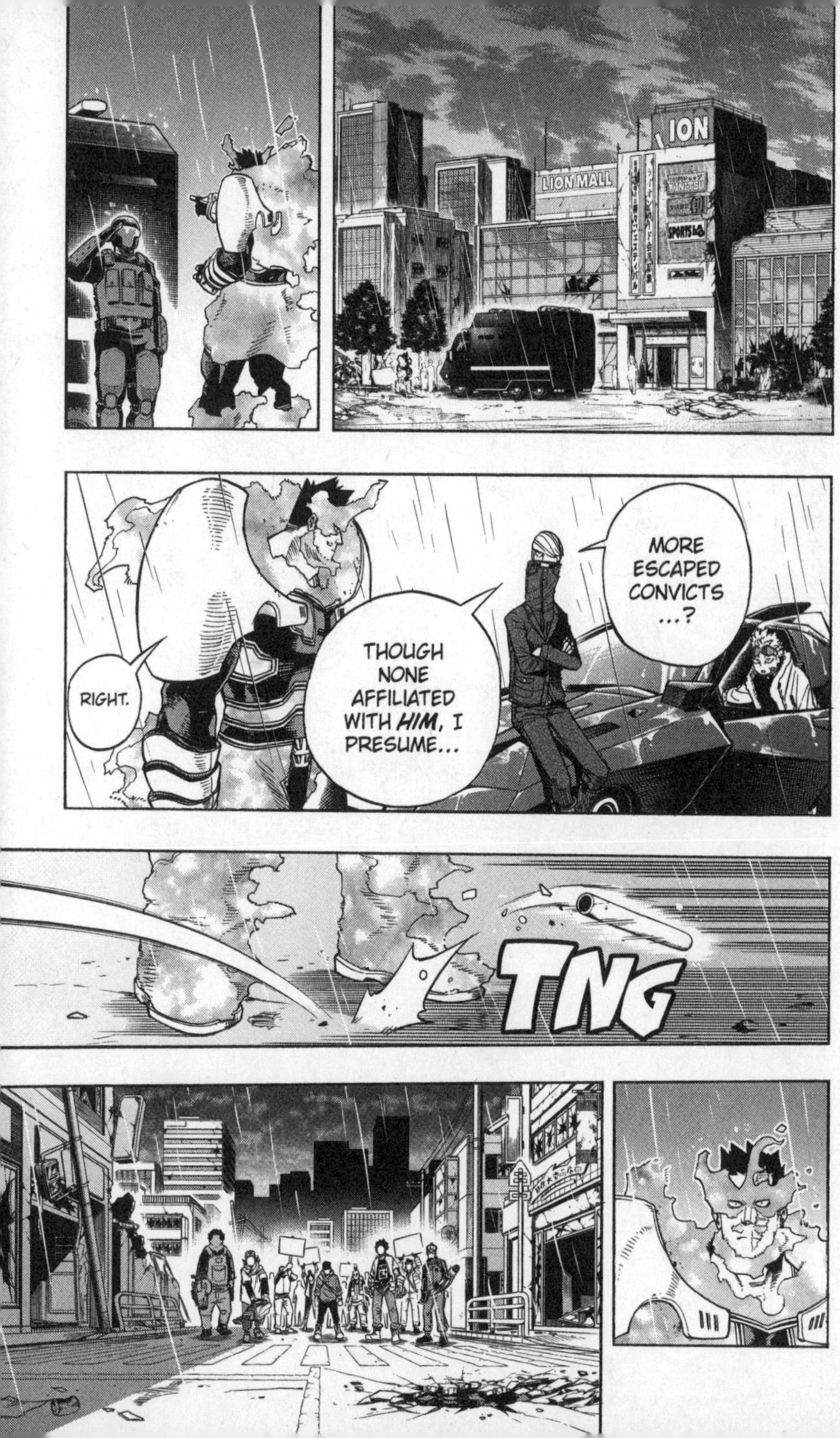
ION
LION MALL
MORE ESCAPED CONVICTS ...?
THOUGH NONE AFFILIATED WITH *HIM*, I PRESUME...
RIGHT.
TNG

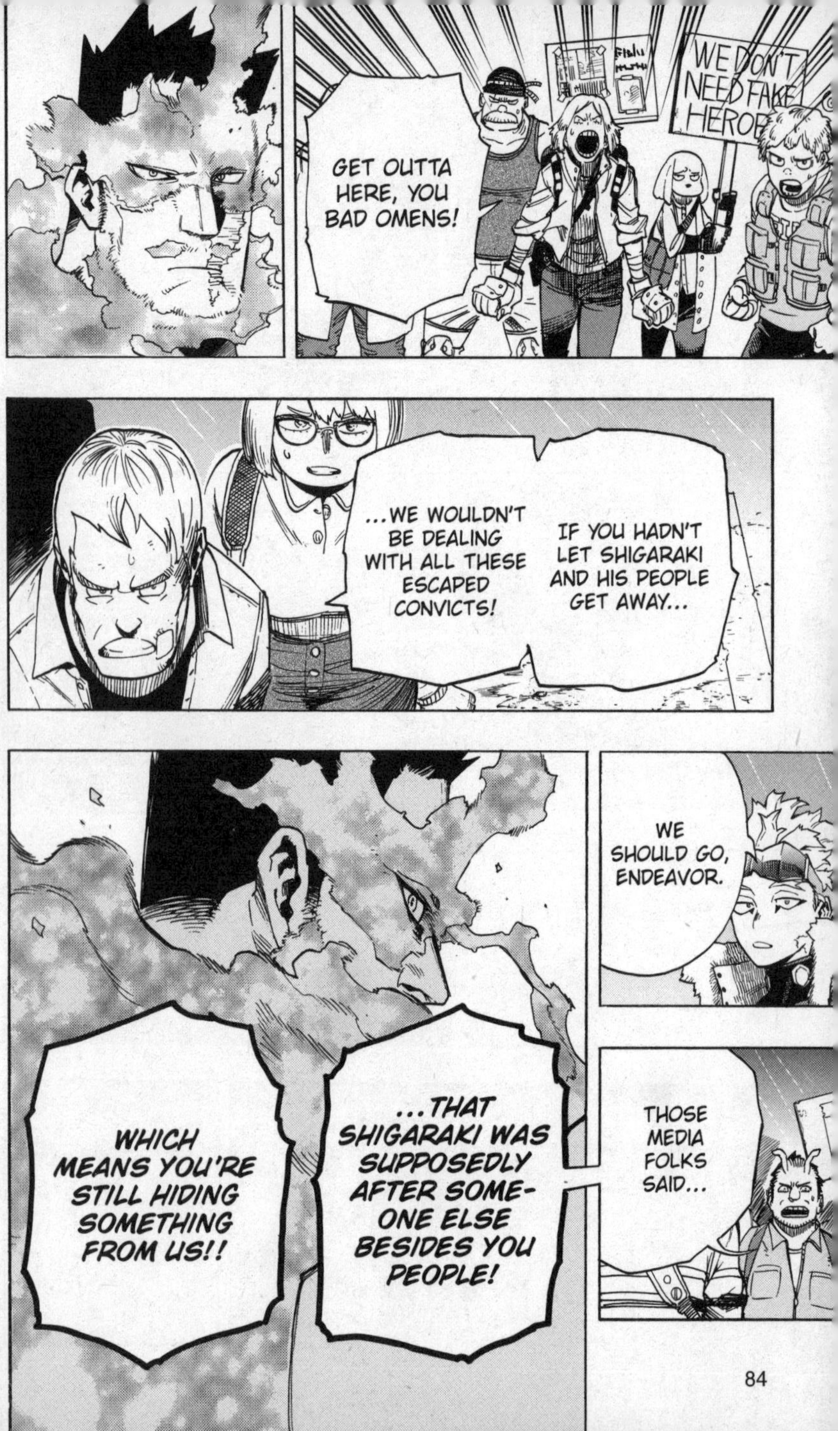
WE DON'T NEED FAKE HEROE
GET OUTTA HERE, YOU BAD OMENS!
IF YOU HADN'T LET SHIGARAKI AND HIS PEOPLE GET AWAY...
...WE WOULDN'T BE DEALING WITH ALL THESE ESCAPED CONVICTS!
WE SHOULD GO, ENDEAVOR.
THOSE MEDIA FOLKS SAID...
...THAT SHIGARAKI WAS SUPPOSEDLY AFTER SOME-ONE ELSE BESIDES YOU PEOPLE!
WHICH MEANS YOU'RE STILL HIDING SOMETHING FROM US!!

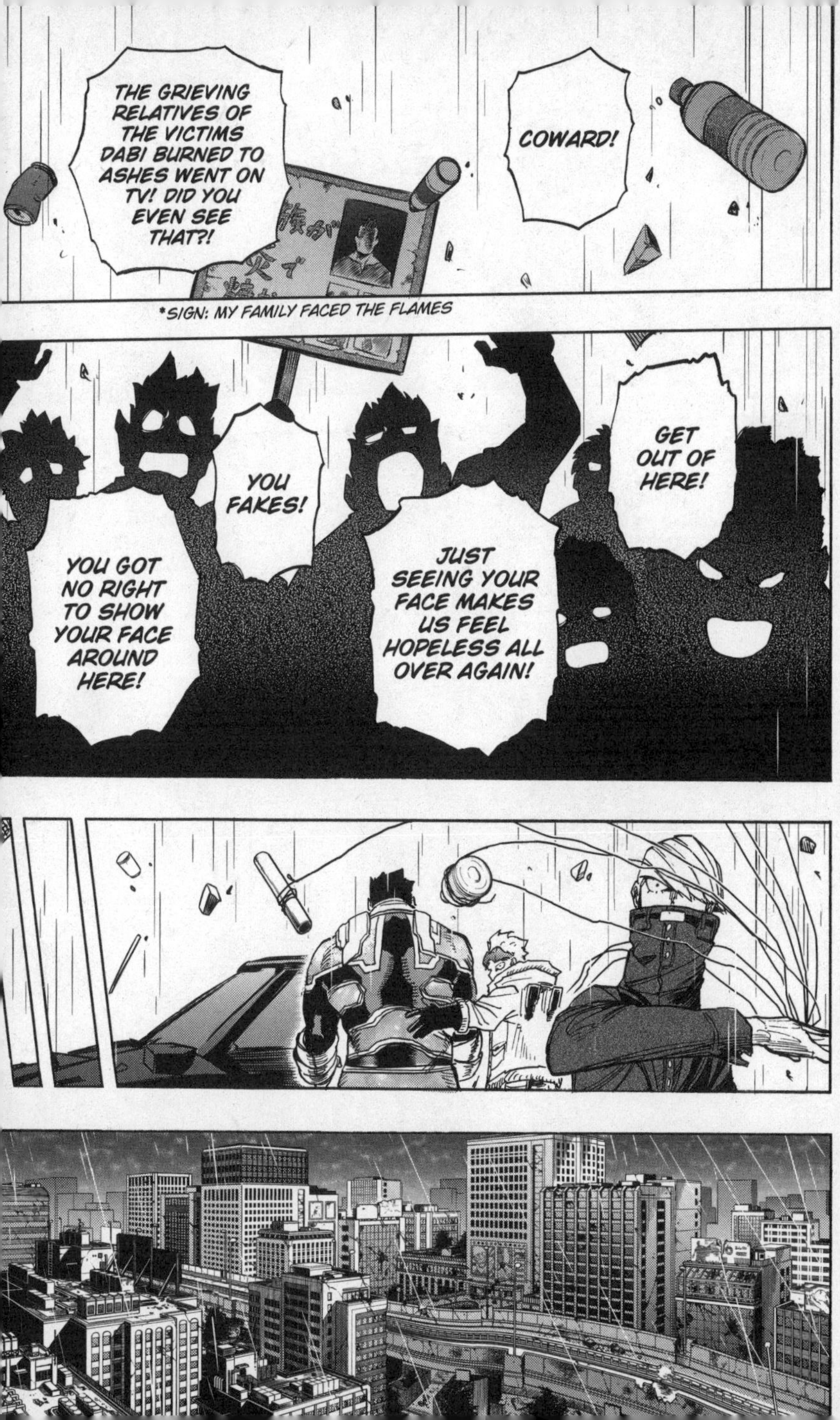
COWARD!
THE GRIEVING RELATIVES OF THE VICTIMS DABI BURNED TO ASHES WENT ON TV! DID YOU EVEN SEE THAT?!
*SIGN: MY FAMILY FACED THE FLAMES
GET OUT OF HERE!
JUST SEEING YOUR FACE MAKES US FEEL HOPELESS ALL OVER AGAIN!
YOU FAKES!
YOU GOT NO RIGHT TO SHOW YOUR FACE AROUND HERE!

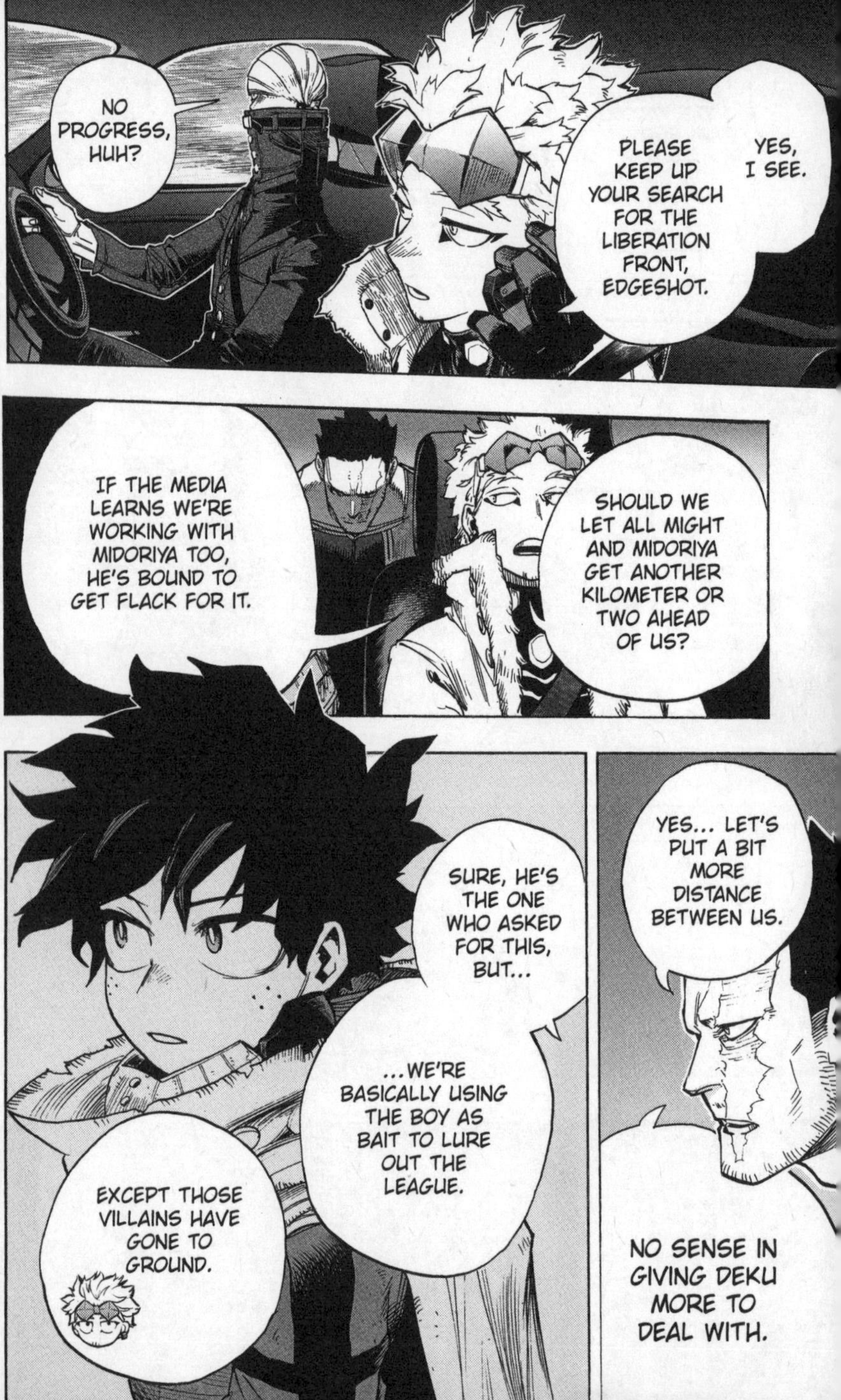
YES, I SEE.
PLEASE KEEP UP YOUR SEARCH FOR THE LIBERATION FRONT, EDGESHOT.
NO PROGRESS, HUH?
SHOULD WE LET ALL MIGHT AND MIDORIYA GET ANOTHER KILOMETER OR TWO AHEAD OF US?
IF THE MEDIA LEARNS WE'RE WORKING WITH MIDORIYA TOO, HE'S BOUND TO GET FLACK FOR IT.
YES... LET'S PUT A BIT MORE DISTANCE BETWEEN US.
NO SENSE IN GIVING DEKU MORE TO DEAL WITH.
SURE, HE'S THE ONE WHO ASKED FOR THIS, BUT...
...WE'RE BASICALLY USING THE BOY AS BAIT TO LURE OUT THE LEAGUE.
EXCEPT THOSE VILLAINS HAVE GONE TO GROUND.

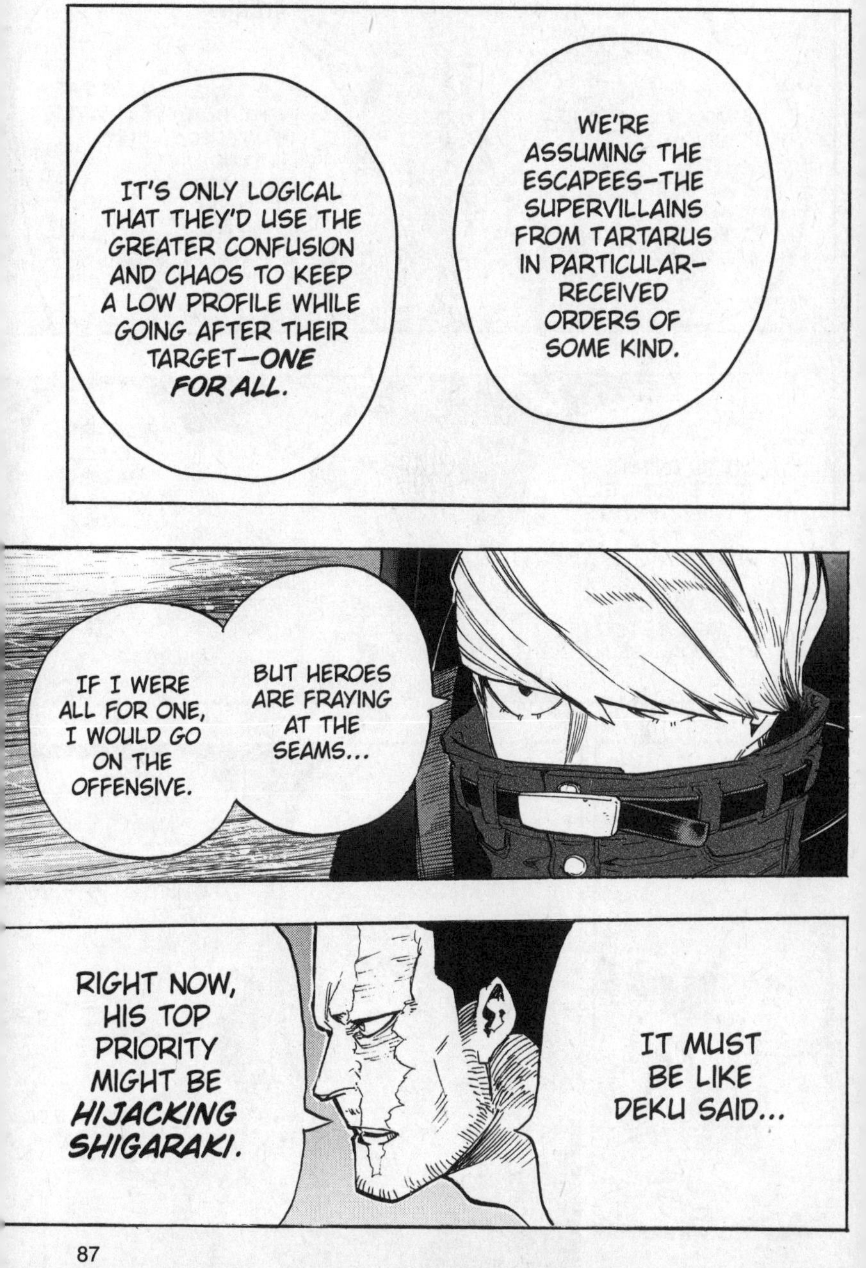
WE'RE ASSUMING THE ESCAPEES—THE SUPERVILLAINS FROM TARTARUS IN PARTICULAR—RECEIVED ORDERS OF SOME KIND.
IT'S ONLY LOGICAL THAT THEY'D USE THE GREATER CONFUSION AND CHAOS TO KEEP A LOW PROFILE WHILE GOING AFTER THEIR TARGET—*ONE FOR ALL*.
BUT HEROES ARE FRAYING AT THE SEAMS...
IF I WERE ALL FOR ONE, I WOULD GO ON THE OFFENSIVE.
IT MUST BE LIKE DEKU SAID...
RIGHT NOW, HIS TOP PRIORITY MIGHT BE *HIJACKING SHIGARAKI*.

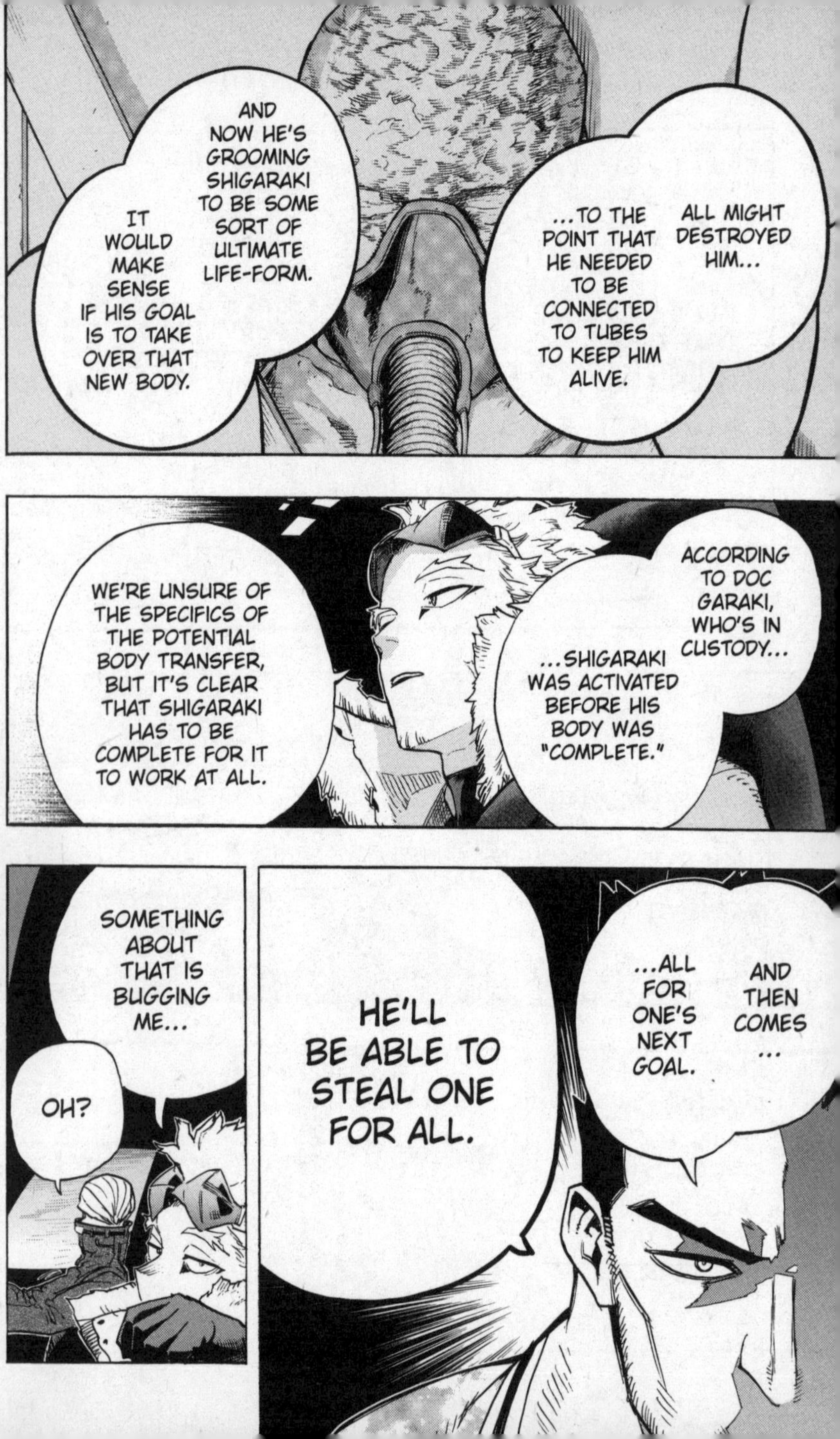
ALL MIGHT DESTROYED HIM...
...TO THE POINT THAT HE NEEDED TO BE CONNECTED TO TUBES TO KEEP HIM ALIVE.
AND NOW HE'S GROOMING SHIGARAKI TO BE SOME SORT OF ULTIMATE LIFE-FORM.
IT WOULD MAKE SENSE IF HIS GOAL IS TO TAKE OVER THAT NEW BODY.
ACCORDING TO DOC GARAKI, WHO'S IN CUSTODY...
...SHIGARAKI WAS ACTIVATED BEFORE HIS BODY WAS "COMPLETE."
WE'RE UNSURE OF THE SPECIFICS OF THE POTENTIAL BODY TRANSFER, BUT IT'S CLEAR THAT SHIGARAKI HAS TO BE COMPLETE FOR IT TO WORK AT ALL.
AND THEN COMES...
...ALL FOR ONE'S NEXT GOAL.
HE'LL BE ABLE TO STEAL ONE FOR ALL.
SOMETHING ABOUT THAT IS BUGGING ME...
OH?

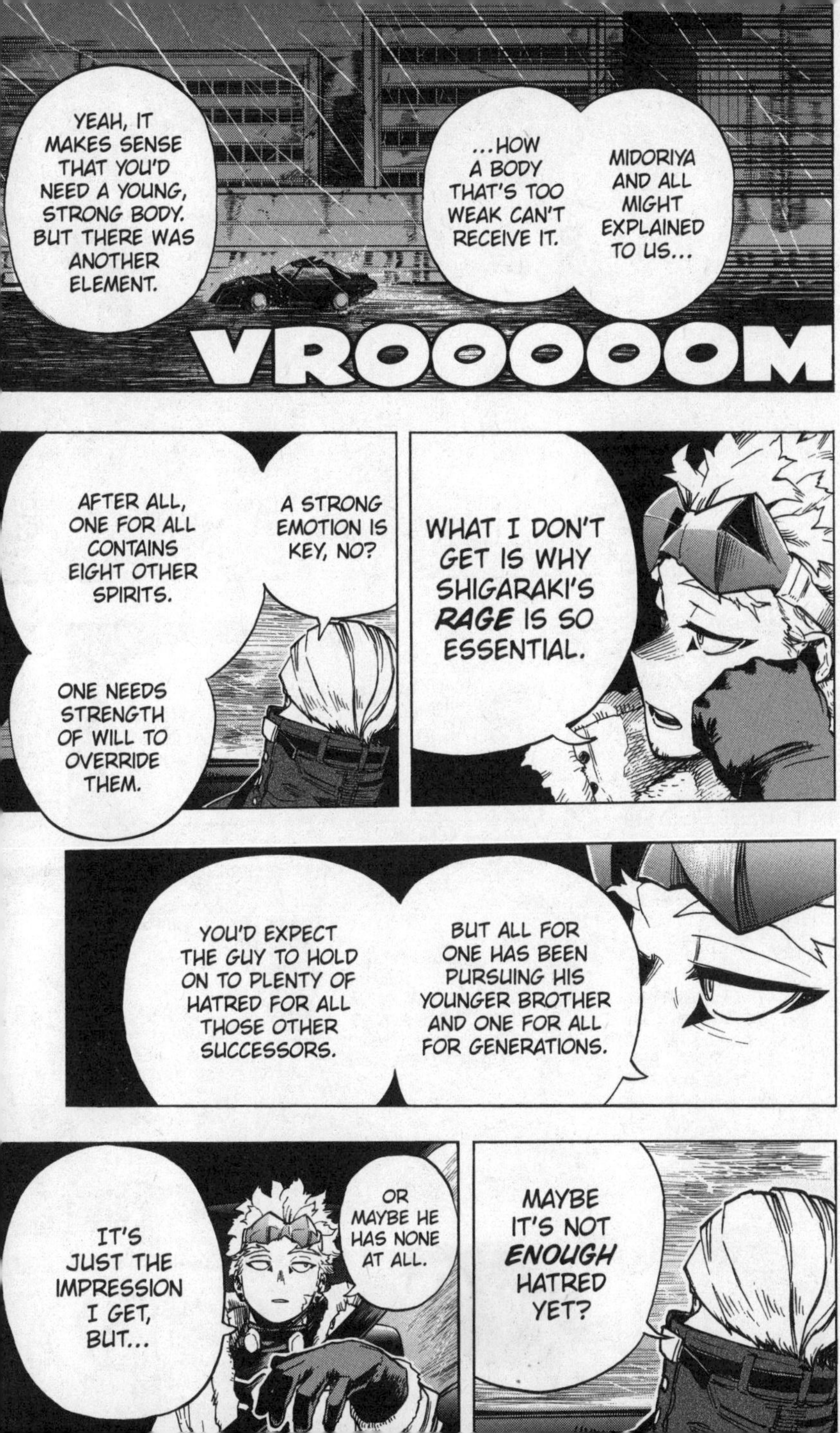
MIDORIYA AND ALL MIGHT EXPLAINED TO US...
...HOW A BODY THAT'S TOO WEAK CAN'T RECEIVE IT.
YEAH, IT MAKES SENSE THAT YOU'D NEED A YOUNG, STRONG BODY. BUT THERE WAS ANOTHER ELEMENT.
VROOOOOM
WHAT I DON'T GET IS WHY SHIGARAKI'S *RAGE* IS SO ESSENTIAL.
A STRONG EMOTION IS KEY, NO?
AFTER ALL, ONE FOR ALL CONTAINS EIGHT OTHER SPIRITS.
ONE NEEDS STRENGTH OF WILL TO OVERRIDE THEM.
BUT ALL FOR ONE HAS BEEN PURSUING HIS YOUNGER BROTHER AND ONE FOR ALL FOR GENERATIONS.
YOU'D EXPECT THE GUY TO HOLD ON TO PLENTY OF HATRED FOR ALL THOSE OTHER SUCCESSORS.
MAYBE IT'S NOT *ENOUGH* HATRED YET?
OR MAYBE HE HAS NONE AT ALL.
IT'S JUST THE IMPRESSION I GET, BUT...

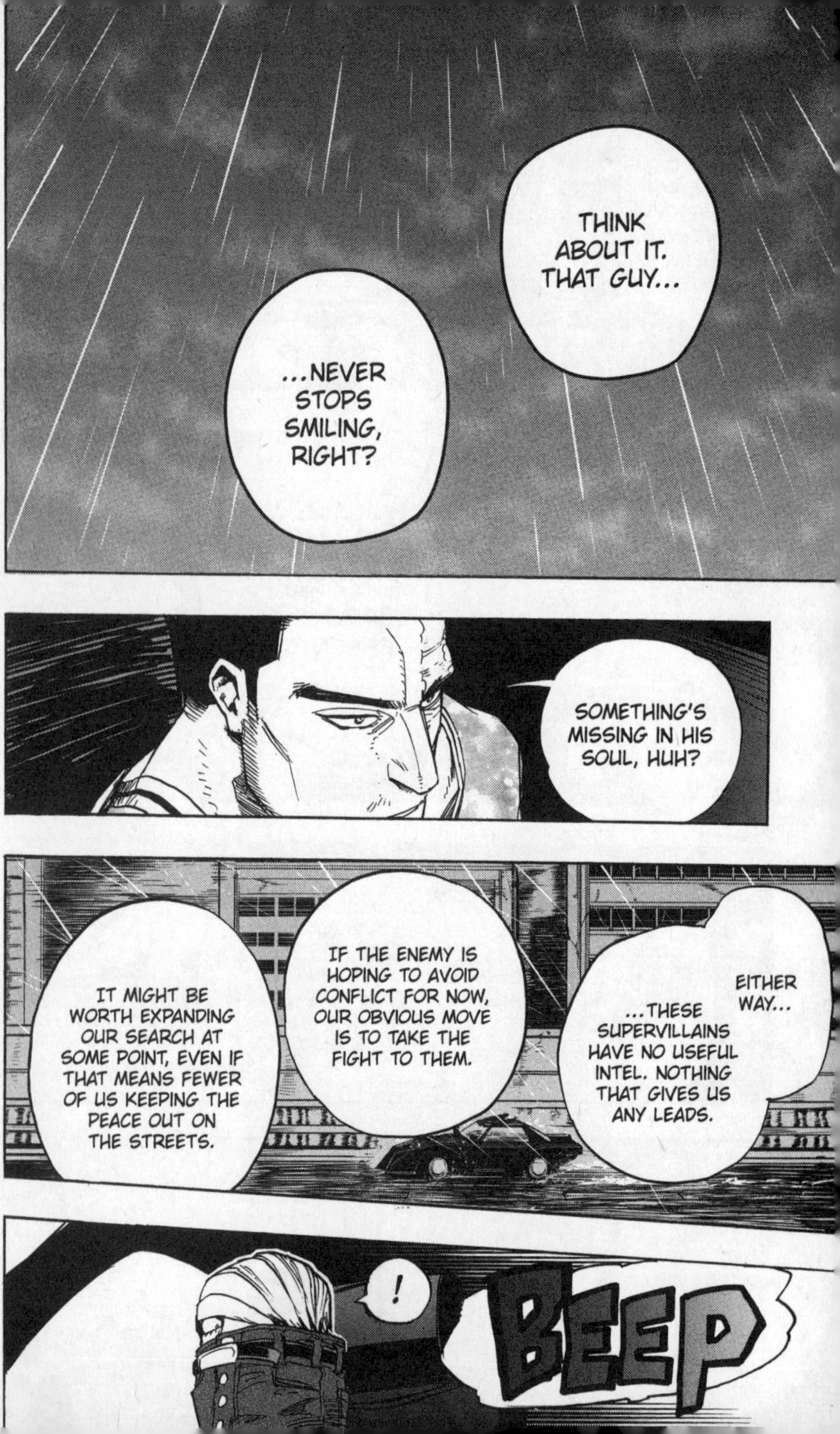
THINK ABOUT IT. THAT GUY...
...NEVER STOPS SMILING, RIGHT?
SOMETHING'S MISSING IN HIS SOUL, HUH?
EITHER WAY...
...THESE SUPERVILLAINS HAVE NO USEFUL INTEL. NOTHING THAT GIVES US ANY LEADS.
IF THE ENEMY IS HOPING TO AVOID CONFLICT FOR NOW, OUR OBVIOUS MOVE IS TO TAKE THE FIGHT TO THEM.
IT MIGHT BE WORTH EXPANDING OUR SEARCH AT SOME POINT, EVEN IF THAT MEANS FEWER OF US KEEPING THE PEACE OUT ON THE STREETS.
BEEP
!

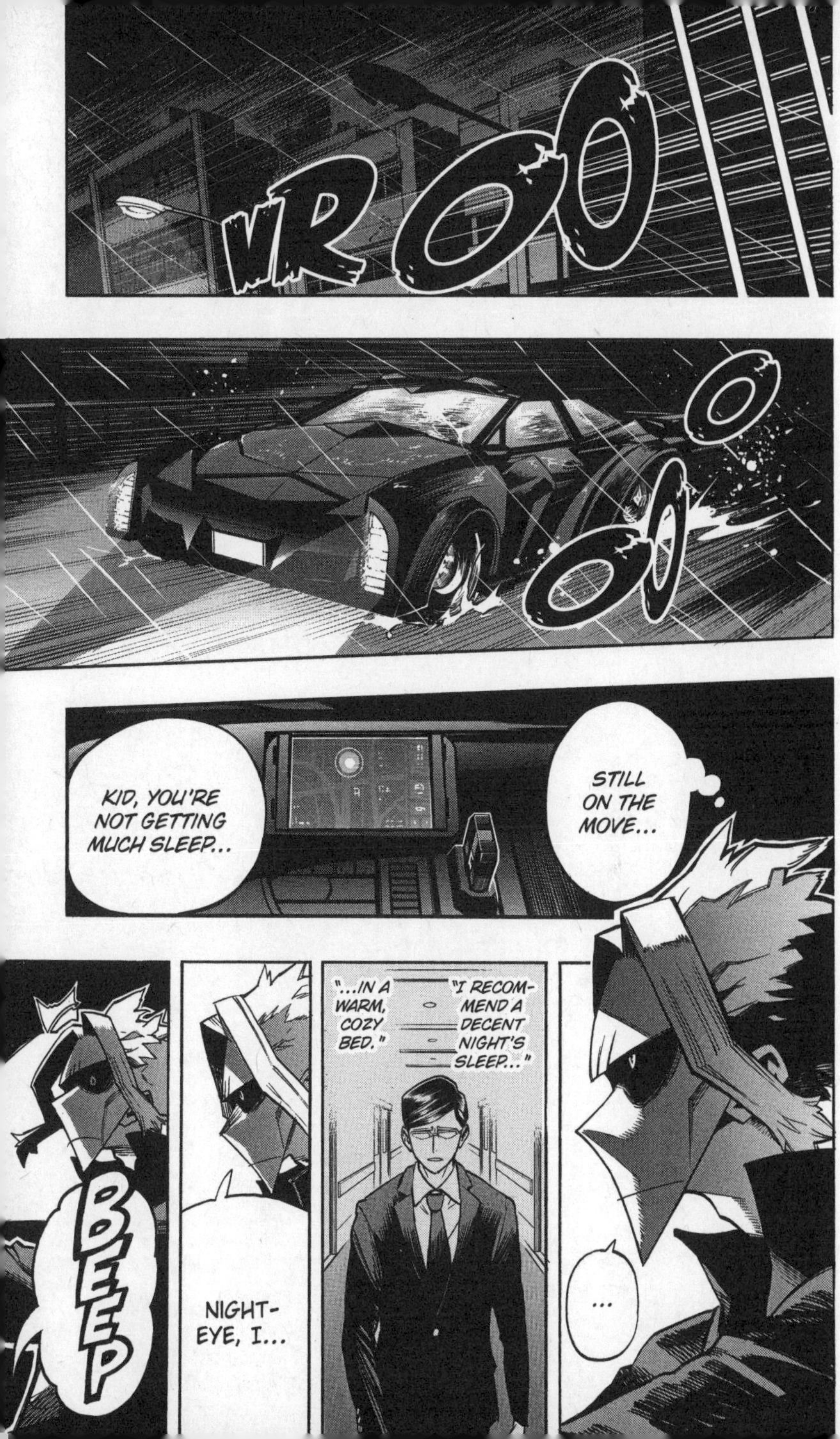
VROOO
OOO
STILL ON THE MOVE...
KID, YOU'RE NOT GETTING MUCH SLEEP...
...
"I RECOMMEND A DECENT NIGHT'S SLEEP..."
"...IN A WARM, COZY BED."
NIGHT-EYE, I...
BEEP

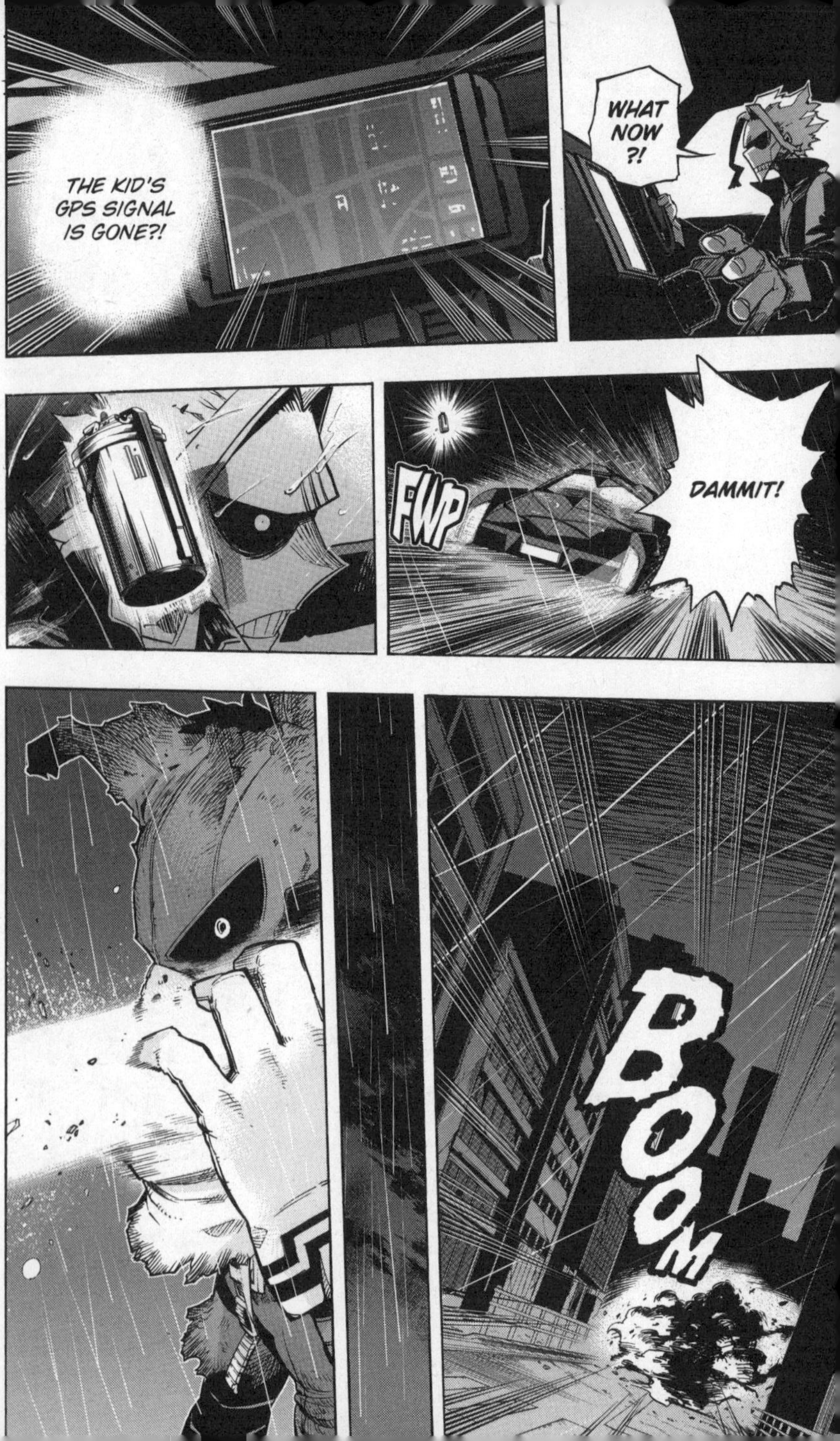
WHAT NOW ?!
THE KID'S GPS SIGNAL IS GONE?!
DAMMIT!
FWP
BOOM

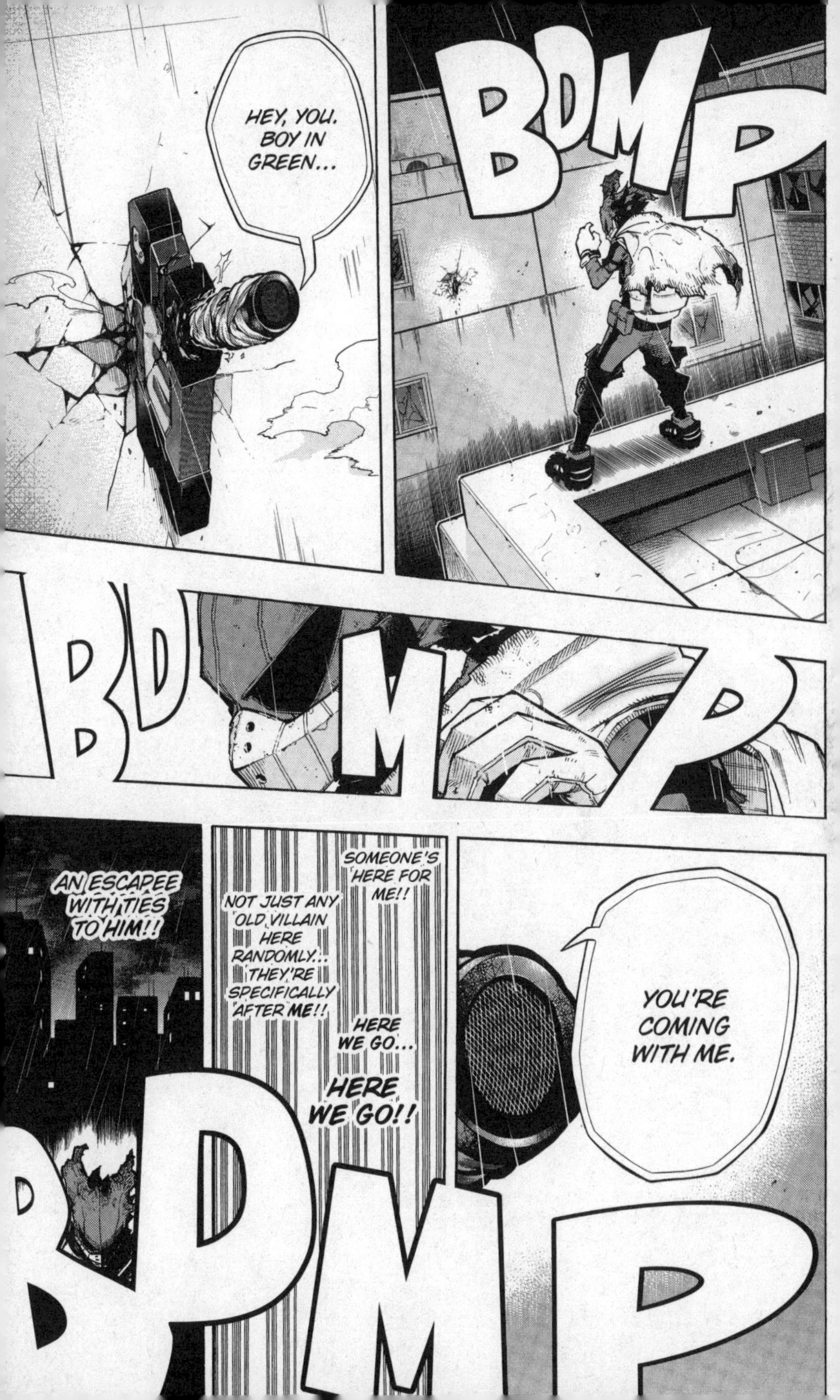
BDOMP
HEY, YOU. BOY IN GREEN...
BDOMP
YOU'RE COMING WITH ME.
SOMEONE'S HERE FOR ME!!
NOT JUST ANY OLD VILLAIN HERE RANDOMLY... THEY'RE SPECIFICALLY AFTER ME!!
HERE WE GO...
HERE WE GO!!
AN ESCAPEE WITH TIES TO HIM!!
BDOMP

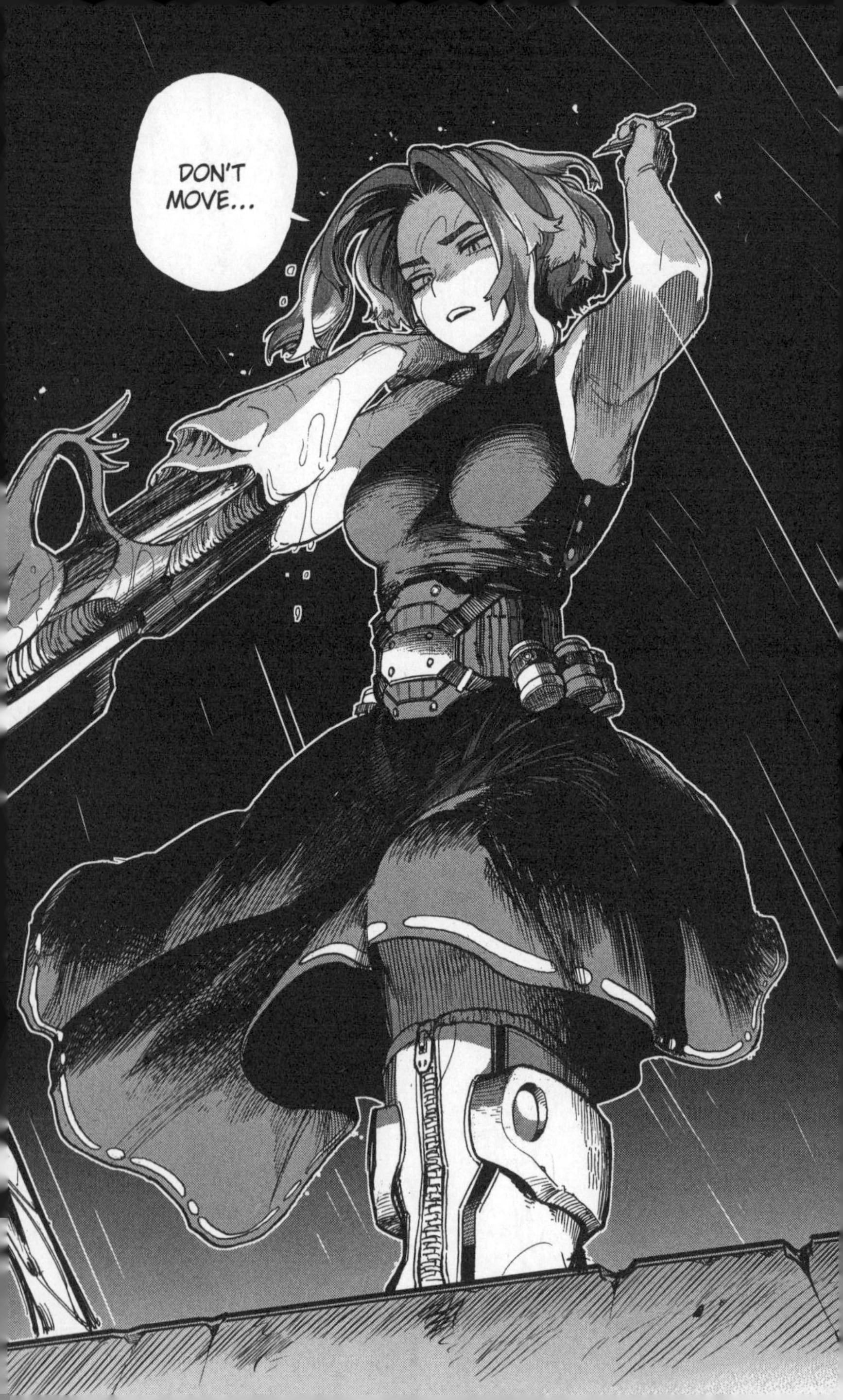
DON'T MOVE...

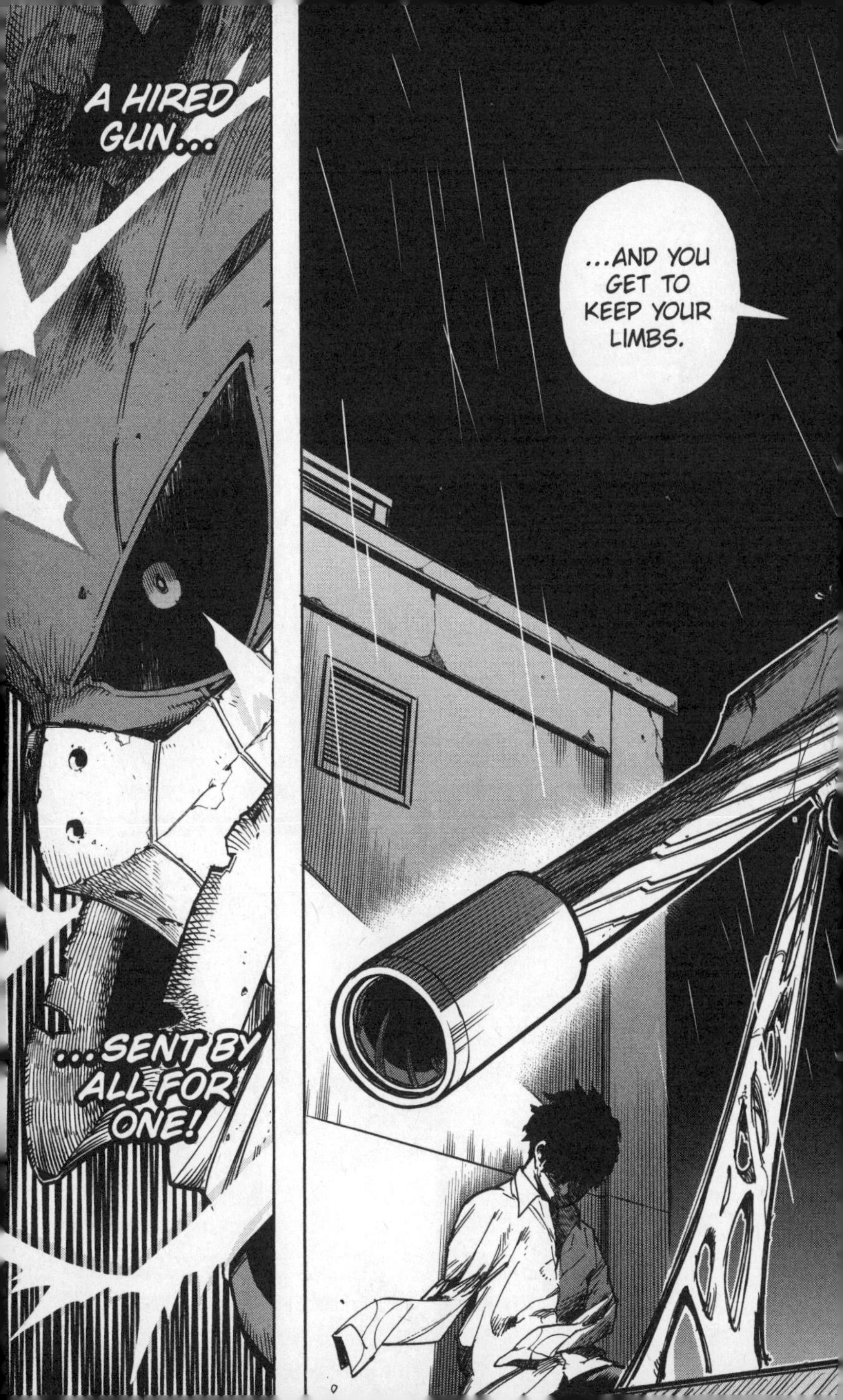
...AND YOU GET TO KEEP YOUR LIMBS.
A HIRED GUN...
...SENT BY ALL FOR ONE!

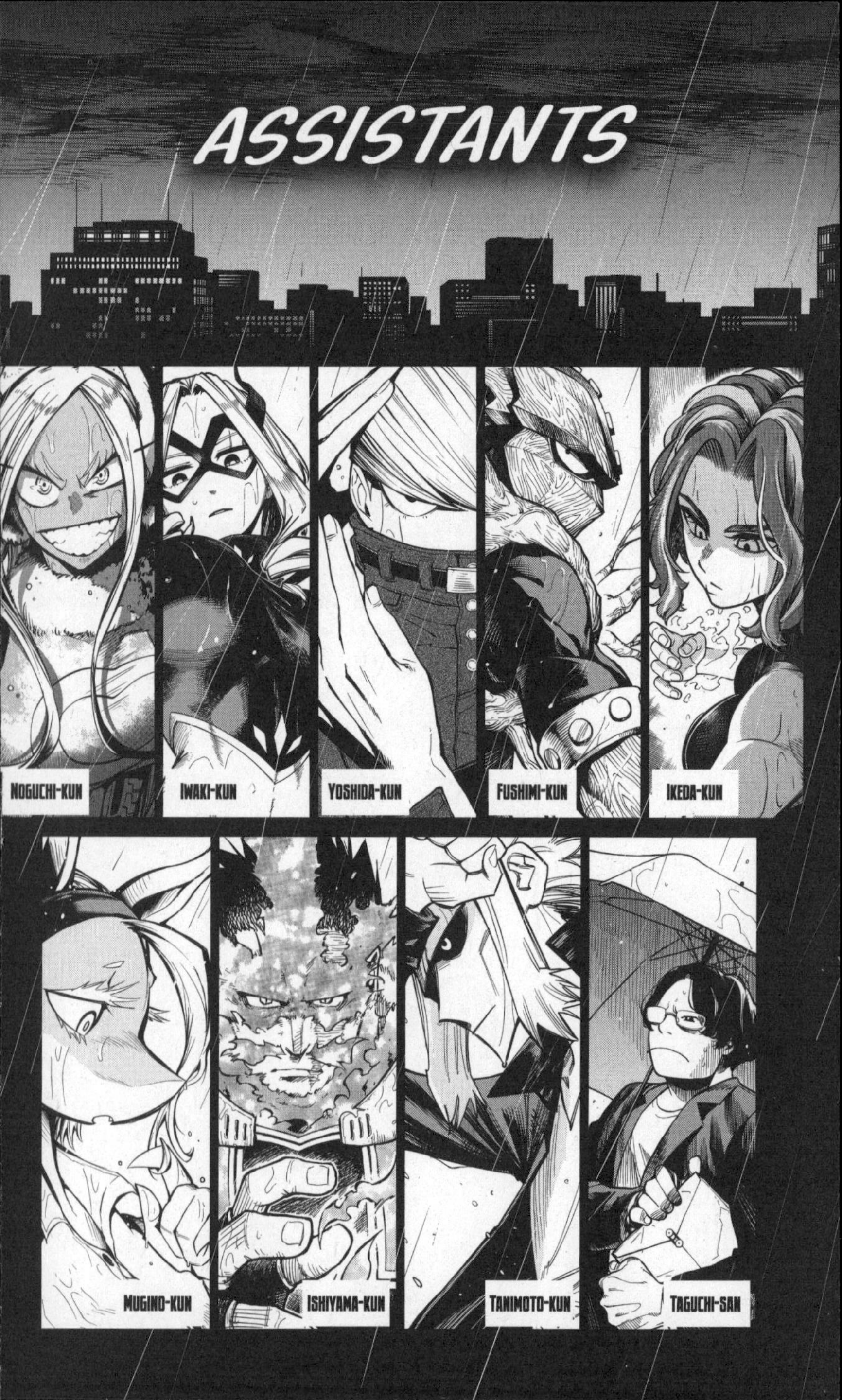
ASSISTANTS
IKEDA-KUN
FUSHIMI-KUN
YOSHIDA-KUN
IWAKI-KUN
NOGUCHI-KUN
TAGUCHI-SAN
TANIMOTO-KUN
ISHIYAMA-KUN
MUGINO-KUN

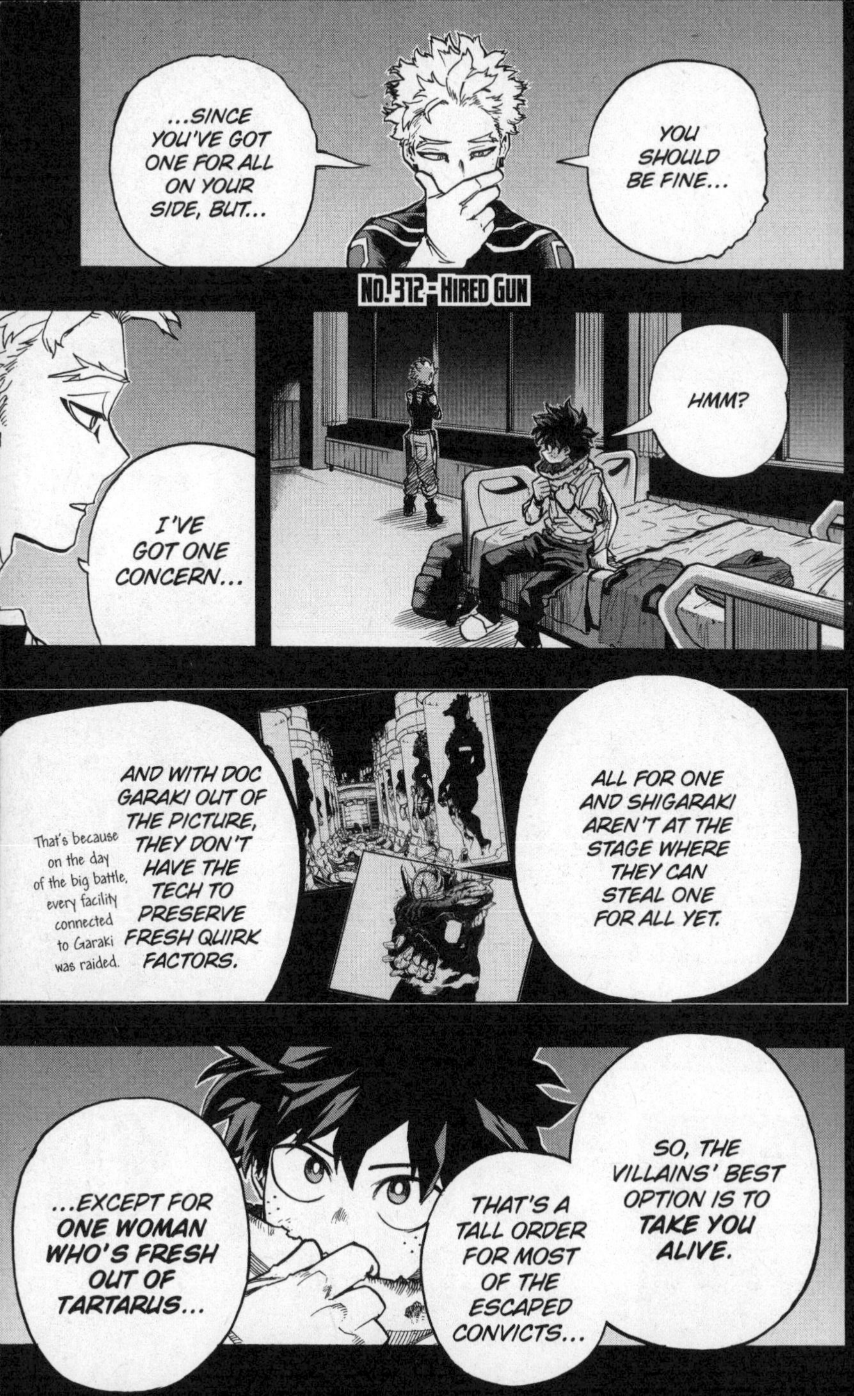
YOU SHOULD BE FINE...
...SINCE YOU'VE GOT ONE FOR ALL ON YOUR SIDE, BUT...
NO. 312 - HIRED GUN
HMM?
I'VE GOT ONE CONCERN...
ALL FOR ONE AND SHIGARAKI AREN'T AT THE STAGE WHERE THEY CAN STEAL ONE FOR ALL YET.
AND WITH DOC GARAKI OUT OF THE PICTURE, THEY DON'T HAVE THE TECH TO PRESERVE FRESH QUIRK FACTORS.
That's because on the day of the big battle, every facility connected to Garaki was raided.
SO, THE VILLAINS' BEST OPTION IS TO TAKE YOU ALIVE.
THAT'S A TALL ORDER FOR MOST OF THE ESCAPED CONVICTS...
...EXCEPT FOR ONE WOMAN WHO'S FRESH OUT OF TARTARUS...

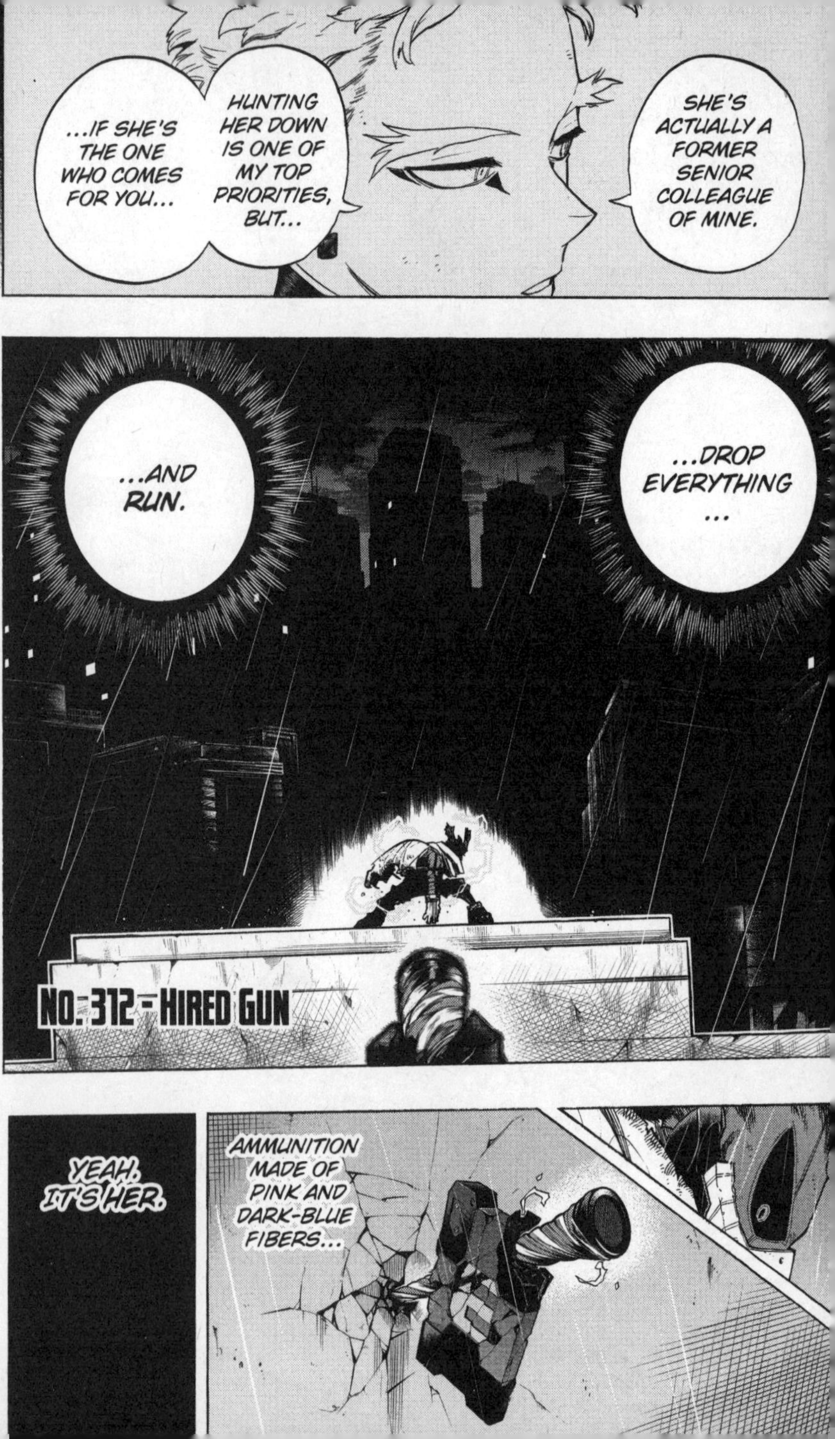
SHE'S ACTUALLY A FORMER SENIOR COLLEAGUE OF MINE.
HUNTING HER DOWN IS ONE OF MY TOP PRIORITIES, BUT...
...IF SHE'S THE ONE WHO COMES FOR YOU...
...DROP EVERYTHING ...
...AND RUN.
No. 312 - Hired Gun
AMMUNITION MADE OF PINK AND DARK-BLUE FIBERS...
YEAH. IT'S HER.

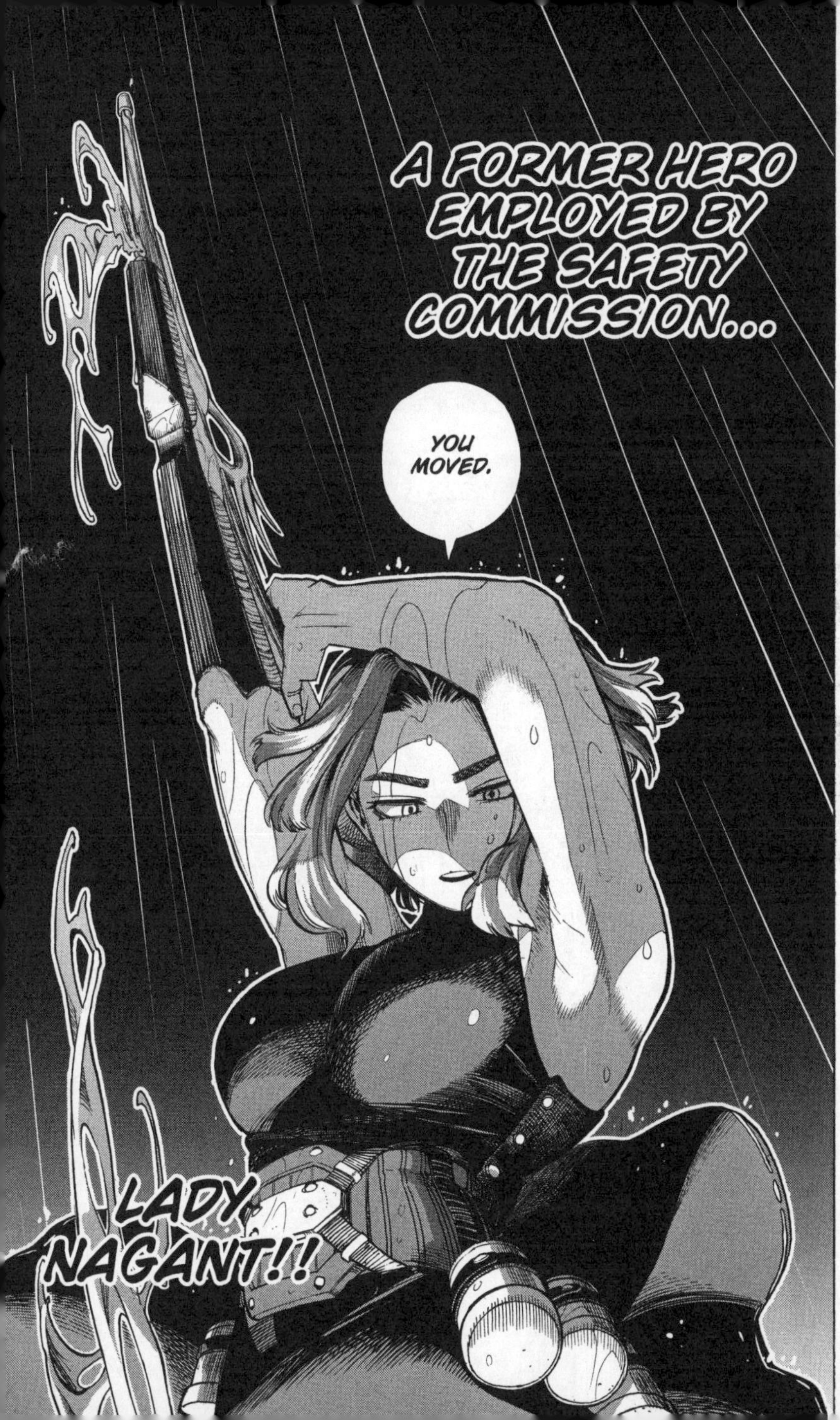
A FORMER HERO EMPLOYED BY THE SAFETY COMMISSION...
YOU MOVED.
LADY NAGANT!!

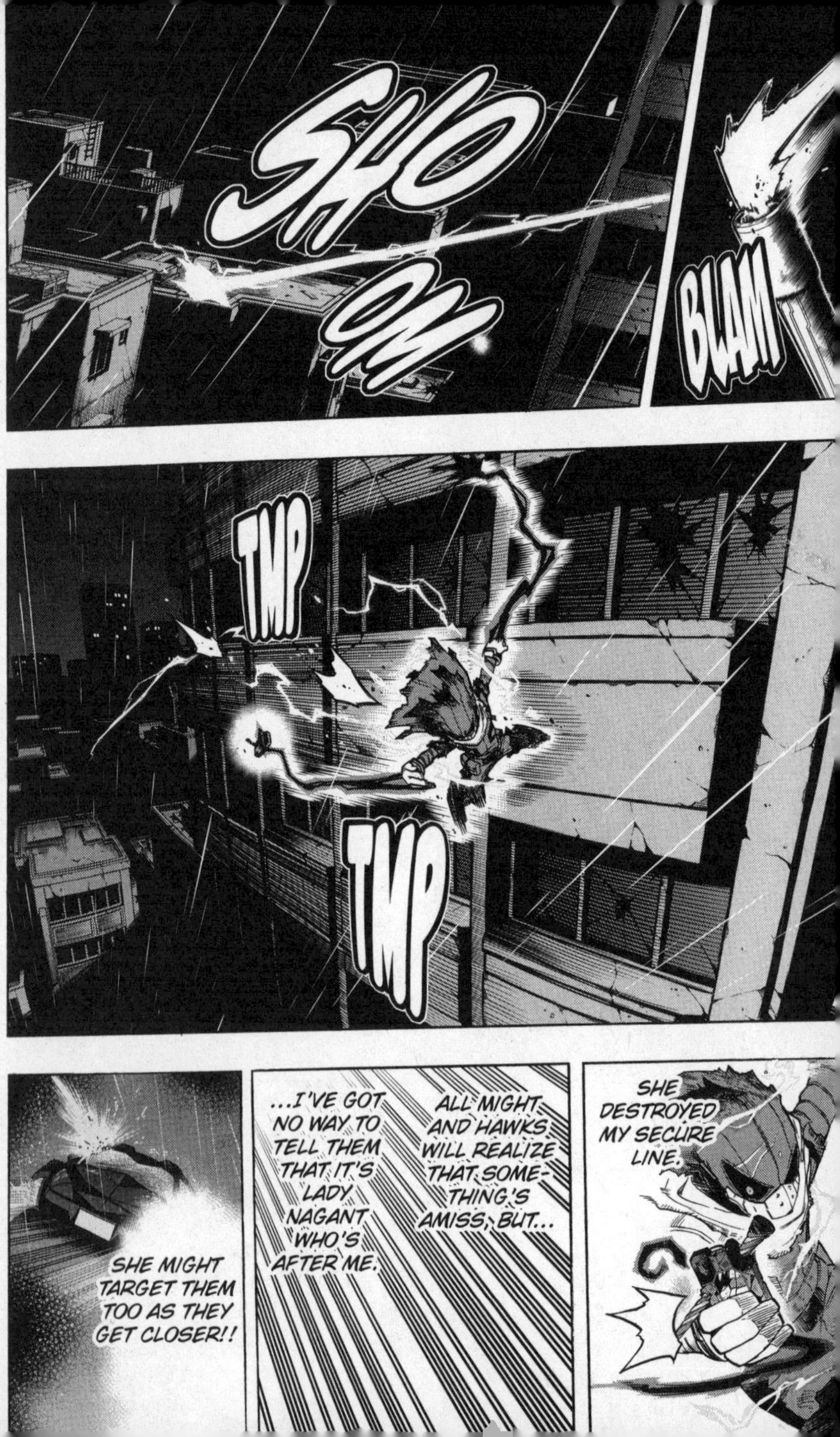
BLAM
SHOOM
TMP
TMP
SHE DESTROYED MY SECURE LINE.
ALL MIGHT AND HAWKS WILL REALIZE THAT SOME-THING'S AMISS, BUT...
...I'VE GOT NO WAY TO TELL THEM THAT IT'S LADY NAGANT WHO'S AFTER ME.
SHE MIGHT TARGET THEM TOO AS THEY GET CLOSER!!

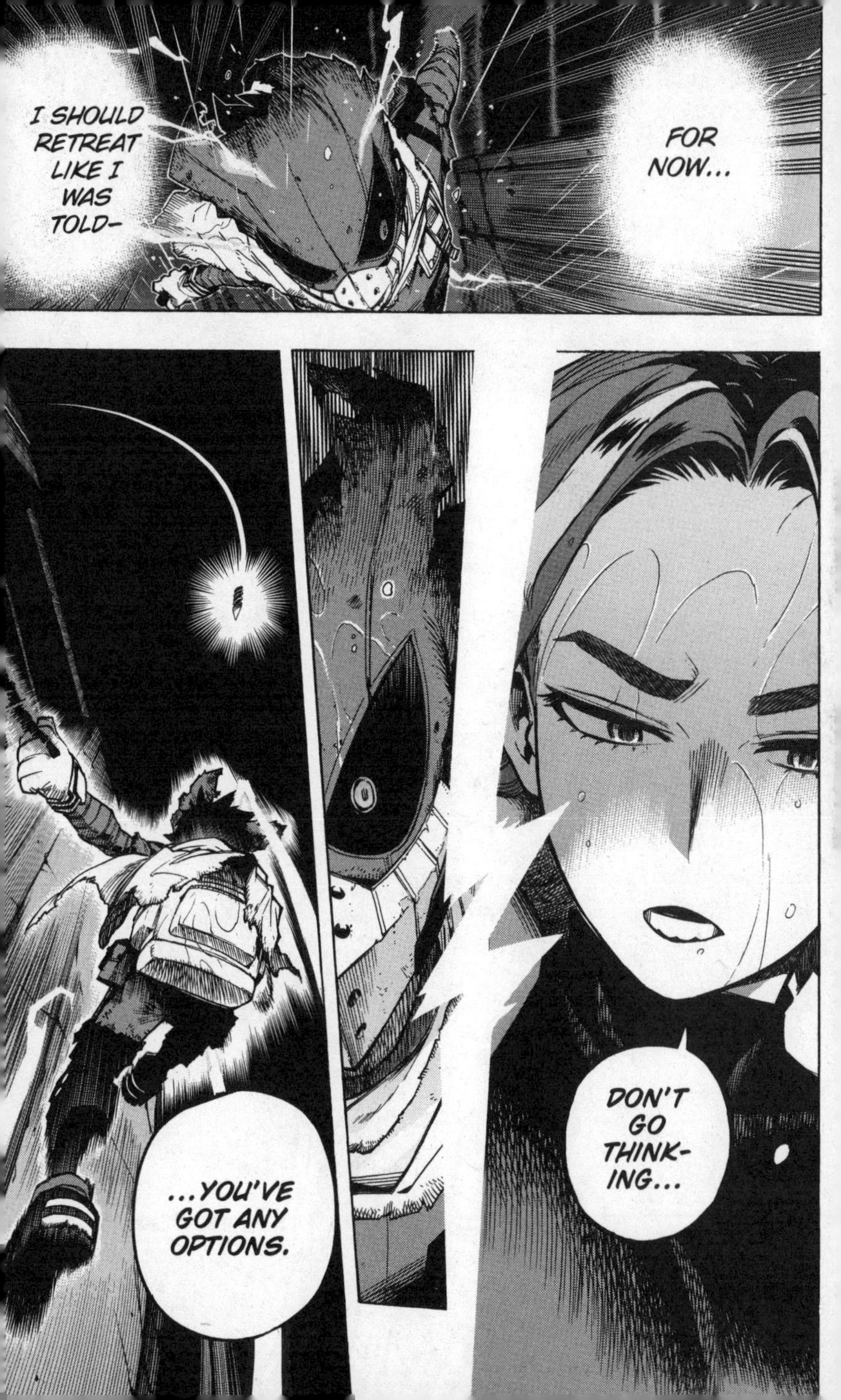

I SHOULD RETREAT LIKE I WAS TOLD-
FOR NOW...
DON'T GO THINKING...
...YOU'VE GOT ANY OPTIONS.

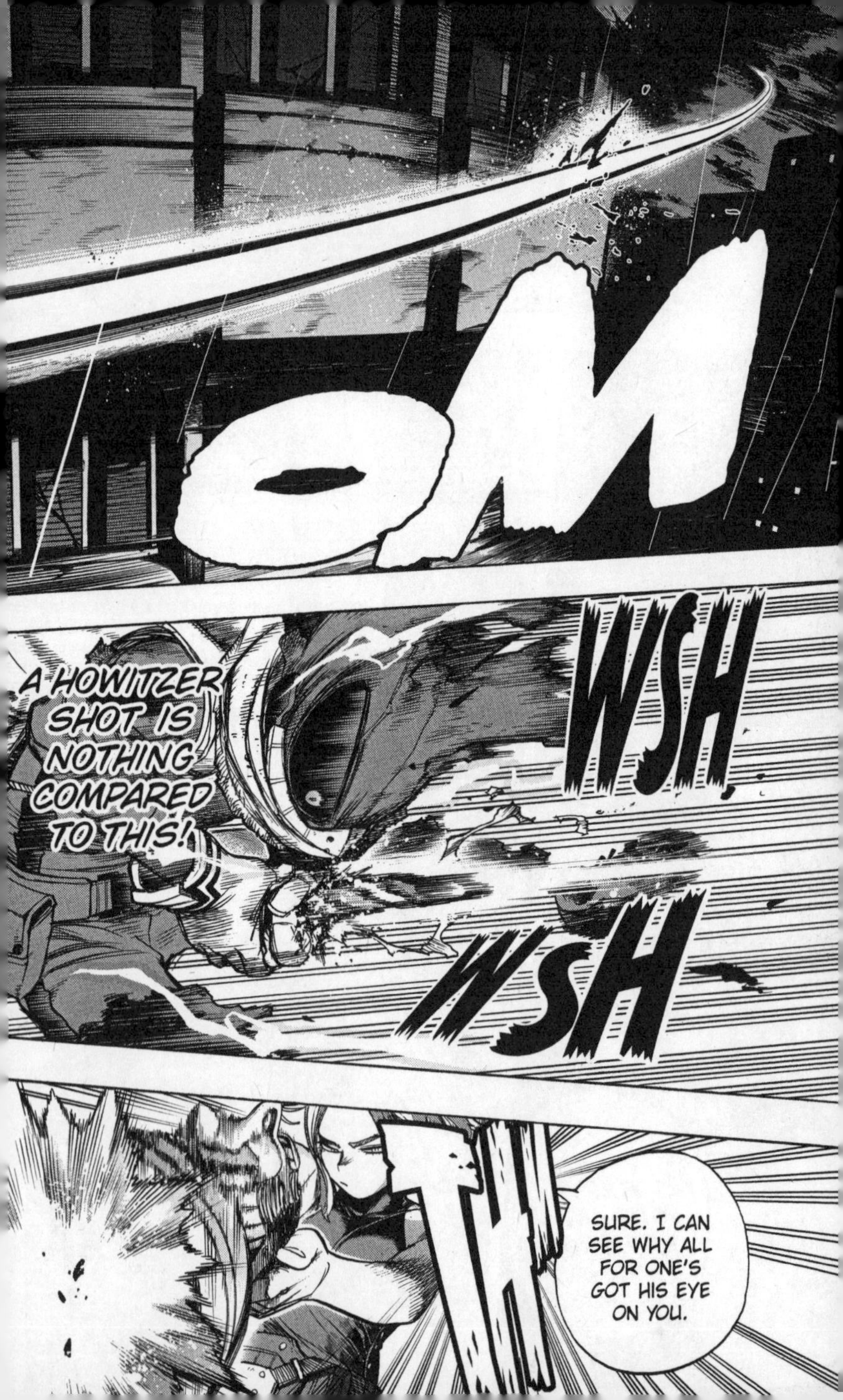
WSH
A HOWITZER SHOT IS NOTHING COMPARED TO THIS!
WSH
SURE. I CAN SEE WHY ALL FOR ONE'S GOT HIS EYE ON YOU.

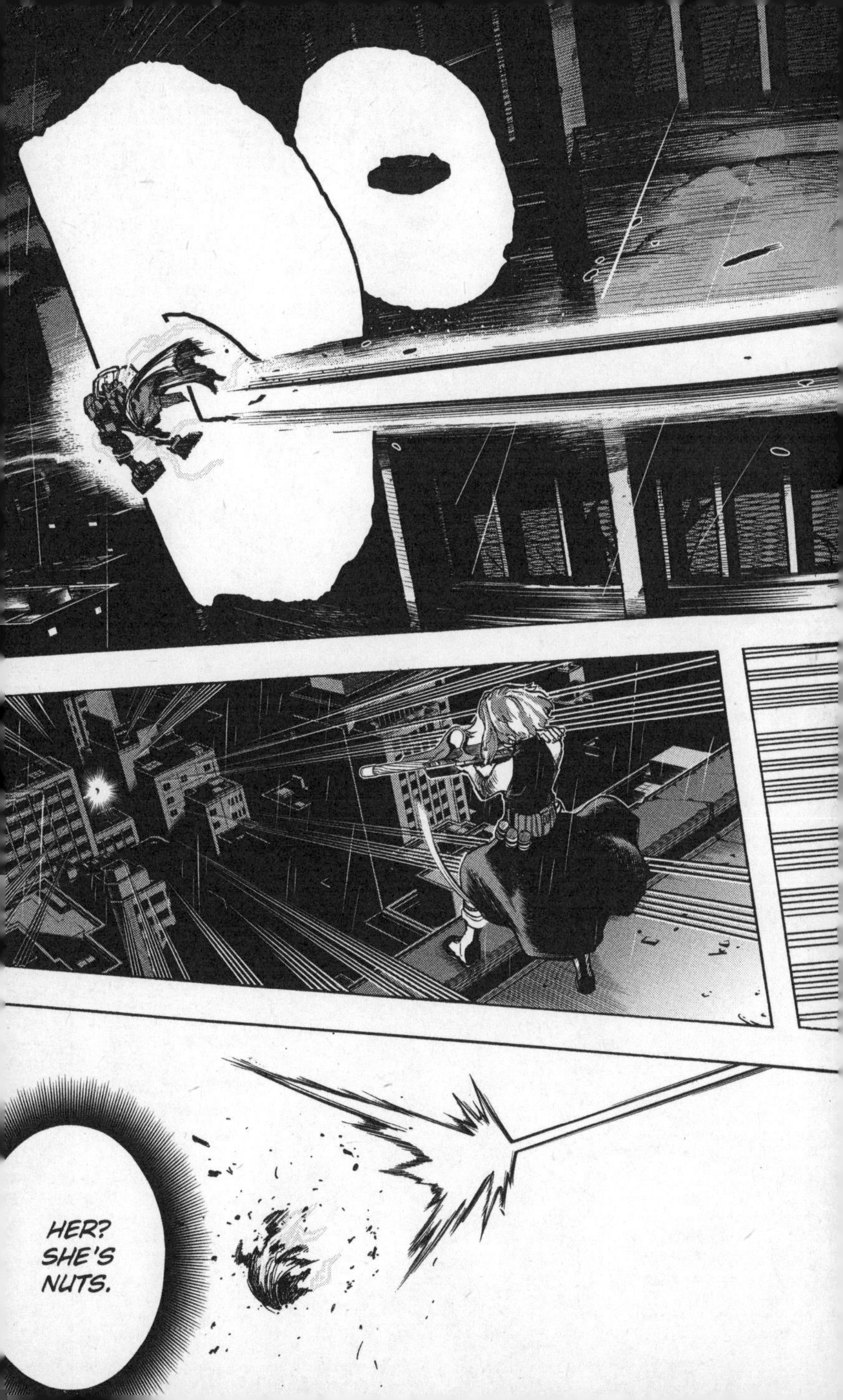
HER? SHE'S NUTS.

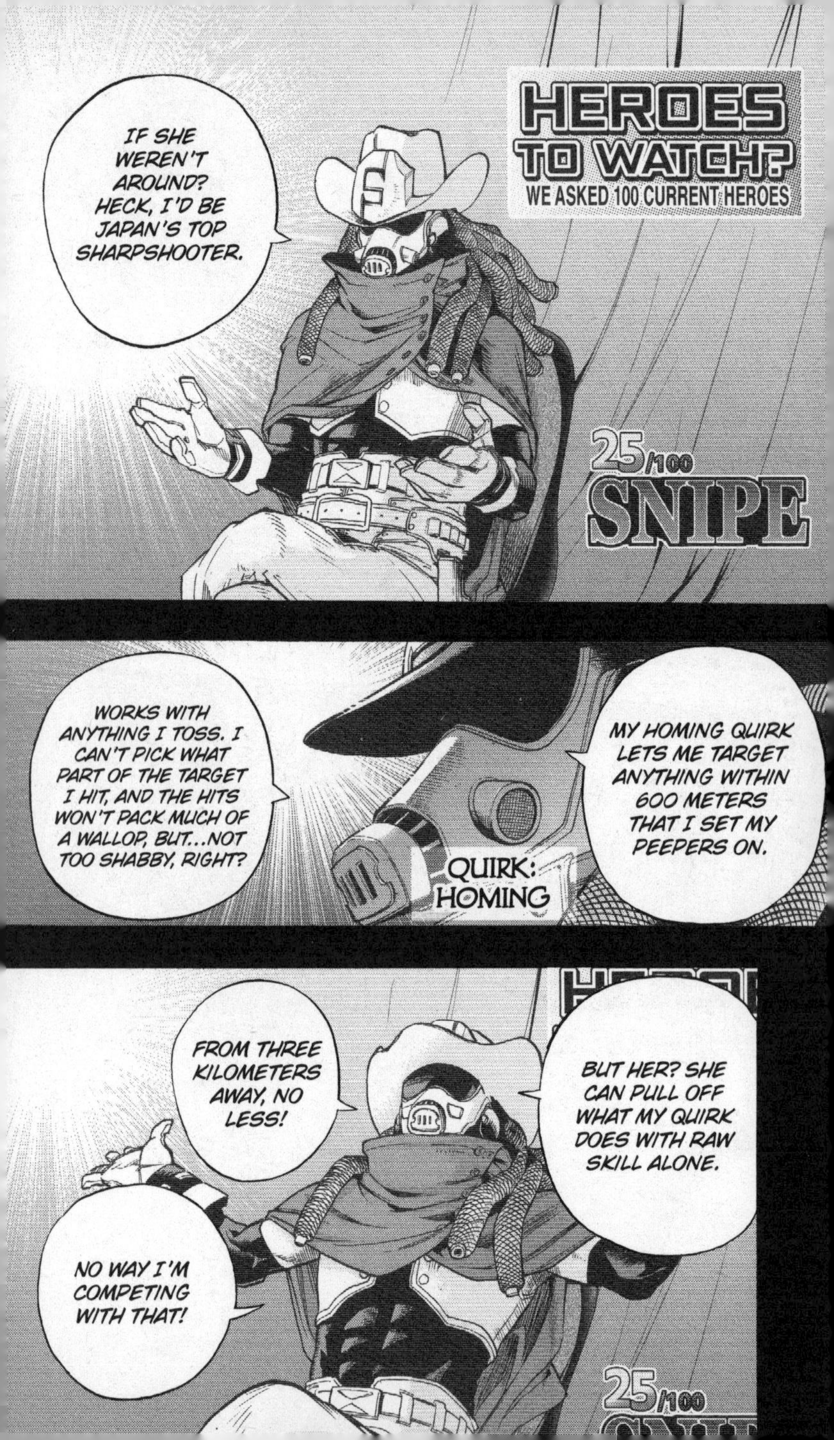
HEROES TO WATCH?
WE ASKED 100 CURRENT HEROES
IF SHE WEREN'T AROUND? HECK, I'D BE JAPAN'S TOP SHARPSHOOTER.
25/100
SNIPE
MY HOMING QUIRK LETS ME TARGET ANYTHING WITHIN 600 METERS THAT I SET MY PEEPERS ON.
QUIRK: HOMING
WORKS WITH ANYTHING I TOSS. I CAN'T PICK WHAT PART OF THE TARGET I HIT, AND THE HITS WON'T PACK MUCH OF A WALLOP, BUT...NOT TOO SHABBY, RIGHT?
BUT HER? SHE CAN PULL OFF WHAT MY QUIRK DOES WITH RAW SKILL ALONE.
FROM THREE KILOMETERS AWAY, NO LESS!
NO WAY I'M COMPETING WITH THAT!
25/100

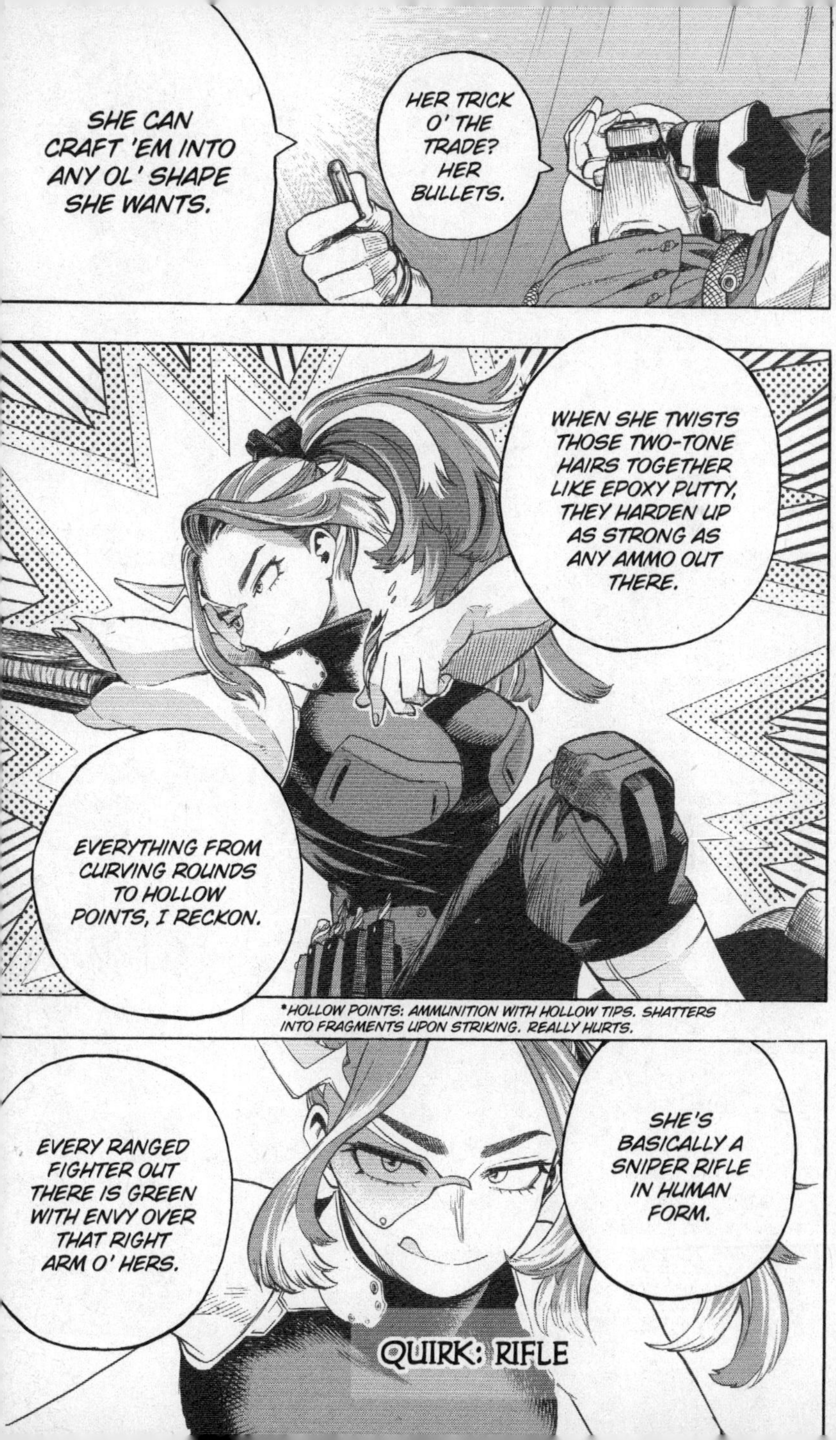
HER TRICK O' THE TRADE? HER BULLETS.
SHE CAN CRAFT 'EM INTO ANY OL' SHAPE SHE WANTS.
WHEN SHE TWISTS THOSE TWO-TONE HAIRS TOGETHER LIKE EPOXY PUTTY, THEY HARDEN UP AS STRONG AS ANY AMMO OUT THERE.
EVERYTHING FROM CURVING ROUNDS TO HOLLOW POINTS, I RECKON.
*HOLLOW POINTS: AMMUNITION WITH HOLLOW TIPS. SHATTERS INTO FRAGMENTS UPON STRIKING. REALLY HURTS.
SHE'S BASICALLY A SNIPER RIFLE IN HUMAN FORM.
EVERY RANGED FIGHTER OUT THERE IS GREEN WITH ENVY OVER THAT RIGHT ARM O' HERS.
QUIRK: RIFLE

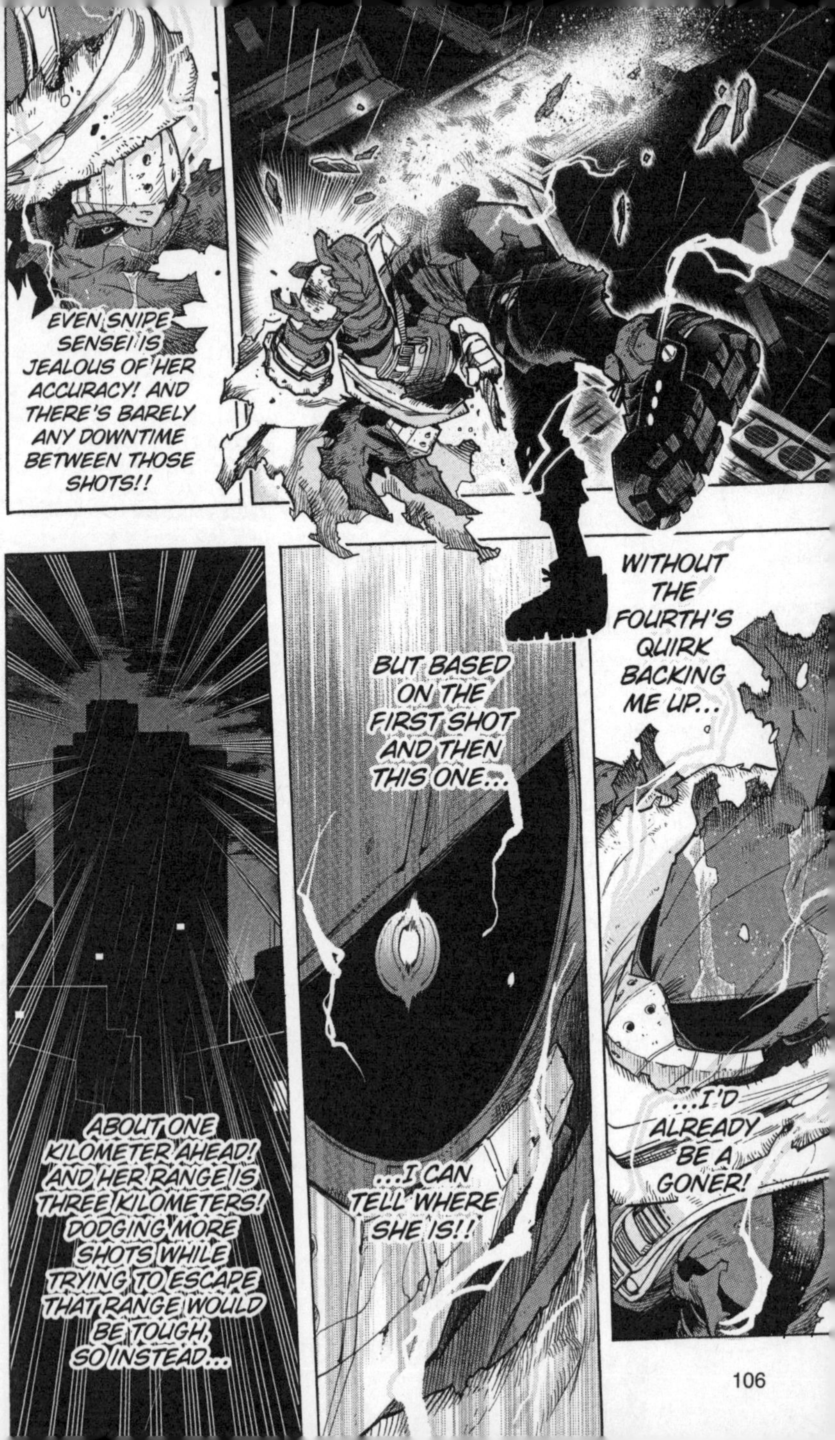
EVEN SNIPE SENSEI IS JEALOUS OF HER ACCURACY! AND THERE'S BARELY ANY DOWNTIME BETWEEN THOSE SHOTS!!
WITHOUT THE FOURTH'S QUIRK BACKING ME UP...
...I'D ALREADY BE A GONER!
BUT BASED ON THE FIRST SHOT AND THEN THIS ONE...
...I CAN TELL WHERE SHE IS!!
ABOUT ONE KILOMETER AHEAD! AND HER RANGE IS THREE KILOMETERS! DODGING MORE SHOTS WHILE TRYING TO ESCAPE THAT RANGE WOULD BE TOUGH, SO INSTEAD...

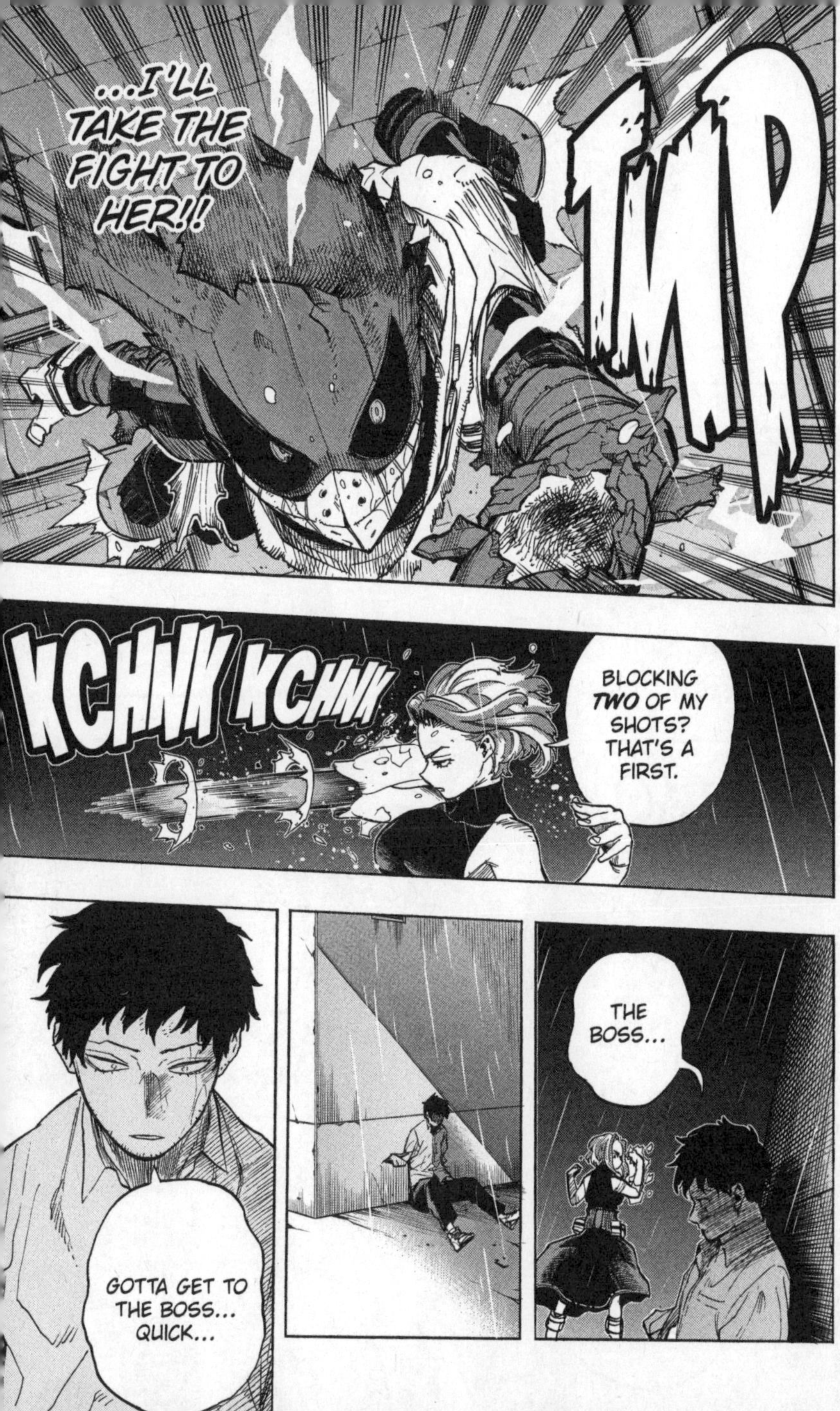
TMP
...I'LL TAKE THE FIGHT TO HER!!
BLOCKING TWO OF MY SHOTS? THAT'S A FIRST.
KCHNK KCHNK
THE BOSS...
GOTTA GET TO THE BOSS... QUICK...

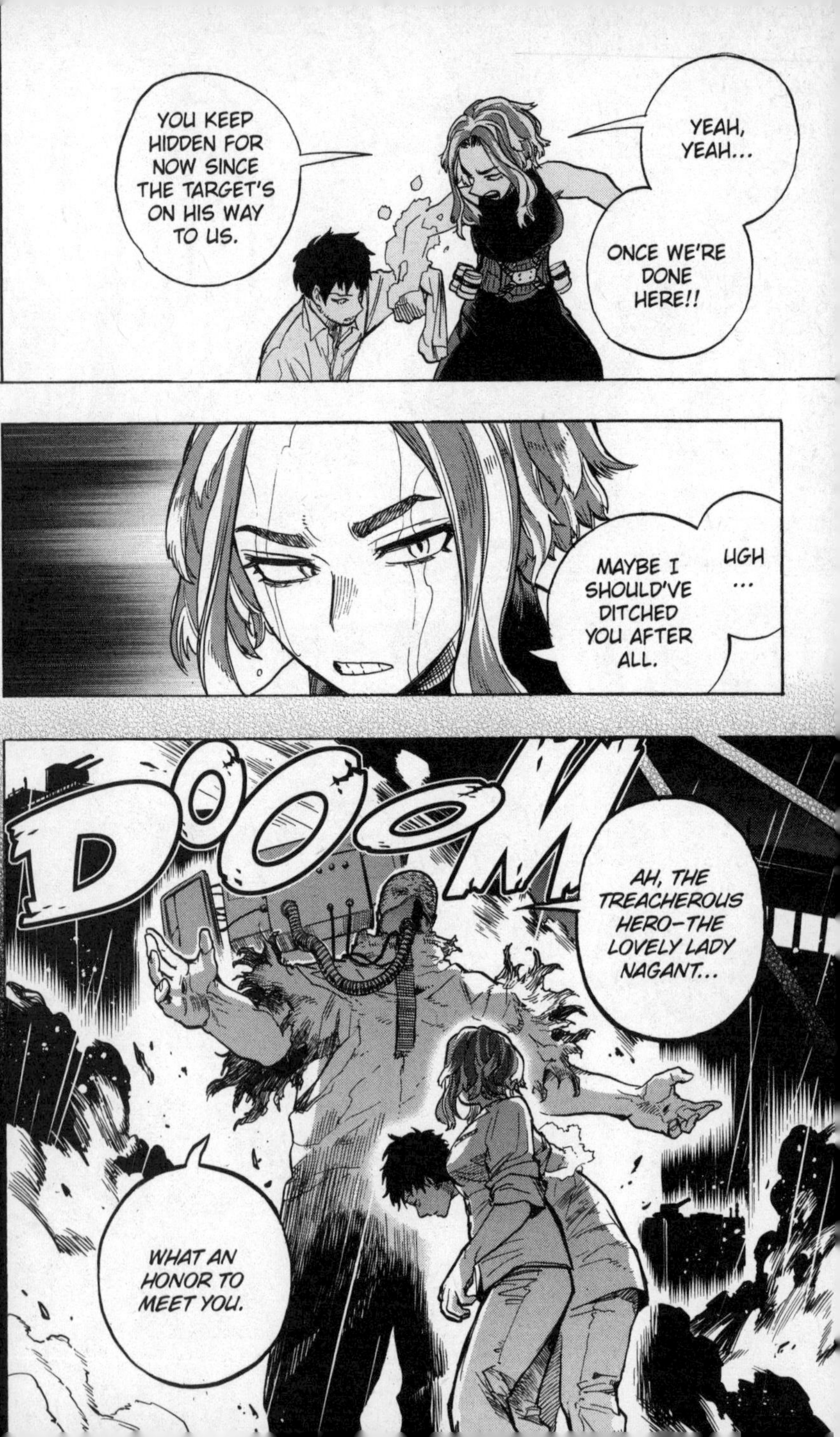
YEAH, YEAH...
ONCE WE'RE DONE HERE!!
YOU KEEP HIDDEN FOR NOW SINCE THE TARGET'S ON HIS WAY TO US.
UGH ...
MAYBE I SHOULD'VE DITCHED YOU AFTER ALL.
DOOOM
AH, THE TREACHEROUS HERO—THE LOVELY LADY NAGANT...
WHAT AN HONOR TO MEET YOU.

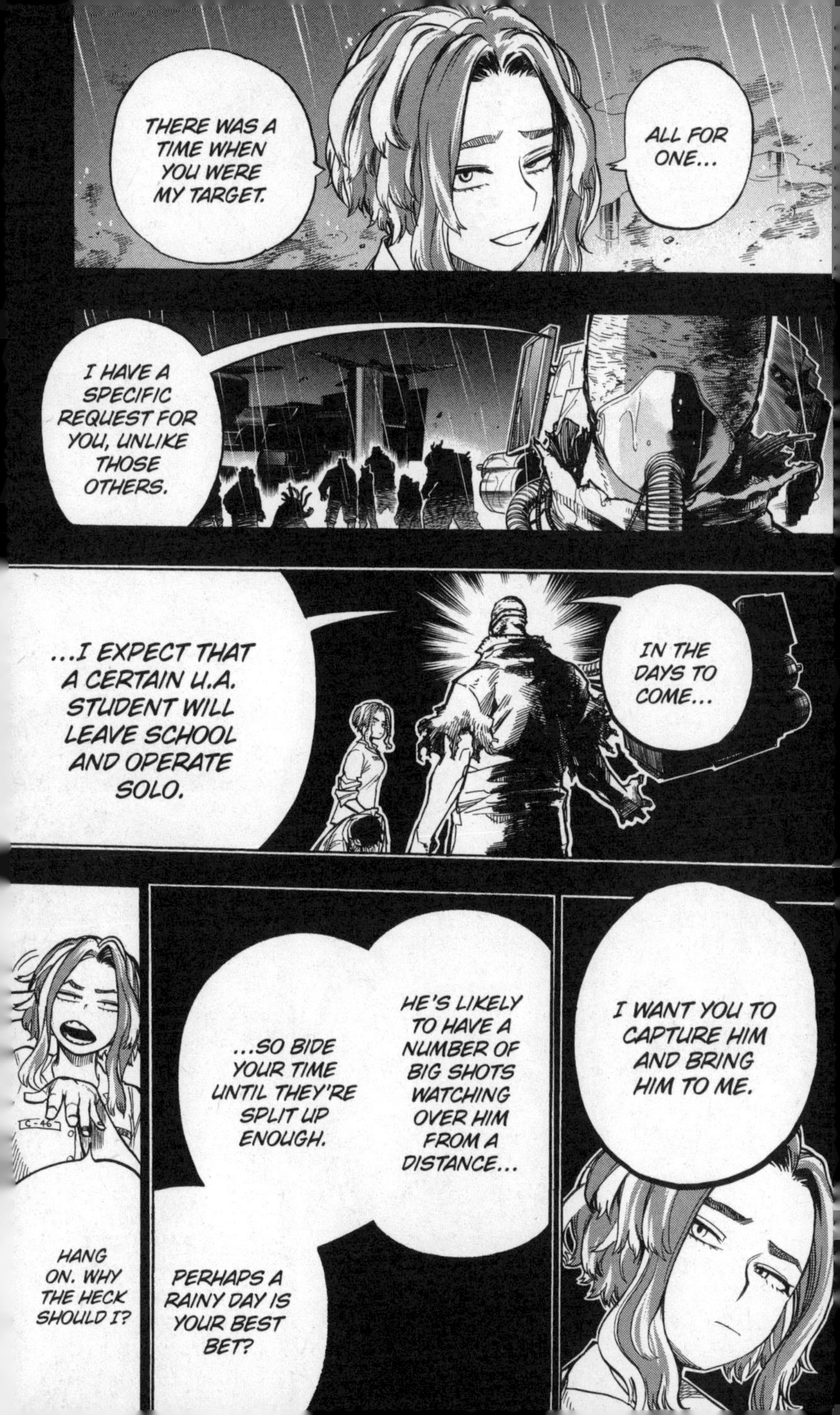
ALL FOR ONE...
THERE WAS A TIME WHEN YOU WERE MY TARGET.
I HAVE A SPECIFIC REQUEST FOR YOU, UNLIKE THOSE OTHERS.
IN THE DAYS TO COME...
...I EXPECT THAT A CERTAIN U.A. STUDENT WILL LEAVE SCHOOL AND OPERATE SOLO.
I WANT YOU TO CAPTURE HIM AND BRING HIM TO ME.
HE'S LIKELY TO HAVE A NUMBER OF BIG SHOTS WATCHING OVER HIM FROM A DISTANCE...
...SO BIDE YOUR TIME UNTIL THEY'RE SPLIT UP ENOUGH.
PERHAPS A RAINY DAY IS YOUR BEST BET?
C-46
HANG ON. WHY THE HECK SHOULD I?

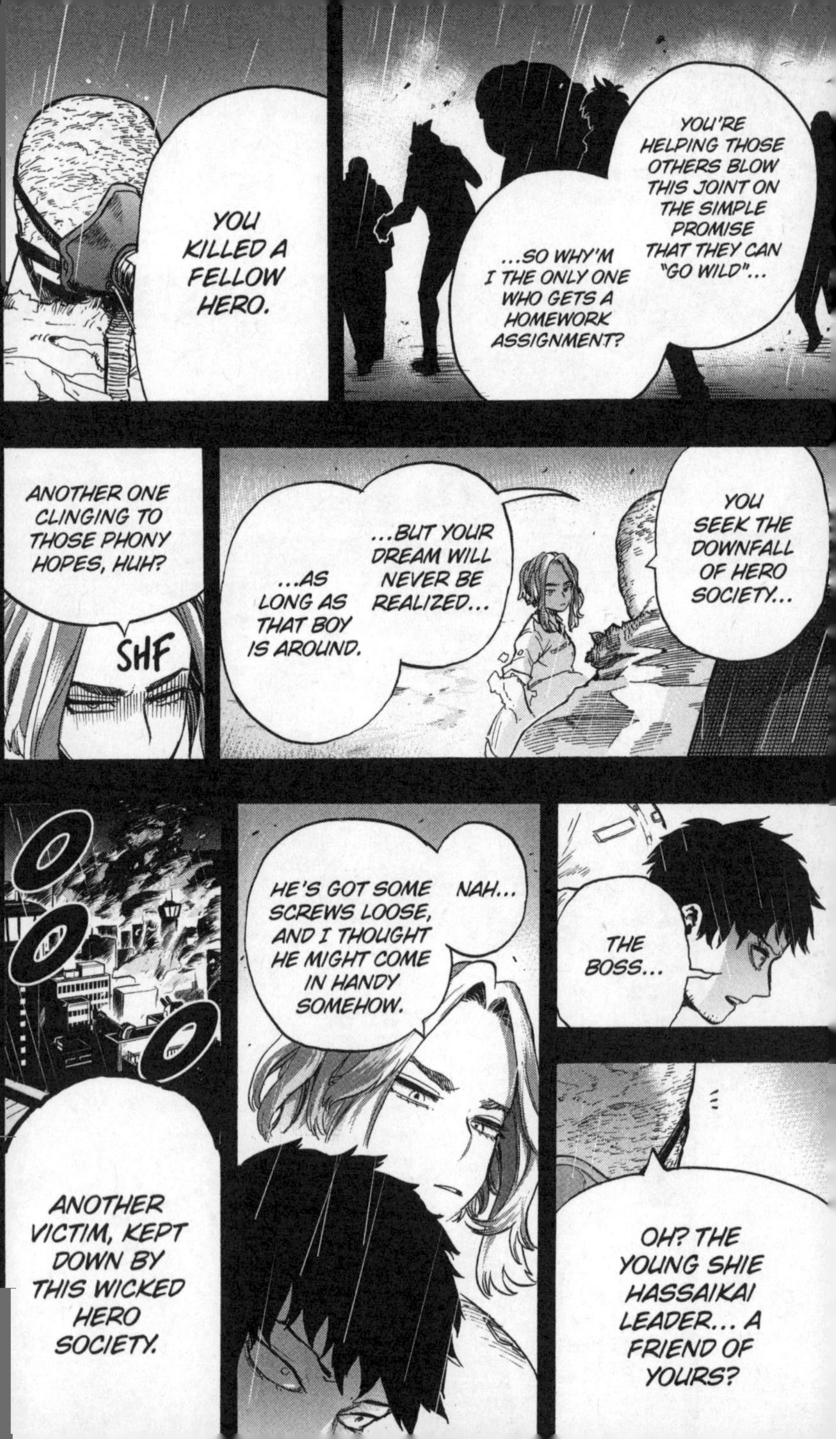
YOU'RE HELPING THOSE OTHERS BLOW THIS JOINT ON THE SIMPLE PROMISE THAT THEY CAN "GO WILD"...
...SO WHY'M I THE ONLY ONE WHO GETS A HOMEWORK ASSIGNMENT?
YOU KILLED A FELLOW HERO.
YOU SEEK THE DOWNFALL OF HERO SOCIETY...
...BUT YOUR DREAM WILL NEVER BE REALIZED...
...AS LONG AS THAT BOY IS AROUND.
ANOTHER ONE CLINGING TO THOSE PHONY HOPES, HUH?
SHF
THE BOSS...
OH? THE YOUNG SHIE HASSAIKAI LEADER... A FRIEND OF YOURS?
NAH...
HE'S GOT SOME SCREWS LOOSE, AND I THOUGHT HE MIGHT COME IN HANDY SOMEHOW.
ANOTHER VICTIM, KEPT DOWN BY THIS WICKED HERO SOCIETY.

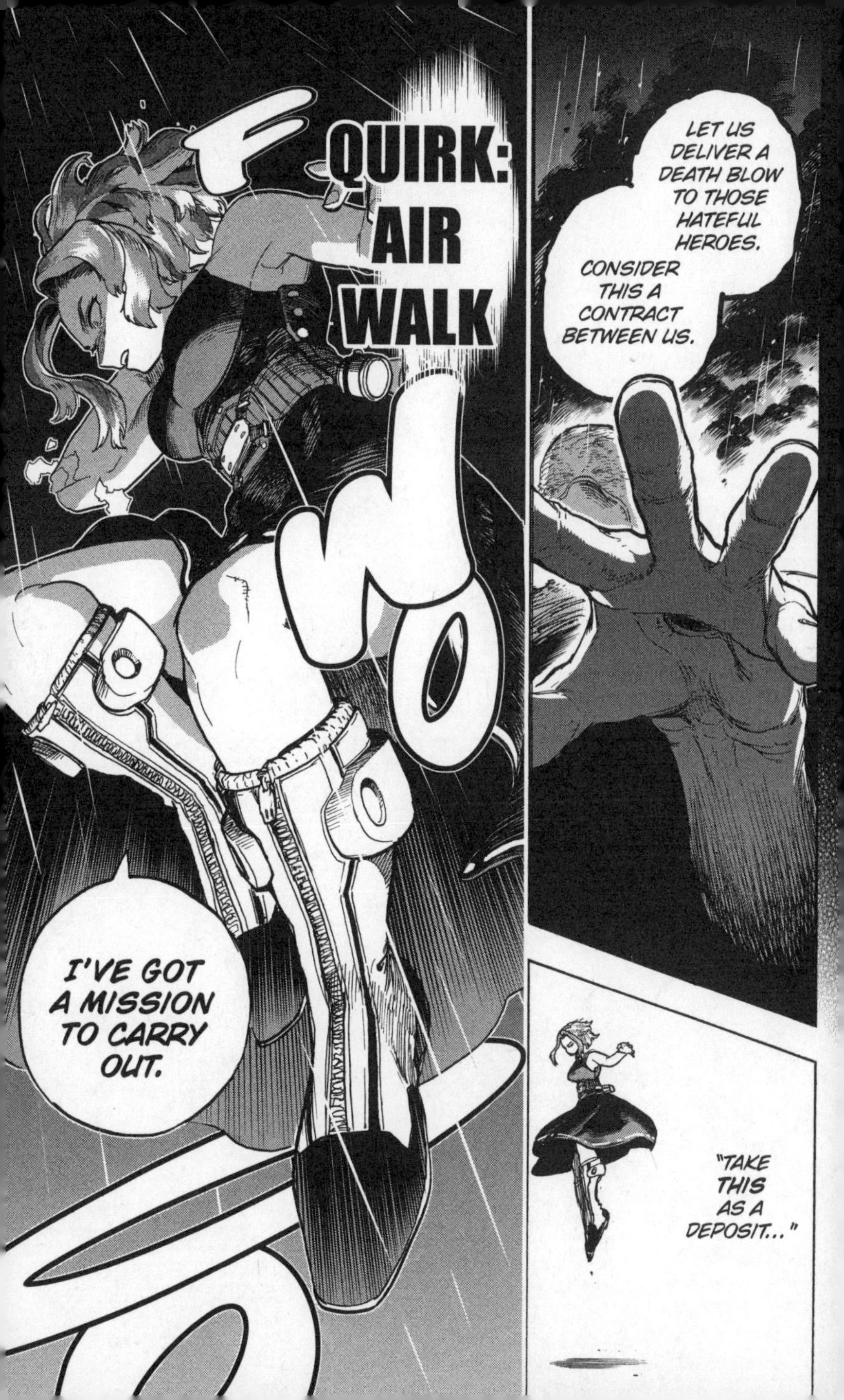
LET US DELIVER A DEATH BLOW TO THOSE HATEFUL HEROES.
CONSIDER THIS A CONTRACT BETWEEN US.
"TAKE THIS AS A DEPOSIT..."
QUIRK: AIR WALK
FWOO
I'VE GOT A MISSION TO CARRY OUT.

KAINA TSUTSUMI (LATE THIRTIES... THAT'S ALL YOU GET)

Birthday: 10/10
Height: 171 cm
Favorite Things: Pretty stuff, cutesy stuff

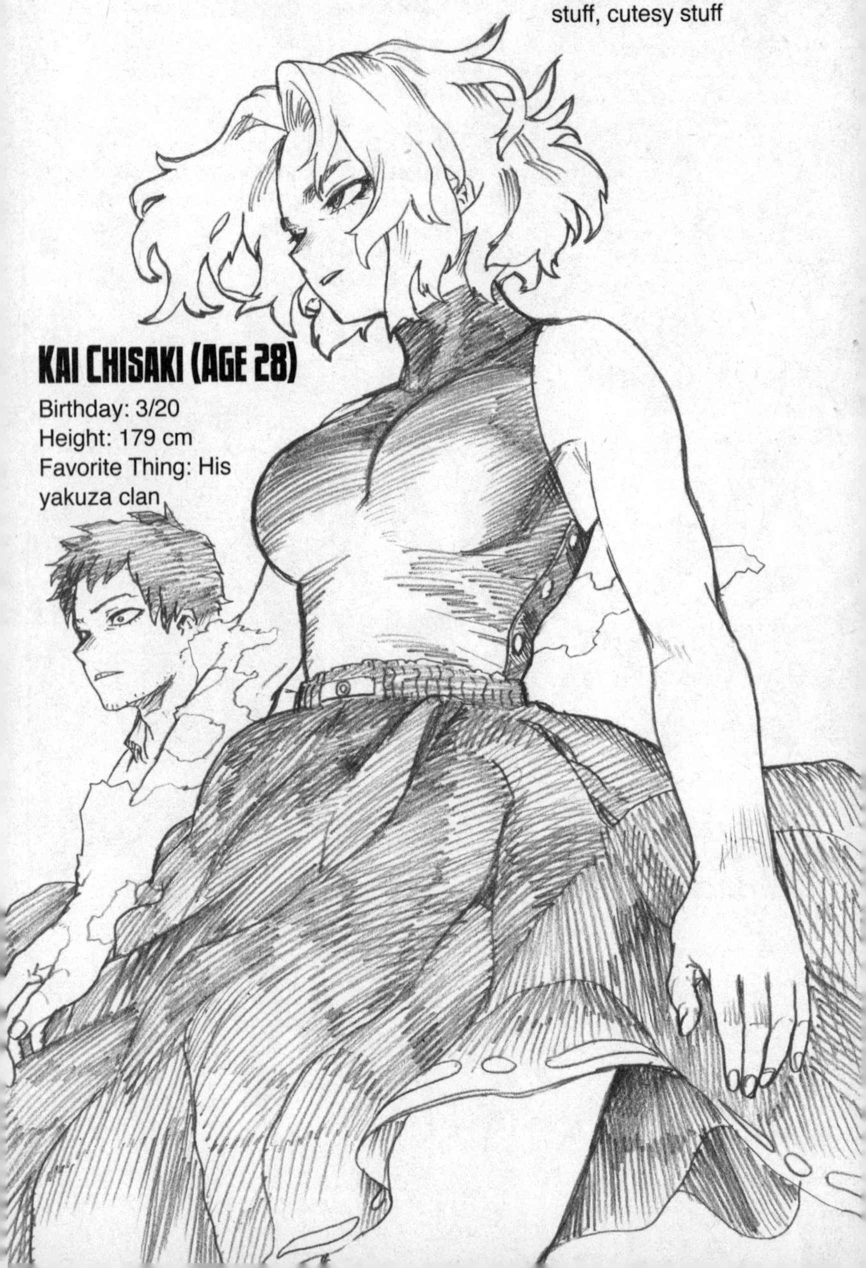

KAI CHISAKI (AGE 28)

Birthday: 3/20
Height: 179 cm
Favorite Thing: His yakuza clan

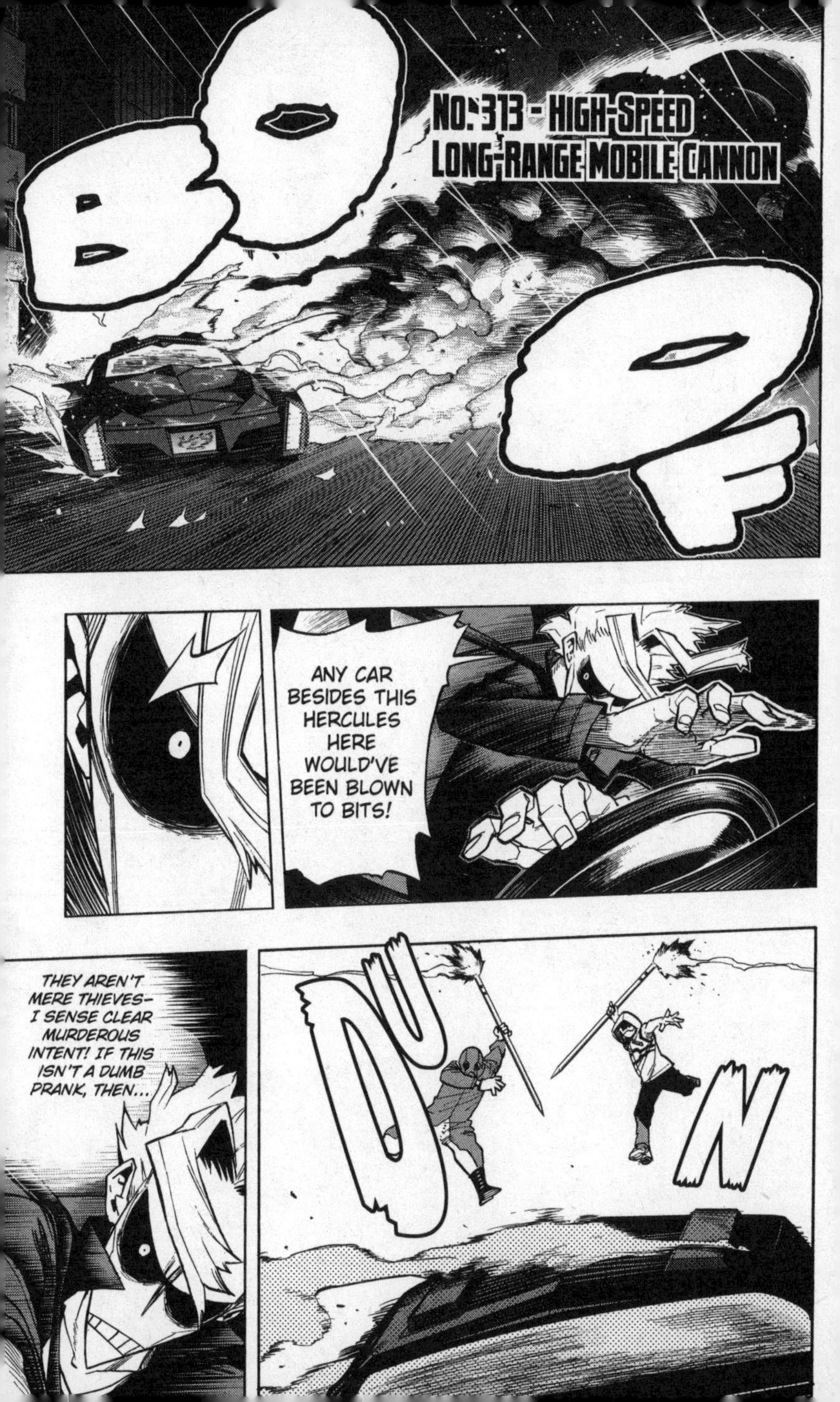
NO. 313 - HIGH-SPEED LONG-RANGE MOBILE CANNON
ANY CAR BESIDES THIS HERCULES HERE WOULD'VE BEEN BLOWN TO BITS!
THEY AREN'T MERE THIEVES- I SENSE CLEAR MURDEROUS INTENT! IF THIS ISN'T A DUMB PRANK, THEN...

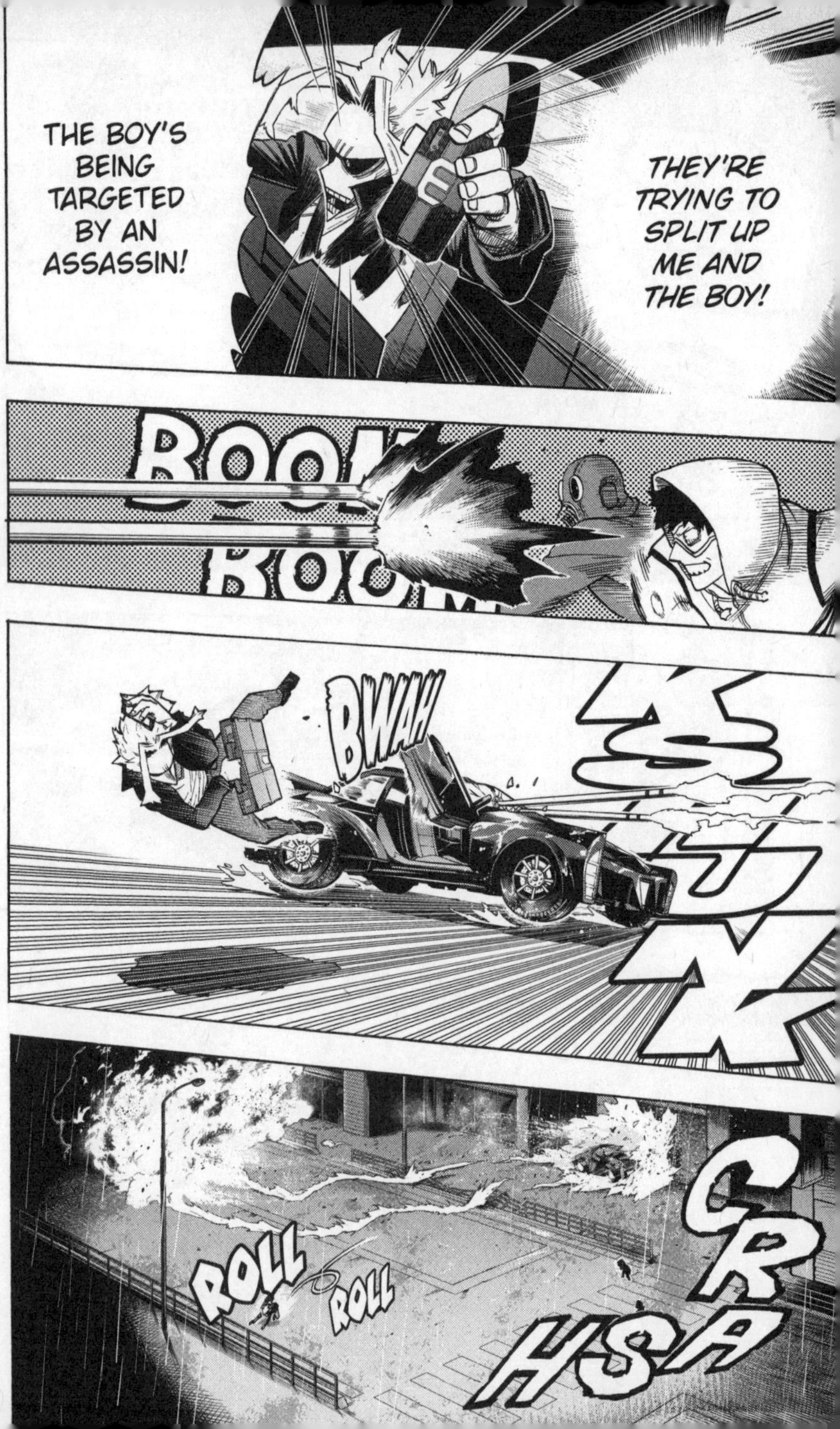
THEY'RE TRYING TO SPLIT UP ME AND THE BOY!
THE BOY'S BEING TARGETED BY AN ASSASSIN!
BOOM
BOOM
KSHUNK
BWAH
CRASH
ROLL
ROLL

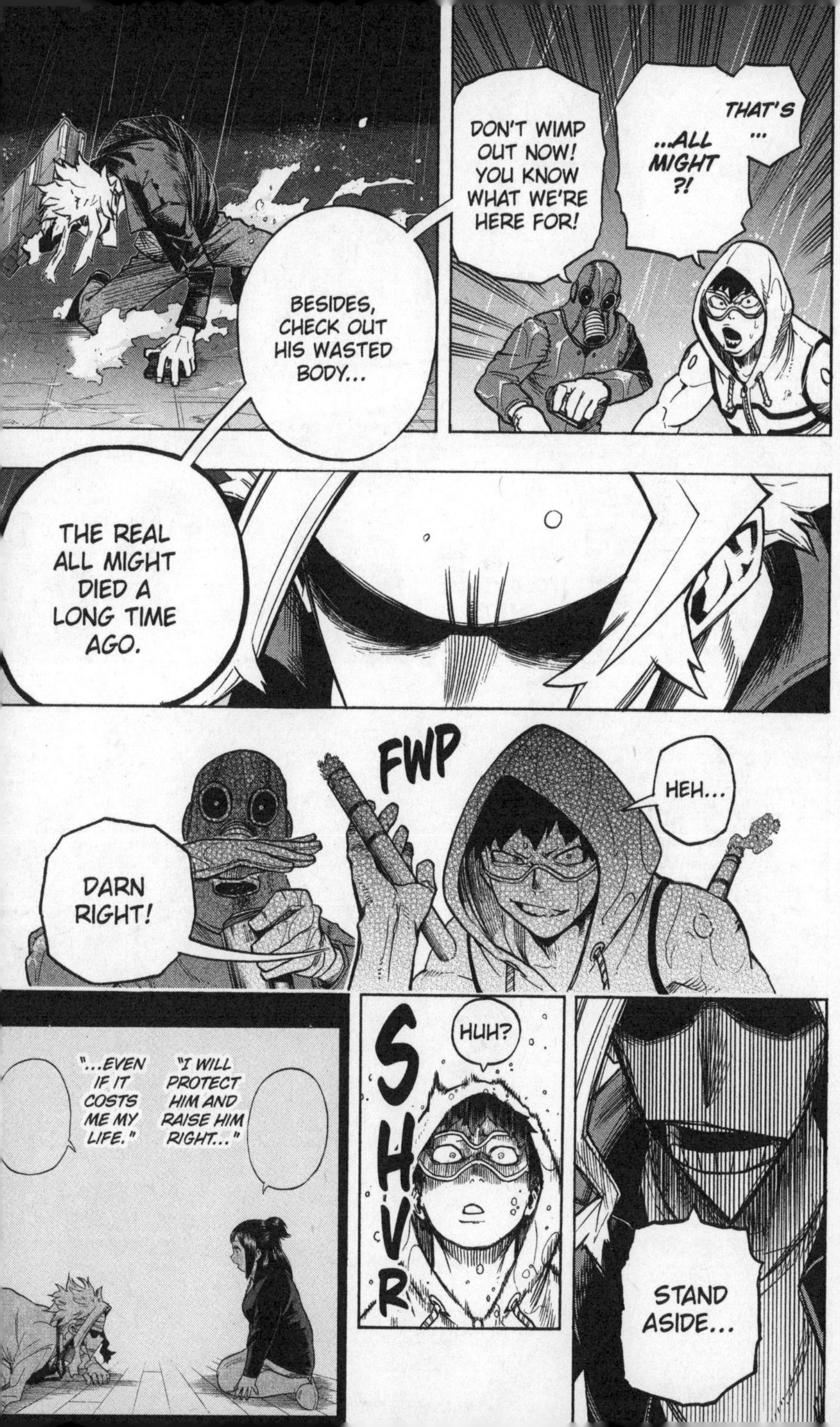
THAT'S ... ...ALL MIGHT ?!
DON'T WIMP OUT NOW! YOU KNOW WHAT WE'RE HERE FOR!
BESIDES, CHECK OUT HIS WASTED BODY...
THE REAL ALL MIGHT DIED A LONG TIME AGO.
HEH...
FWP
DARN RIGHT!
STAND ASIDE...
HUH?
SHVR
"I WILL PROTECT HIM AND RAISE HIM RIGHT..."
"...EVEN IF IT COSTS ME MY LIFE."

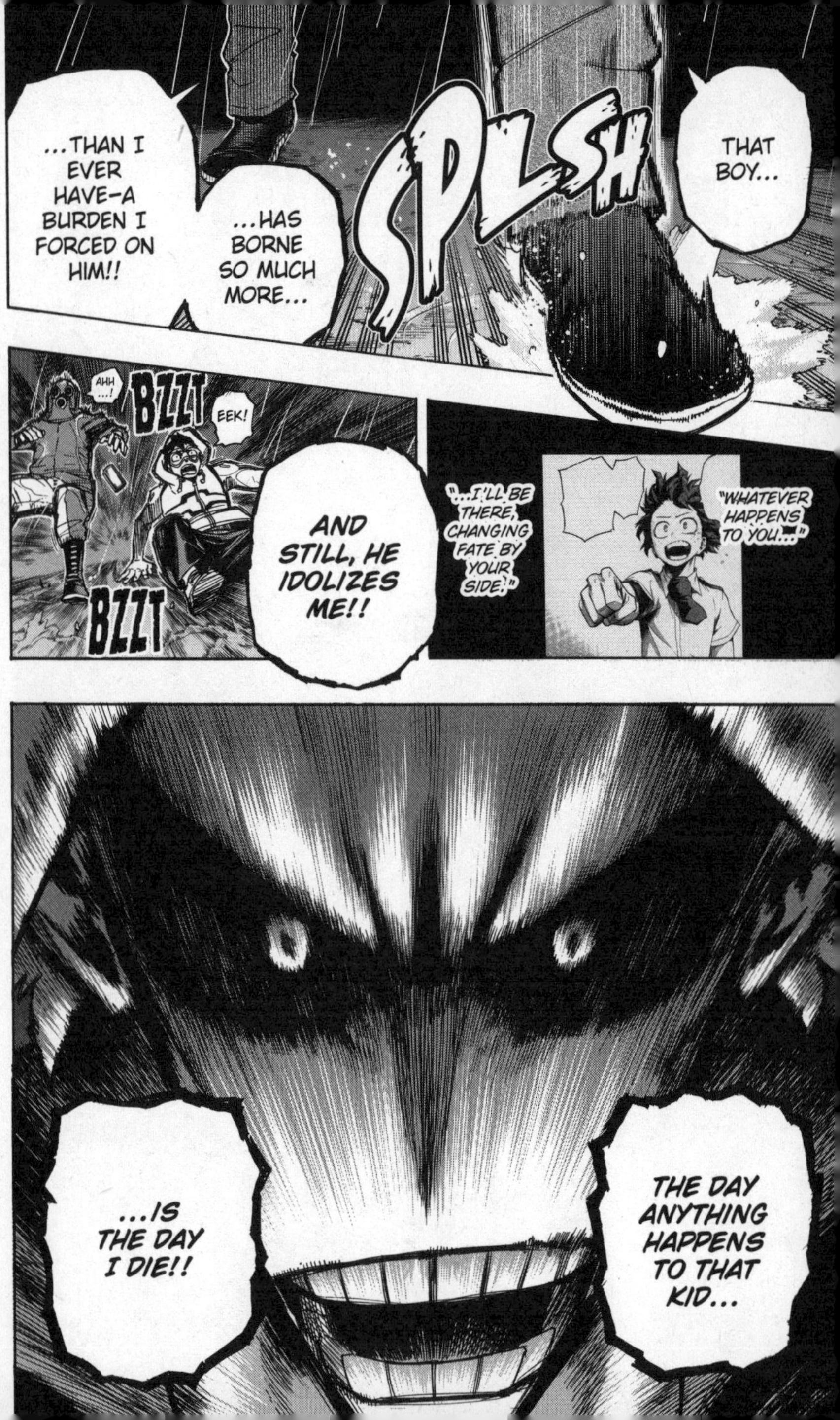
THAT BOY...
SPLSH
...HAS BORNE SO MUCH MORE...
...THAN I EVER HAVE—A BURDEN I FORCED ON HIM!!
"WHATEVER HAPPENS TO YOU..."
"...I'LL BE THERE, CHANGING FATE BY YOUR SIDE."
AND STILL, HE IDOLIZES ME!!
EEK!
BZZT
AHH ...!
BZZT
THE DAY ANYTHING HAPPENS TO THAT KID...
...IS THE DAY I DIE!!

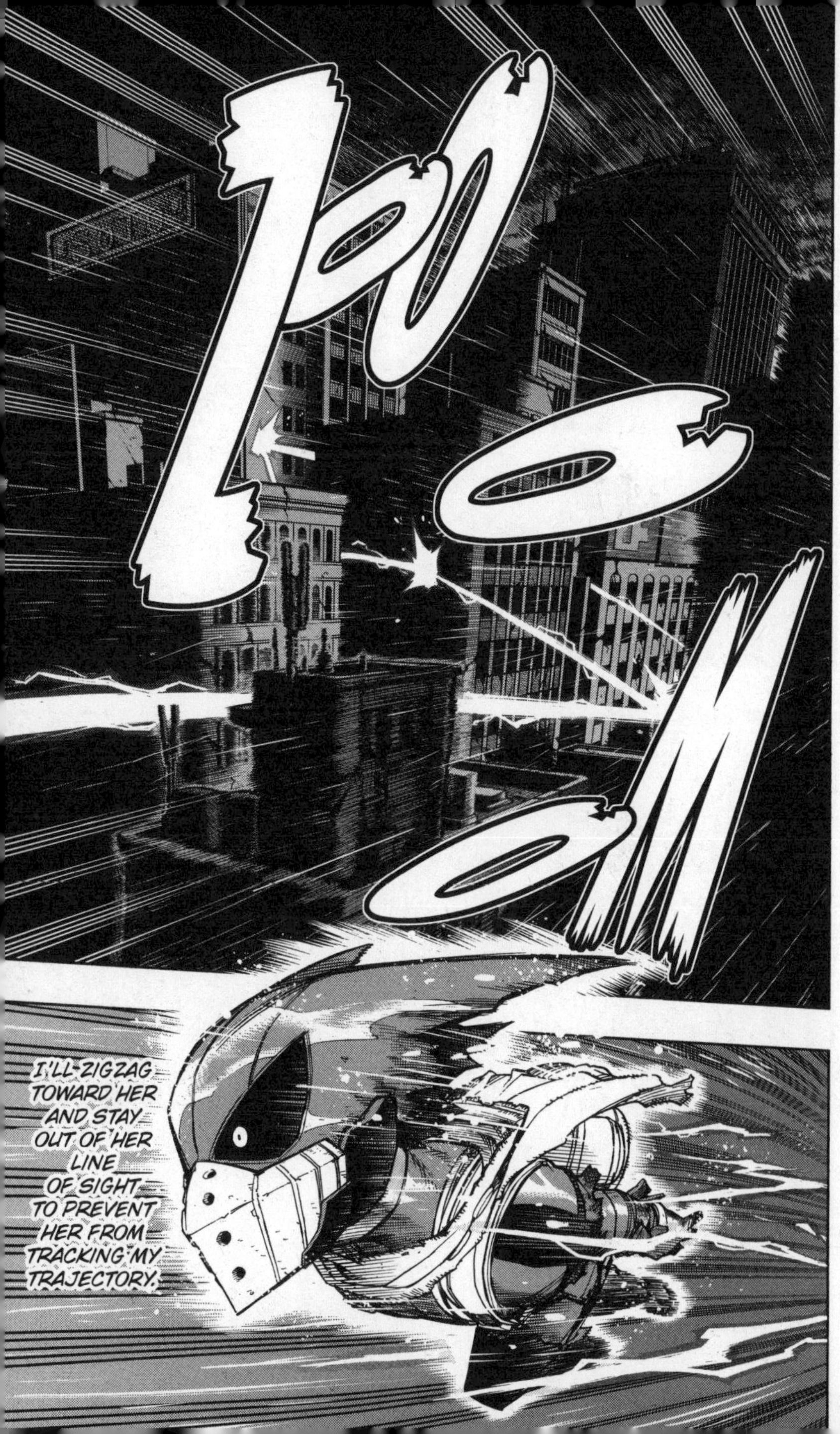
I'LL ZIGZAG TOWARD HER AND STAY OUT OF HER LINE OF SIGHT TO PREVENT HER FROM TRACKING MY TRAJECTORY.

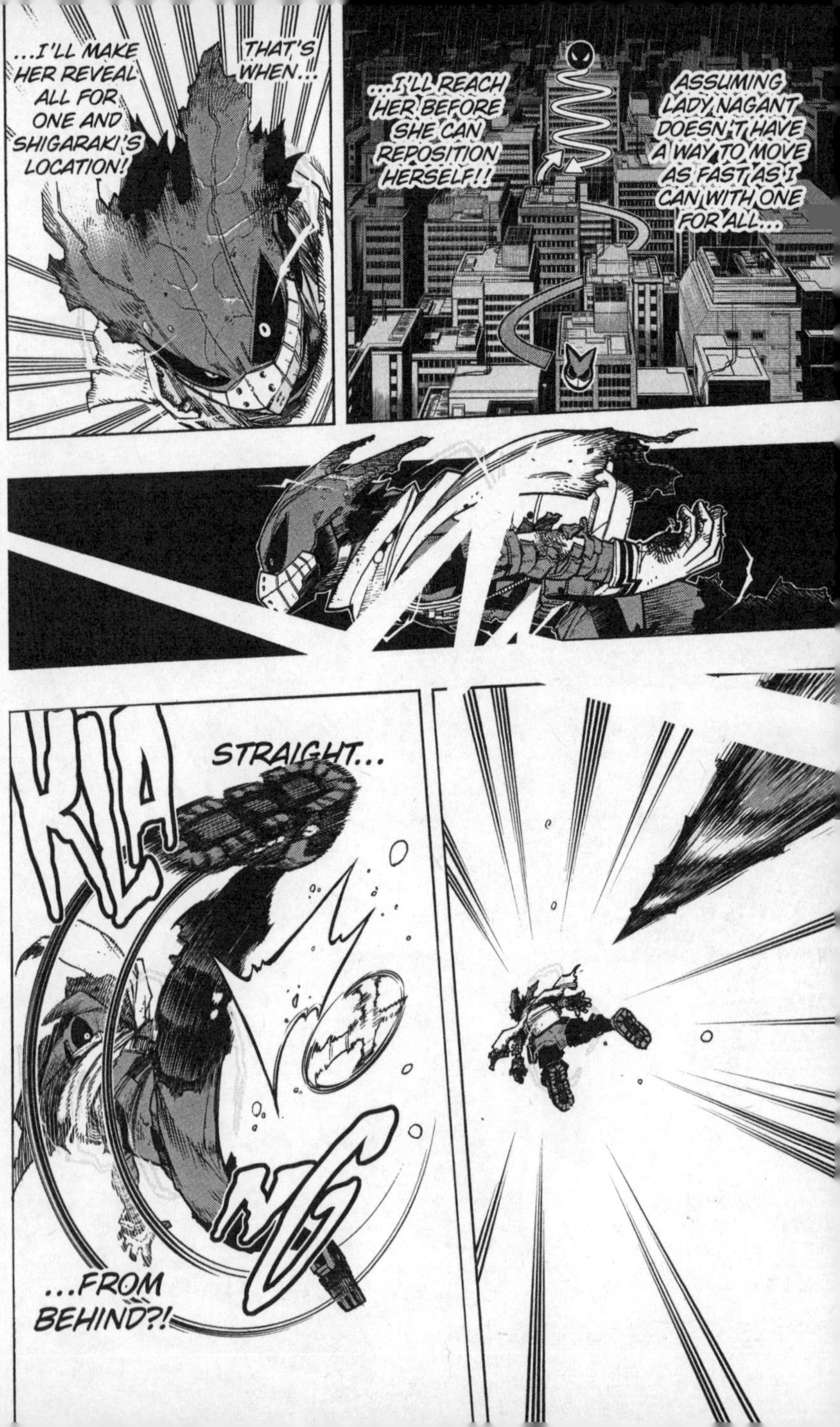
ASSUMING LADY NAGANT DOESN'T HAVE A WAY TO MOVE AS FAST AS I CAN WITH ONE FOR ALL...
...I'LL REACH HER BEFORE SHE CAN REPOSITION HERSELF!!
THAT'S WHEN...
...I'LL MAKE HER REVEAL ALL FOR ONE AND SHIGARAKI'S LOCATION!
STRAIGHT...
KA
NG
...FROM BEHIND?!

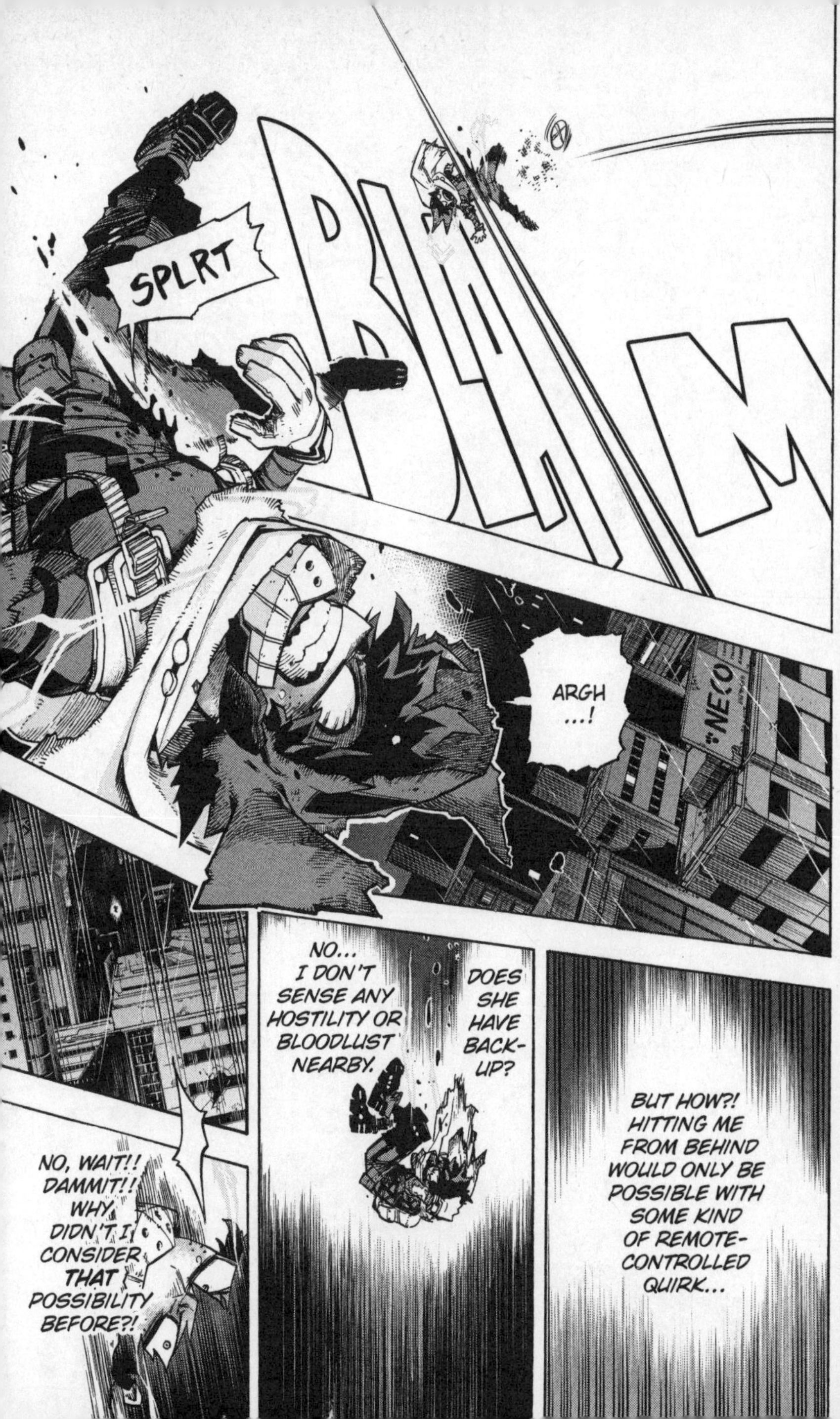
BLAM
SPLRT
ARGH ...!
BUT HOW?! HITTING ME FROM BEHIND WOULD ONLY BE POSSIBLE WITH SOME KIND OF REMOTE-CONTROLLED QUIRK...
DOES SHE HAVE BACK-UP?
NO... I DON'T SENSE ANY HOSTILITY OR BLOODLUST NEARBY.
NO, WAIT!! DAMMIT!! WHY DIDN'T I CONSIDER THAT POSSIBILITY BEFORE?!

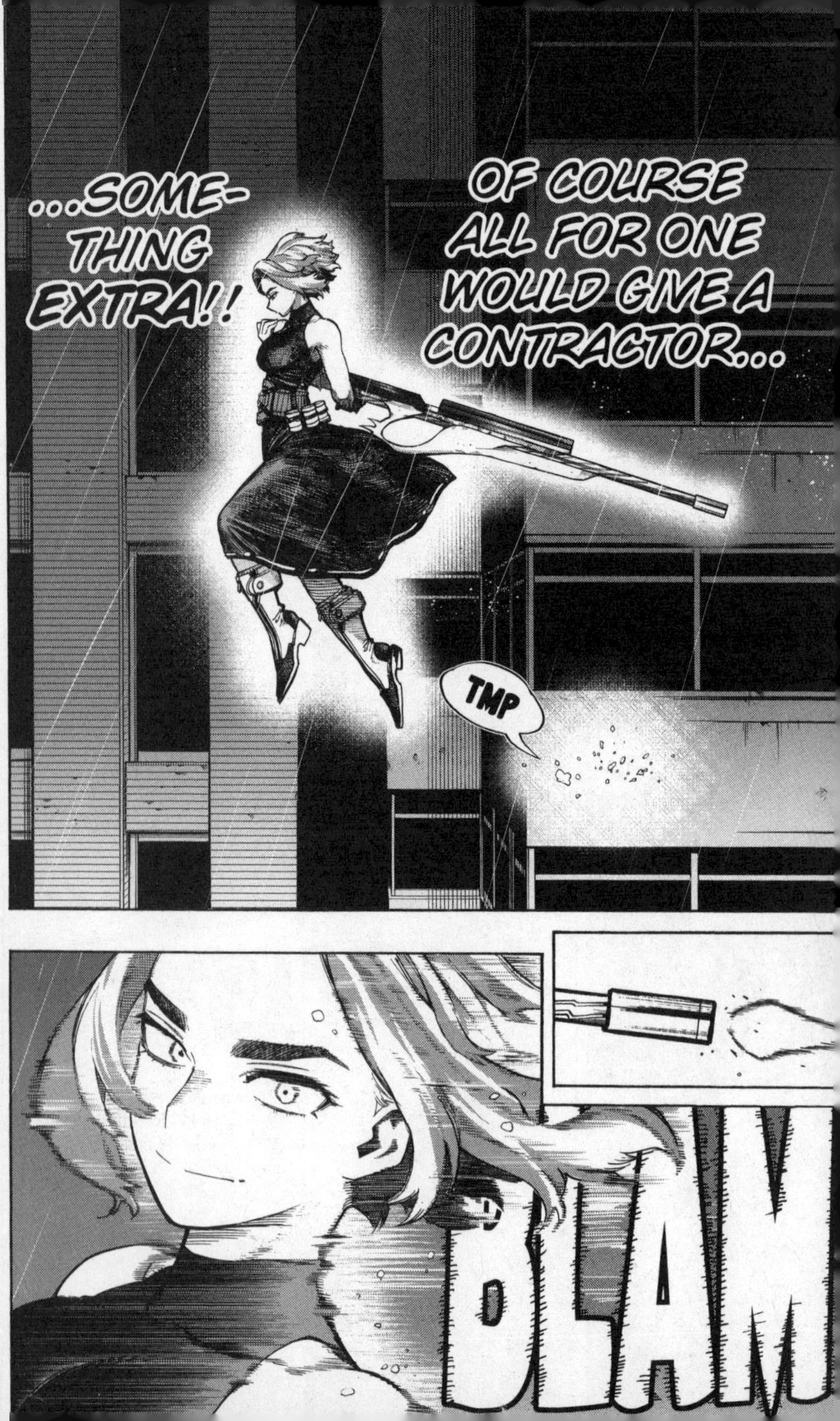
OF COURSE ALL FOR ONE WOULD GIVE A CONTRACTOR...
...SOME-THING EXTRA!!
TMP
BLAM

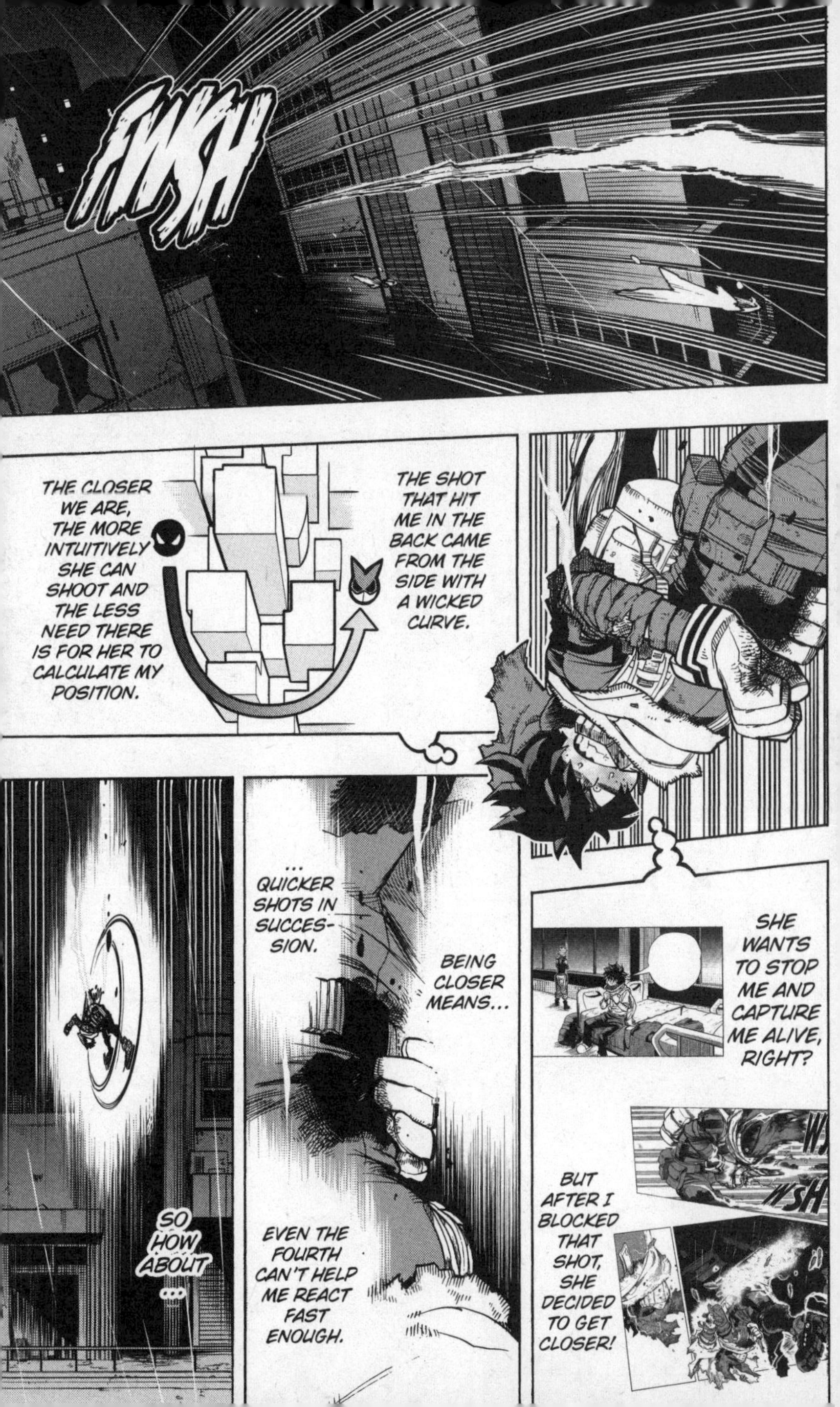
FWSH
THE SHOT THAT HIT ME IN THE BACK CAME FROM THE SIDE WITH A WICKED CURVE.
THE CLOSER WE ARE, THE MORE INTUITIVELY SHE CAN SHOOT AND THE LESS NEED THERE IS FOR HER TO CALCULATE MY POSITION.
SHE WANTS TO STOP ME AND CAPTURE ME ALIVE, RIGHT?
WSH
BUT AFTER I BLOCKED THAT SHOT, SHE DECIDED TO GET CLOSER!
BEING CLOSER MEANS...
...QUICKER SHOTS IN SUCCESSION.
EVEN THE FOURTH CAN'T HELP ME REACT FAST ENOUGH.
SO HOW ABOUT ...

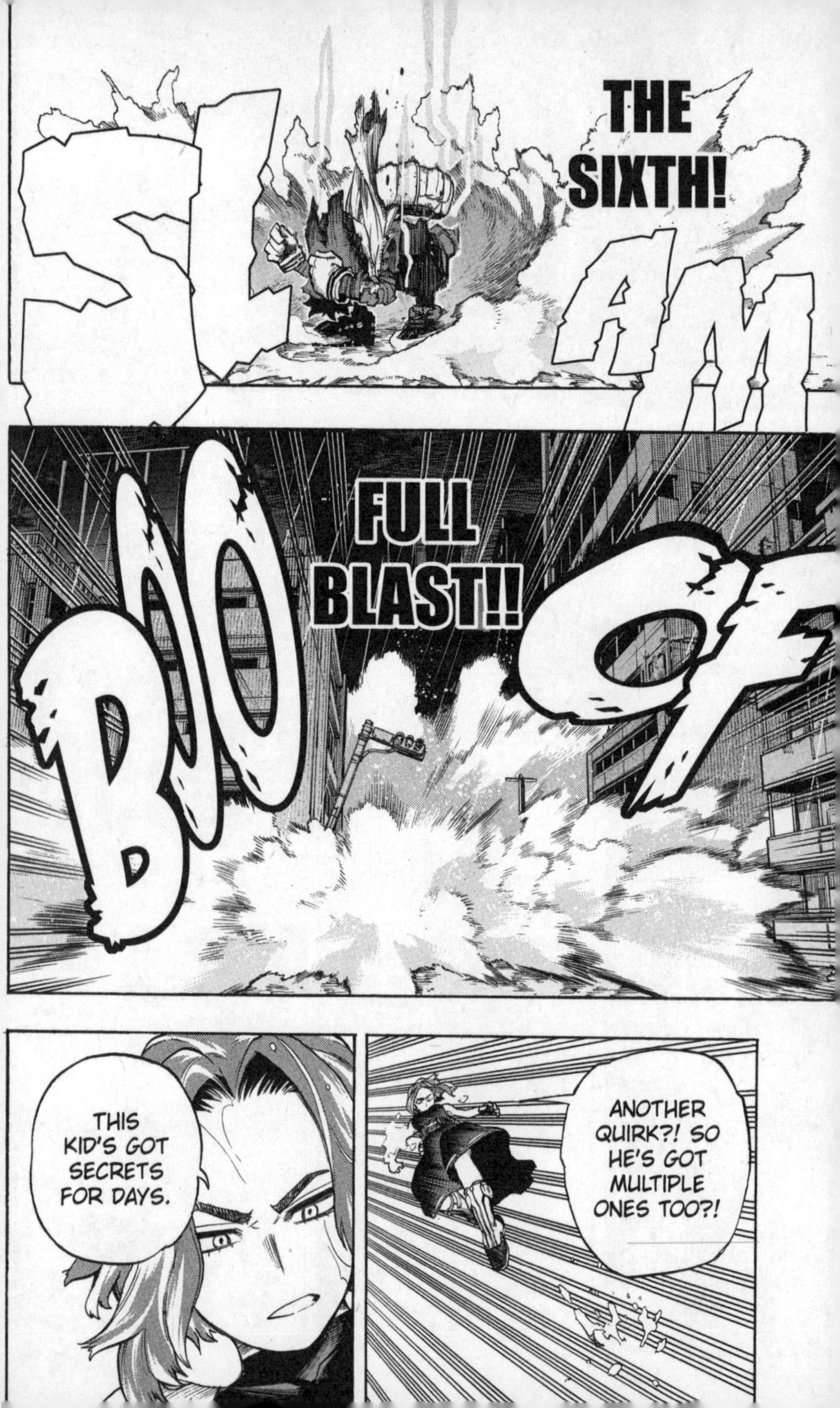
THE SIXTH!
SLAM
FULL BLAST!!
ANOTHER QUIRK?! SO HE'S GOT MULTIPLE ONES TOO?!
THIS KID'S GOT SECRETS FOR DAYS.

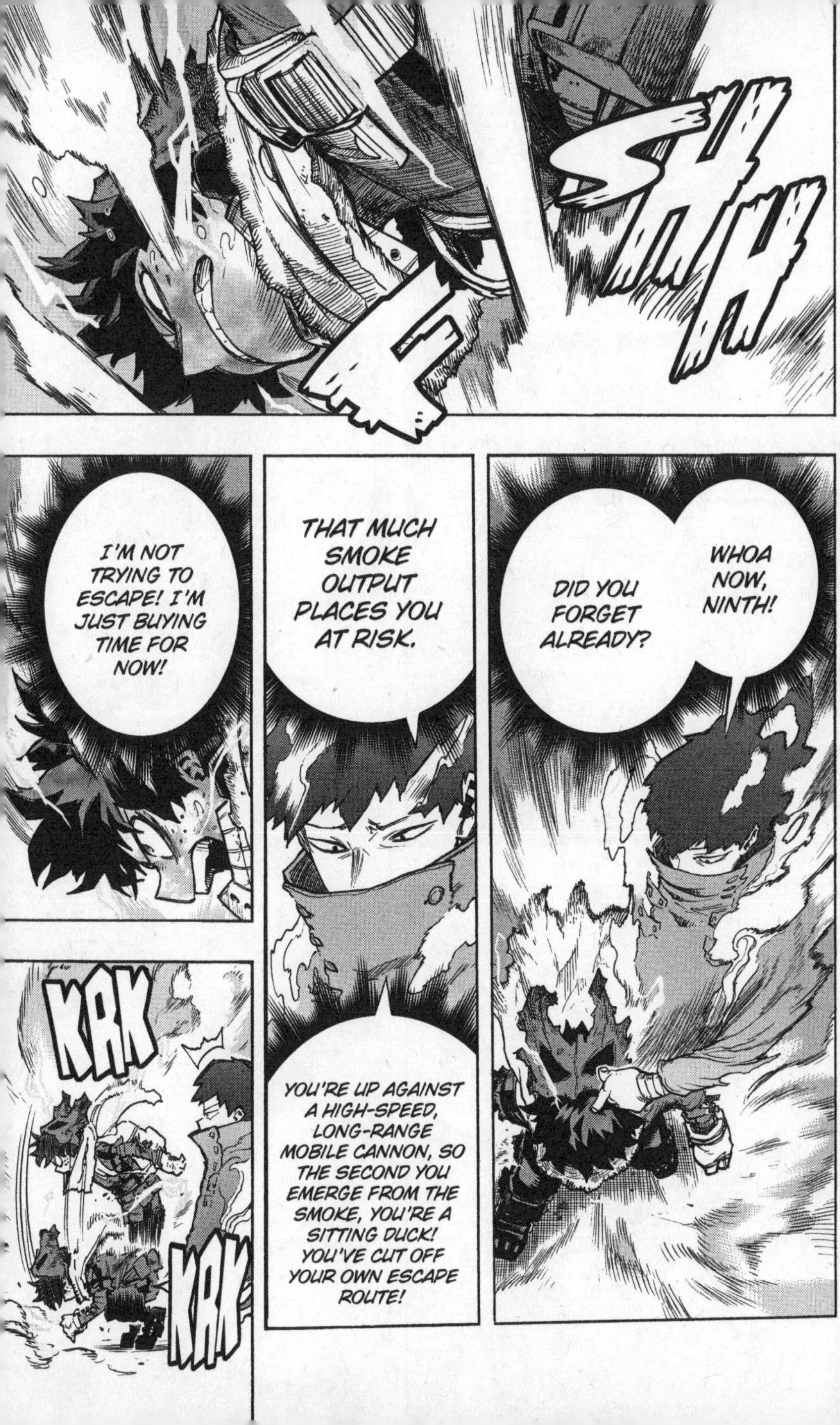
SHH
WHOA NOW, NINTH!
DID YOU FORGET ALREADY?
THAT MUCH SMOKE OUTPUT PLACES YOU AT RISK.
YOU'RE UP AGAINST A HIGH-SPEED, LONG-RANGE MOBILE CANNON, SO THE SECOND YOU EMERGE FROM THE SMOKE, YOU'RE A SITTING DUCK! YOU'VE CUT OFF YOUR OWN ESCAPE ROUTE!
I'M NOT TRYING TO ESCAPE! I'M JUST BUYING TIME FOR NOW!
KRK
KRK

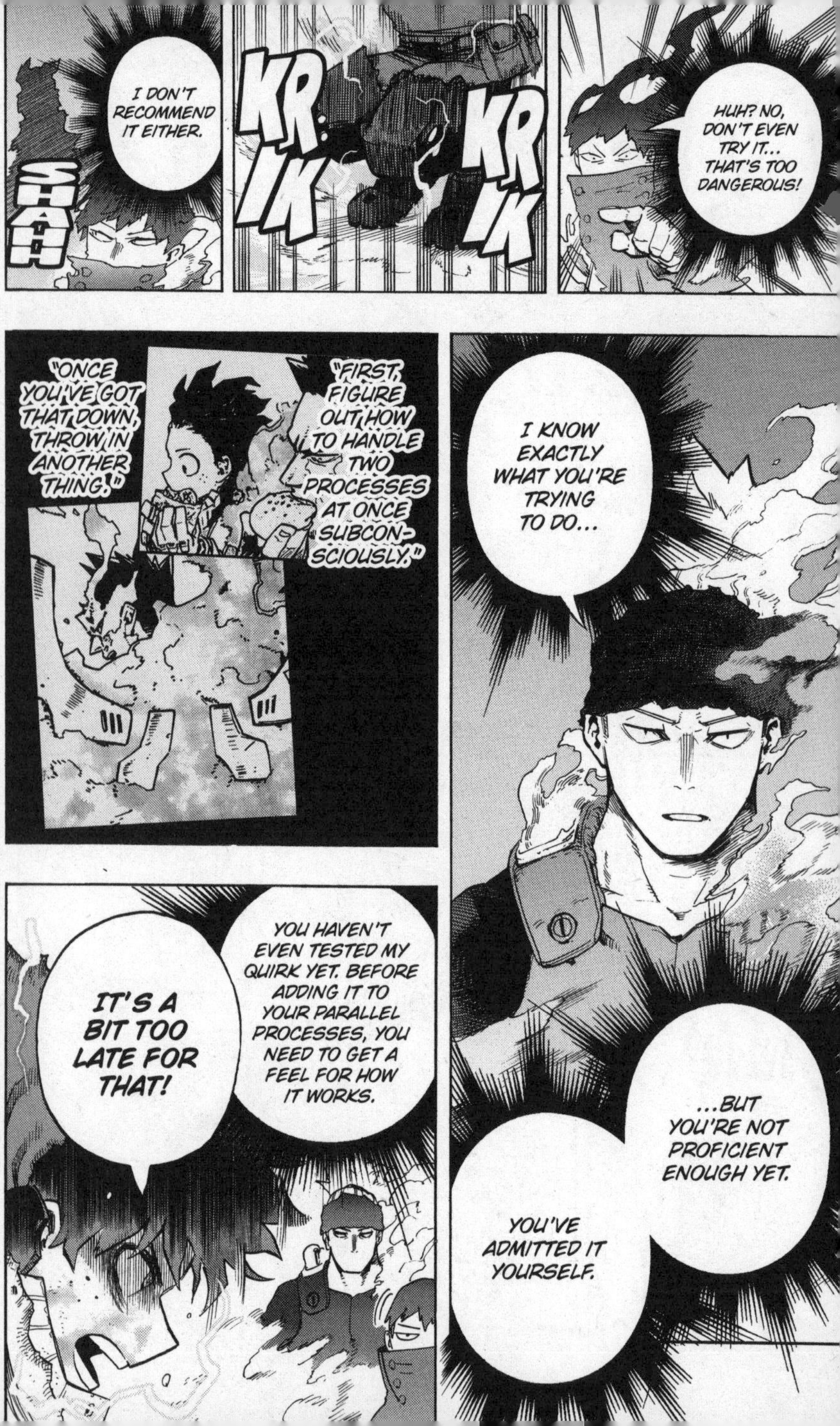
HUH? NO, DON'T EVEN TRY IT... THAT'S TOO DANGEROUS!
KR KR IK IK
I DON'T RECOMMEND IT EITHER.
SHAAH
I KNOW EXACTLY WHAT YOU'RE TRYING TO DO...
...BUT YOU'RE NOT PROFICIENT ENOUGH YET.
YOU'VE ADMITTED IT YOURSELF.
"FIRST, FIGURE OUT HOW TO HANDLE TWO PROCESSES AT ONCE SUBCONSCIOUSLY."
"ONCE YOU'VE GOT THAT DOWN, THROW IN ANOTHER THING."
YOU HAVEN'T EVEN TESTED MY QUIRK YET. BEFORE ADDING IT TO YOUR PARALLEL PROCESSES, YOU NEED TO GET A FEEL FOR HOW IT WORKS.
IT'S A BIT TOO LATE FOR THAT!

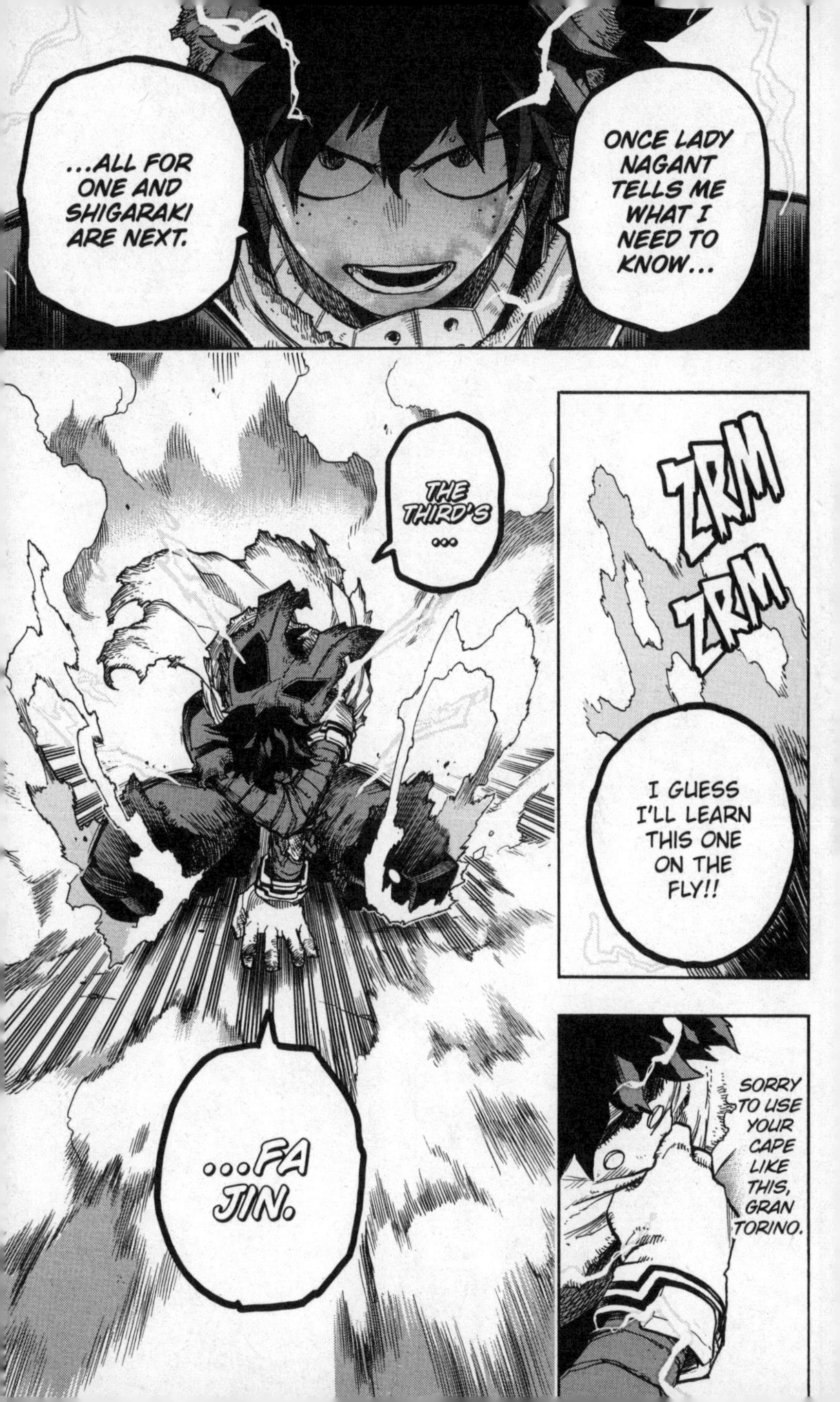
ONCE LADY NAGANT TELLS ME WHAT I NEED TO KNOW...
...ALL FOR ONE AND SHIGARAKI ARE NEXT.
ZRM
ZRM
I GUESS I'LL LEARN THIS ONE ON THE FLY!!
SORRY TO USE YOUR CAPE LIKE THIS, GRAN TORINO.
THE THIRD'S...
...FA JIN.

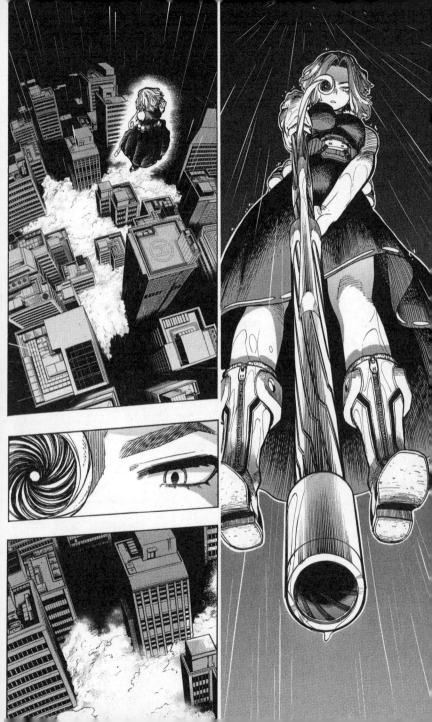

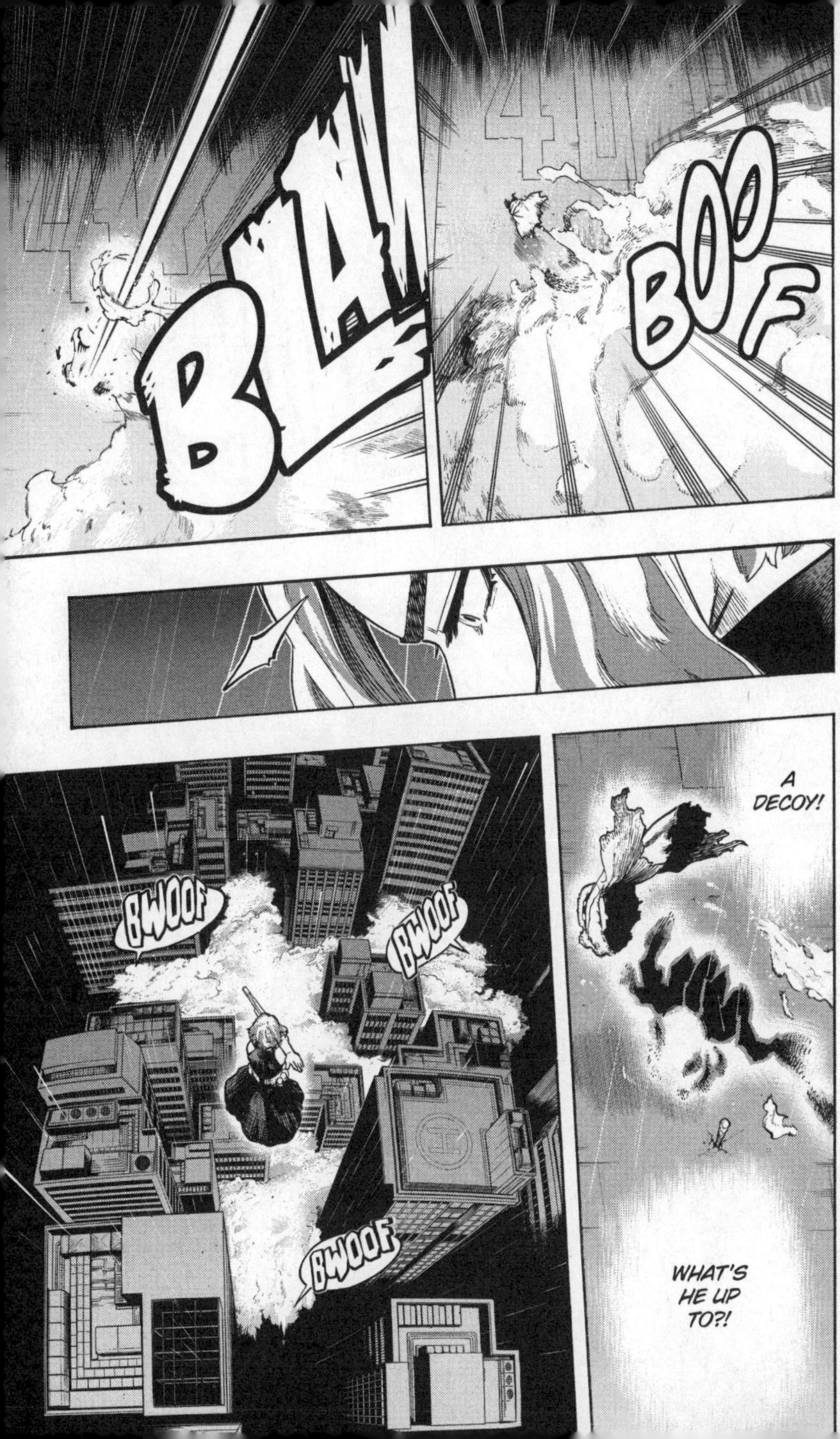
BOOF
BLA
A DECOY!
WHAT'S HE UP TO?!
BWOOF
BWOOF
BWOOF

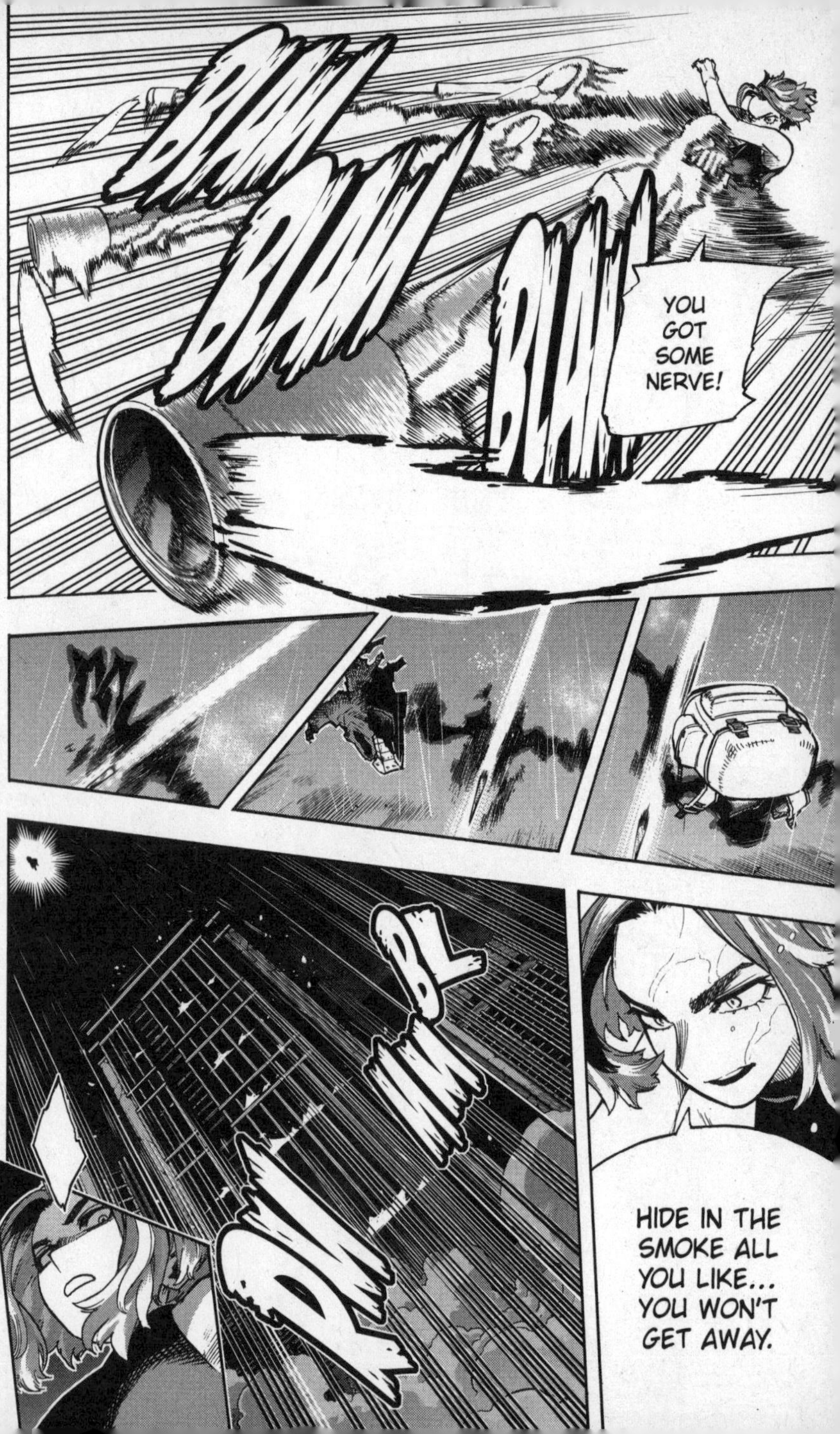
YOU GOT SOME NERVE!
HIDE IN THE SMOKE ALL YOU LIKE... YOU WON'T GET AWAY.

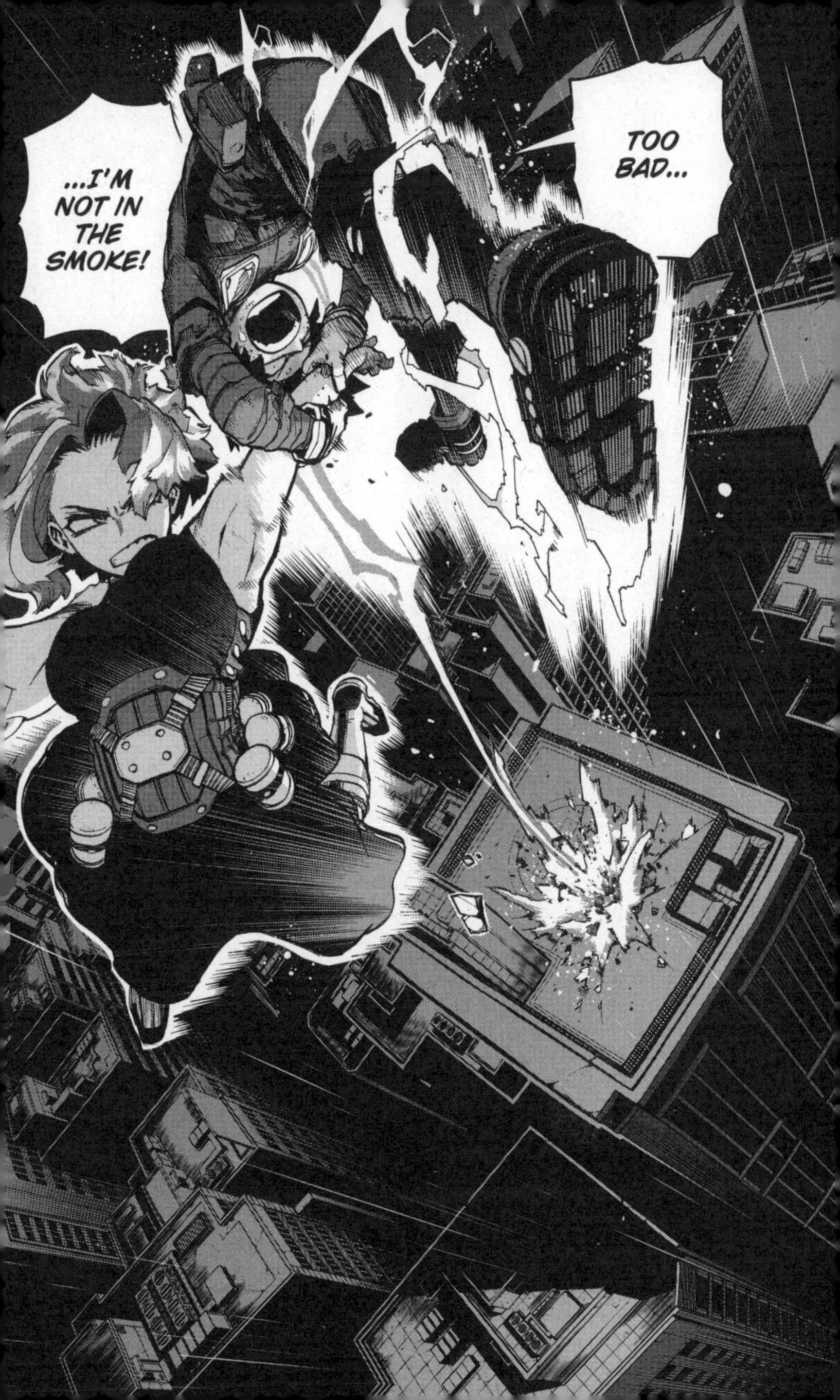
TOO BAD...
...I'M NOT IN THE SMOKE!

DEKU'S MOVEMENTS

① The closer he gets, the more Deku stands a chance! So he spread his smoke screen really wide to draw her in.

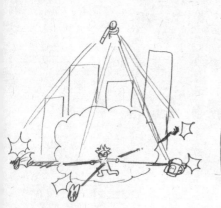

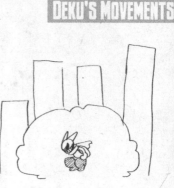

② He shot out decoys in every direction. Because Nagant shot every decoy basically simultaneously, Deku deduced that she was directly above the smoke screen.

Oops?

③ Without visual confirmation, he couldn't get a precise lock on her position! If he were to leap out too early, she could still hit him from a dead angle! Facing the wrong direction by even a little could mean game over! So…

Huh?
Hah!
Hnnngh!

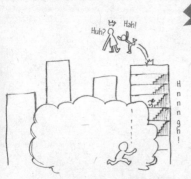

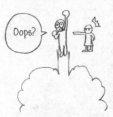

④ He entered a building at the edge of the smoke screen and dashed up the stairs! This way, he could get the drop on Nagant while ensuring that she couldn't catch him by surprise!

No. 314 - The Lovely Lady Nagant

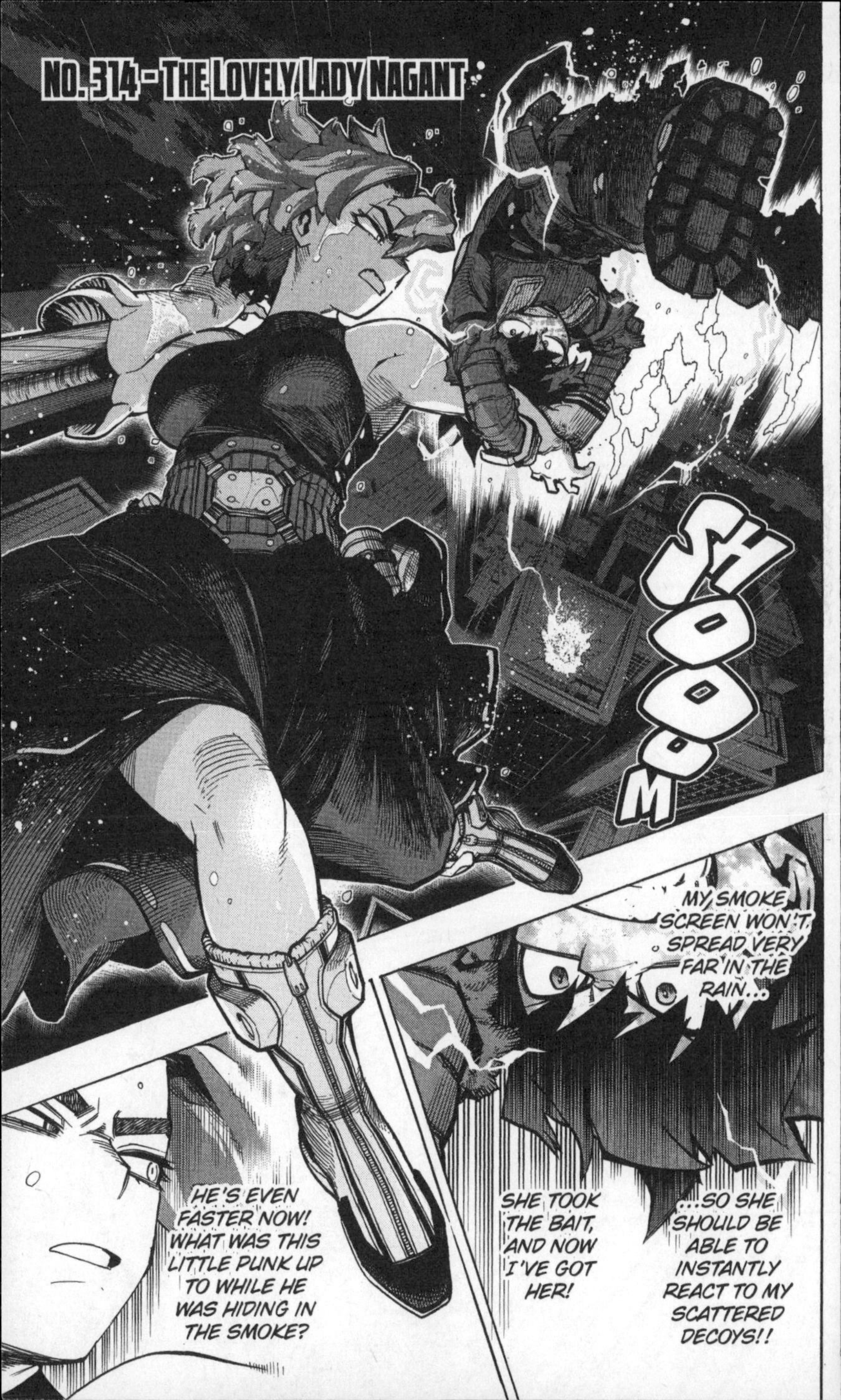
SHOOOOM
MY, SMOKE SCREEN WON'T SPREAD VERY FAR IN THE RAIN...
...SO SHE SHOULD BE ABLE TO INSTANTLY REACT TO MY SCATTERED DECOYS!!
SHE TOOK THE BAIT, AND NOW I'VE GOT HER!
HE'S EVEN FASTER NOW! WHAT WAS THIS LITTLE PUNK UP TO WHILE HE WAS HIDING IN THE SMOKE?

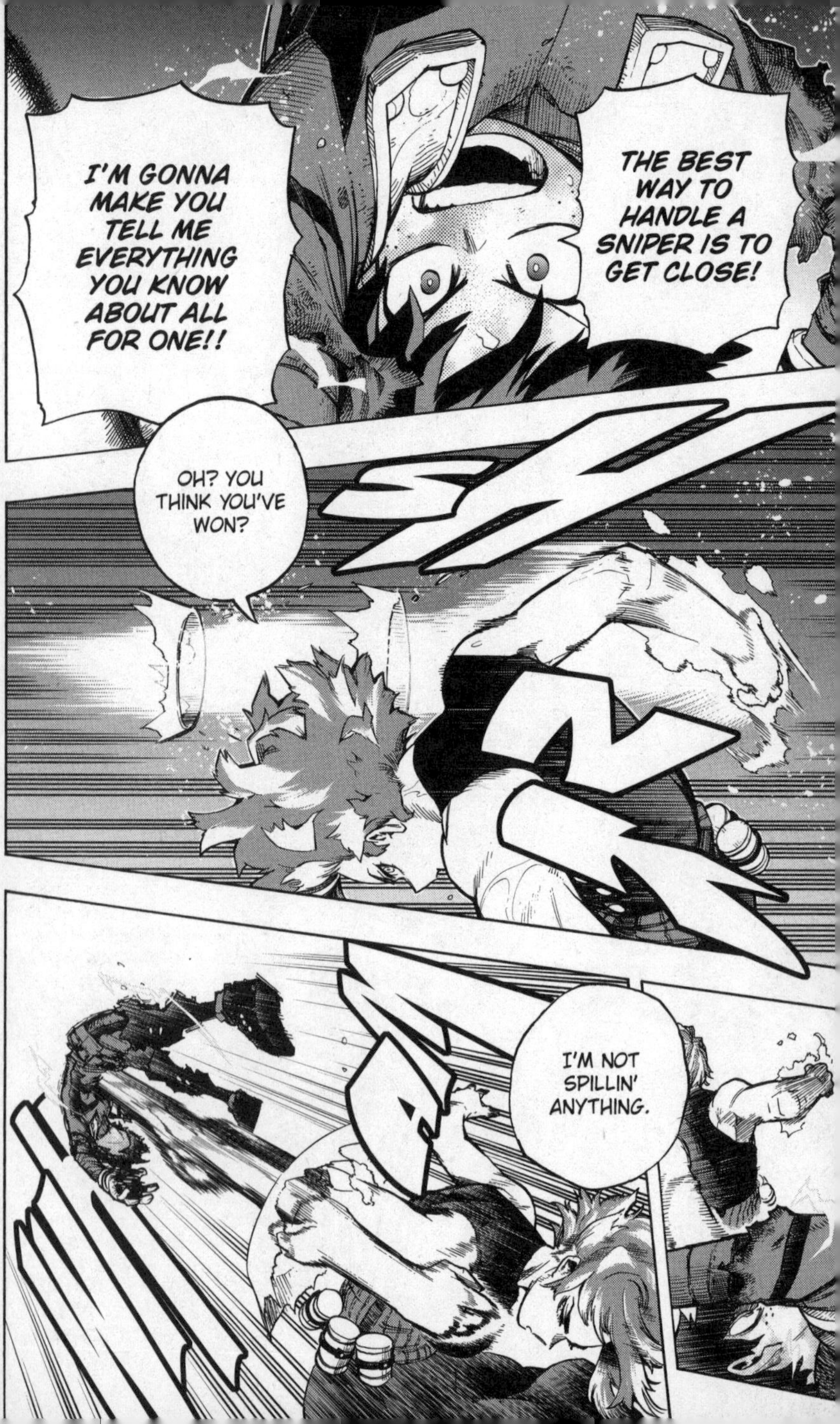
THE BEST WAY TO HANDLE A SNIPER IS TO GET CLOSE!
I'M GONNA MAKE YOU TELL ME EVERYTHING YOU KNOW ABOUT ALL FOR ONE!!
OH? YOU THINK YOU'VE WON?
I'M NOT SPILLIN' ANYTHING.

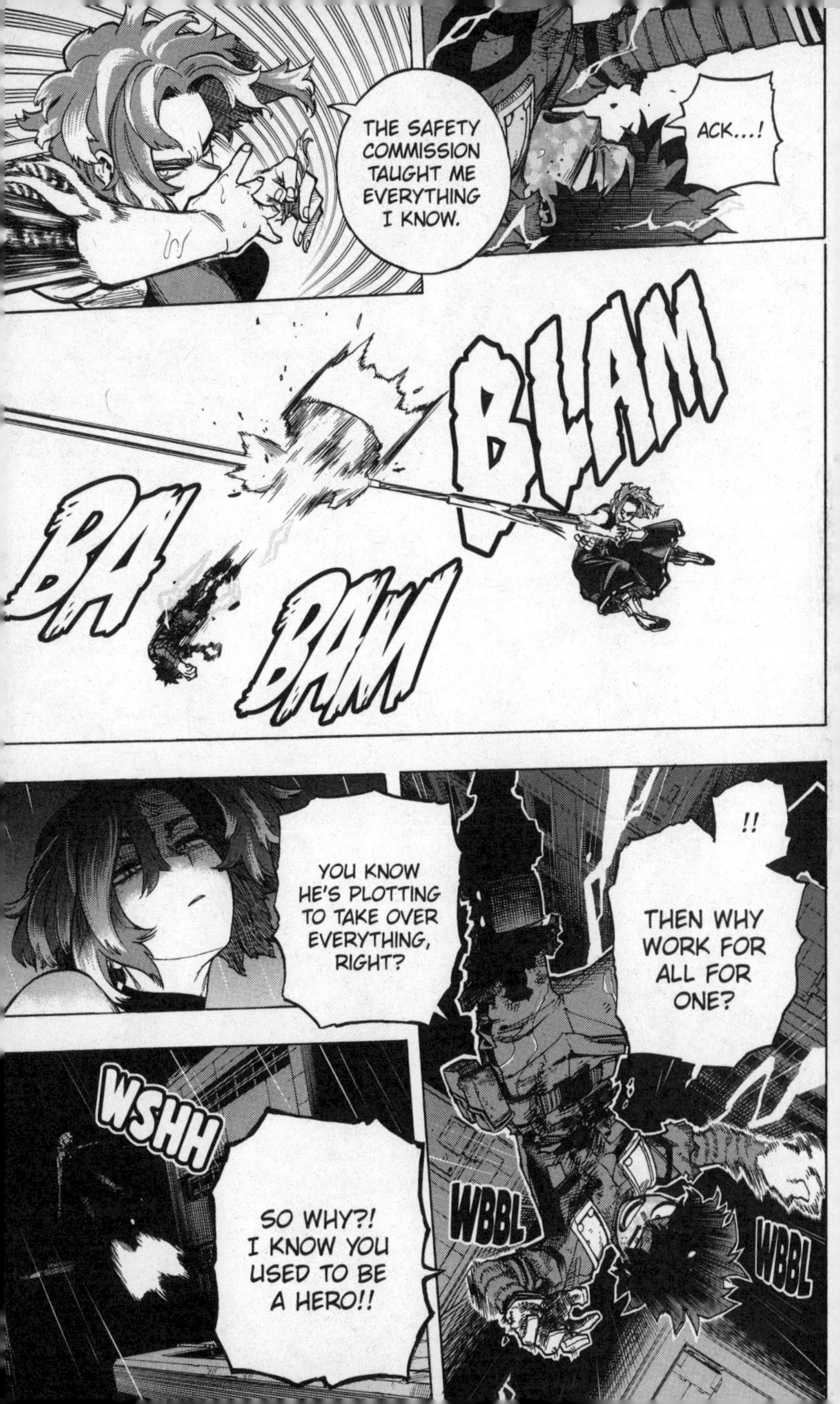
ACK...!
THE SAFETY COMMISSION TAUGHT ME EVERYTHING I KNOW.
BLAM
BA
BAM
!!
THEN WHY WORK FOR ALL FOR ONE?
WBBL
WBBL
YOU KNOW HE'S PLOTTING TO TAKE OVER EVERYTHING, RIGHT?
WSHH
SO WHY?! I KNOW YOU USED TO BE A HERO!!

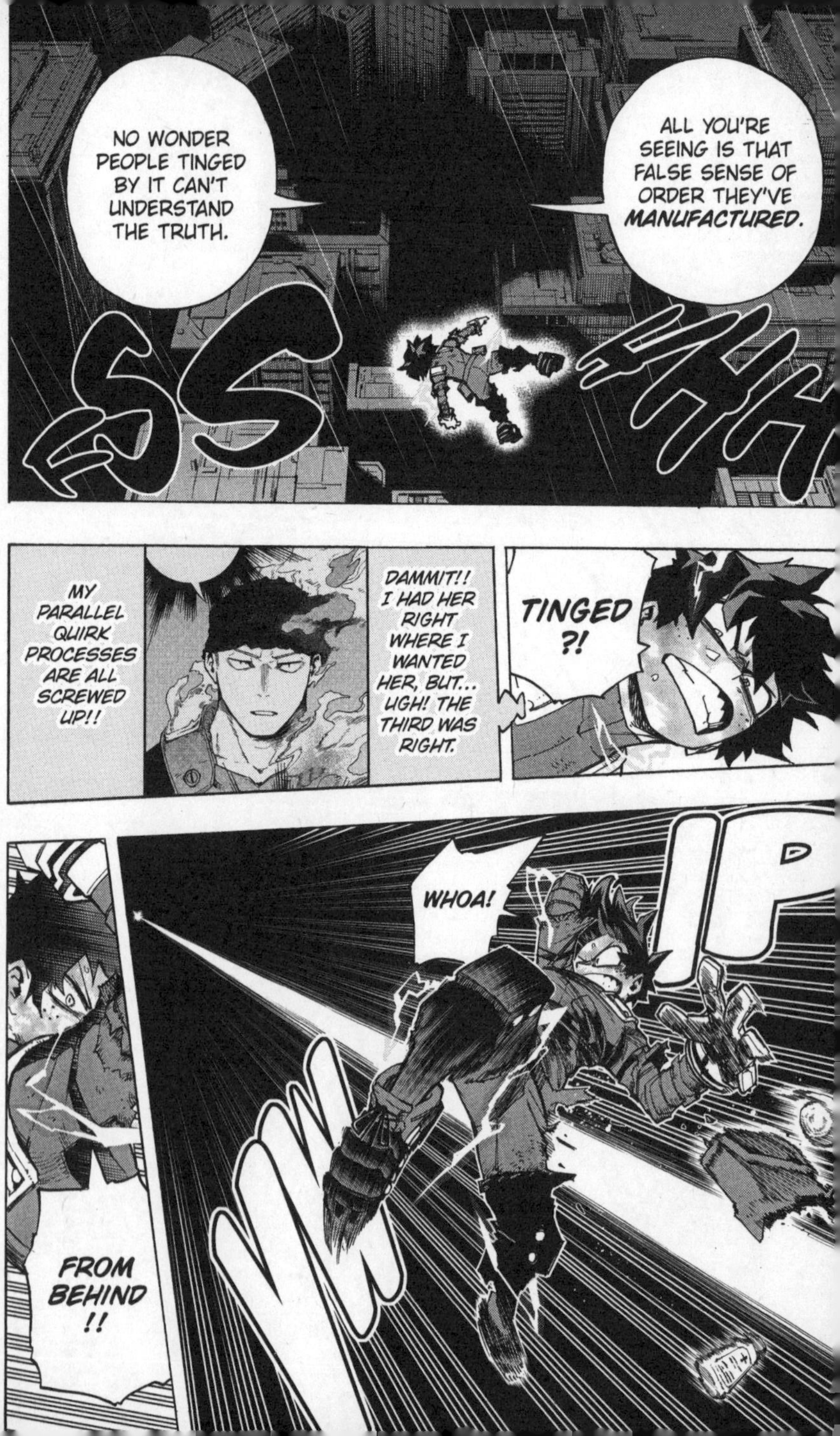
ALL YOU'RE SEEING IS THAT FALSE SENSE OF ORDER THEY'VE *MANUFACTURED*.
NO WONDER PEOPLE TINGED BY IT CAN'T UNDERSTAND THE TRUTH.
FSSHHH
TINGED ?!
DAMMIT!! I HAD HER RIGHT WHERE I WANTED HER, BUT... UGH! THE THIRD WAS RIGHT.
MY PARALLEL QUIRK PROCESSES ARE ALL SCREWED UP!!
WHOA!
FROM BEHIND !!

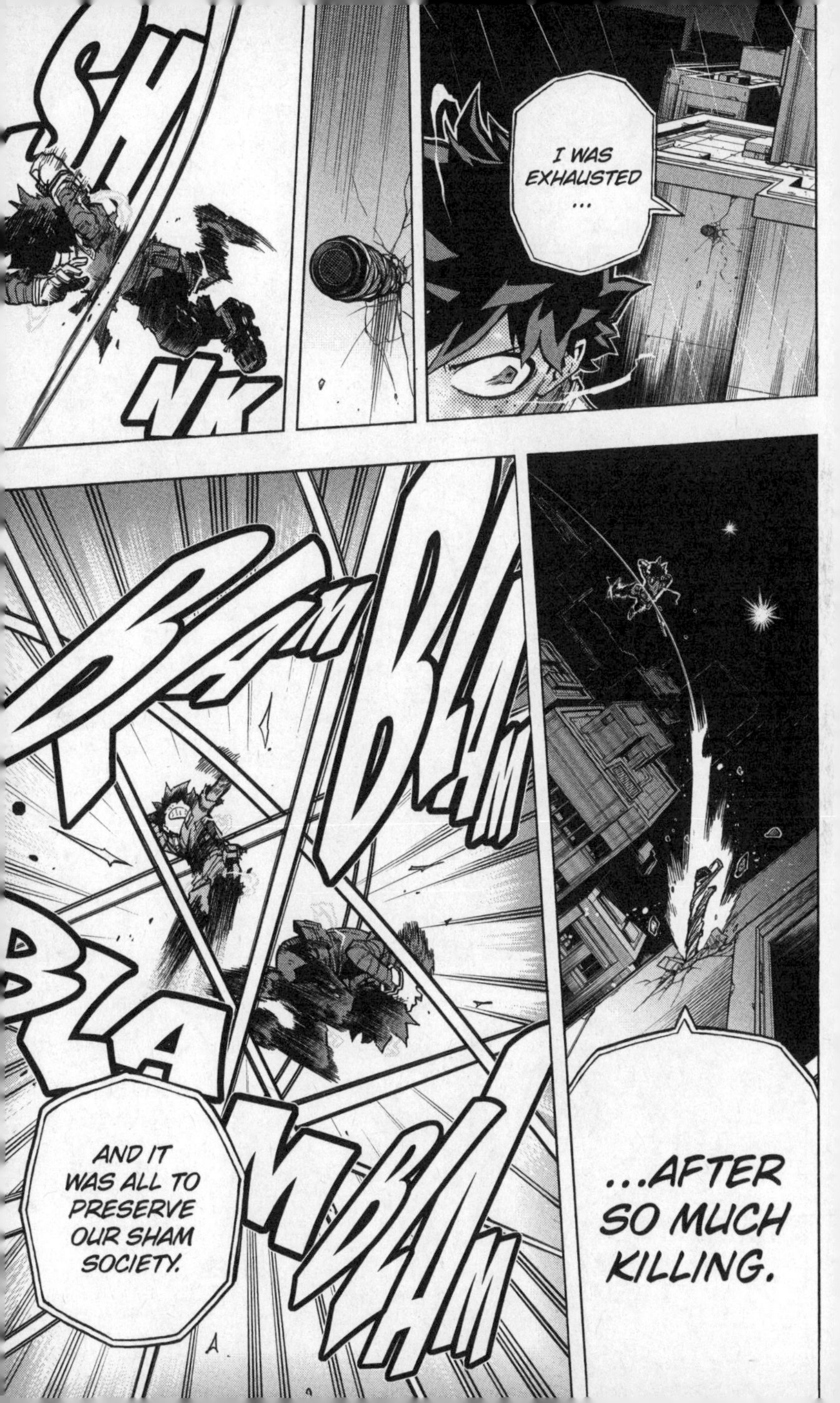
I WAS EXHAUSTED...
SH
NK
...AFTER SO MUCH KILLING.
BAM
BAM
BLAM
AND IT WAS ALL TO PRESERVE OUR SHAM SOCIETY.
BAM
BAM

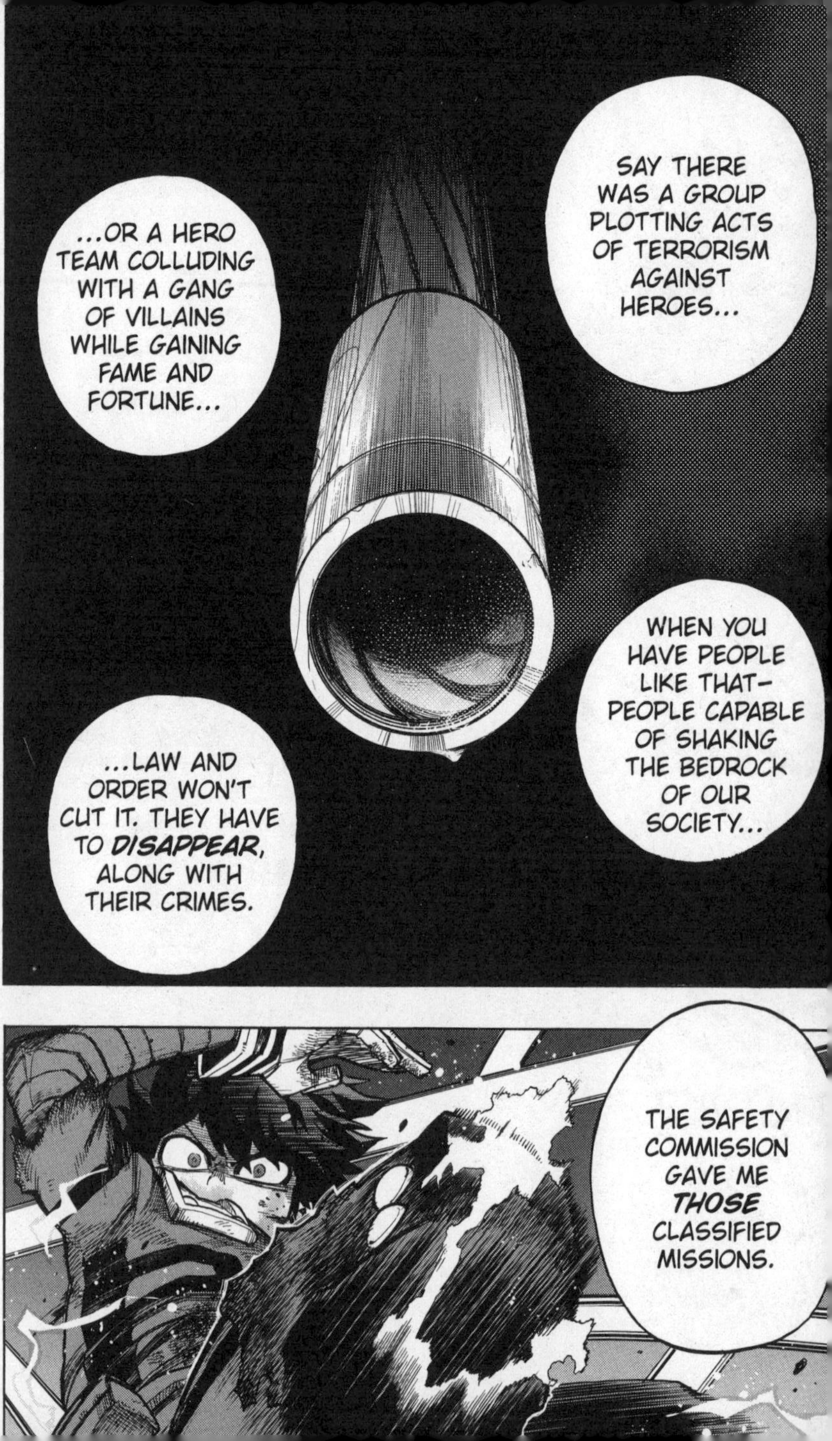
SAY THERE WAS A GROUP PLOTTING ACTS OF TERRORISM AGAINST HEROES...
...OR A HERO TEAM COLLUDING WITH A GANG OF VILLAINS WHILE GAINING FAME AND FORTUNE...
WHEN YOU HAVE PEOPLE LIKE THAT– PEOPLE CAPABLE OF SHAKING THE BEDROCK OF OUR SOCIETY...
...LAW AND ORDER WON'T CUT IT. THEY HAVE TO *DISAPPEAR*, ALONG WITH THEIR CRIMES.
THE SAFETY COMMISSION GAVE ME *THOSE* CLASSIFIED MISSIONS.

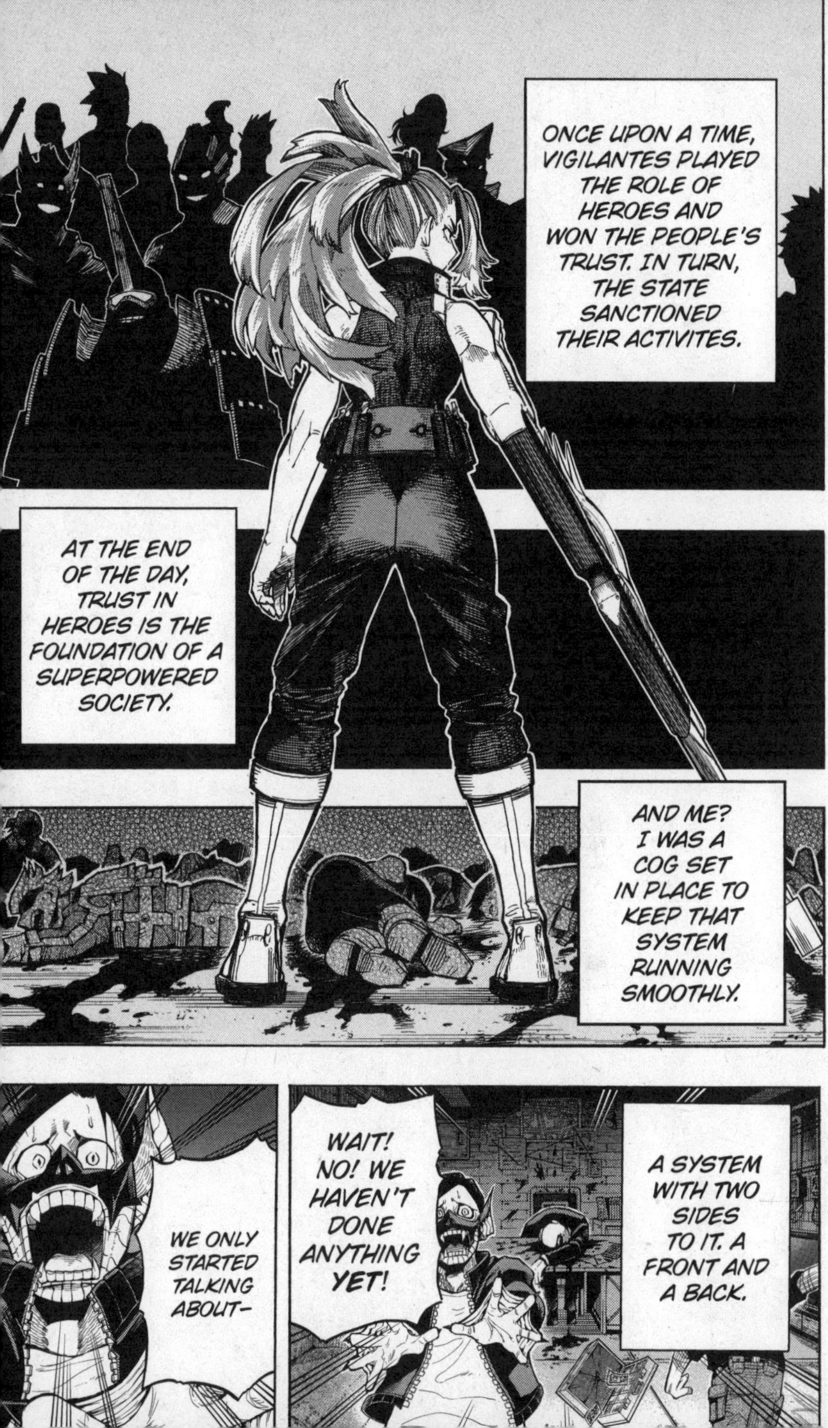
ONCE UPON A TIME, VIGILANTES PLAYED THE ROLE OF HEROES AND WON THE PEOPLE'S TRUST. IN TURN, THE STATE SANCTIONED THEIR ACTIVITES.
AT THE END OF THE DAY, TRUST IN HEROES IS THE FOUNDATION OF A SUPERPOWERED SOCIETY.
AND ME? I WAS A COG SET IN PLACE TO KEEP THAT SYSTEM RUNNING SMOOTHLY.
A SYSTEM WITH TWO SIDES TO IT. A FRONT AND A BACK.
WAIT! NO! WE HAVEN'T DONE ANYTHING YET!
WE ONLY STARTED TALKING ABOUT-

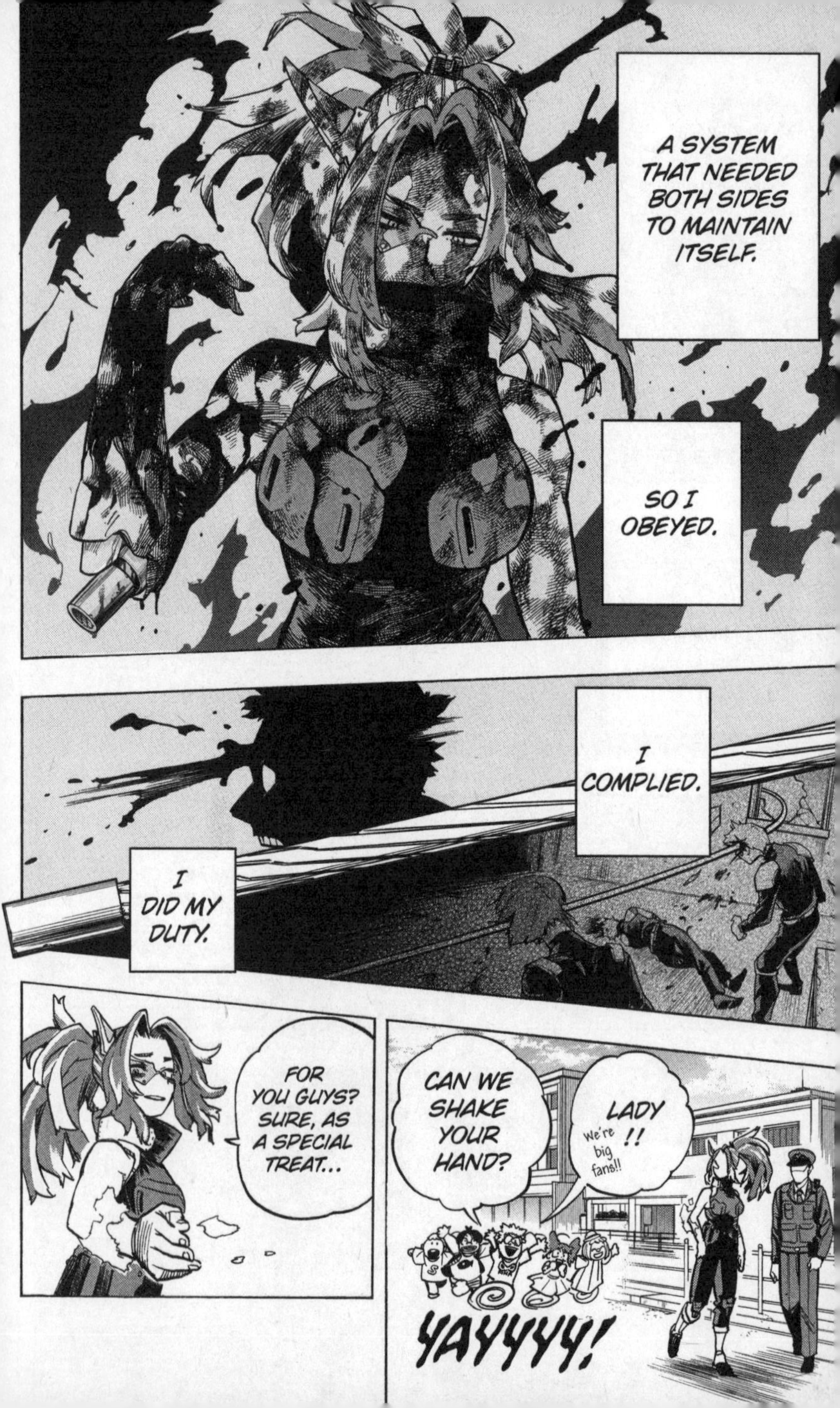
A SYSTEM THAT NEEDED BOTH SIDES TO MAINTAIN ITSELF.
SO I OBEYED.
I COMPLIED.
I DID MY DUTY.
LADY!!
We're big fans!!
CAN WE SHAKE YOUR HAND?
YAYYYY!
FOR YOU GUYS? SURE, AS A SPECIAL TREAT...

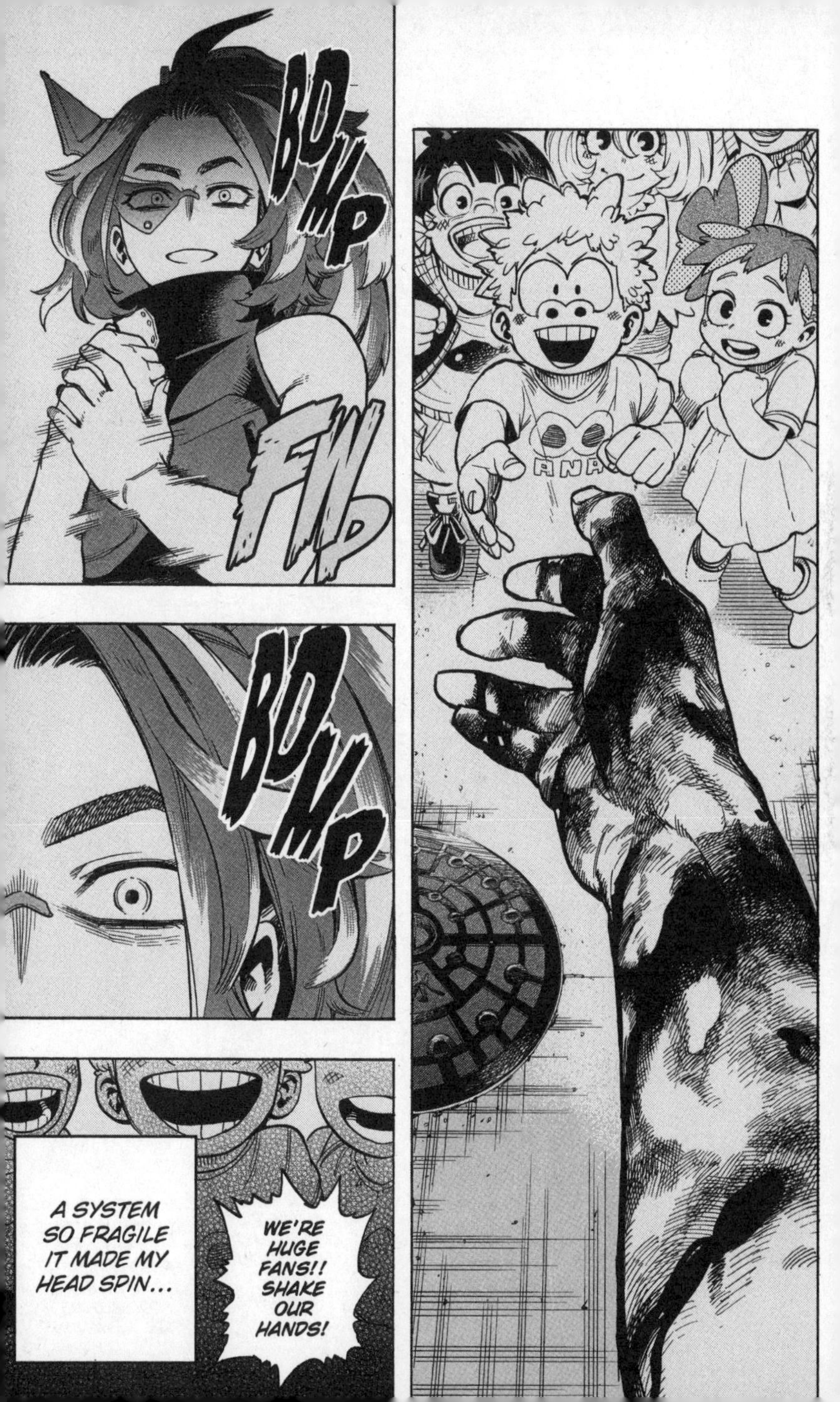
BUMP
FWP
BUMP
WE'RE HUGE FANS!! SHAKE OUR HANDS!
A SYSTEM SO FRAGILE IT MADE MY HEAD SPIN...

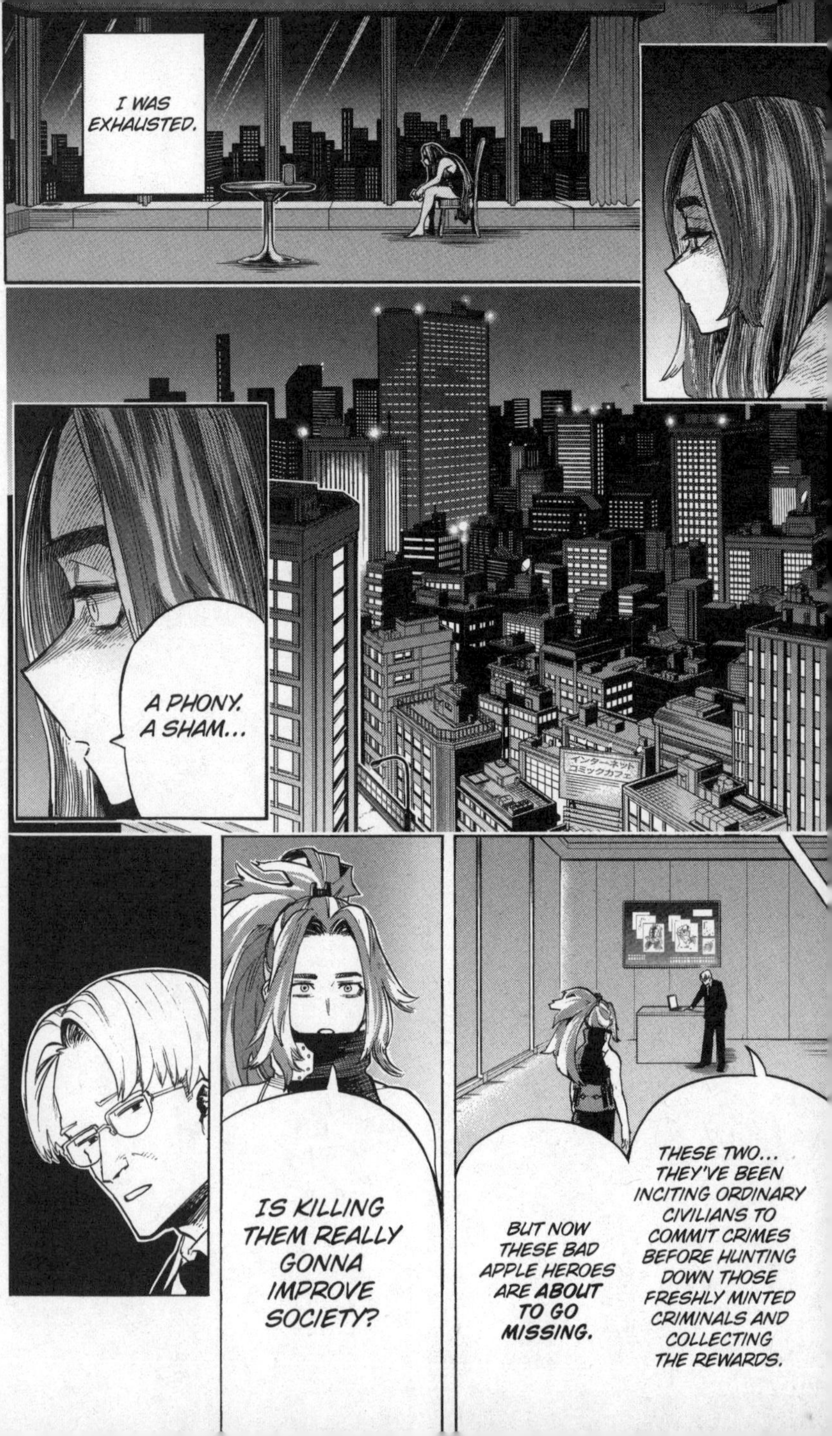
I WAS EXHAUSTED.
A PHONY. A SHAM...
インターネット
コミックカフェ
THESE TWO... THEY'VE BEEN INCITING ORDINARY CIVILIANS TO COMMIT CRIMES BEFORE HUNTING DOWN THOSE FRESHLY MINTED CRIMINALS AND COLLECTING THE REWARDS.
BUT NOW THESE BAD APPLE HEROES ARE ABOUT TO GO MISSING.
IS KILLING THEM REALLY GONNA IMPROVE SOCIETY?

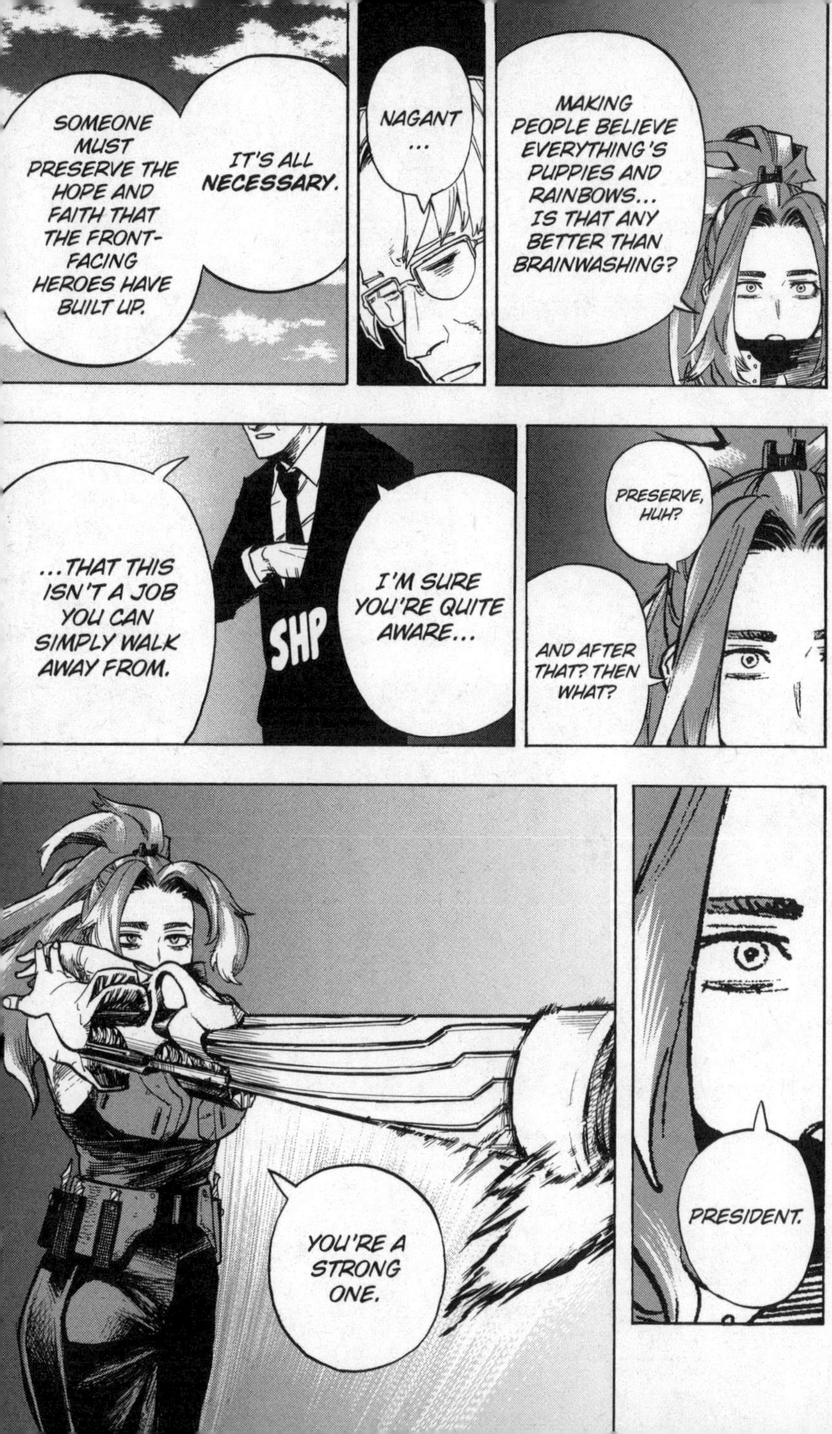
MAKING PEOPLE BELIEVE EVERYTHING'S PUPPIES AND RAINBOWS... IS THAT ANY BETTER THAN BRAINWASHING?
NAGANT...
IT'S ALL NECESSARY.
SOMEONE MUST PRESERVE THE HOPE AND FAITH THAT THE FRONT-FACING HEROES HAVE BUILT UP.
PRESERVE, HUH?
AND AFTER THAT? THEN WHAT?
I'M SURE YOU'RE QUITE AWARE...
...THAT THIS ISN'T A JOB YOU CAN SIMPLY WALK AWAY FROM.
SHP
PRESIDENT.
YOU'RE A STRONG ONE.

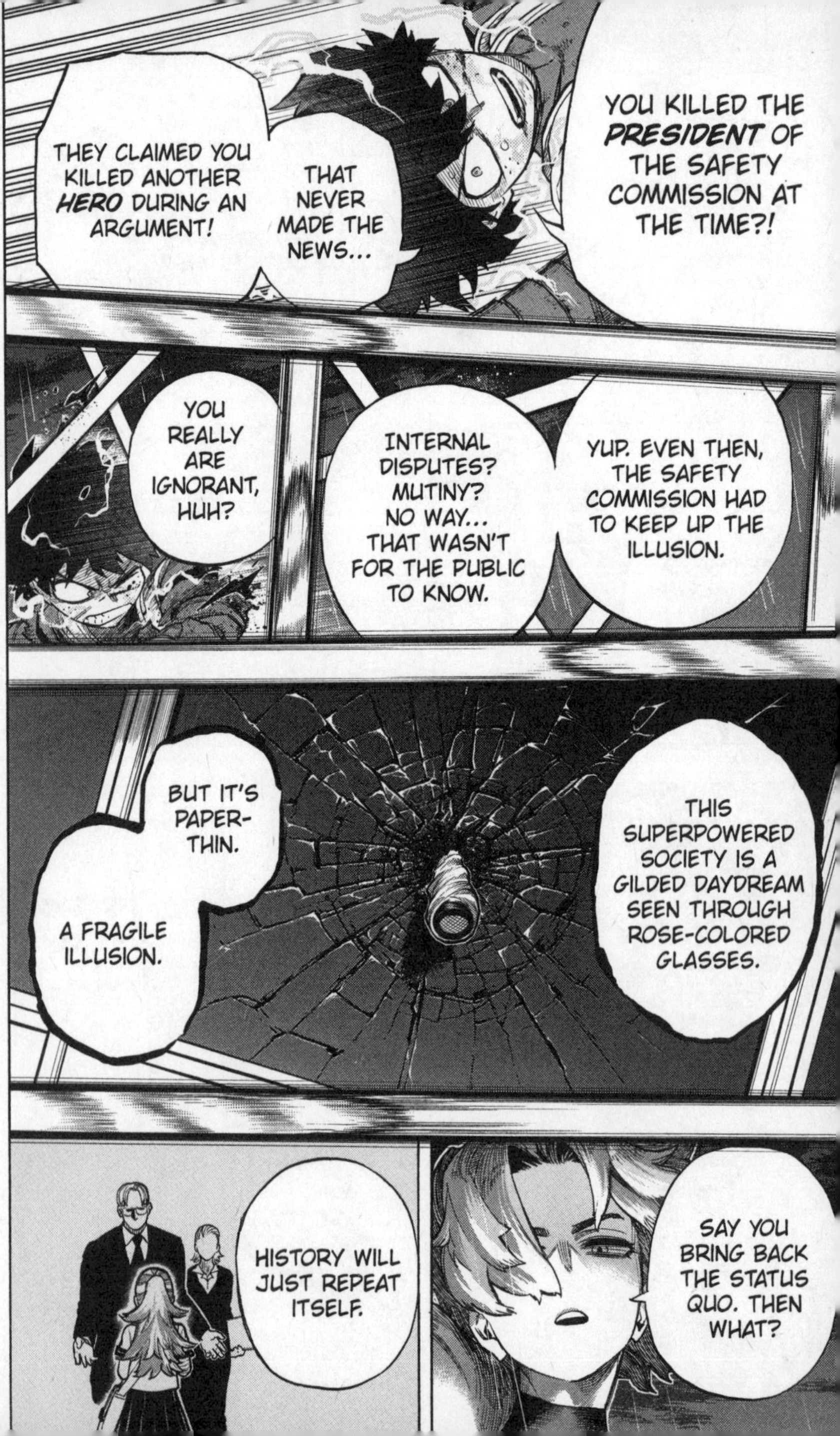

YOU KILLED THE PRESIDENT OF THE SAFETY COMMISSION AT THE TIME?!
THAT NEVER MADE THE NEWS...
THEY CLAIMED YOU KILLED ANOTHER HERO DURING AN ARGUMENT!
YUP. EVEN THEN, THE SAFETY COMMISSION HAD TO KEEP UP THE ILLUSION.
INTERNAL DISPUTES? MUTINY? NO WAY... THAT WASN'T FOR THE PUBLIC TO KNOW.
YOU REALLY ARE IGNORANT, HUH?
THIS SUPERPOWERED SOCIETY IS A GILDED DAYDREAM SEEN THROUGH ROSE-COLORED GLASSES.
BUT IT'S PAPER-THIN.
A FRAGILE ILLUSION.
SAY YOU BRING BACK THE STATUS QUO. THEN WHAT?
HISTORY WILL JUST REPEAT ITSELF.

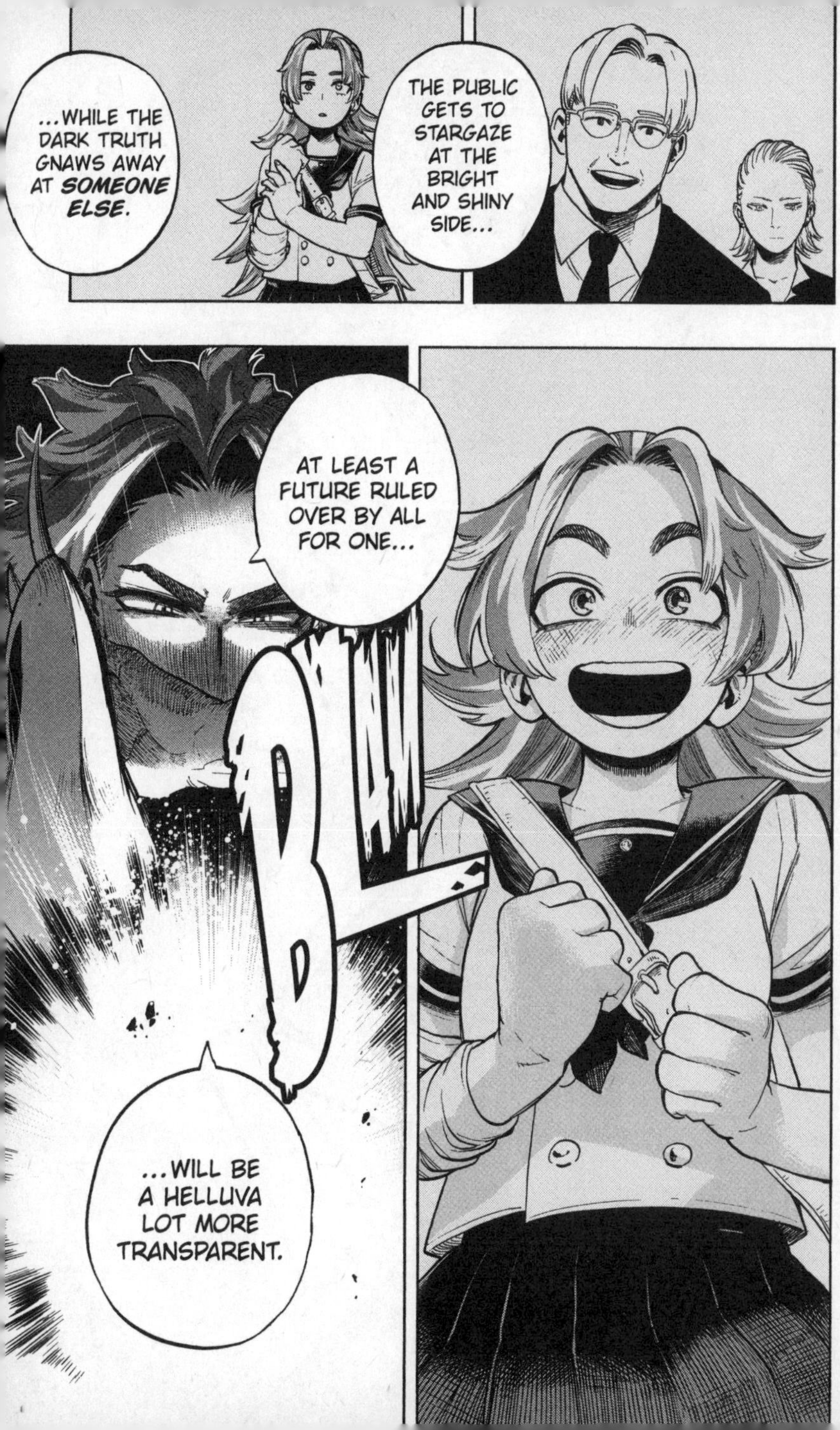
THE PUBLIC GETS TO STARGAZE AT THE BRIGHT AND SHINY SIDE...
...WHILE THE DARK TRUTH GNAWS AWAY AT **SOMEONE ELSE**.
AT LEAST A FUTURE RULED OVER BY ALL FOR ONE...
BLAM
...WILL BE A HELLUVA LOT MORE TRANSPARENT.

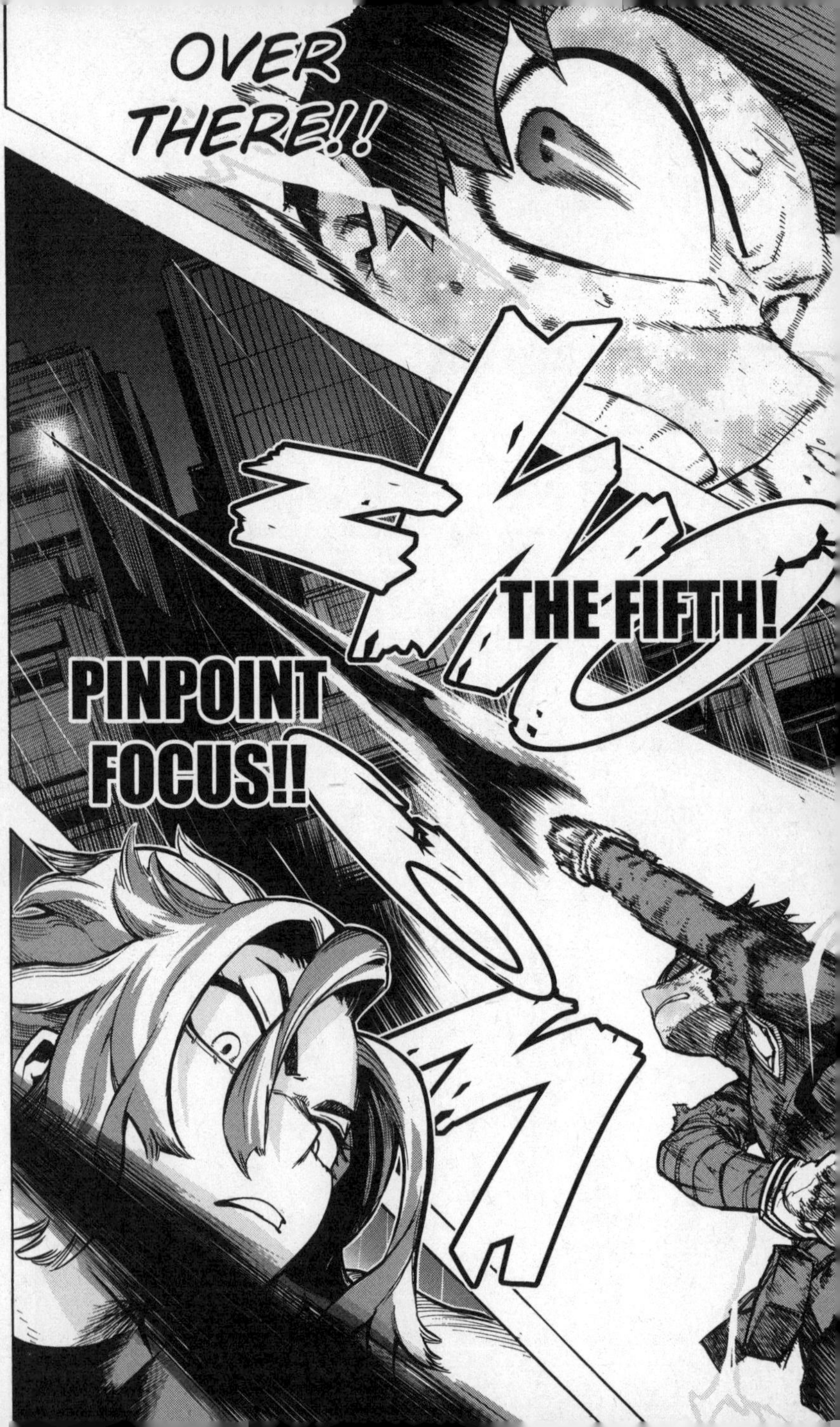
OVER THERE!!
THE FIFTH!
PINPOINT FOCUS!!

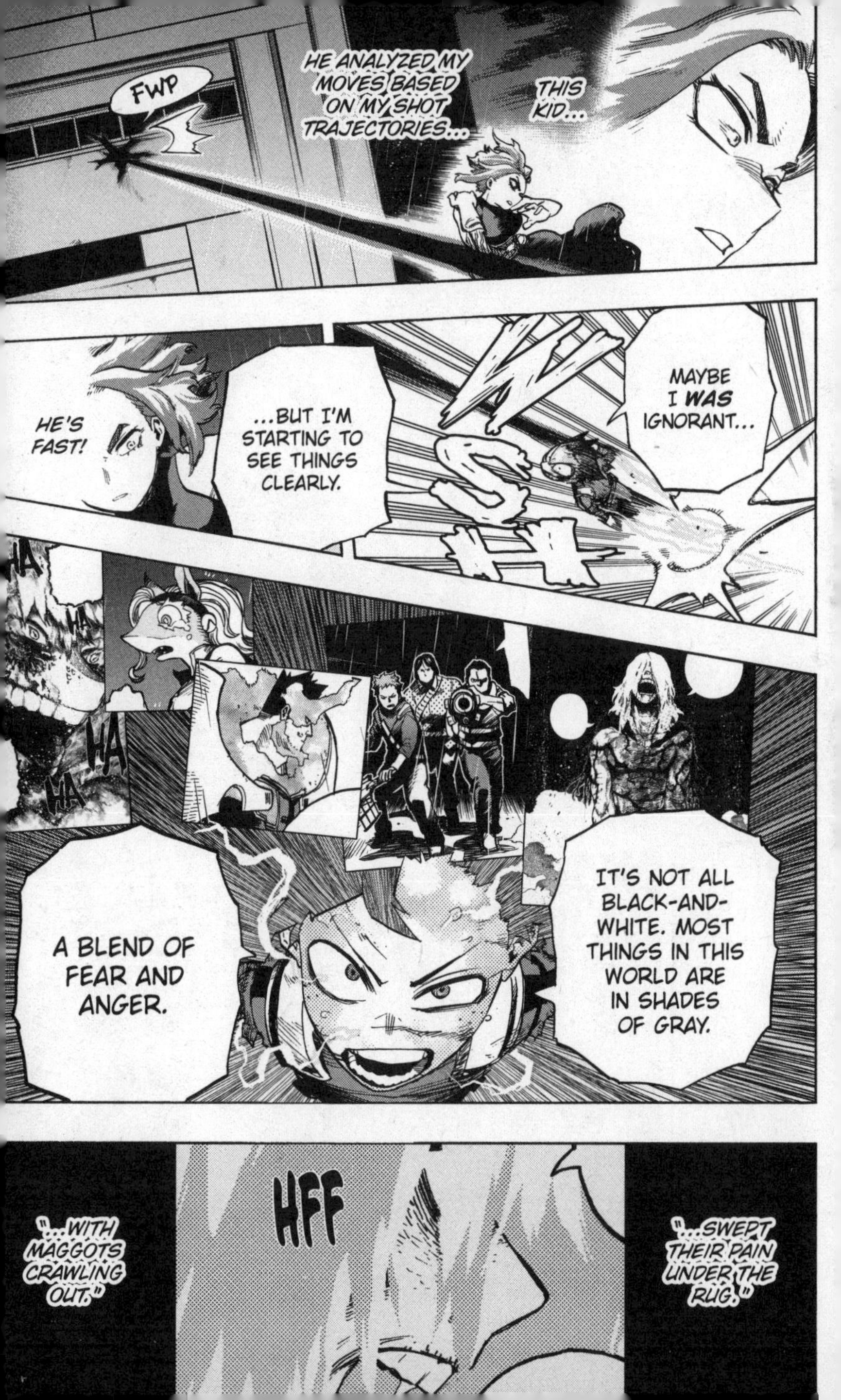
THIS KID...
HE ANALYZED MY MOVES BASED ON MY SHOT TRAJECTORIES...
FWP
MAYBE I **WAS** IGNORANT...
...BUT I'M STARTING TO SEE THINGS CLEARLY.
HE'S FAST!
HA
HA
HA
HA
IT'S NOT ALL BLACK-AND-WHITE. MOST THINGS IN THIS WORLD ARE IN SHADES OF GRAY.
A BLEND OF FEAR AND ANGER.
"...SWEPT THEIR PAIN UNDER THE RUG."
HFF
"...WITH MAGGOTS CRAWLING OUT."

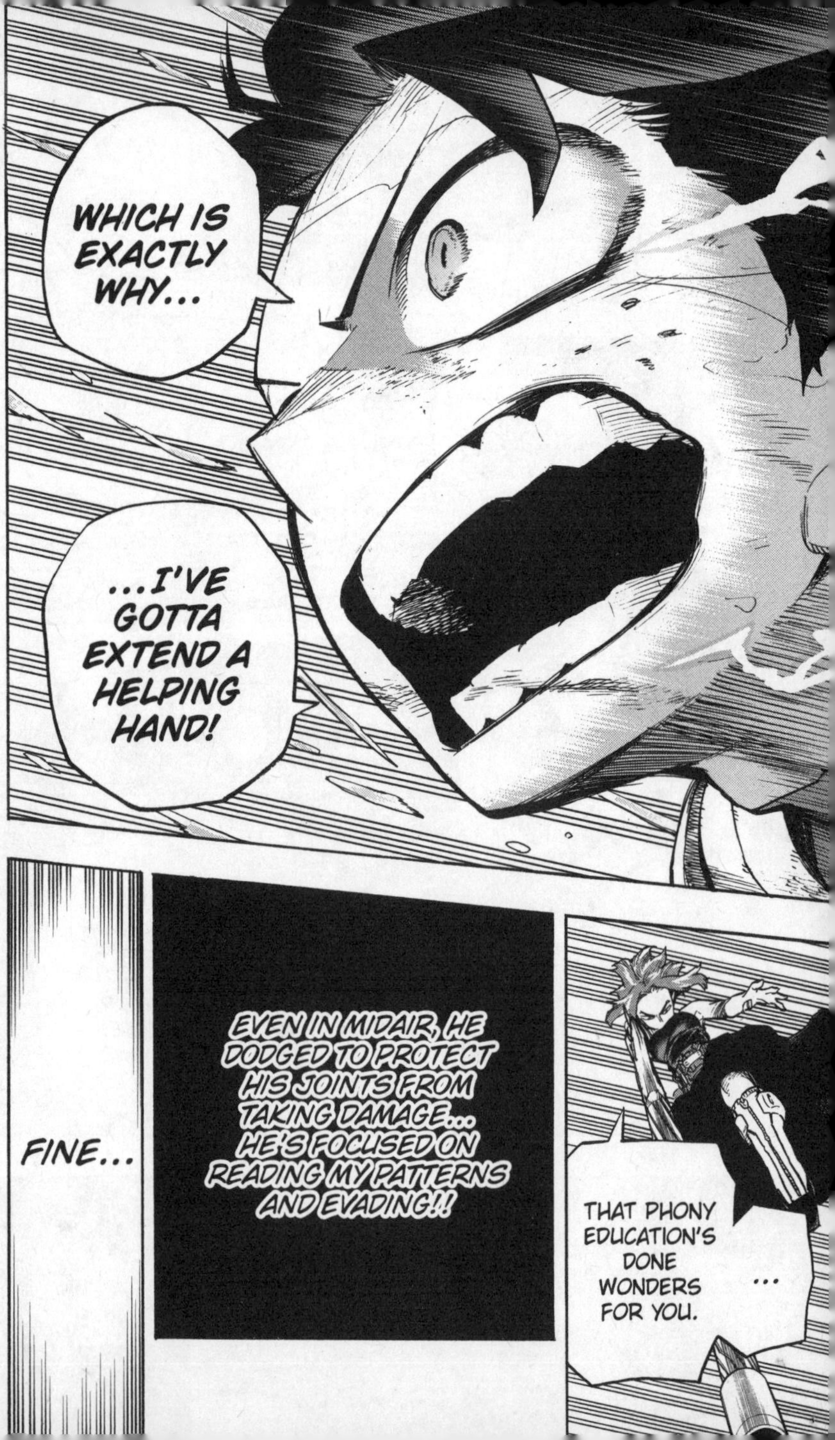
WHICH IS EXACTLY WHY...
...I'VE GOTTA EXTEND A HELPING HAND!
THAT PHONY EDUCATION'S DONE WONDERS FOR YOU.
...
EVEN IN MIDAIR, HE DODGED TO PROTECT HIS JOINTS FROM TAKING DAMAGE... HE'S FOCUSED ON READING MY PATTERNS AND EVADING!!
FINE...

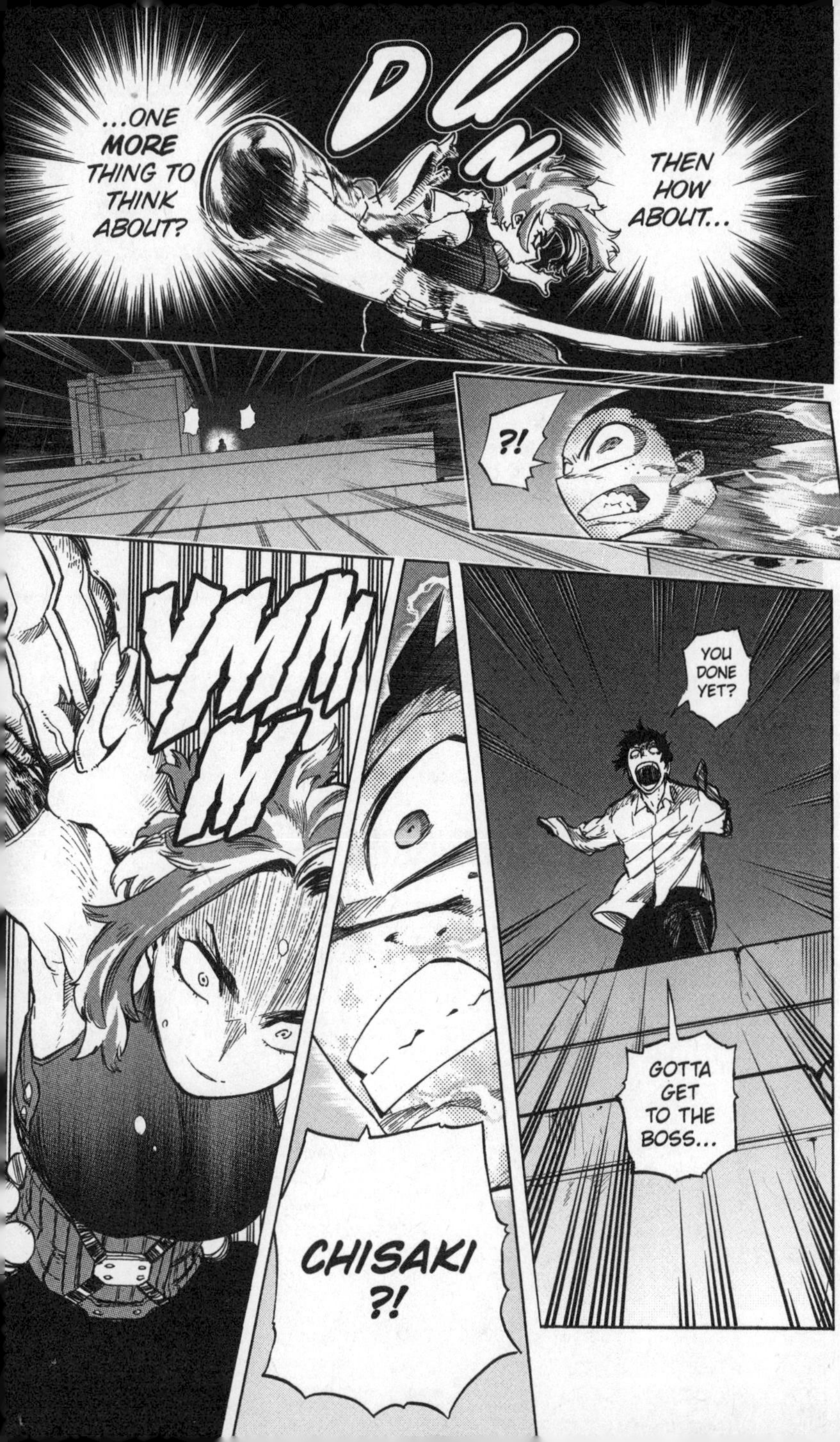
THEN HOW ABOUT...
DUN
...ONE MORE THING TO THINK ABOUT?
?!
YOU DONE YET?
GOTTA GET TO THE BOSS...
CHISAKI ?!
VMMMM

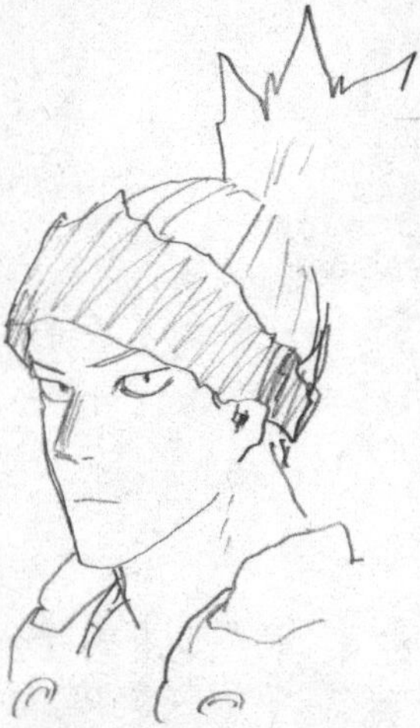

FA JIN

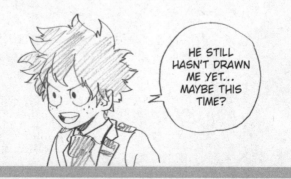

The real-life concept of fa jin is all about aligning the body in such a way as to emit explosive force (jin) through minimal movement. Probably. That's the rough idea, anyway.

The Third's Fa Jin Quirk allows one to store up power (jin) and release it with minimal movement. So it's similar to the real-life thing in terms of releasing that force, but still pretty different.

I wavered between calling it "Charge-Up" and "Fa Jin."

THE CONTRIBUTION

As always, I've received a fantastic guest drawing from *Vigilantes* artist Betten Sensei! It's over on page 166!! I wonder who he chose to draw this time?! It always gets my heart pounding.

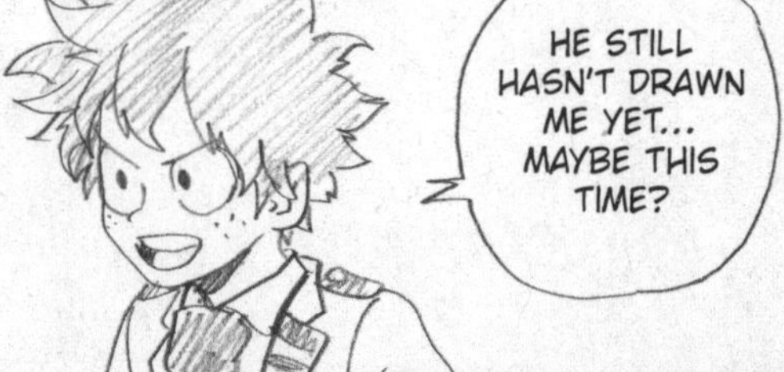
HE STILL HASN'T DRAWN ME YET... MAYBE THIS TIME?

No. 315 - Platitudes

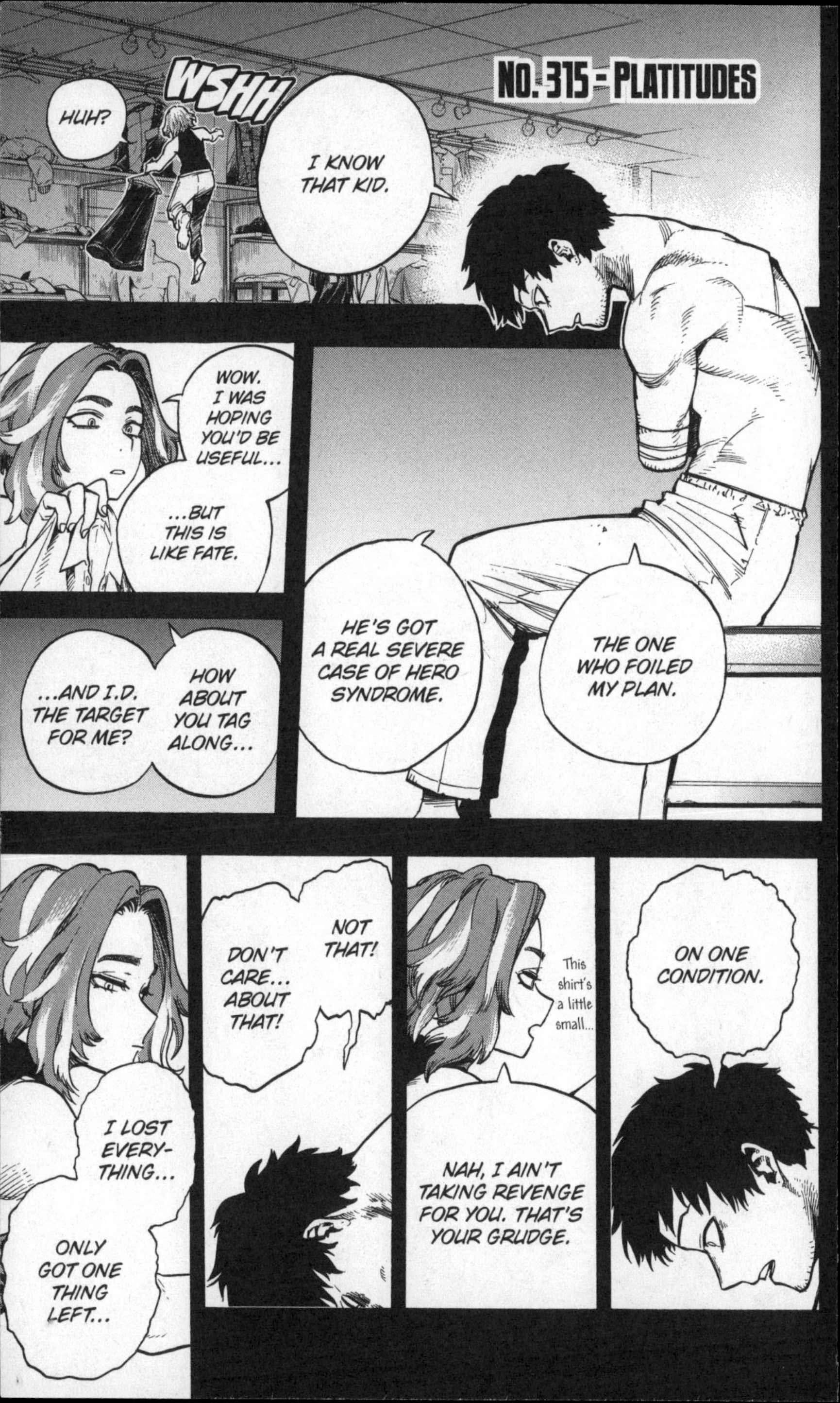

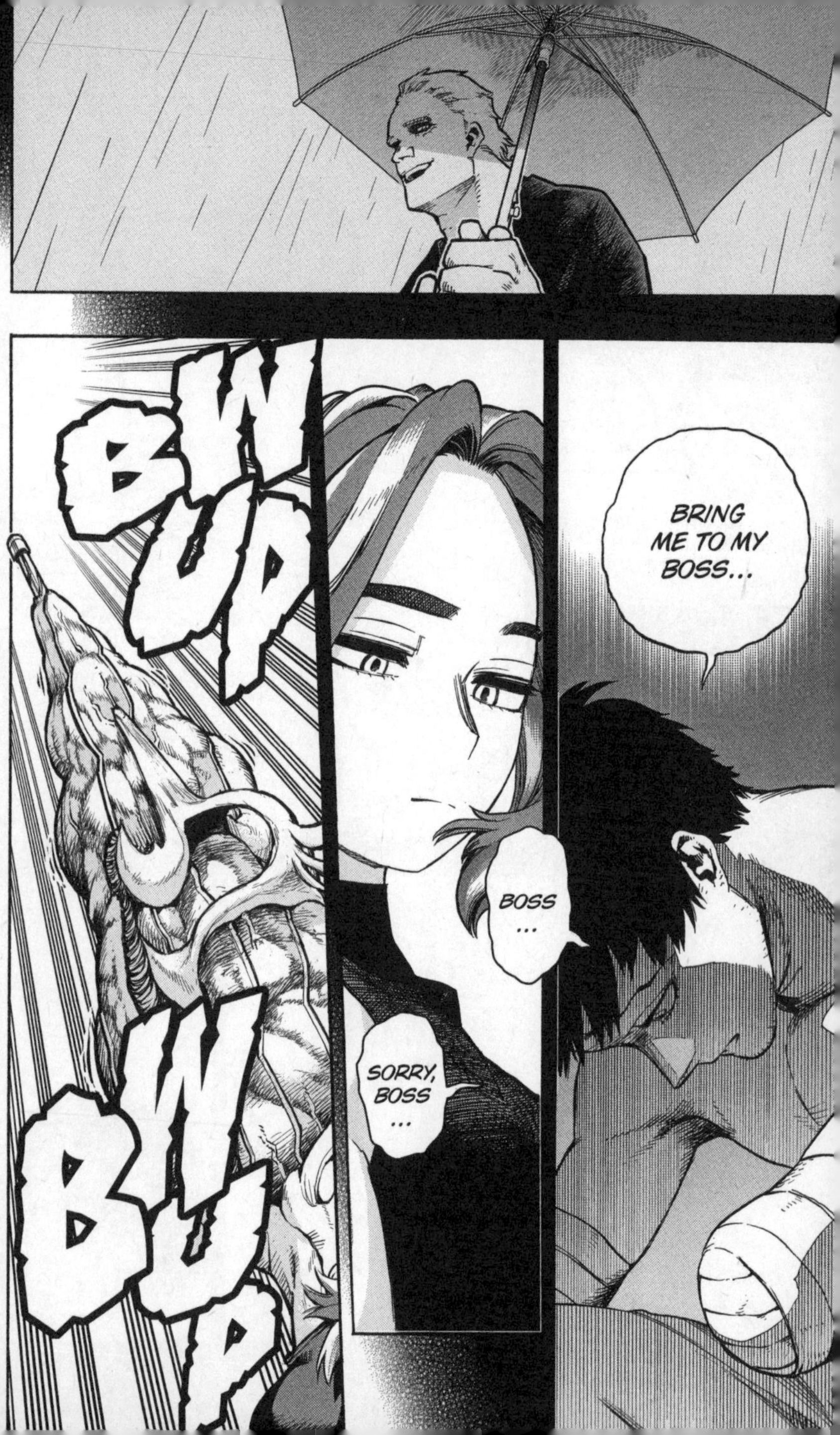
BRING ME TO MY BOSS...
BOSS ...
SORRY, BOSS ...
BWUP
BWUP

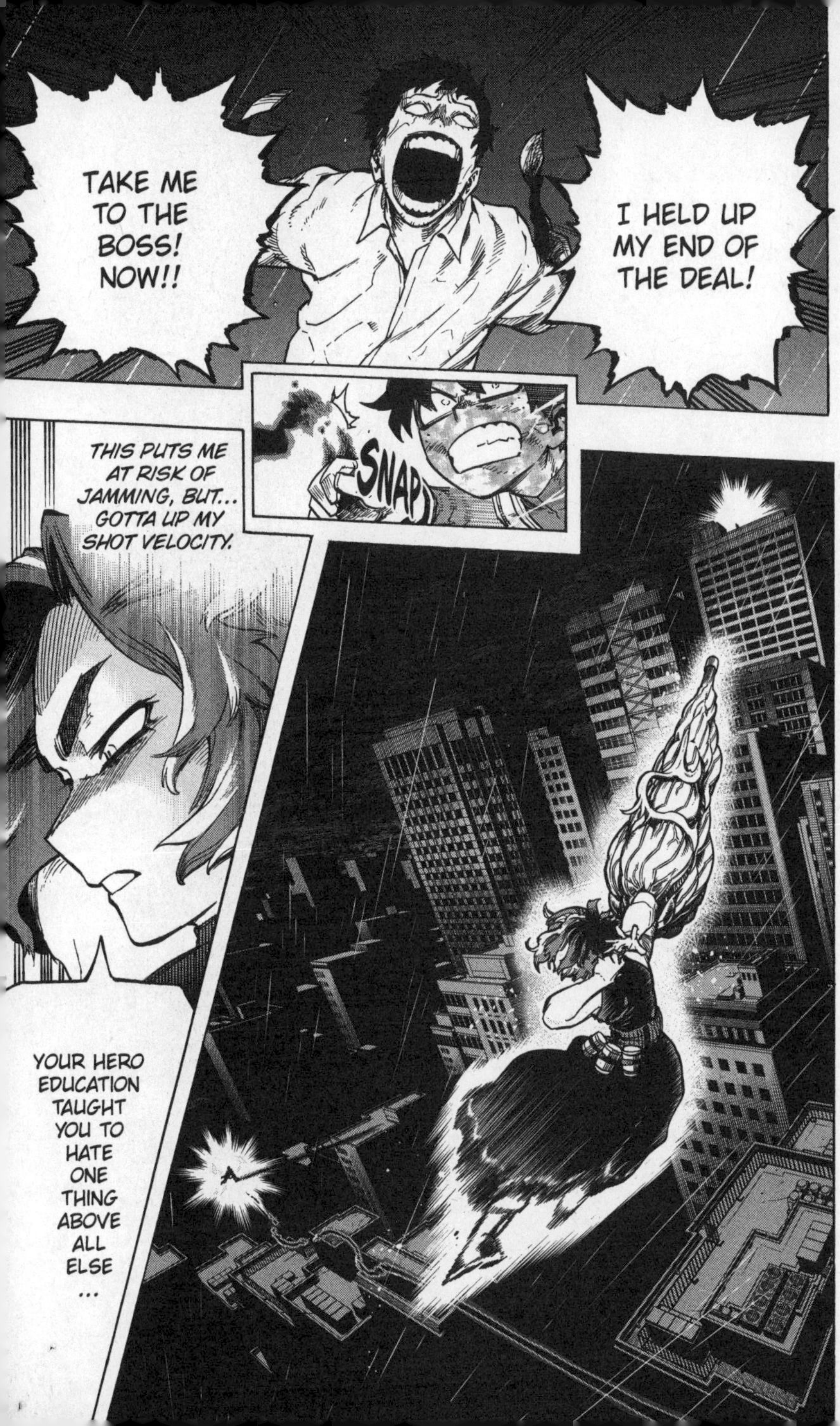
I HELD UP MY END OF THE DEAL!
TAKE ME TO THE BOSS! NOW!!
SNAP
THIS PUTS ME AT RISK OF JAMMING, BUT... GOTTA UP MY SHOT VELOCITY.
YOUR HERO EDUCATION TAUGHT YOU TO HATE ONE THING ABOVE ALL ELSE ...

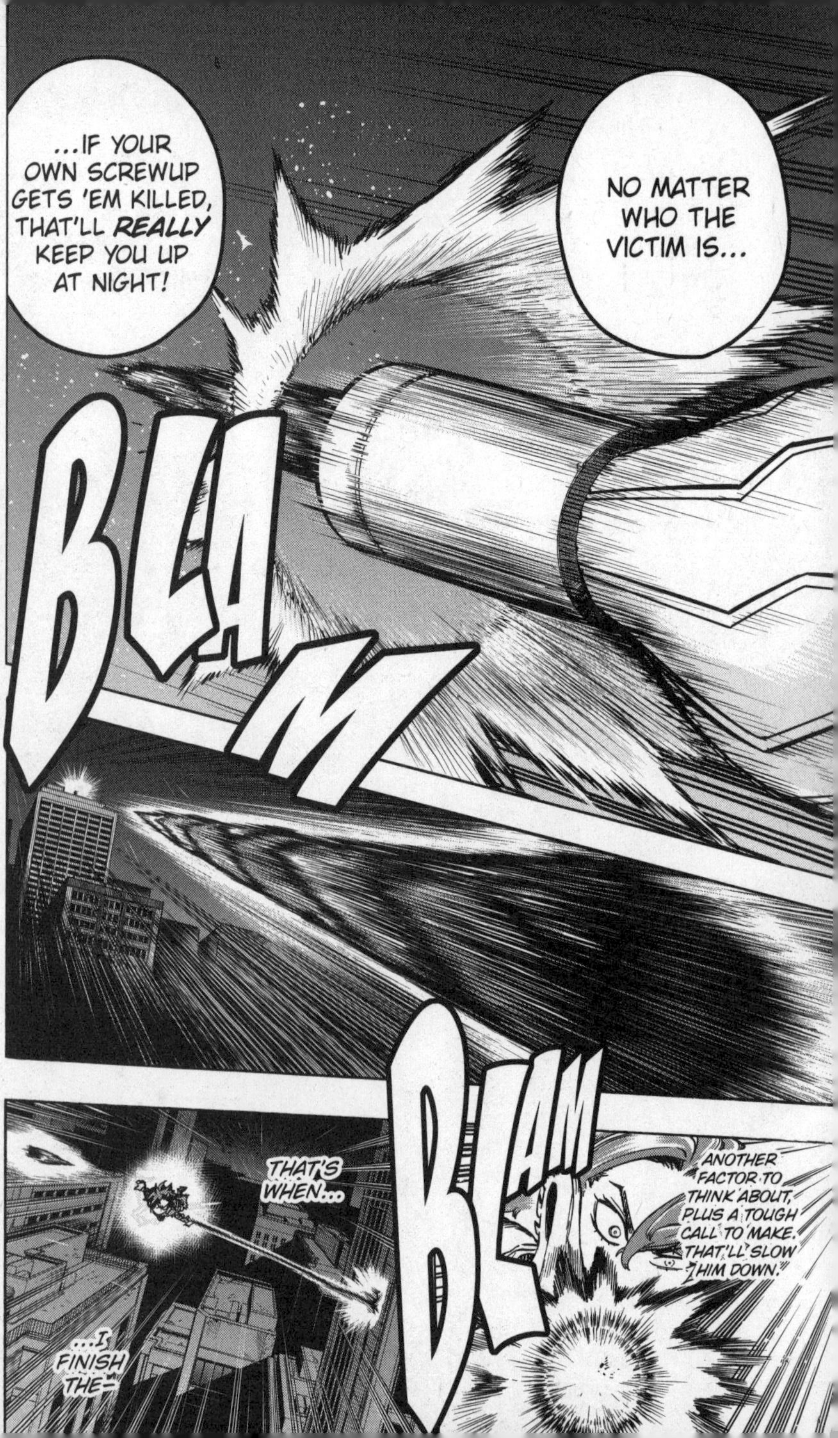
NO MATTER WHO THE VICTIM IS...
...IF YOUR OWN SCREWUP GETS 'EM KILLED, THAT'LL *REALLY* KEEP YOU UP AT NIGHT!
BLAM
ANOTHER FACTOR TO THINK ABOUT, PLUS A TOUGH CALL TO MAKE. THAT'LL SLOW HIM DOWN.
BLAM
THAT'S WHEN...
...I FINISH THE–

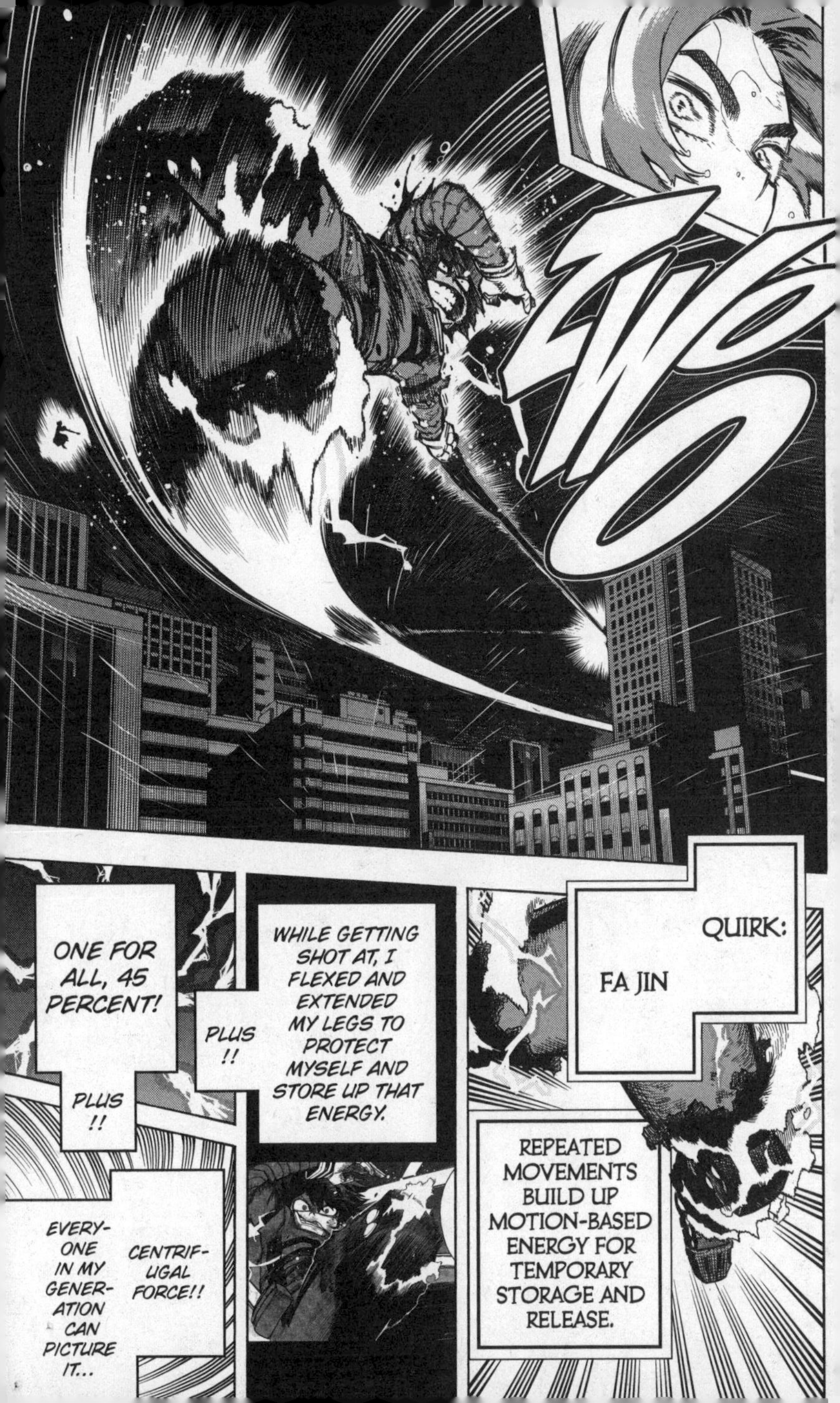
QUIRK: FA JIN
REPEATED MOVEMENTS BUILD UP MOTION-BASED ENERGY FOR TEMPORARY STORAGE AND RELEASE.
WHILE GETTING SHOT AT, I FLEXED AND EXTENDED MY LEGS TO PROTECT MYSELF AND STORE UP THAT ENERGY.
PLUS !!
ONE FOR ALL, 45 PERCENT!
PLUS !!
CENTRIF-UGAL FORCE!!
EVERY-ONE IN MY GENER-ATION CAN PICTURE IT...

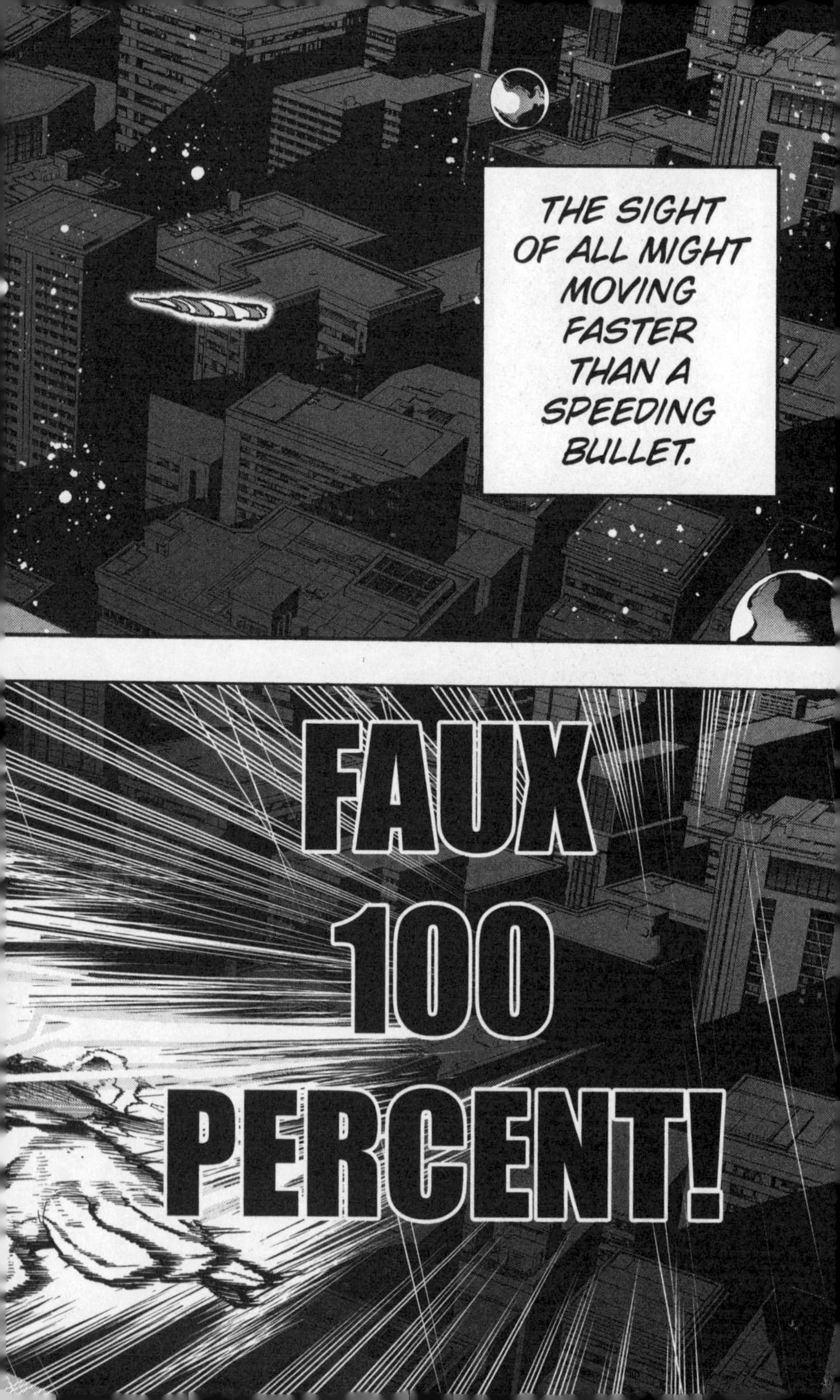
THE SIGHT OF ALL MIGHT MOVING FASTER THAN A SPEEDING BULLET.
FAUX 100 PERCENT!

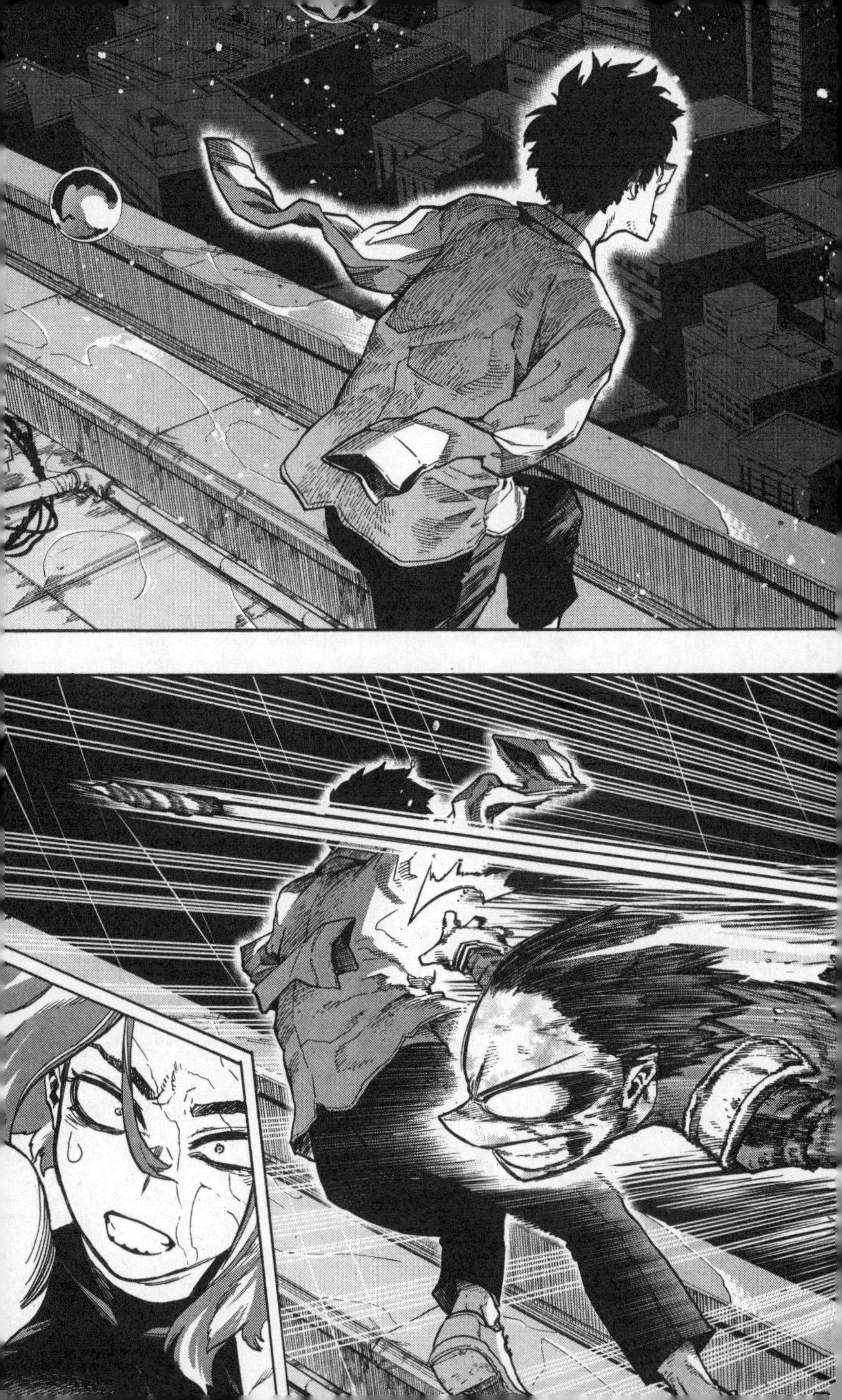

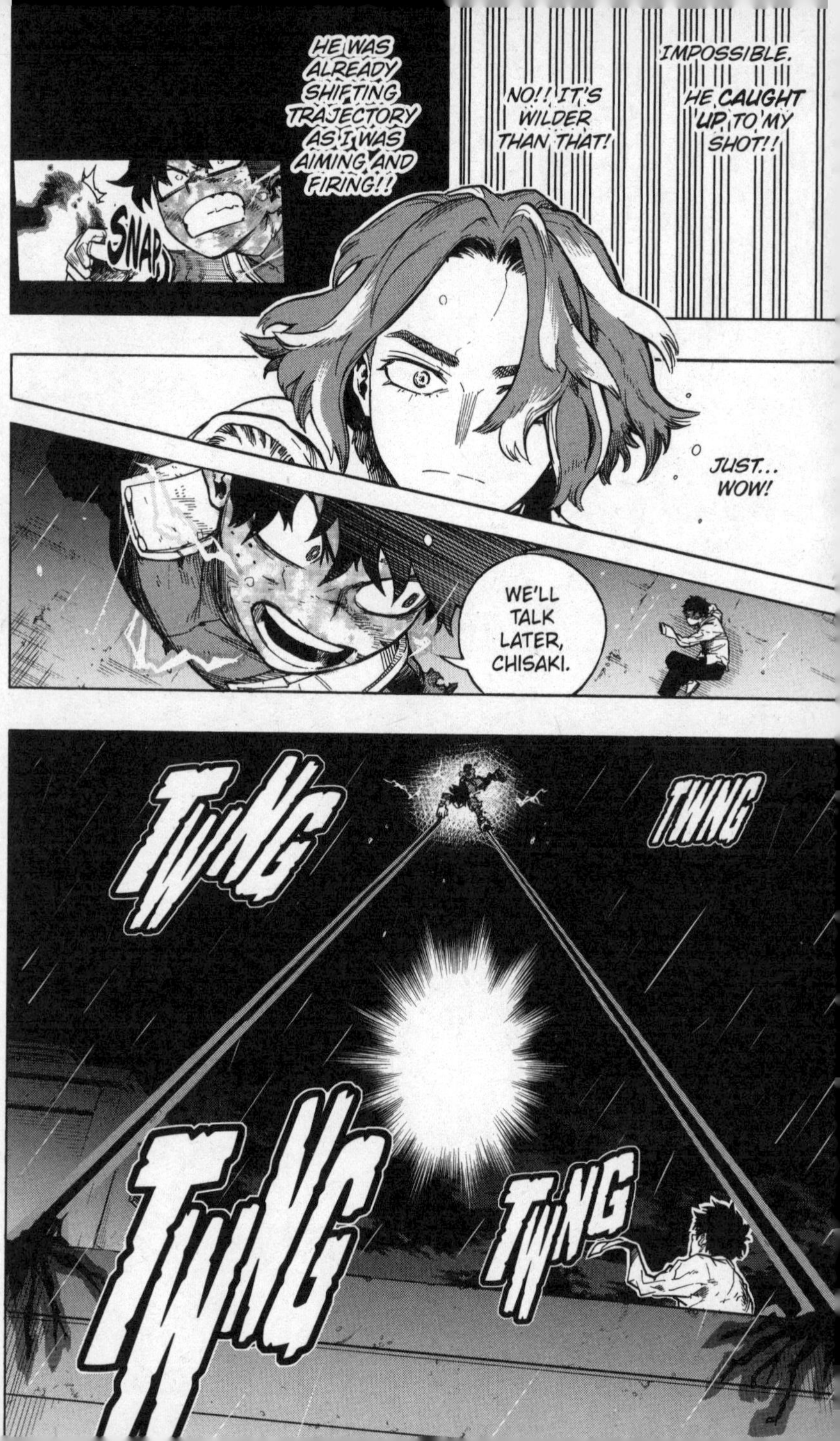
IMPOSSIBLE.
HE CAUGHT UP TO MY SHOT!!
NO!! IT'S WILDER THAN THAT!
HE WAS ALREADY SHIFTING TRAJECTORY AS I WAS AIMING AND FIRING!!
SNAP
JUST... WOW!
WE'LL TALK LATER, CHISAKI.
TWNG
TWNG
TWNG
TWNG

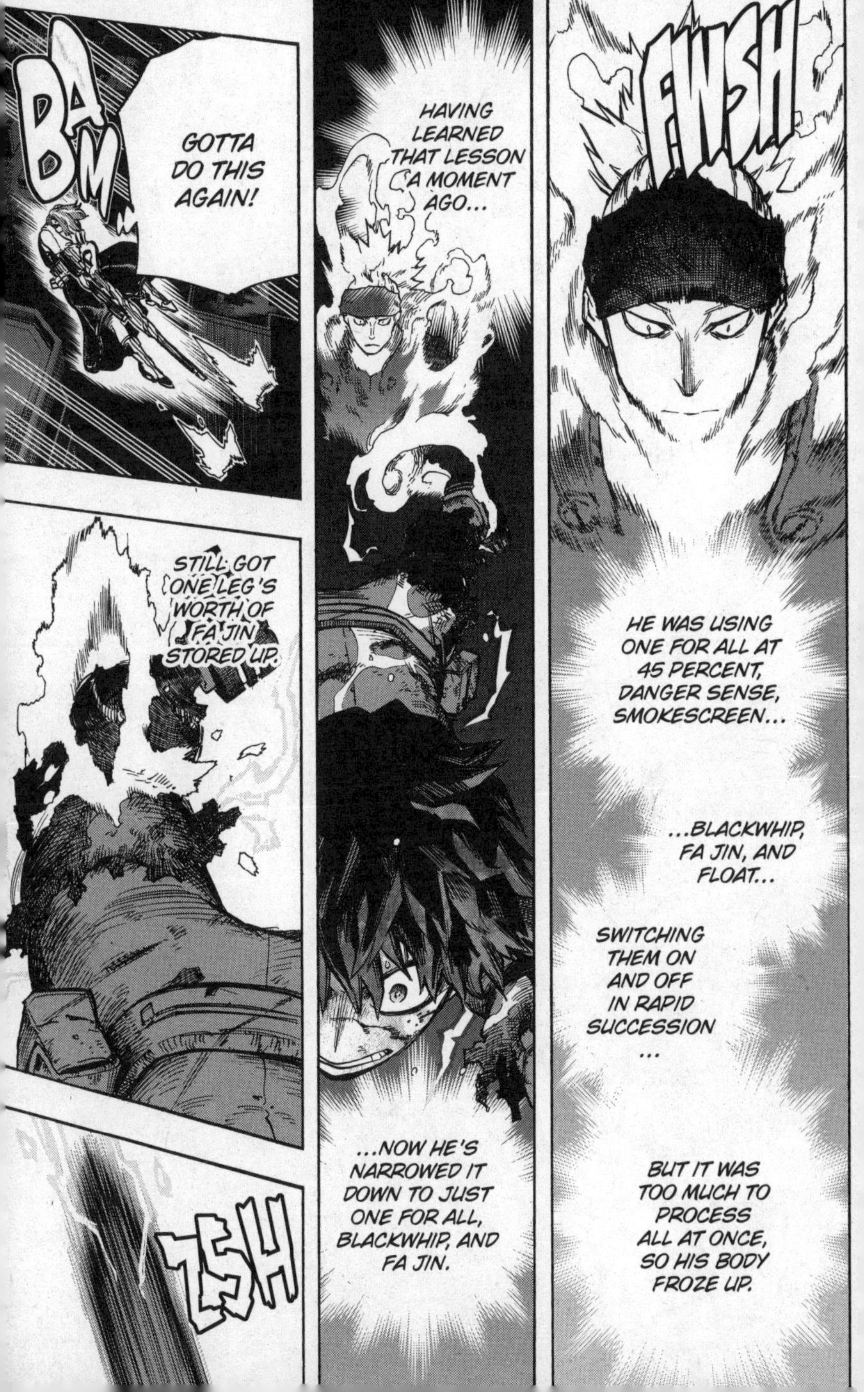
FWSH
HE WAS USING ONE FOR ALL AT 45 PERCENT, DANGER SENSE, SMOKESCREEN...
...BLACKWHIP, FA JIN, AND FLOAT...
SWITCHING THEM ON AND OFF IN RAPID SUCCESSION...
BUT IT WAS TOO MUCH TO PROCESS ALL AT ONCE, SO HIS BODY FROZE UP.
HAVING LEARNED THAT LESSON A MOMENT AGO...
...NOW HE'S NARROWED IT DOWN TO JUST ONE FOR ALL, BLACKWHIP, AND FA JIN.
BAM
GOTTA DO THIS AGAIN!
STILL GOT ONE LEG'S WORTH OF FA JIN STORED UP.
TSH

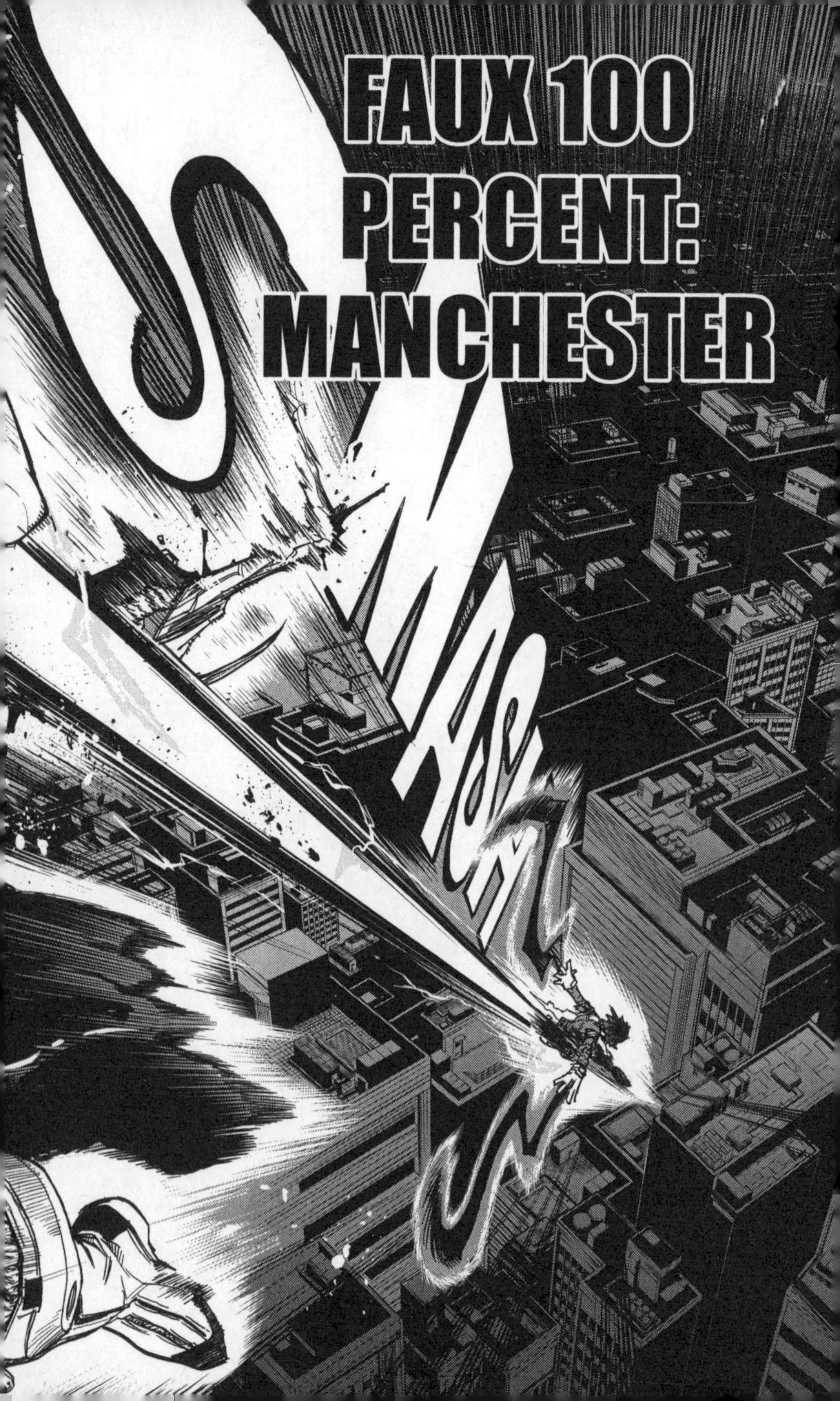
FAUX 100 PERCENT: MANCHESTER

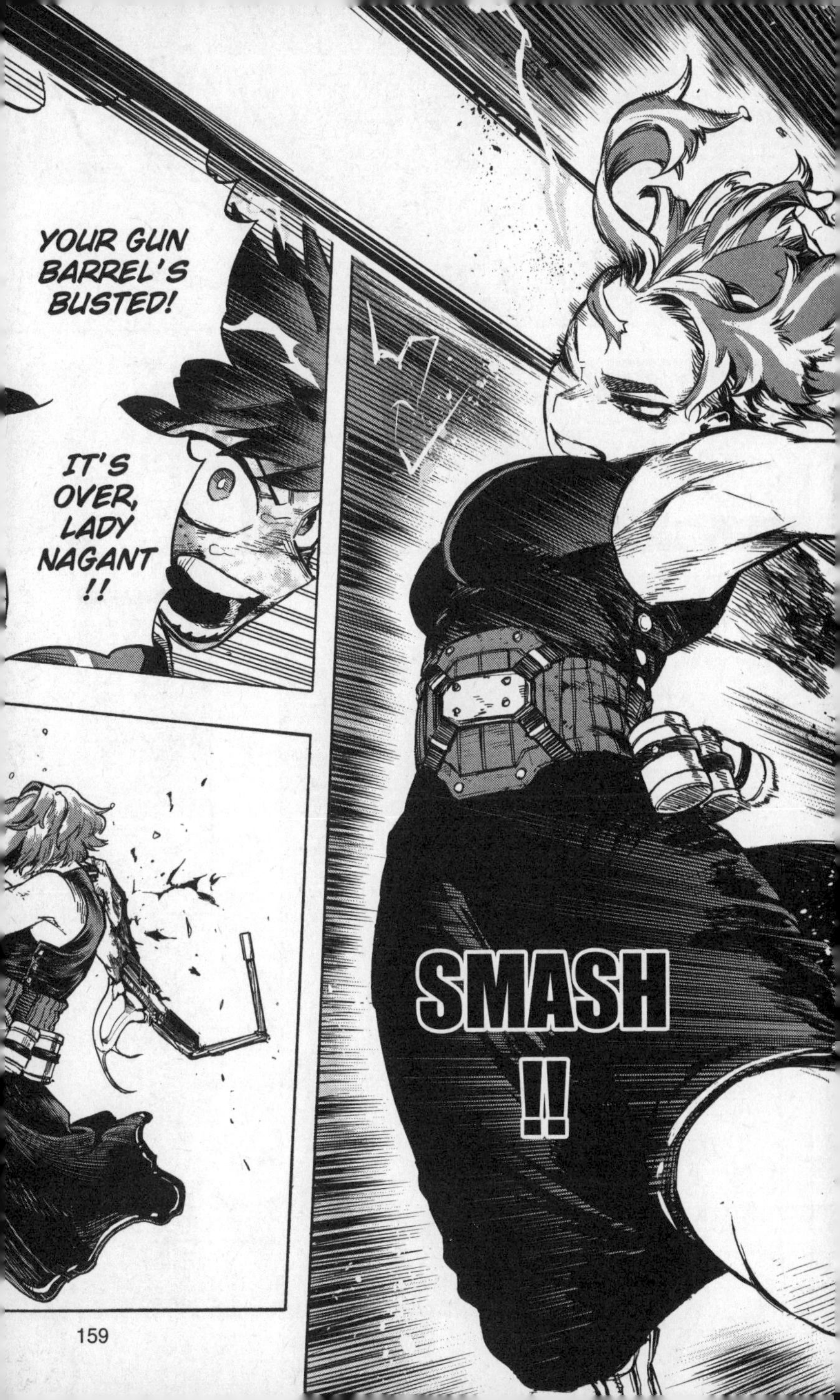

SMASH !!
YOUR GUN BARREL'S BUSTED!
IT'S OVER, LADY NAGANT !!

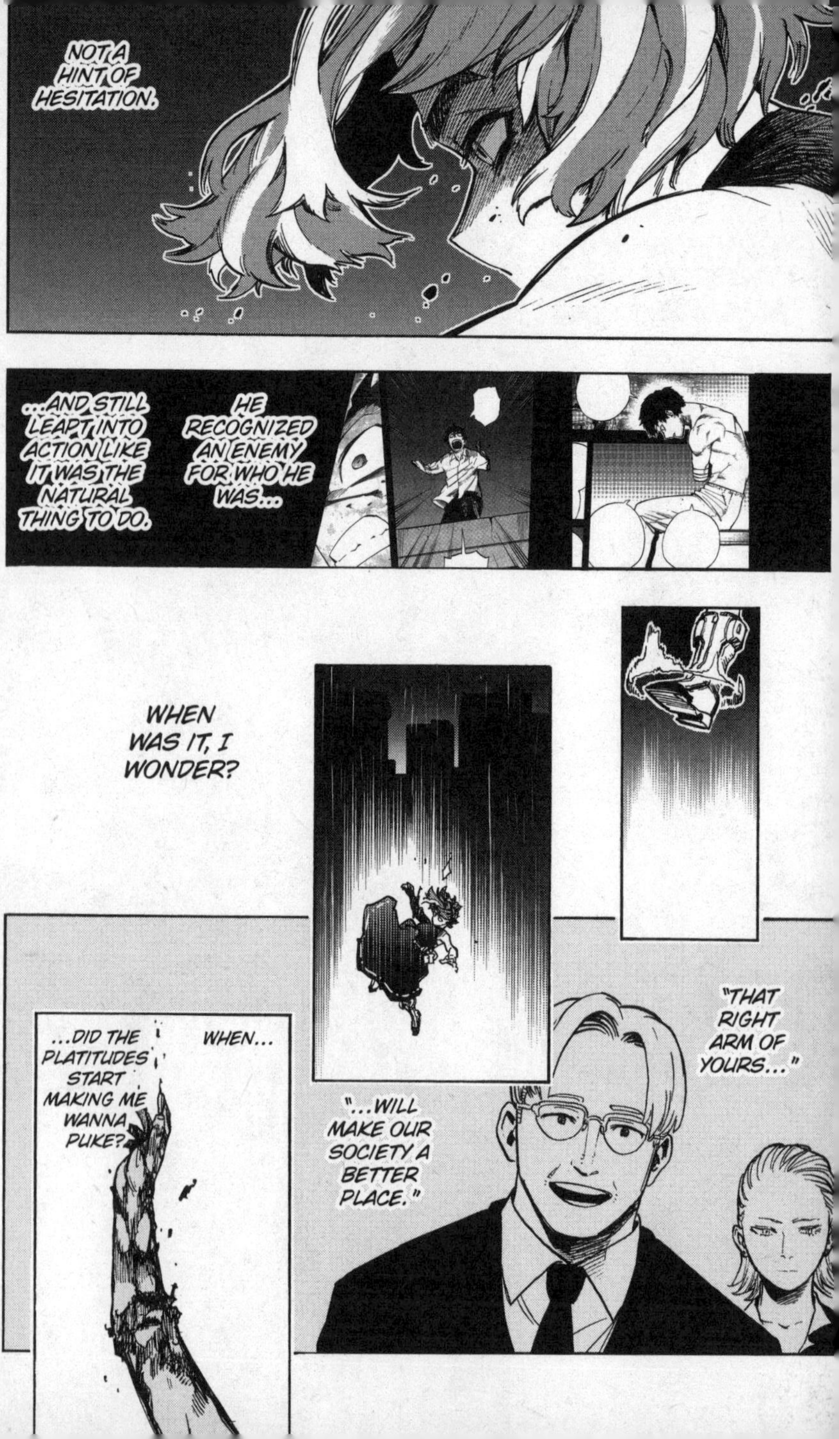
NOT A HINT OF HESITATION.
HE RECOGNIZED AN ENEMY FOR WHO HE WAS...
...AND STILL LEAPT INTO ACTION LIKE IT WAS THE NATURAL THING TO DO.
WHEN WAS IT, I WONDER?
"THAT RIGHT ARM OF YOURS..."
"...WILL MAKE OUR SOCIETY A BETTER PLACE."
WHEN...
...DID THE PLATITUDES START MAKING ME WANNA PUKE?

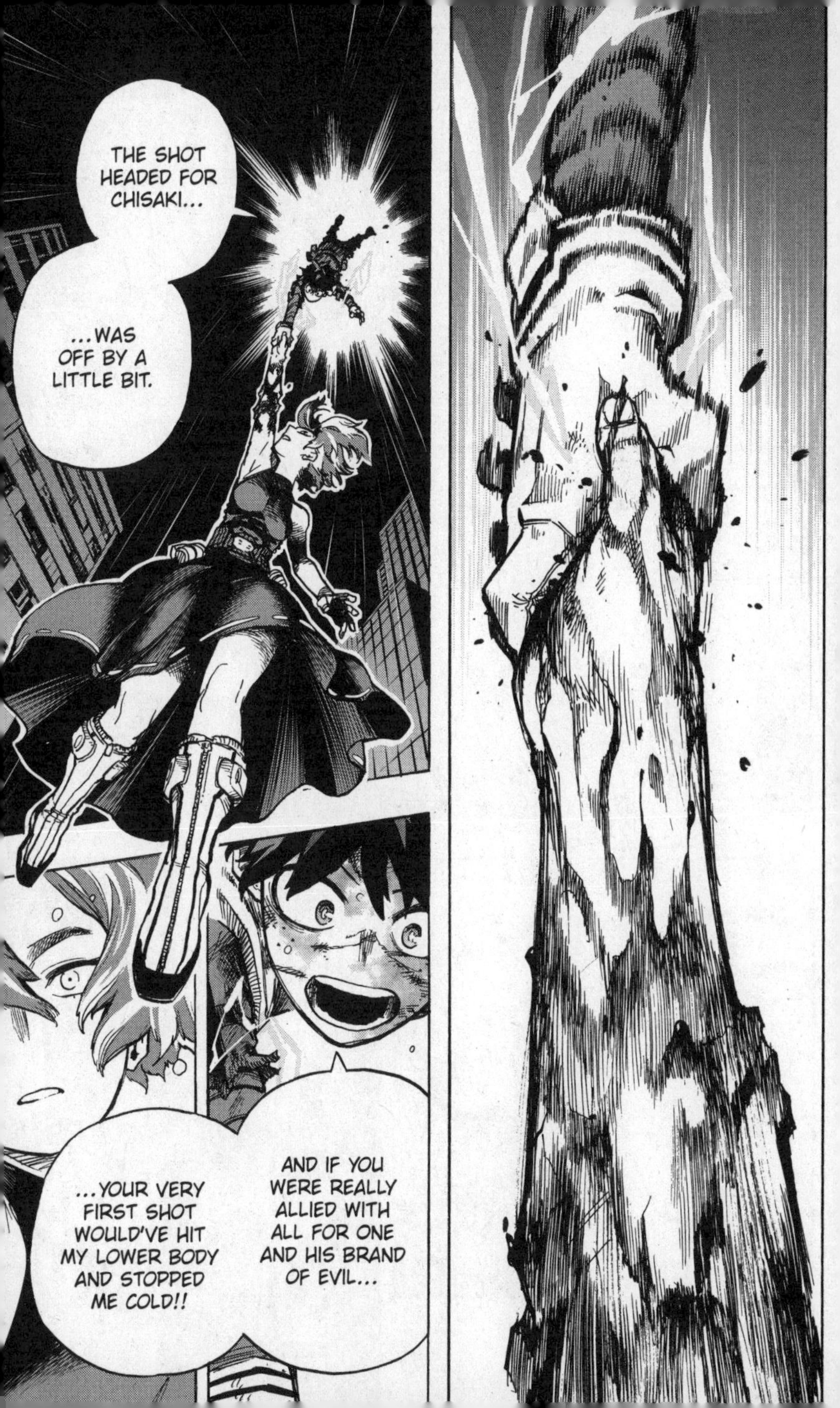
THE SHOT HEADED FOR CHISAKI...
...WAS OFF BY A LITTLE BIT.
AND IF YOU WERE REALLY ALLIED WITH ALL FOR ONE AND HIS BRAND OF EVIL...
...YOUR VERY FIRST SHOT WOULD'VE HIT MY LOWER BODY AND STOPPED ME COLD!!

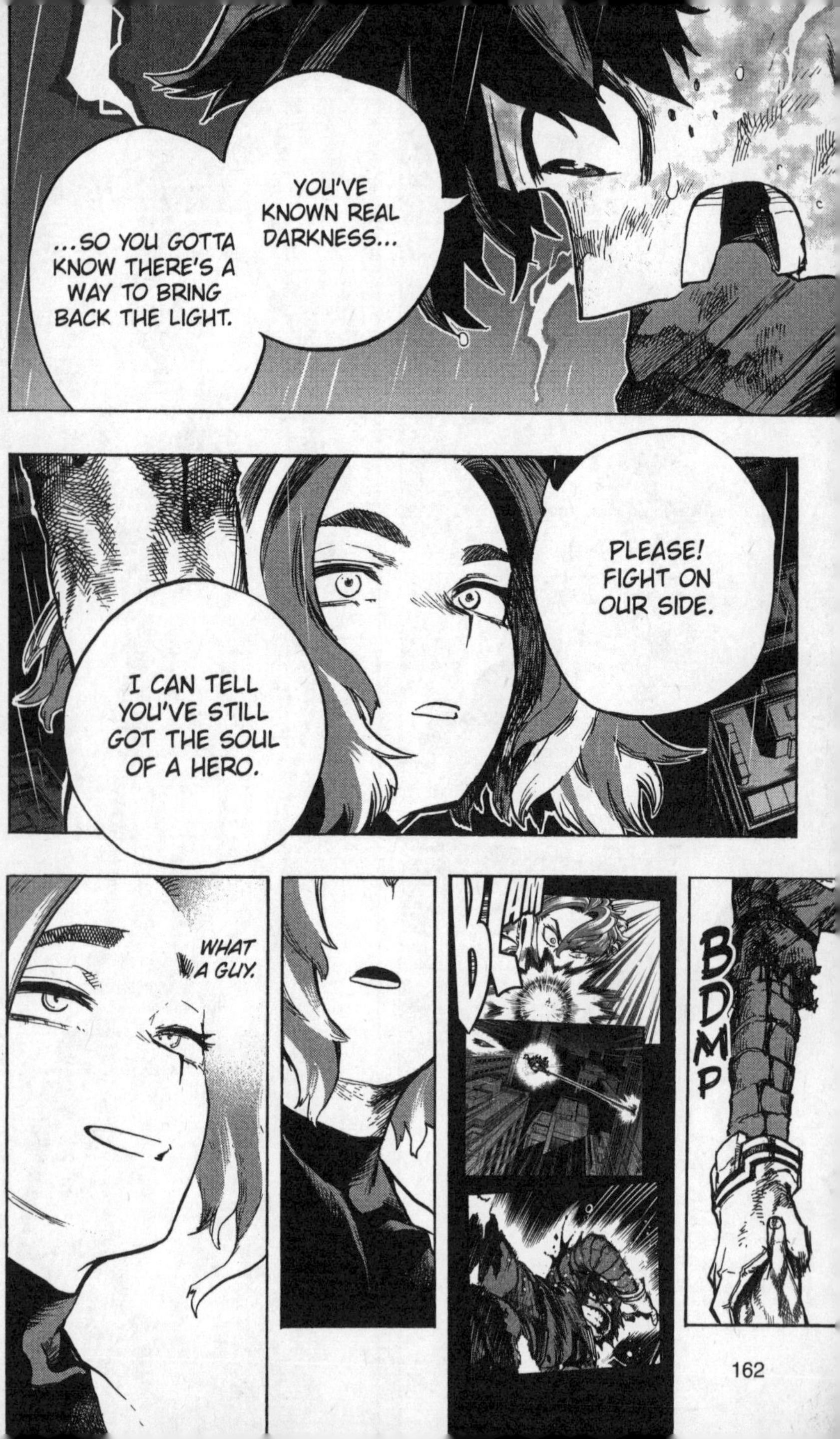
YOU'VE KNOWN REAL DARKNESS...
...SO YOU GOTTA KNOW THERE'S A WAY TO BRING BACK THE LIGHT.
PLEASE! FIGHT ON OUR SIDE.
I CAN TELL YOU'VE STILL GOT THE SOUL OF A HERO.
BDMP
BLAM
WHAT A GUY.

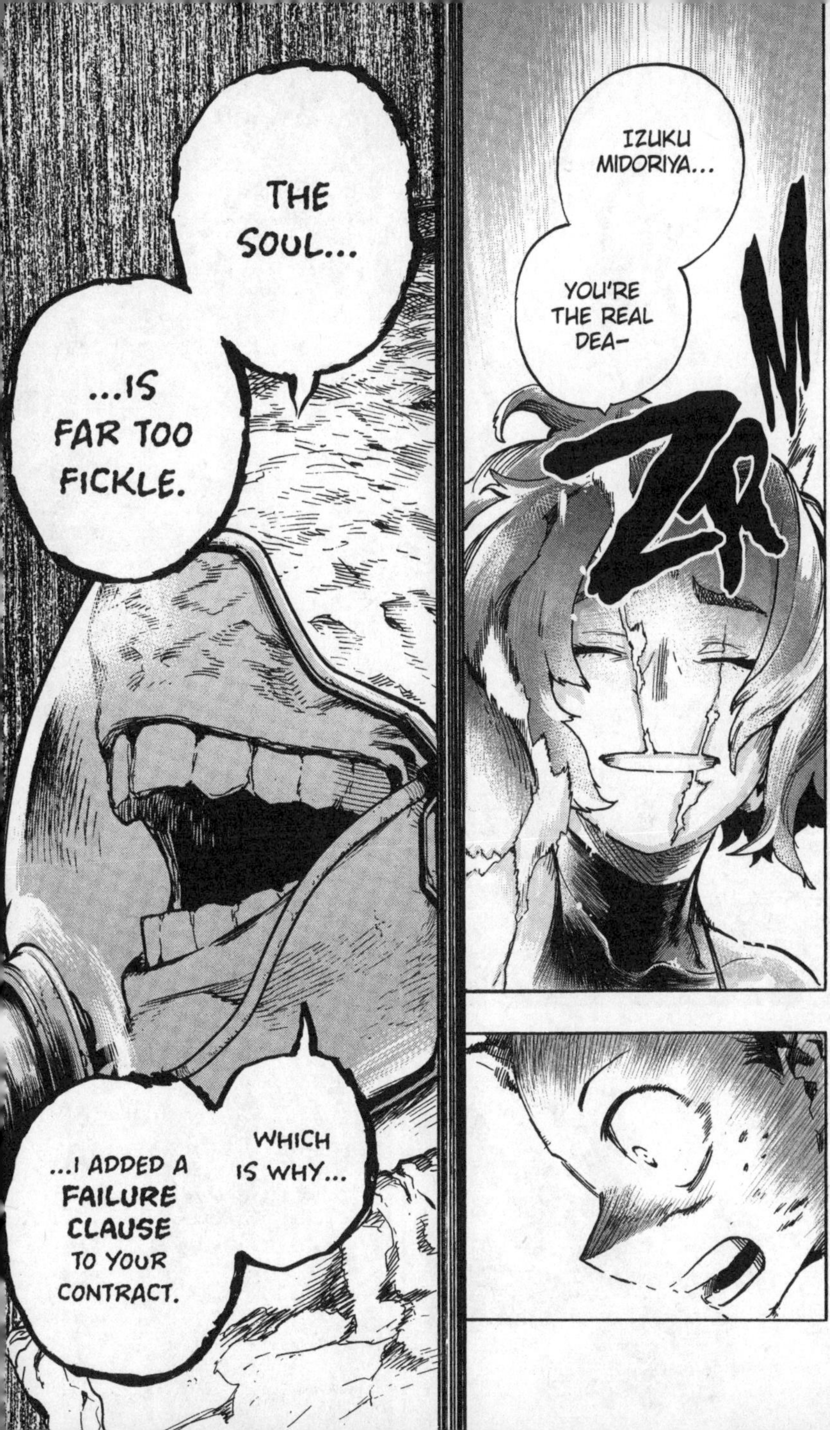

IZUKU MIDORIYA...
YOU'RE THE REAL DEA-
ZRM
THE SOUL...
...IS FAR TOO FICKLE.
WHICH IS WHY...
...I ADDED A FAILURE CLAUSE TO YOUR CONTRACT.

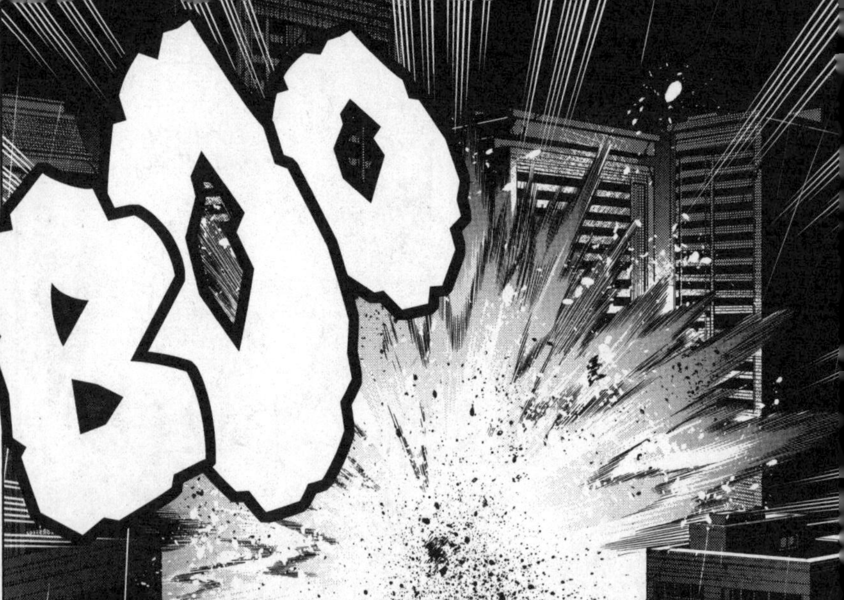
BOOM
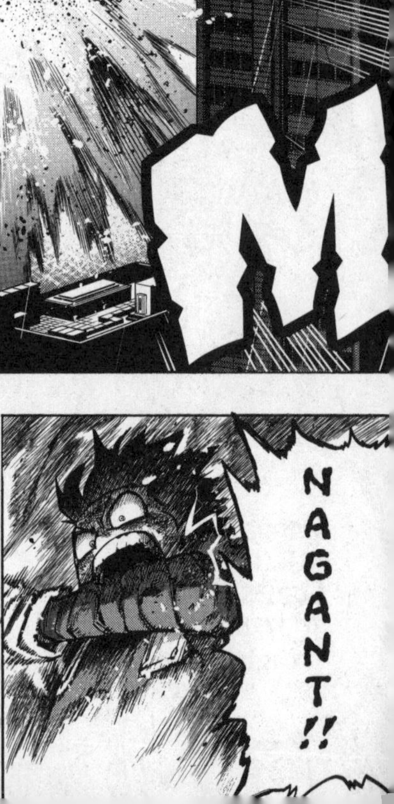
NAGANT!!
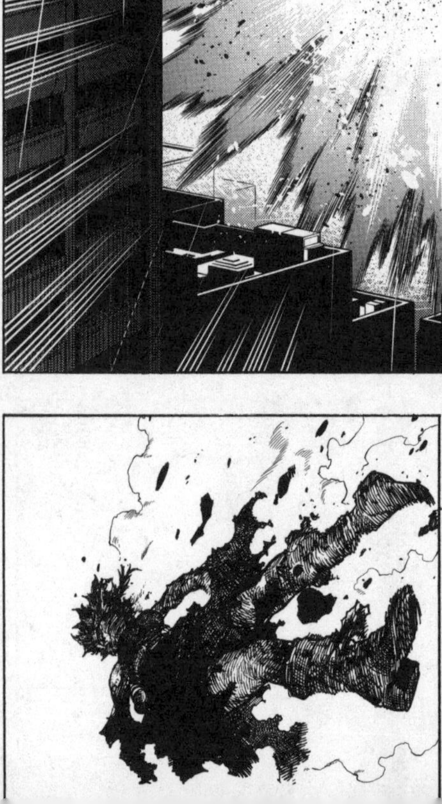

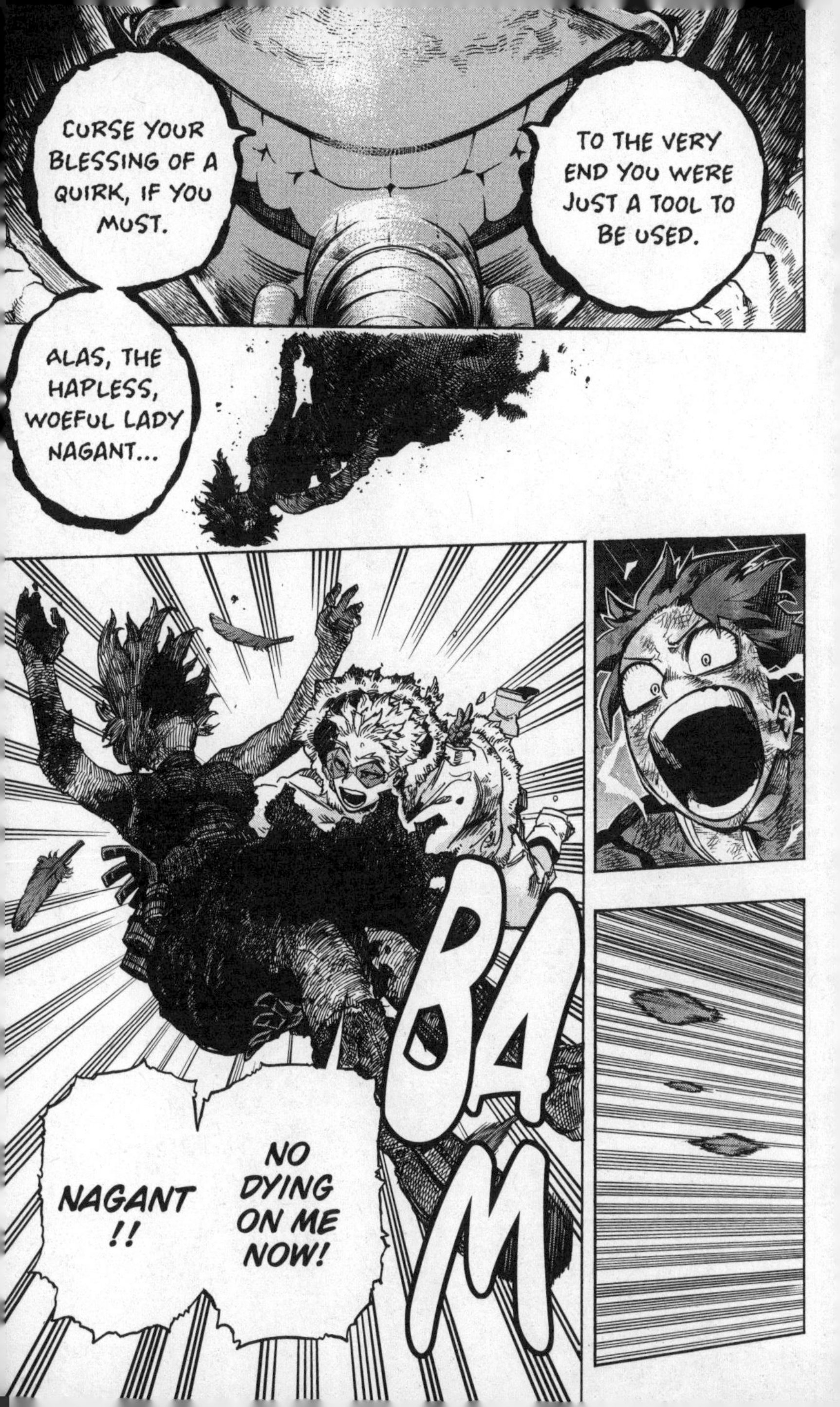

TO THE VERY END YOU WERE JUST A TOOL TO BE USED.
CURSE YOUR BLESSING OF A QUIRK, IF YOU MUST.
ALAS, THE HAPLESS, WOEFUL LADY NAGANT...
BAM
NAGANT !!
NO DYING ON ME NOW!

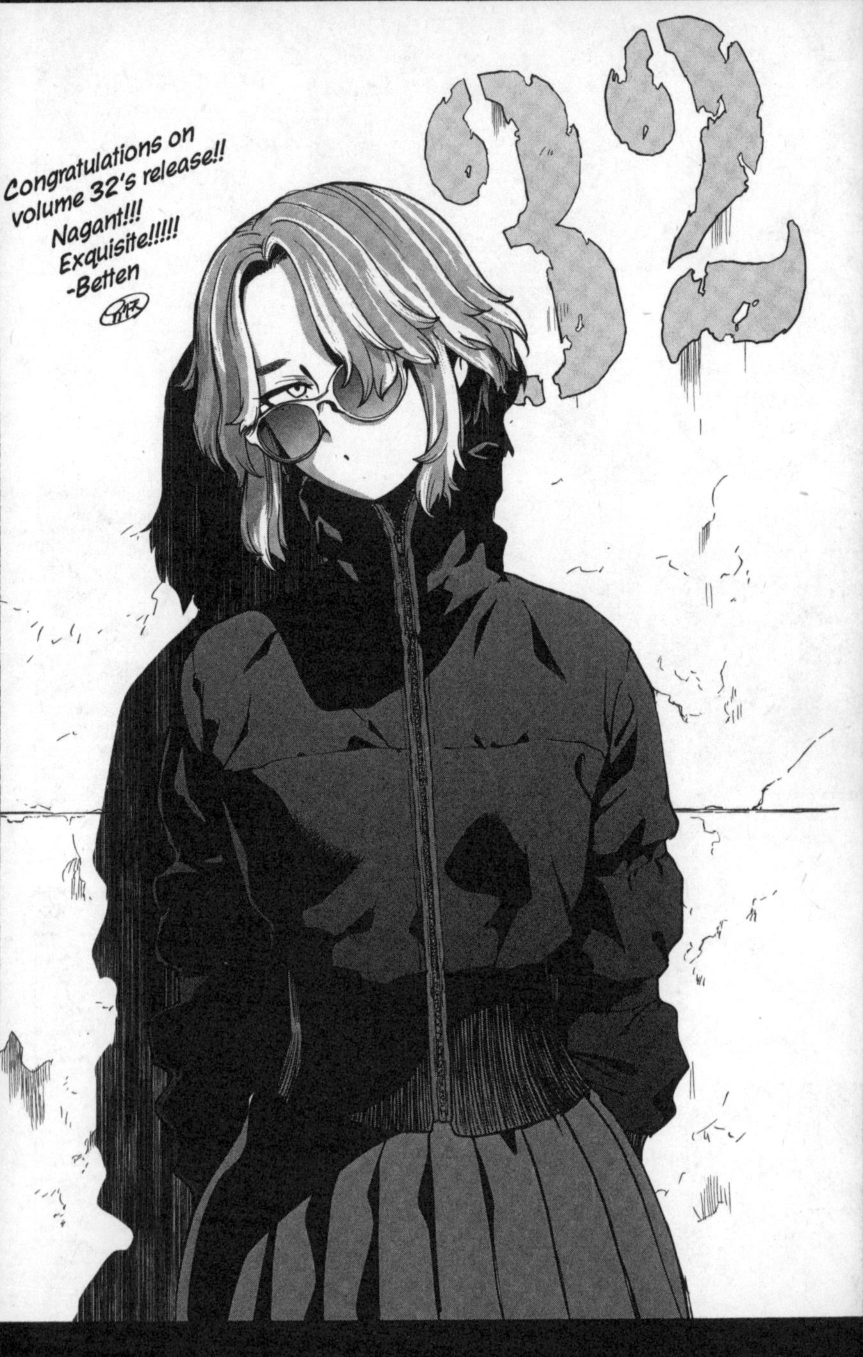
Congratulations on
volume 32's release!!
Nagant!!!
Exquisite!!!!!
-Betten
32

No. 316 - Your Turn

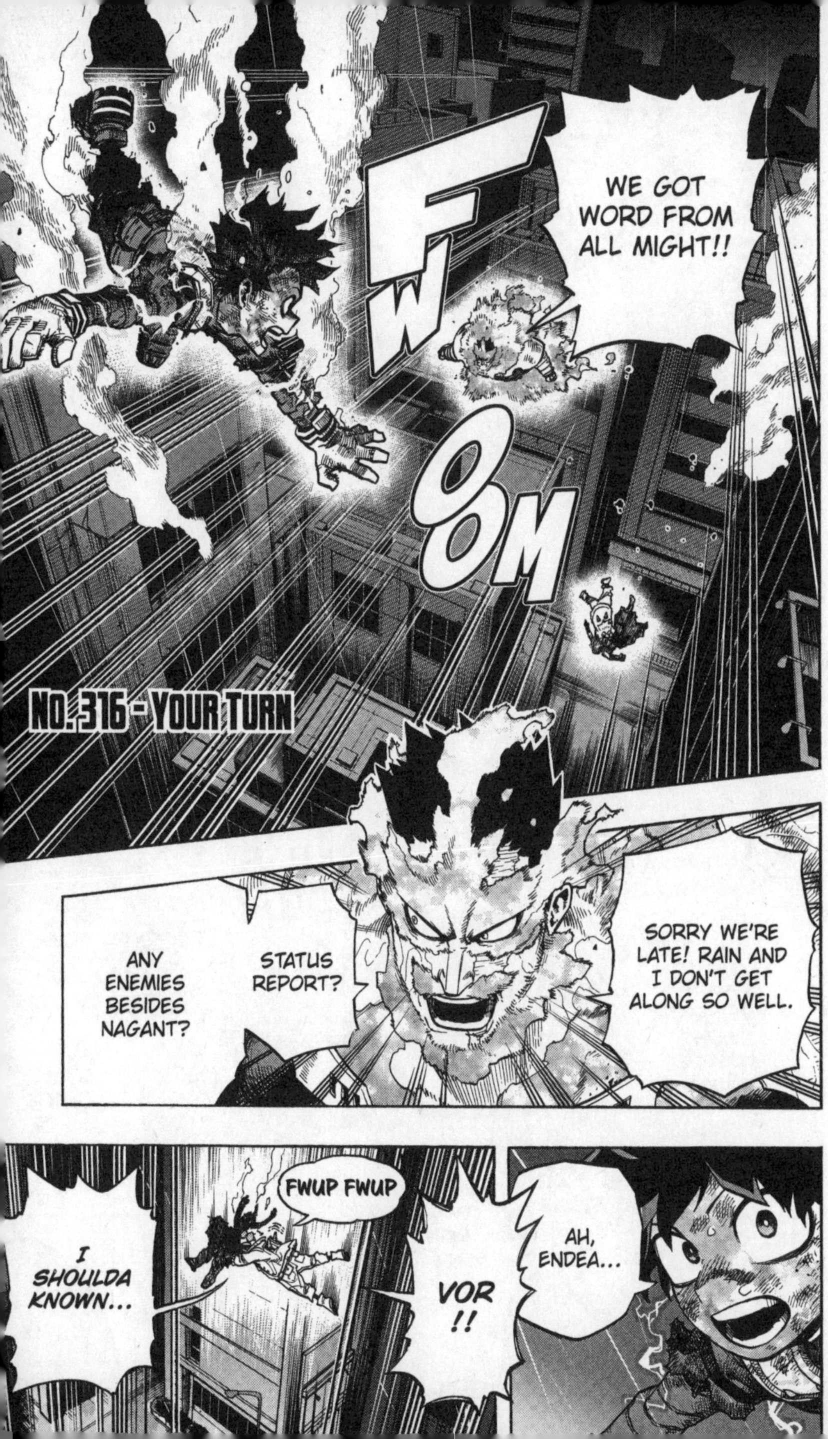
FWOOM
WE GOT WORD FROM ALL MIGHT!!
SORRY WE'RE LATE! RAIN AND I DON'T GET ALONG SO WELL.
STATUS REPORT?
ANY ENEMIES BESIDES NAGANT?
AH, ENDEA...
VOR!!
FWUP FWUP
I SHOULDA KNOWN...

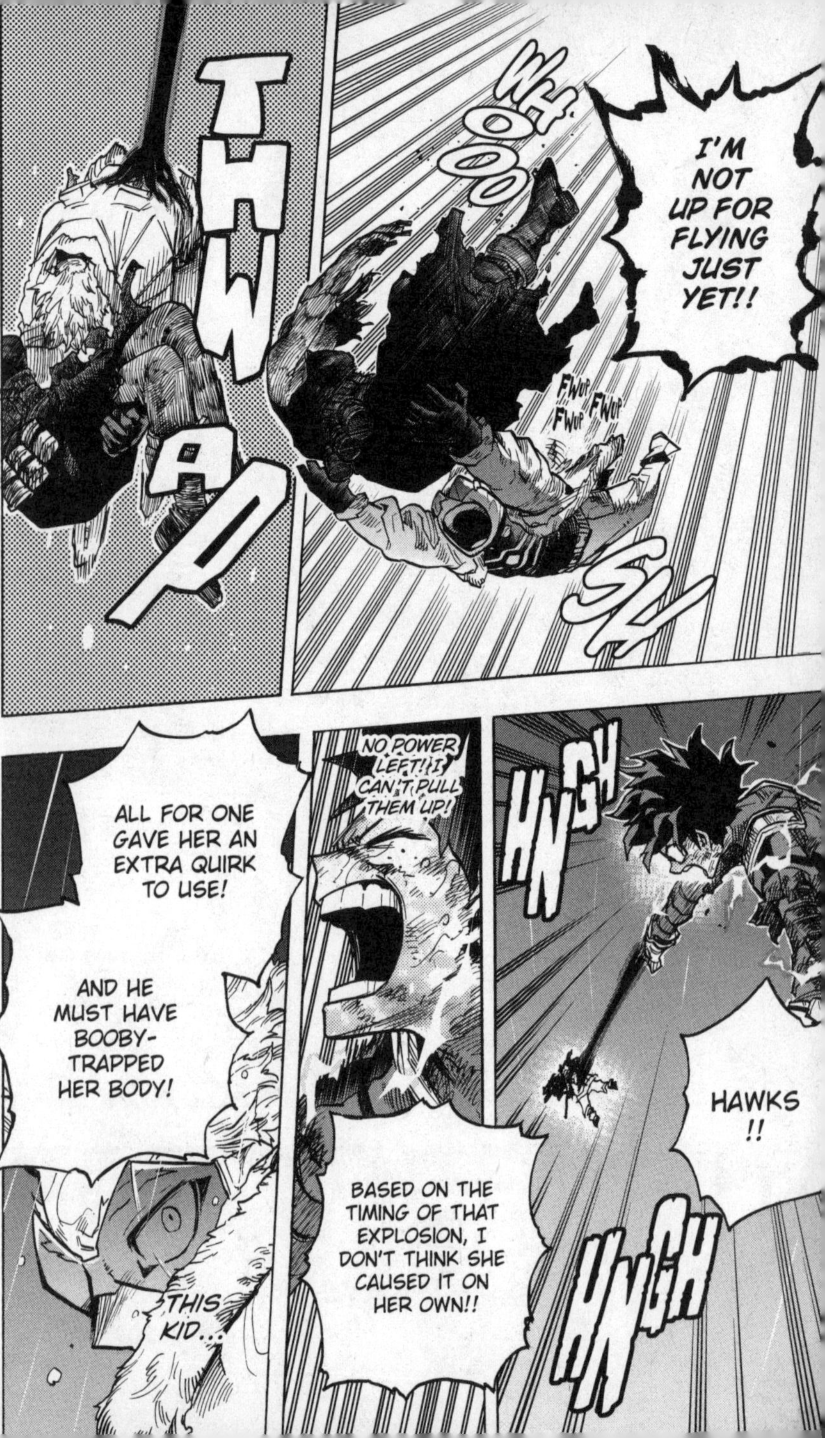
WHOOOO
I'M NOT UP FOR FLYING JUST YET!!
FWUP FWUP FWUP
SHH
THWAP
HNGH
HAWKS !!
HNGH
NO POWER LEFT!! I CAN'T PULL THEM UP!
BASED ON THE TIMING OF THAT EXPLOSION, I DON'T THINK SHE CAUSED IT ON HER OWN!!
ALL FOR ONE GAVE HER AN EXTRA QUIRK TO USE!
AND HE MUST HAVE BOOBY-TRAPPED HER BODY!
THIS KID...

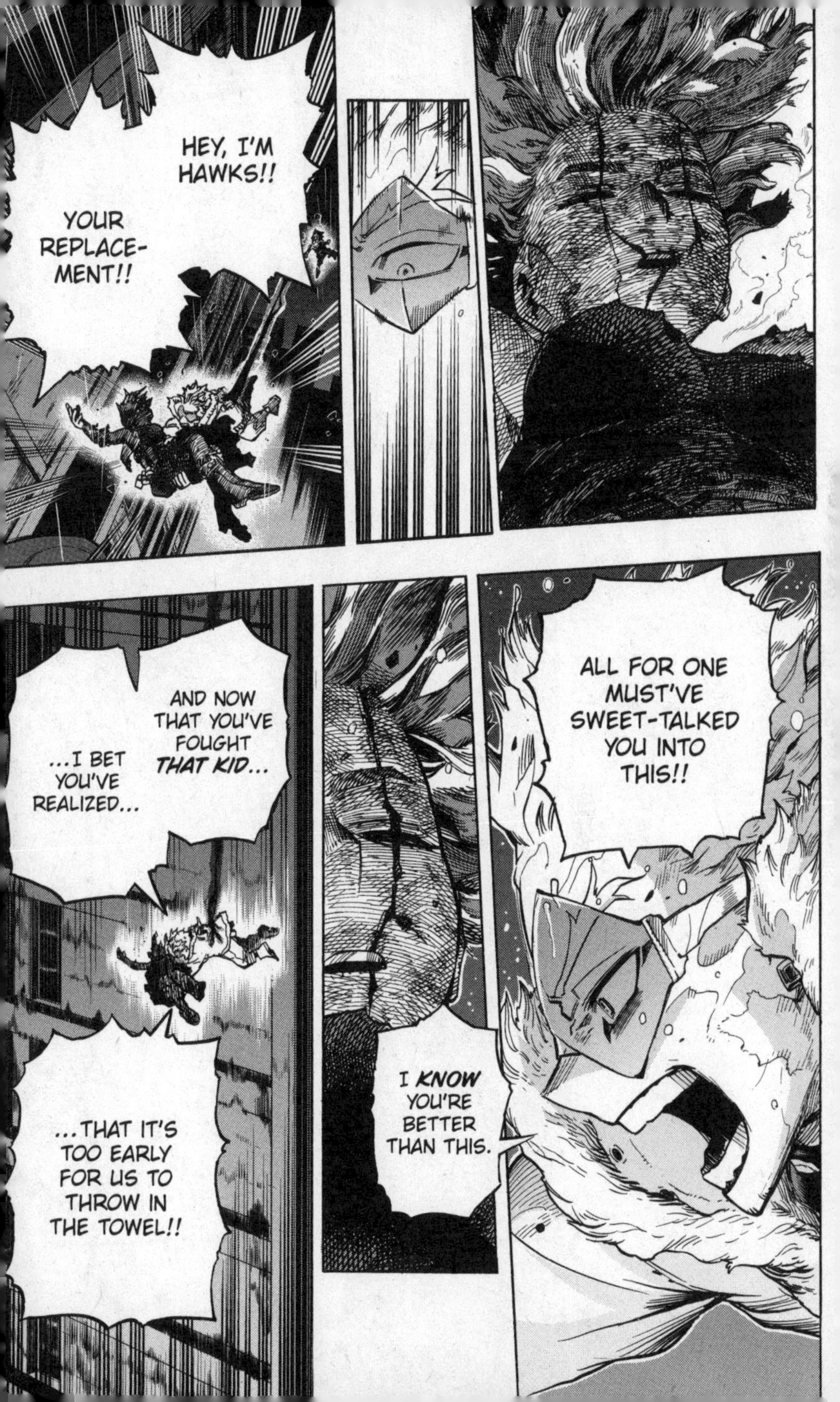

HEY, I'M HAWKS!!
YOUR REPLACE-MENT!!
ALL FOR ONE MUST'VE SWEET-TALKED YOU INTO THIS!!
I *KNOW* YOU'RE BETTER THAN THIS.
AND NOW THAT YOU'VE FOUGHT *THAT KID*...
...I BET YOU'VE REALIZED...
...THAT IT'S TOO EARLY FOR US TO THROW IN THE TOWEL!!

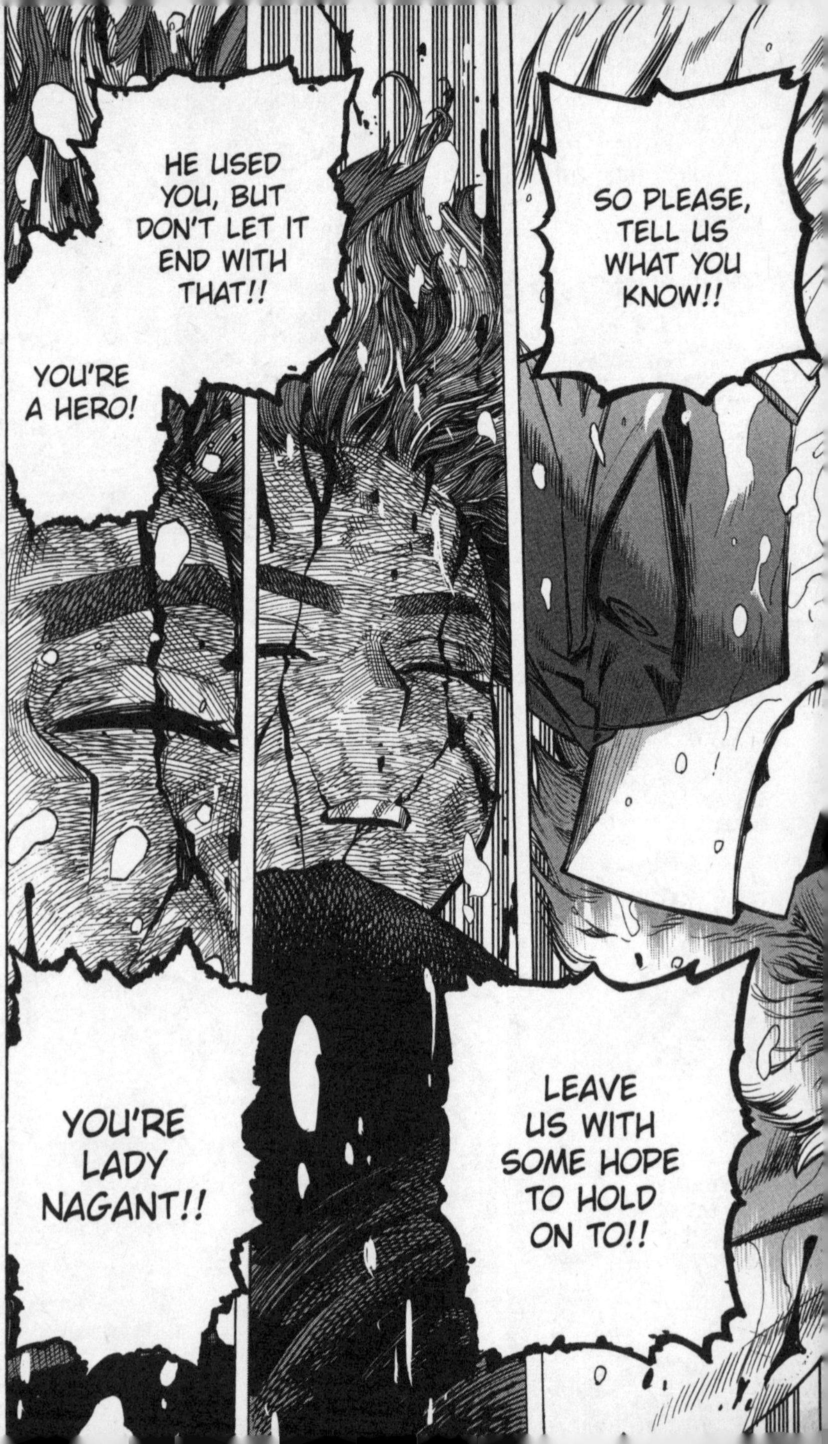

SO PLEASE, TELL US WHAT YOU KNOW!!
HE USED YOU, BUT DON'T LET IT END WITH THAT!!
YOU'RE A HERO!
LEAVE US WITH SOME HOPE TO HOLD ON TO!!
YOU'RE LADY NAGANT!!

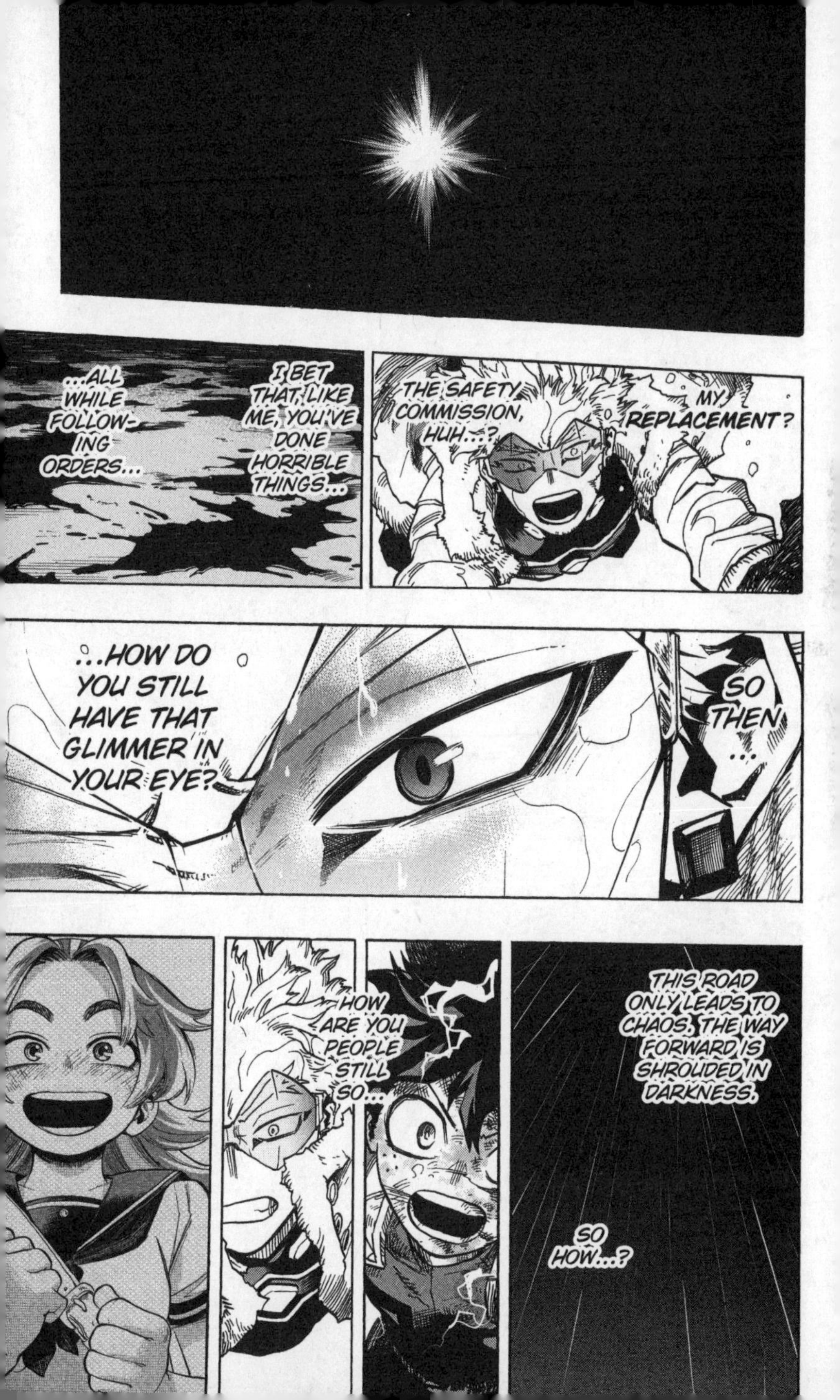

MY REPLACEMENT?
THE SAFETY COMMISSION, HUH...?
I BET THAT, LIKE ME, YOU'VE DONE HORRIBLE THINGS...
...ALL WHILE FOLLOWING ORDERS...
SO THEN...
...HOW DO YOU STILL HAVE THAT GLIMMER IN YOUR EYE?
THIS ROAD ONLY LEADS TO CHAOS. THE WAY FORWARD IS SHROUDED IN DARKNESS.
SO HOW...?
HOW ARE YOU PEOPLE STILL SO...

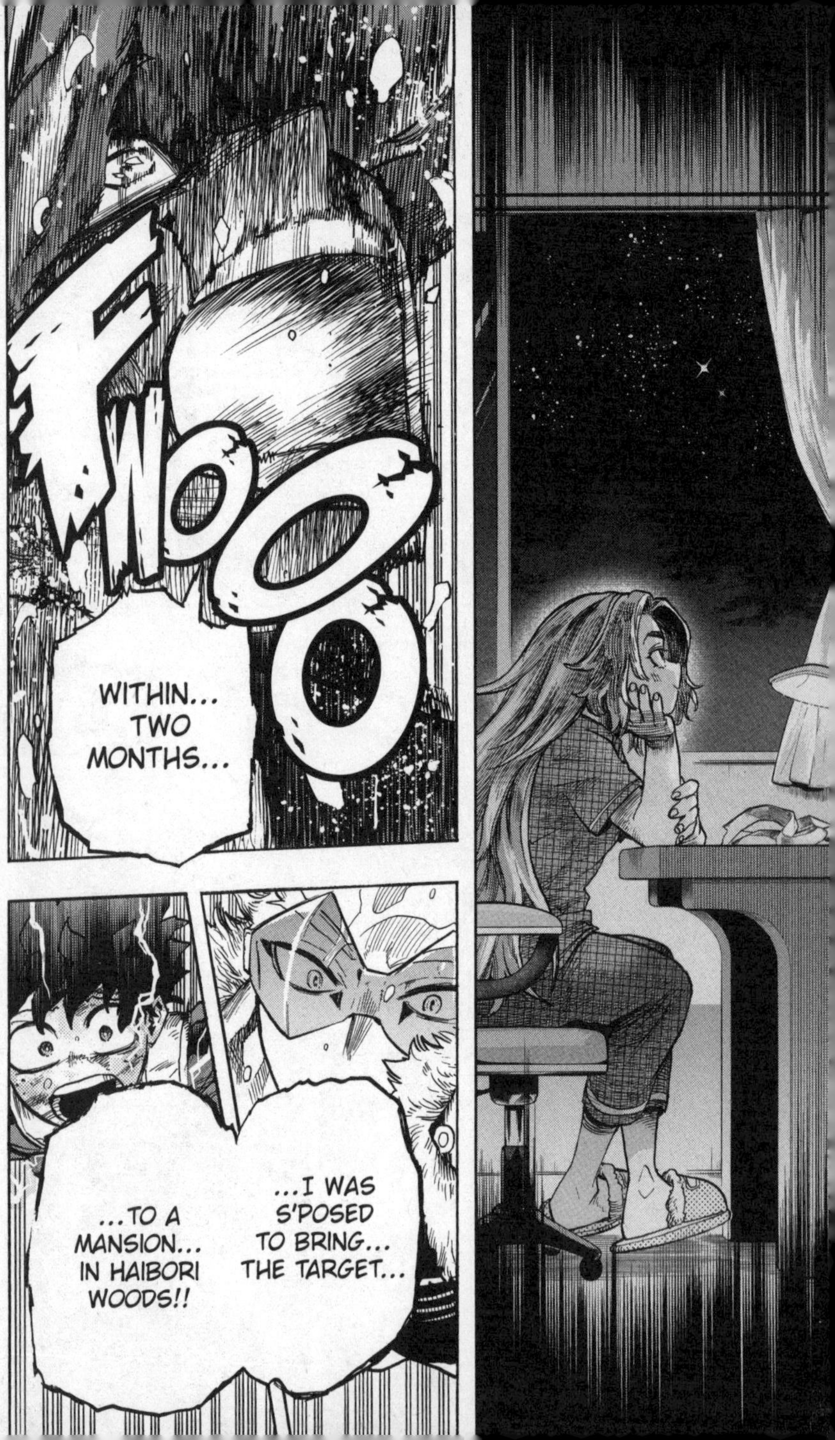
FWOOO
WITHIN... TWO MONTHS...
...I WAS S'POSED TO BRING... THE TARGET...
...TO A MANSION... IN HAIBORI WOODS!!

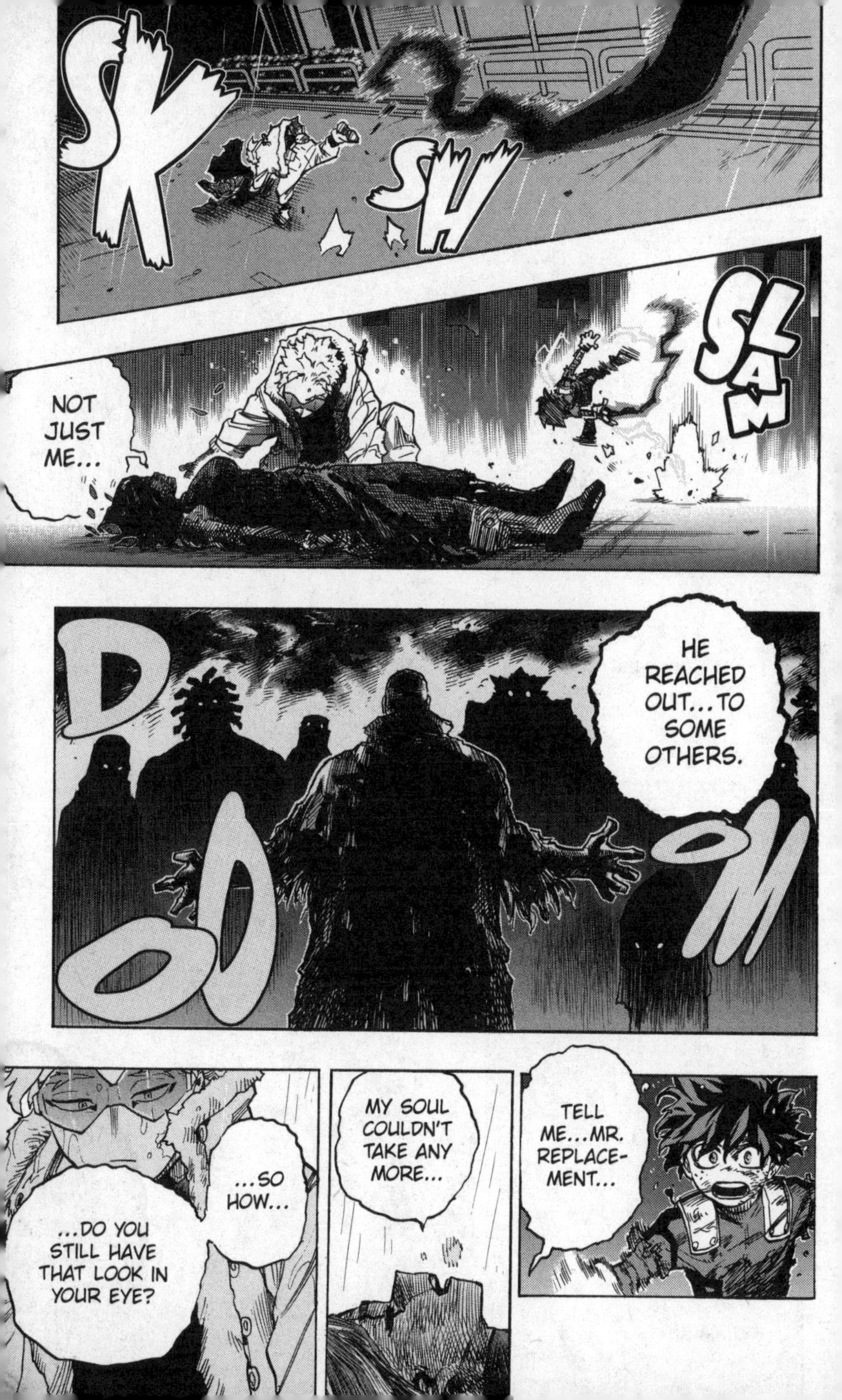
SK
SH
SLAM
NOT JUST ME...
HE REACHED OUT...TO SOME OTHERS.
DOOM
TELL ME...MR. REPLACE-MENT...
MY SOUL COULDN'T TAKE ANY MORE...
...SO HOW...
...DO YOU STILL HAVE THAT LOOK IN YOUR EYE?

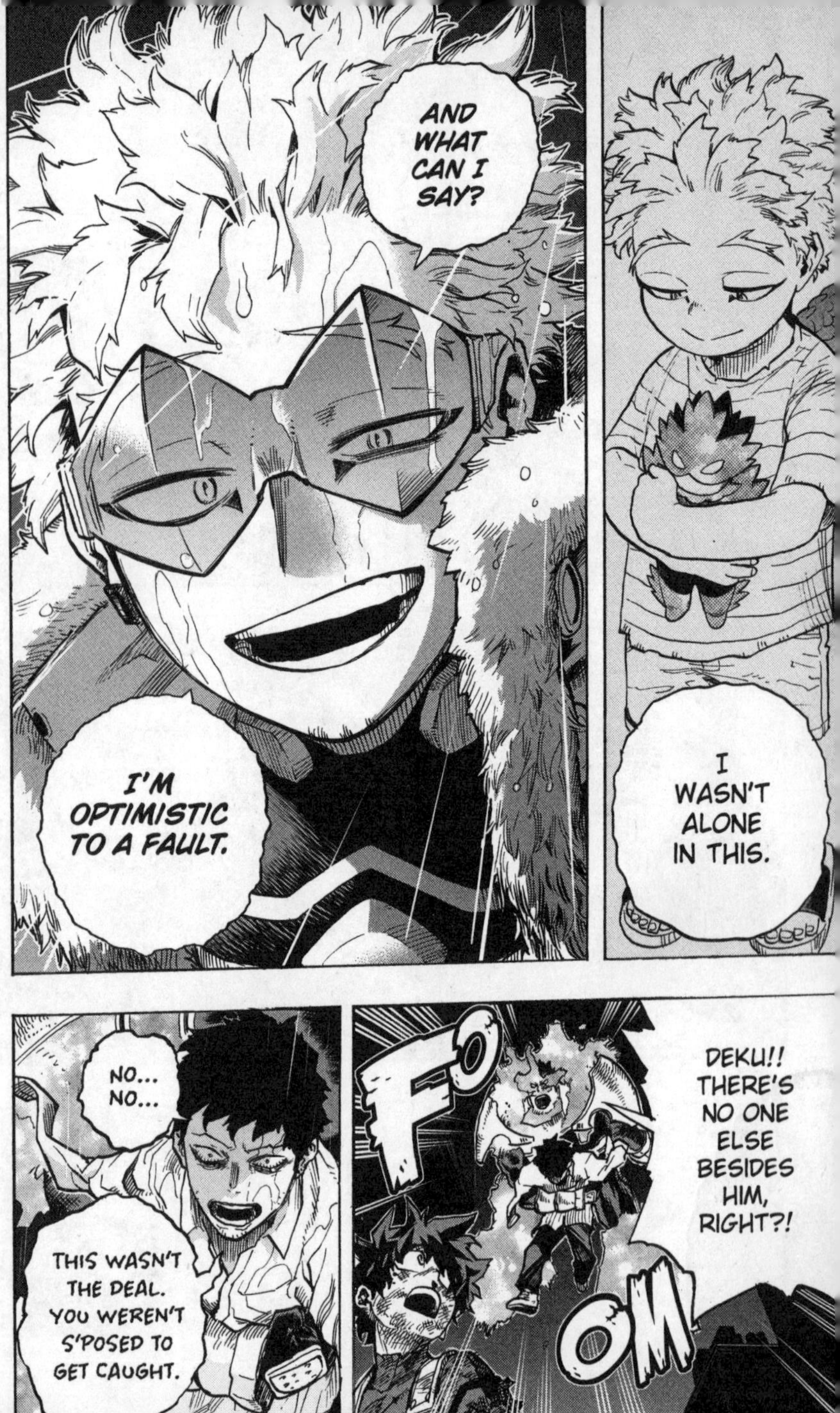
I WASN'T ALONE IN THIS.
AND WHAT CAN I SAY?
I'M OPTIMISTIC TO A FAULT.
FO
OM
DEKU!! THERE'S NO ONE ELSE BESIDES HIM, RIGHT?!
NO... NO...
THIS WASN'T THE DEAL. YOU WEREN'T S'POSED TO GET CAUGHT.

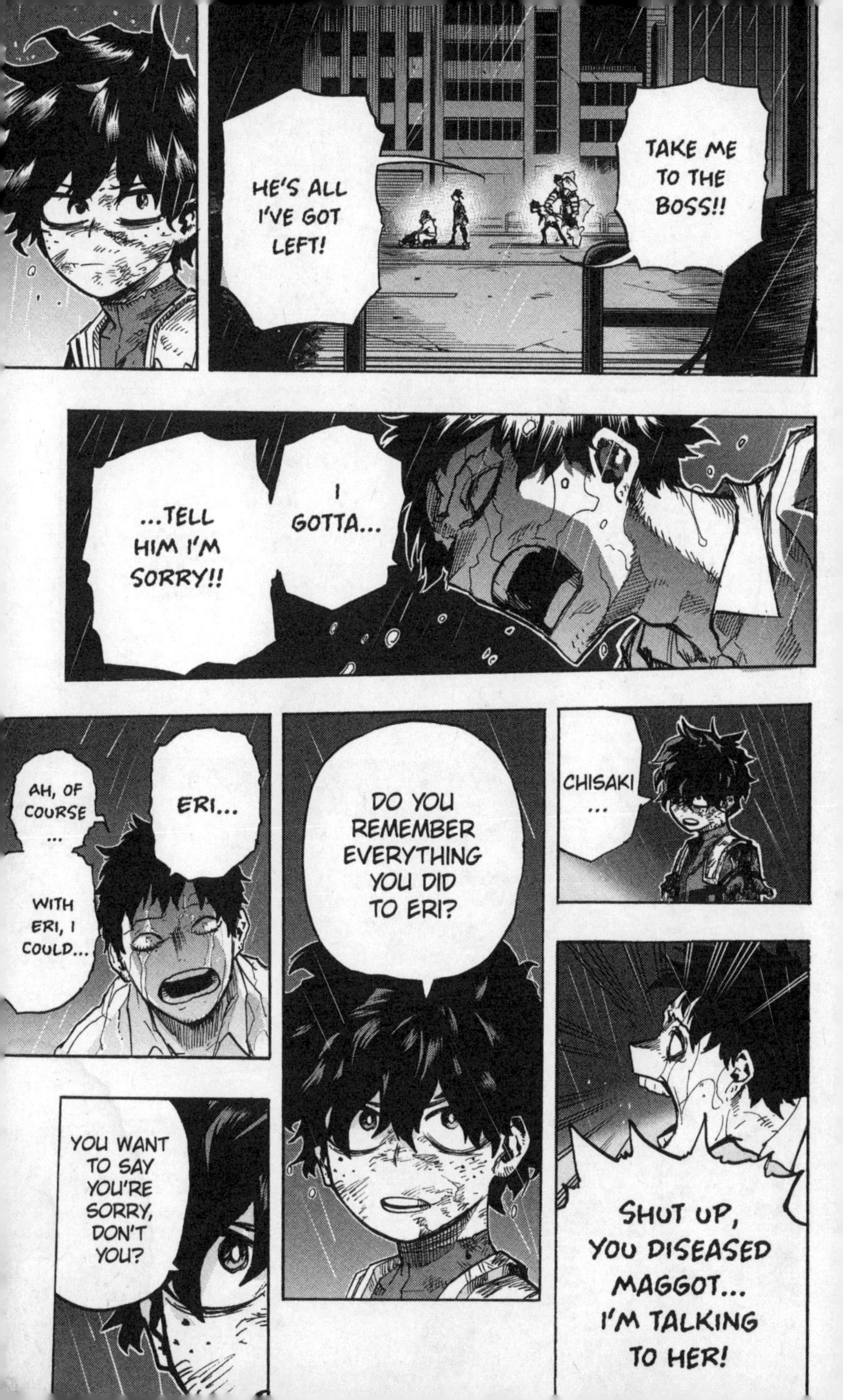
TAKE ME TO THE BOSS!!
HE'S ALL I'VE GOT LEFT!
I GOTTA...
...TELL HIM I'M SORRY!!
CHISAKI ...
SHUT UP, YOU DISEASED MAGGOT... I'M TALKING TO HER!
DO YOU REMEMBER EVERYTHING YOU DID TO ERI?
ERI...
AH, OF COURSE ...
WITH ERI, I COULD...
YOU WANT TO SAY YOU'RE SORRY, DON'T YOU?

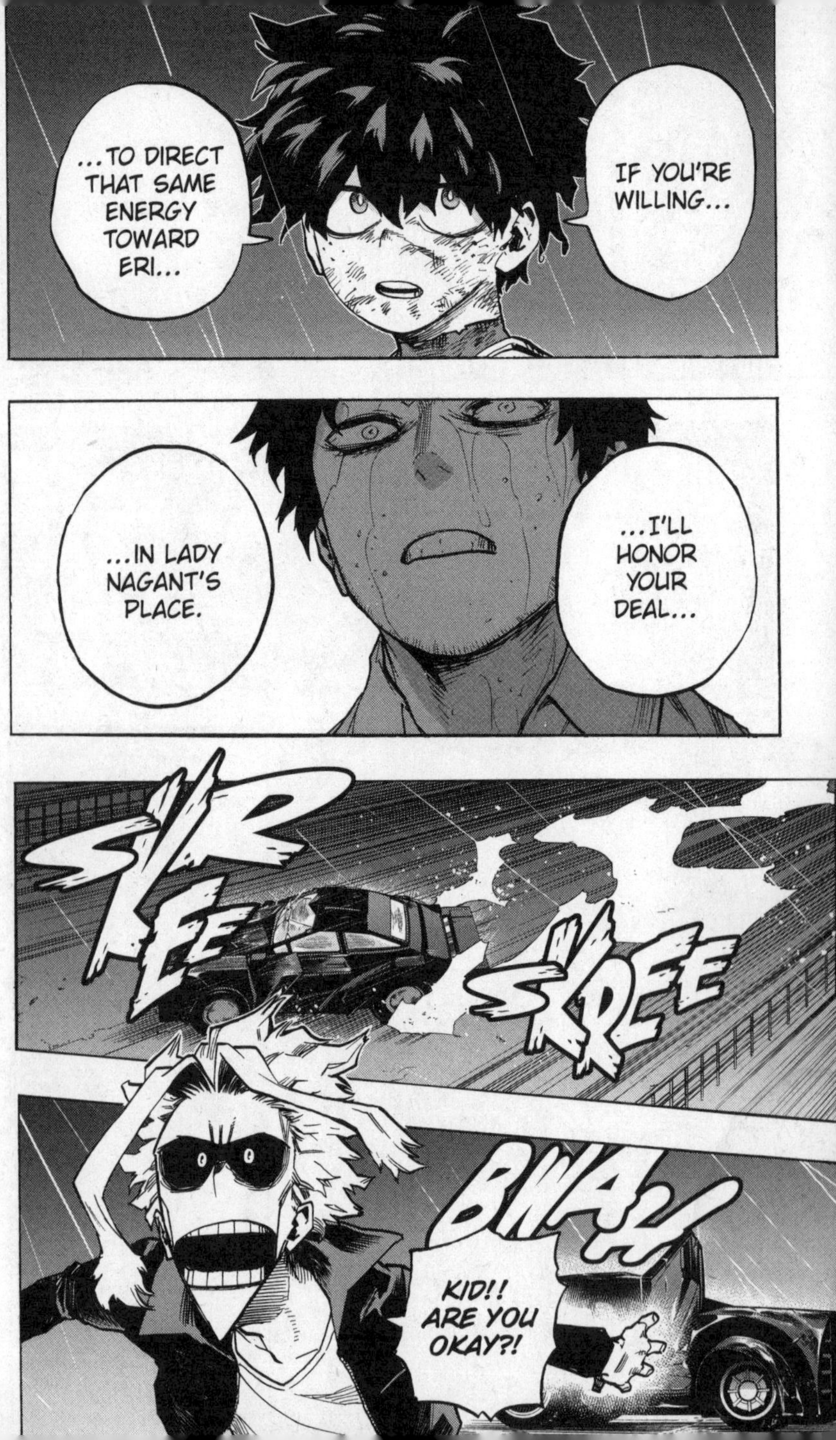
IF YOU'RE WILLING...
...TO DIRECT THAT SAME ENERGY TOWARD ERI...
...I'LL HONOR YOUR DEAL...
...IN LADY NAGANT'S PLACE.
SKREE
KID!! ARE YOU OKAY?!

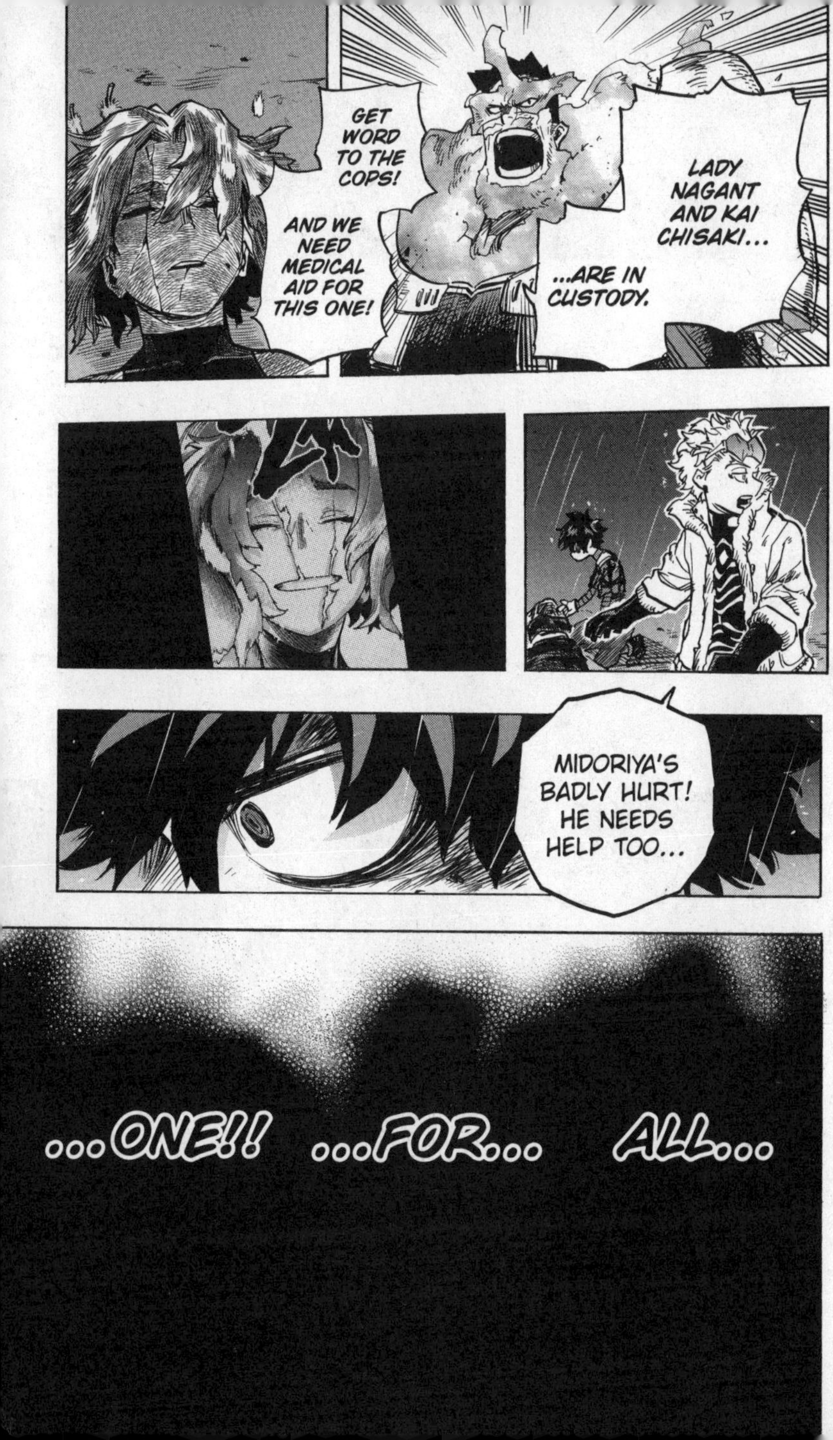
LADY NAGANT AND KAI CHISAKI...
...ARE IN CUSTODY.
GET WORD TO THE COPS!
AND WE NEED MEDICAL AID FOR THIS ONE!
MIDORIYA'S BADLY HURT! HE NEEDS HELP TOO...
ALL...
...FOR...
...ONE!!

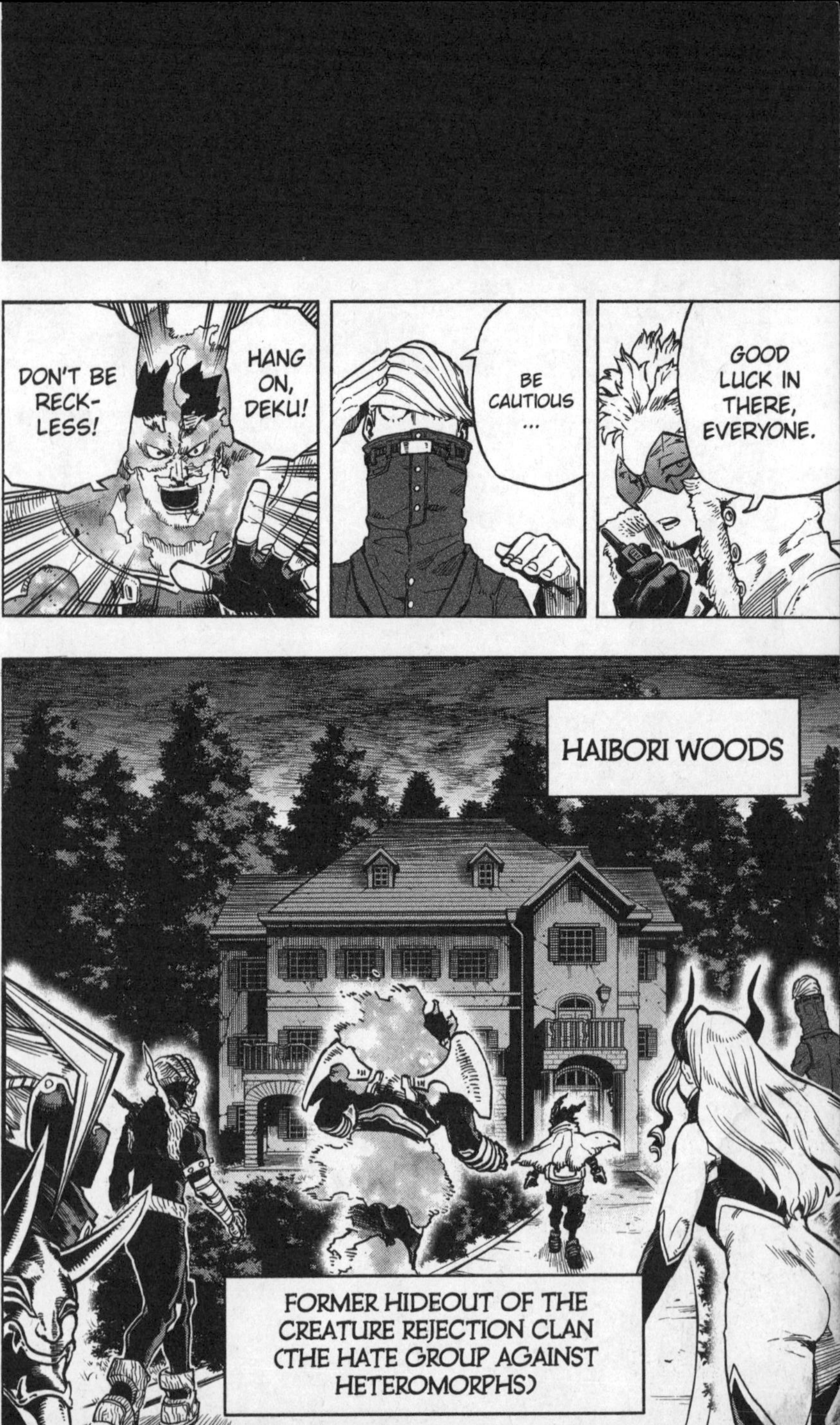
GOOD LUCK IN THERE, EVERYONE.
BE CAUTIOUS ...
HANG ON, DEKU!
DON'T BE RECK-LESS!
HAIBORI WOODS
FORMER HIDEOUT OF THE CREATURE REJECTION CLAN (THE HATE GROUP AGAINST HETEROMORPHS)

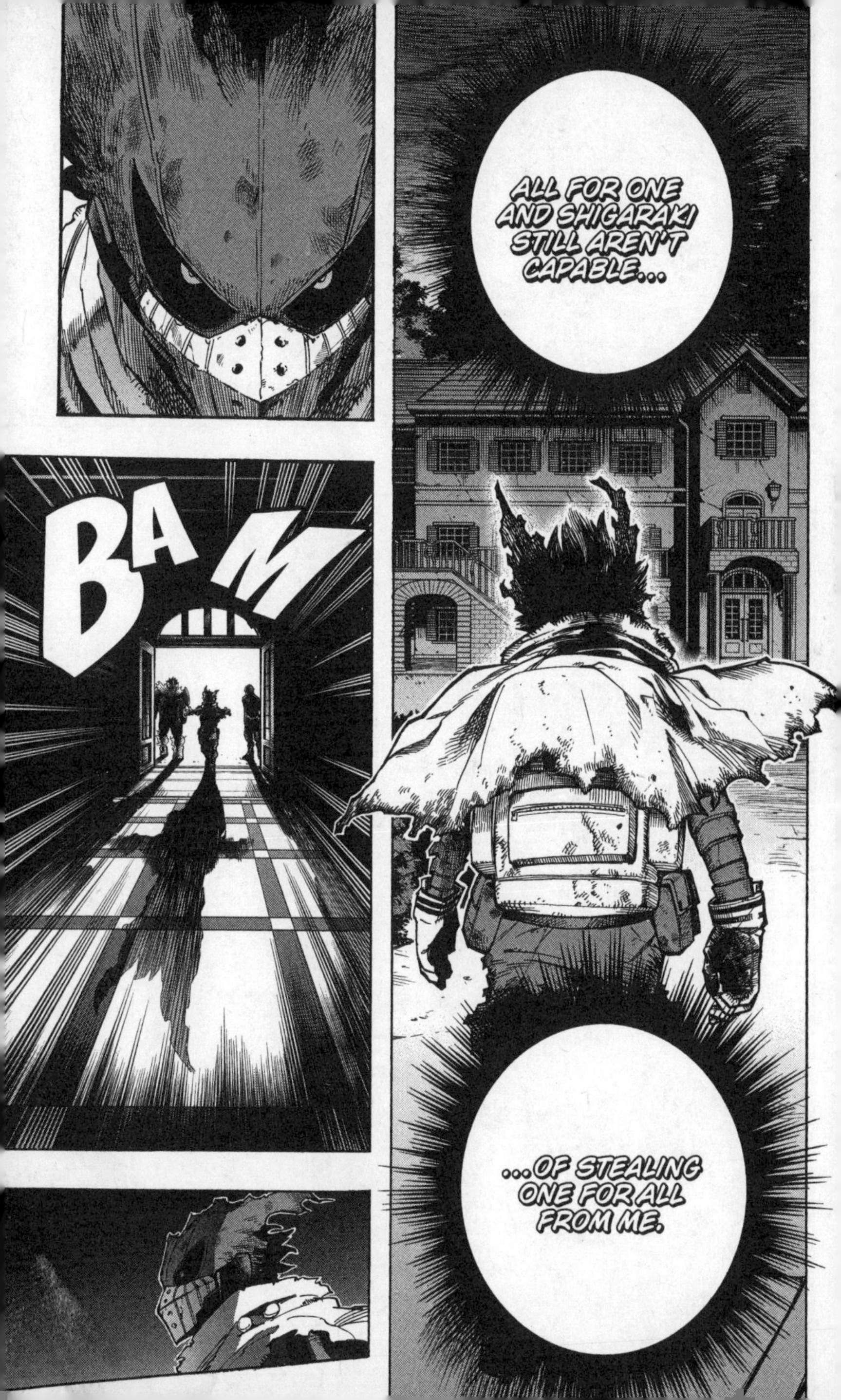
ALL FOR ONE AND SHIGARAKI STILL AREN'T CAPABLE...
...OF STEALING ONE FOR ALL FROM ME.
BAM

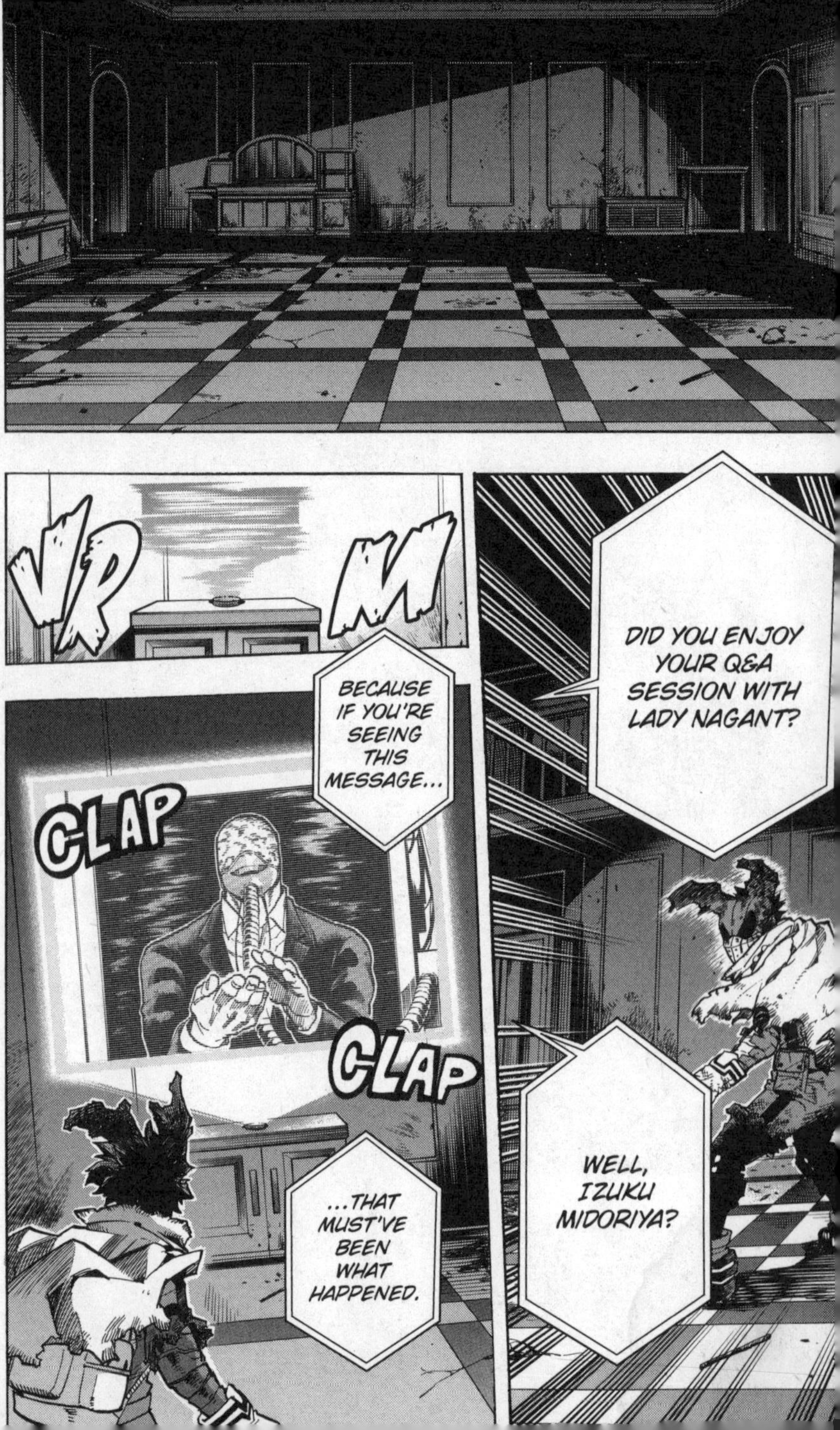
DID YOU ENJOY YOUR Q&A SESSION WITH LADY NAGANT?
WELL, IZUKU MIDORIYA?
VRM
BECAUSE IF YOU'RE SEEING THIS MESSAGE...
CLAP
CLAP
...THAT MUST'VE BEEN WHAT HAPPENED.

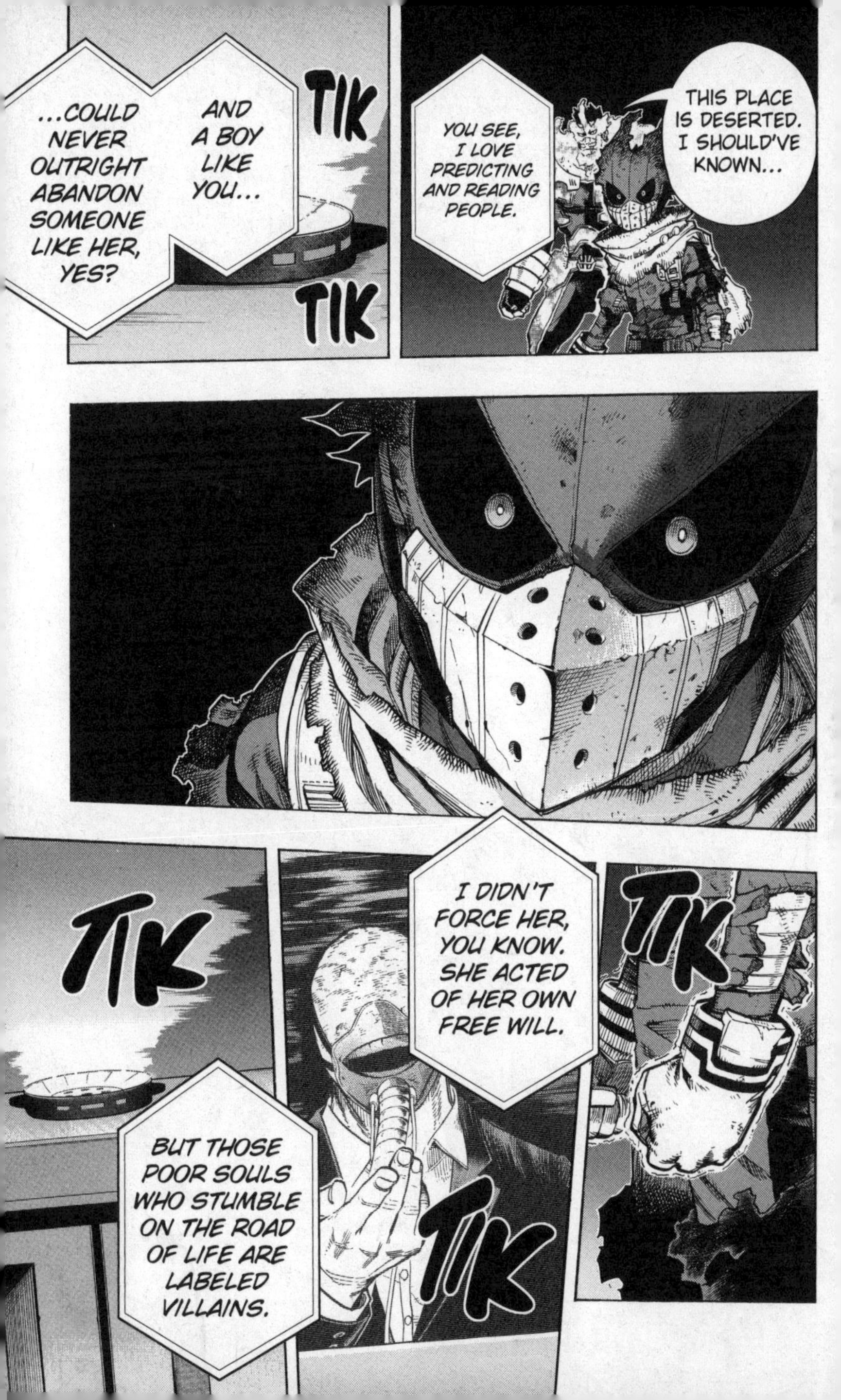
THIS PLACE IS DESERTED. I SHOULD'VE KNOWN...
YOU SEE, I LOVE PREDICTING AND READING PEOPLE.
TIK
TIK
AND A BOY LIKE YOU...
...COULD NEVER OUTRIGHT ABANDON SOMEONE LIKE HER, YES?
TIK
I DIDN'T FORCE HER, YOU KNOW. SHE ACTED OF HER OWN FREE WILL.
BUT THOSE POOR SOULS WHO STUMBLE ON THE ROAD OF LIFE ARE LABELED VILLAINS.
TIK
TIK

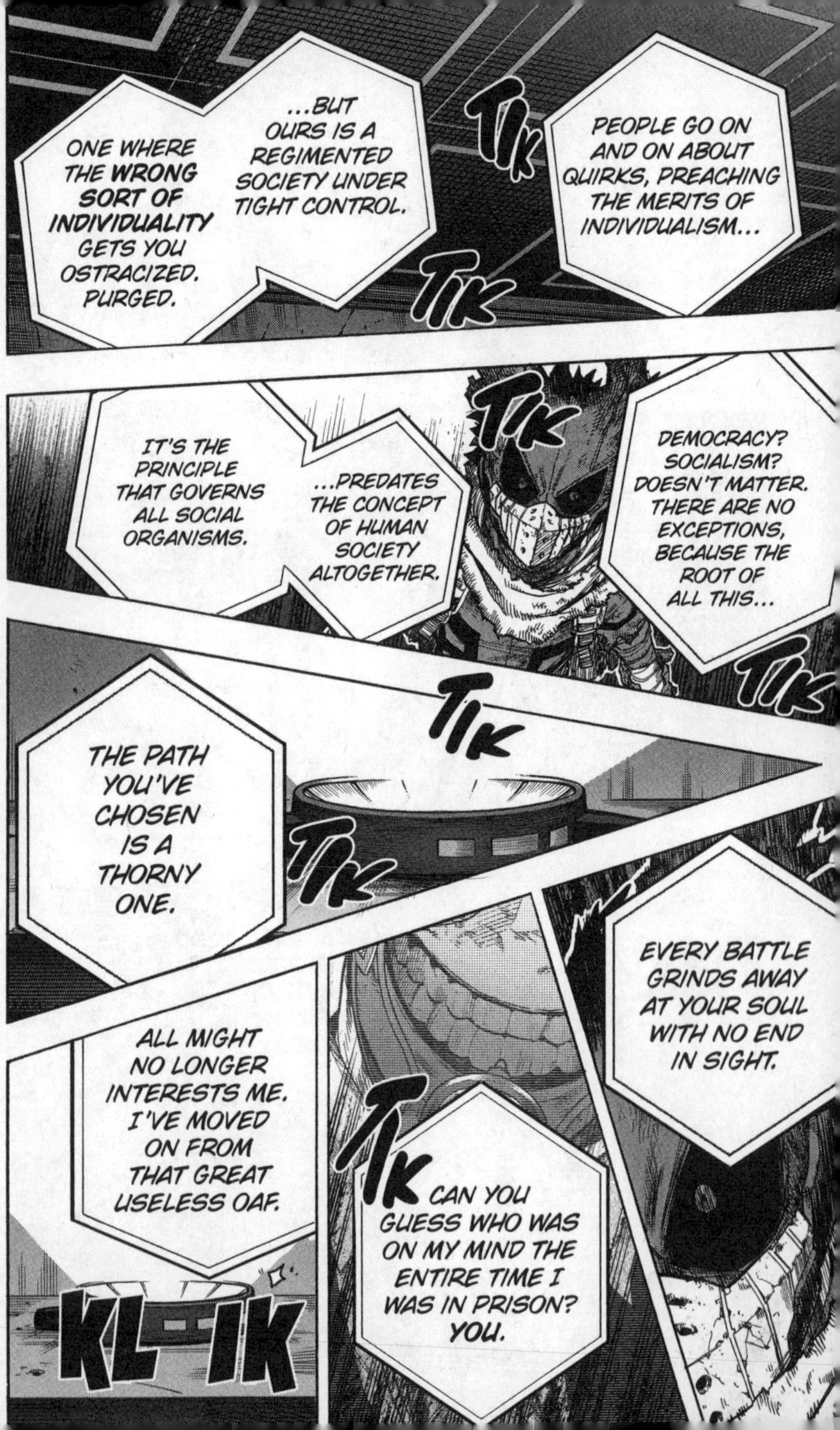
PEOPLE GO ON AND ON ABOUT QUIRKS, PREACHING THE MERITS OF INDIVIDUALISM...
TIK
...BUT OURS IS A REGIMENTED SOCIETY UNDER TIGHT CONTROL.
ONE WHERE THE **WRONG** SORT OF **INDIVIDUALITY** GETS YOU OSTRACIZED. PURGED.
TIK
DEMOCRACY? SOCIALISM? DOESN'T MATTER. THERE ARE NO EXCEPTIONS, BECAUSE THE ROOT OF ALL THIS...
TIK
...PREDATES THE CONCEPT OF HUMAN SOCIETY ALTOGETHER.
IT'S THE PRINCIPLE THAT GOVERNS ALL SOCIAL ORGANISMS.
TIK
TIK
THE PATH YOU'VE CHOSEN IS A THORNY ONE.
TIK
EVERY BATTLE GRINDS AWAY AT YOUR SOUL WITH NO END IN SIGHT.
TIK
CAN YOU GUESS WHO WAS ON MY MIND THE ENTIRE TIME I WAS IN PRISON? **YOU.**
ALL MIGHT NO LONGER INTERESTS ME. I'VE MOVED ON FROM THAT GREAT USELESS OAF.
KL-IK

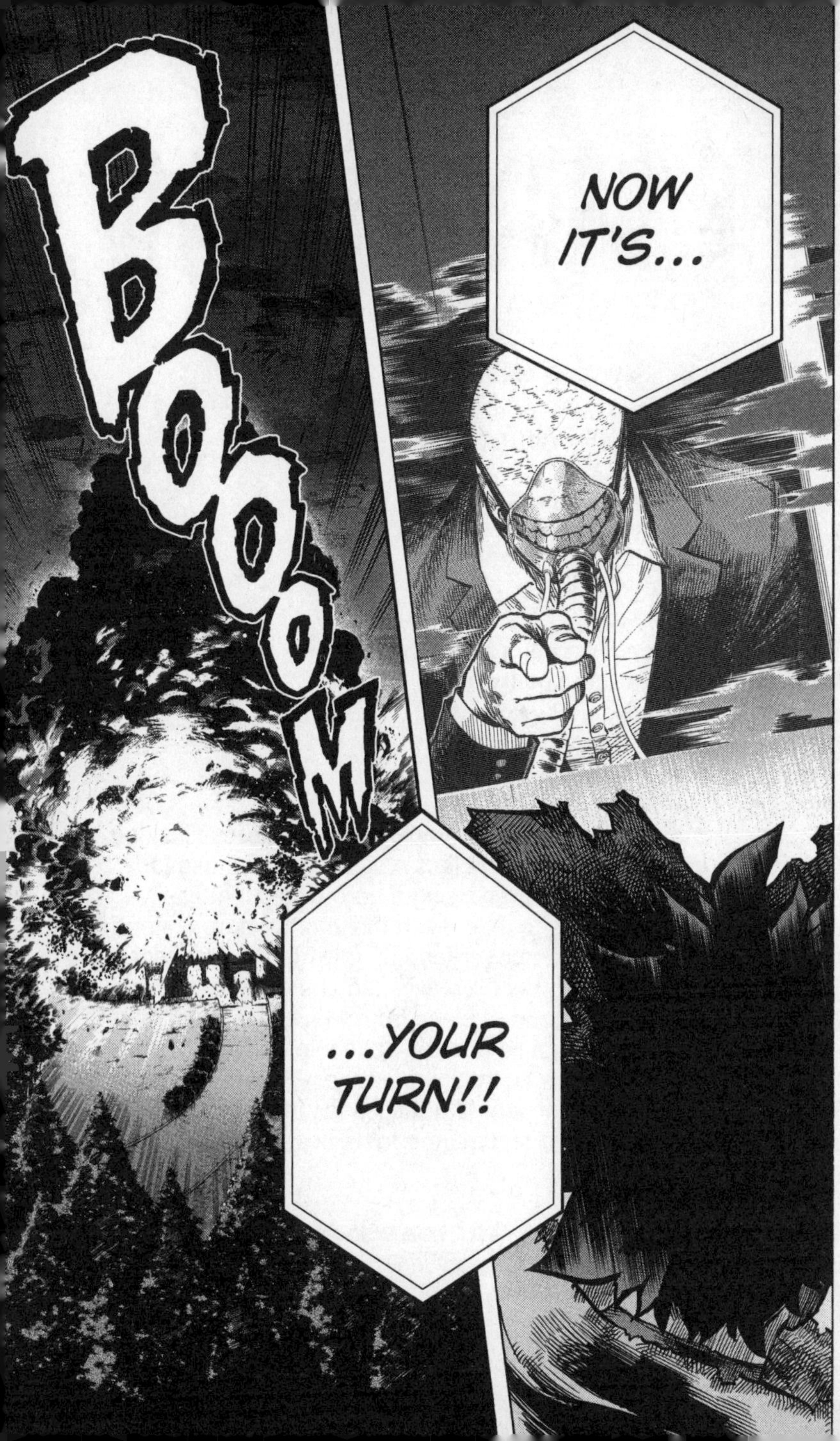
NOW IT'S...
...YOUR TURN!!
BOOOM

THE LADY NAGANT

I could fill an entire volume with Nagant's full backstory, so what you see here is the abridged version.

The decision to imprison Nagant instead of just killing her off was made by the next commission president (pictured on the right).

Madam President. First appeared in volume 20. Got taken out by that copy of Re-Destro in volume 31.

The former president was prone to using people and discarding them, since even before Nagant's time. At first, he made use of shady underworld characters to do the dirty work, but as criminalistic heroes became more frequent, started teaming up, and employing sneakier tactics, the underworld people were less and less able to handle those jobs. That's why the president started using a hero who could easily maneuver through society to take down those other heroes gone bad. Madam President was never fond of how her predecessor played fast and loose with people's lives, so she decided to spare Nagant, throw her in Tartarus (a place from which info could never leak), and cover it up with a lie about a squabble between heroes. In order to prevent another such failure, Madam President set her sights on Takami Keigo as Nagant's successor, since from a young age, he could be educated and trained to dedicate his life to the mission.

Once this series is over, I'd like to write a short story called "The Lovely Lady Nagant: The Brightest Caged Star." It'll probably never happen. Why not? Because I'm exhausted and need to sleep!

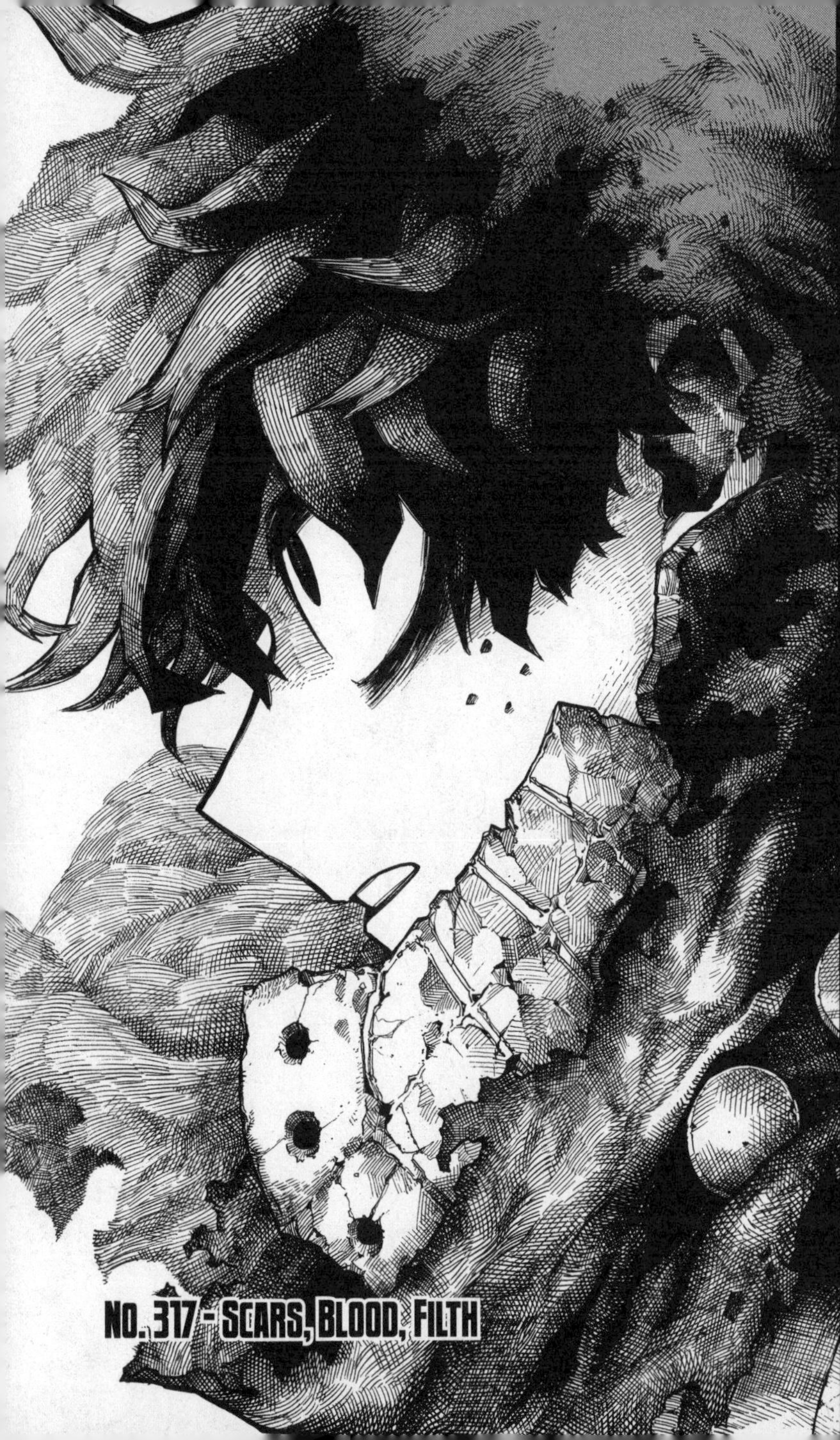
No. 317 - Scars, Blood, Filth

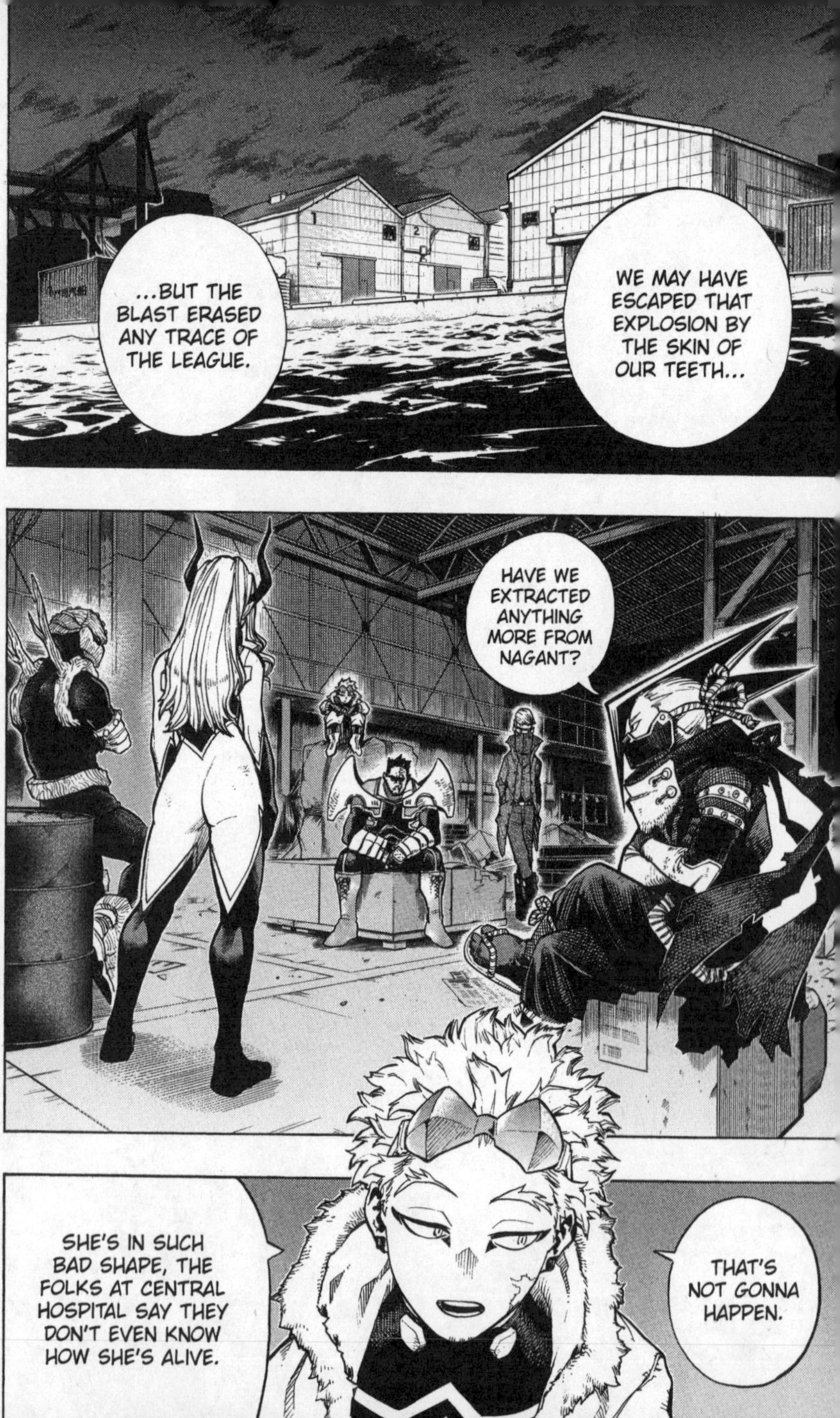
WE MAY HAVE ESCAPED THAT EXPLOSION BY THE SKIN OF OUR TEETH...
...BUT THE BLAST ERASED ANY TRACE OF THE LEAGUE.
HAVE WE EXTRACTED ANYTHING MORE FROM NAGANT?
THAT'S NOT GONNA HAPPEN.
SHE'S IN SUCH BAD SHAPE, THE FOLKS AT CENTRAL HOSPITAL SAY THEY DON'T EVEN KNOW HOW SHE'S ALIVE.

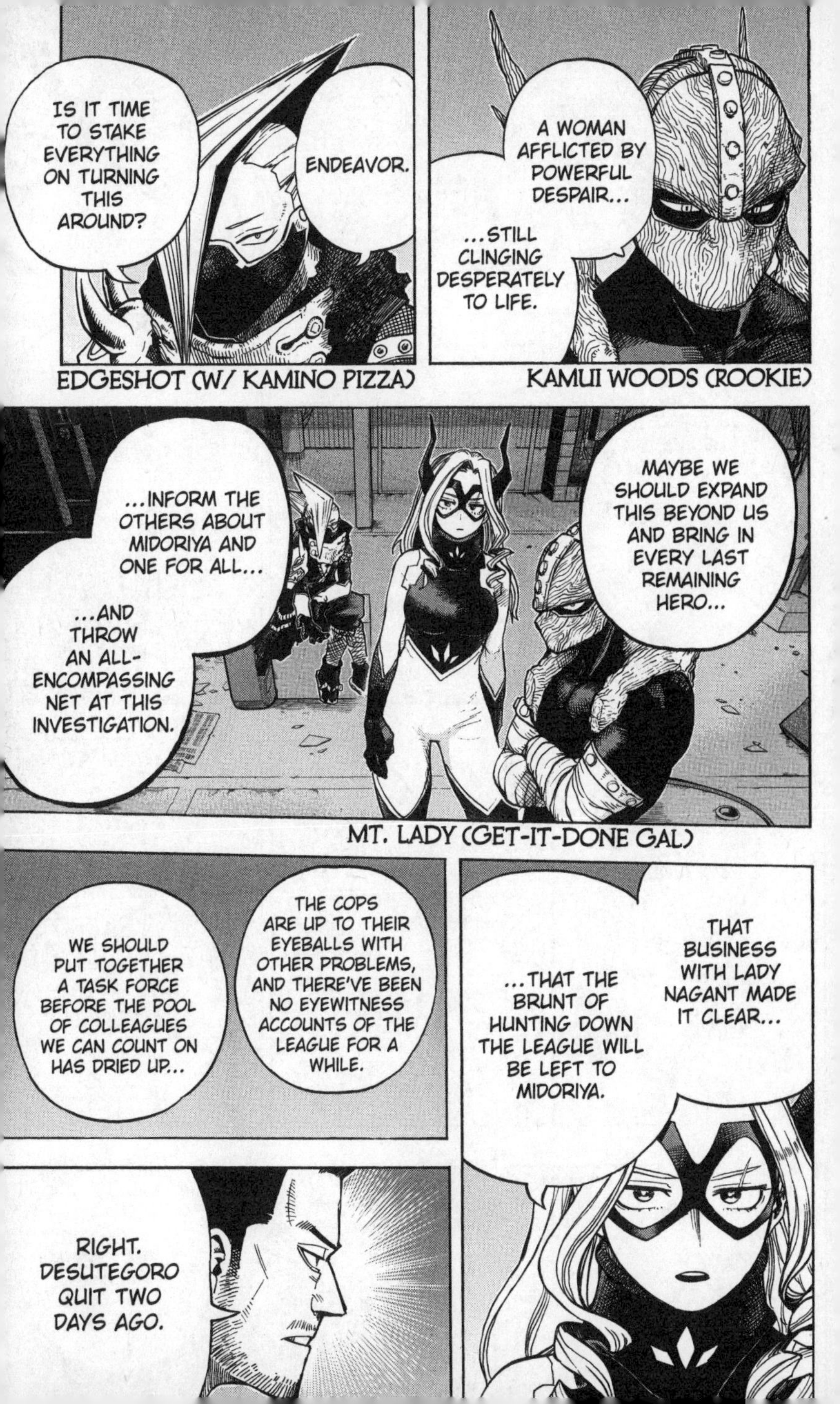

A WOMAN AFFLICTED BY POWERFUL DESPAIR...
...STILL CLINGING DESPERATELY TO LIFE.
KAMUI WOODS (ROOKIE)
ENDEAVOR.
IS IT TIME TO STAKE EVERYTHING ON TURNING THIS AROUND?
EDGESHOT (W/ KAMINO PIZZA)
MAYBE WE SHOULD EXPAND THIS BEYOND US AND BRING IN EVERY LAST REMAINING HERO...
...INFORM THE OTHERS ABOUT MIDORIYA AND ONE FOR ALL...
...AND THROW AN ALL-ENCOMPASSING NET AT THIS INVESTIGATION.
MT. LADY (GET-IT-DONE GAL)
THAT BUSINESS WITH LADY NAGANT MADE IT CLEAR...
...THAT THE BRUNT OF HUNTING DOWN THE LEAGUE WILL BE LEFT TO MIDORIYA.
THE COPS ARE UP TO THEIR EYEBALLS WITH OTHER PROBLEMS, AND THERE'VE BEEN NO EYEWITNESS ACCOUNTS OF THE LEAGUE FOR A WHILE.
WE SHOULD PUT TOGETHER A TASK FORCE BEFORE THE POOL OF COLLEAGUES WE CAN COUNT ON HAS DRIED UP...
RIGHT. DESUTEGORO QUIT TWO DAYS AGO.

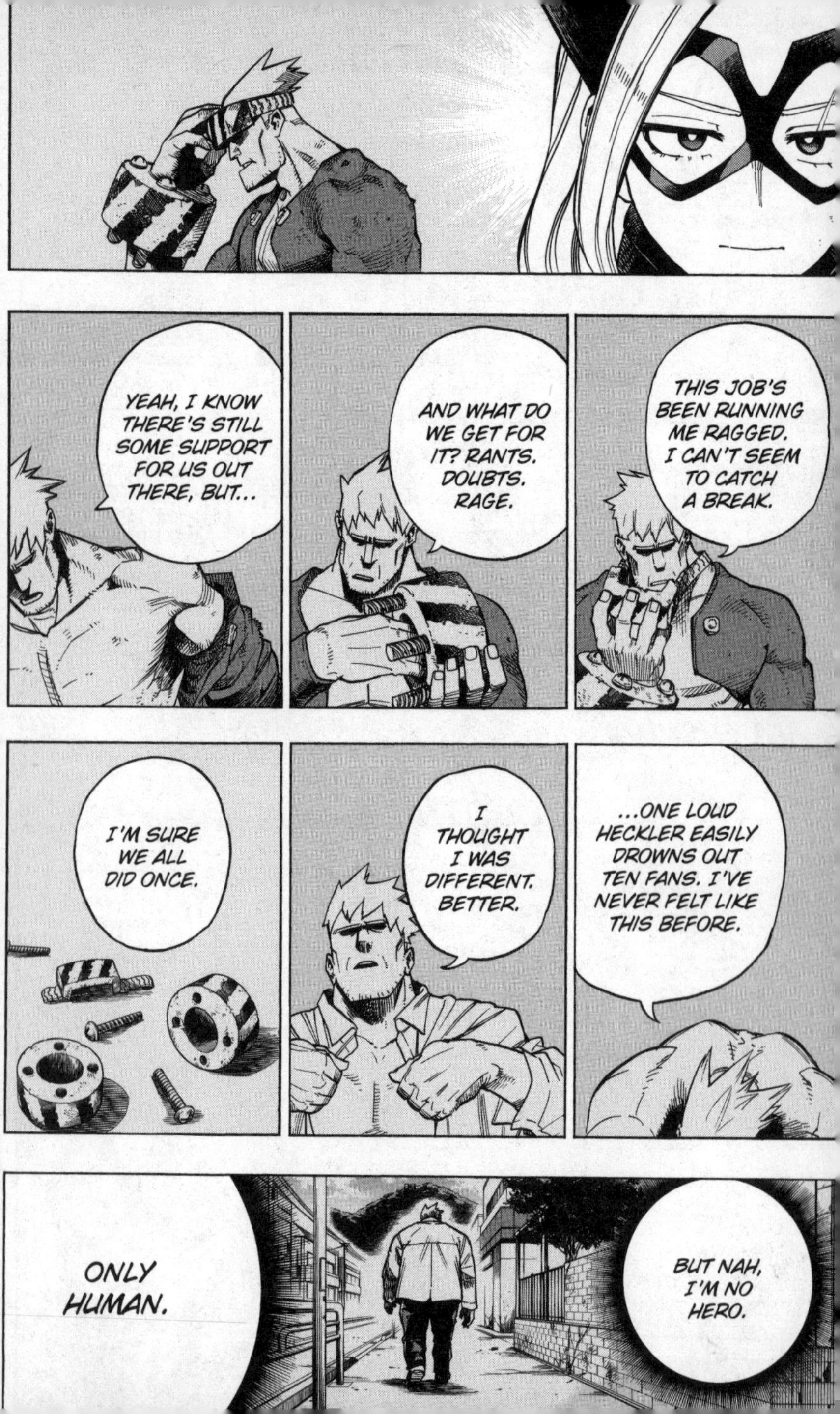
THIS JOB'S BEEN RUNNING ME RAGGED. I CAN'T SEEM TO CATCH A BREAK.
AND WHAT DO WE GET FOR IT? RANTS. DOUBTS. RAGE.
YEAH, I KNOW THERE'S STILL SOME SUPPORT FOR US OUT THERE, BUT...
...ONE LOUD HECKLER EASILY DROWNS OUT TEN FANS. I'VE NEVER FELT LIKE THIS BEFORE.
I THOUGHT I WAS DIFFERENT. BETTER.
I'M SURE WE ALL DID ONCE.
BUT NAH, I'M NO HERO.
ONLY HUMAN.

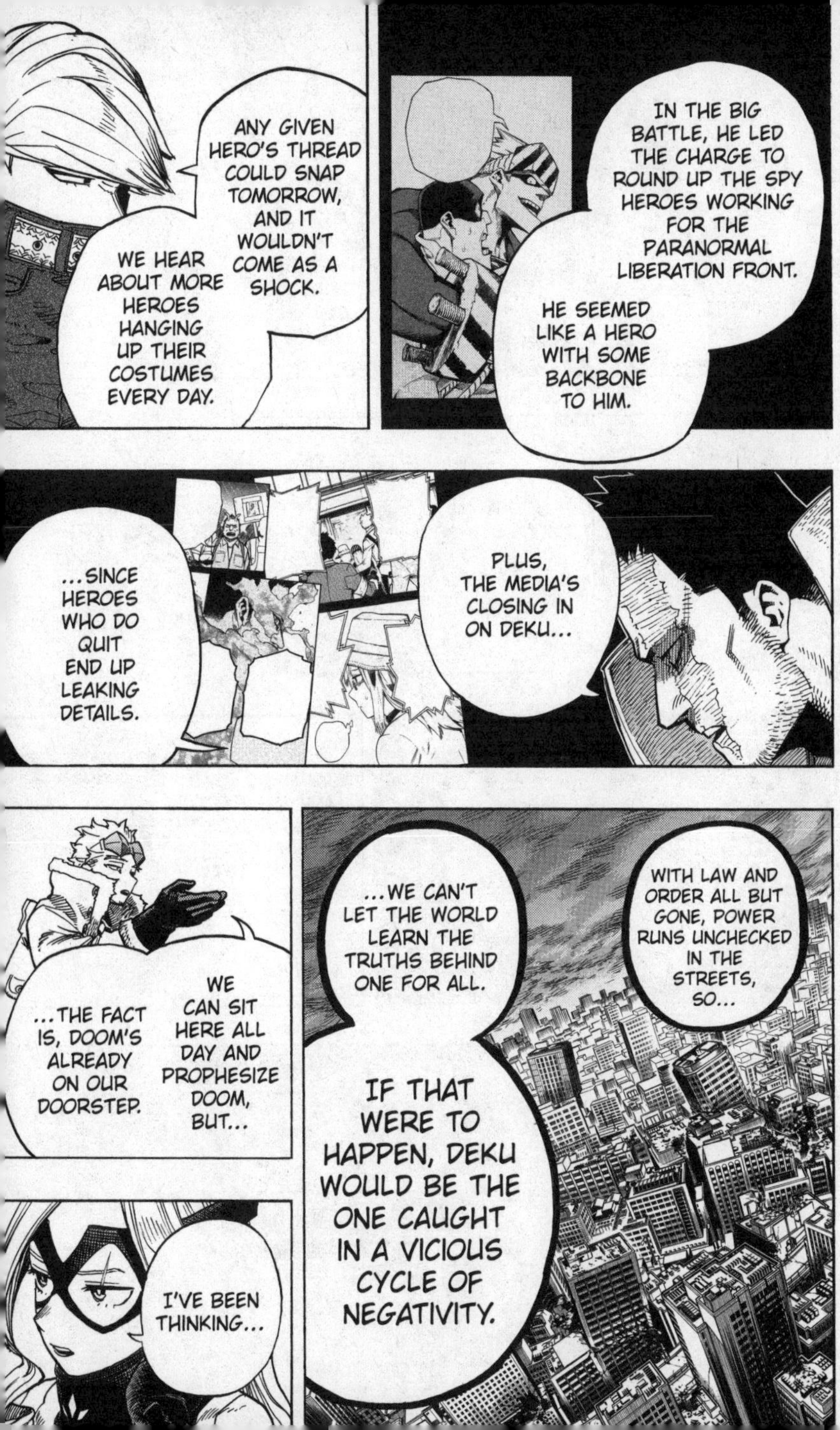
IN THE BIG BATTLE, HE LED THE CHARGE TO ROUND UP THE SPY HEROES WORKING FOR THE PARANORMAL LIBERATION FRONT.
HE SEEMED LIKE A HERO WITH SOME BACKBONE TO HIM.
ANY GIVEN HERO'S THREAD COULD SNAP TOMORROW, AND IT WOULDN'T COME AS A SHOCK.
WE HEAR ABOUT MORE HEROES HANGING UP THEIR COSTUMES EVERY DAY.
PLUS, THE MEDIA'S CLOSING IN ON DEKU...
...SINCE HEROES WHO DO QUIT END UP LEAKING DETAILS.
WITH LAW AND ORDER ALL BUT GONE, POWER RUNS UNCHECKED IN THE STREETS, SO...
...WE CAN'T LET THE WORLD LEARN THE TRUTHS BEHIND ONE FOR ALL.
IF THAT WERE TO HAPPEN, DEKU WOULD BE THE ONE CAUGHT IN A VICIOUS CYCLE OF NEGATIVITY.
WE CAN SIT HERE ALL DAY AND PROPHESIZE DOOM, BUT...
...THE FACT IS, DOOM'S ALREADY ON OUR DOORSTEP.
I'VE BEEN THINKING...

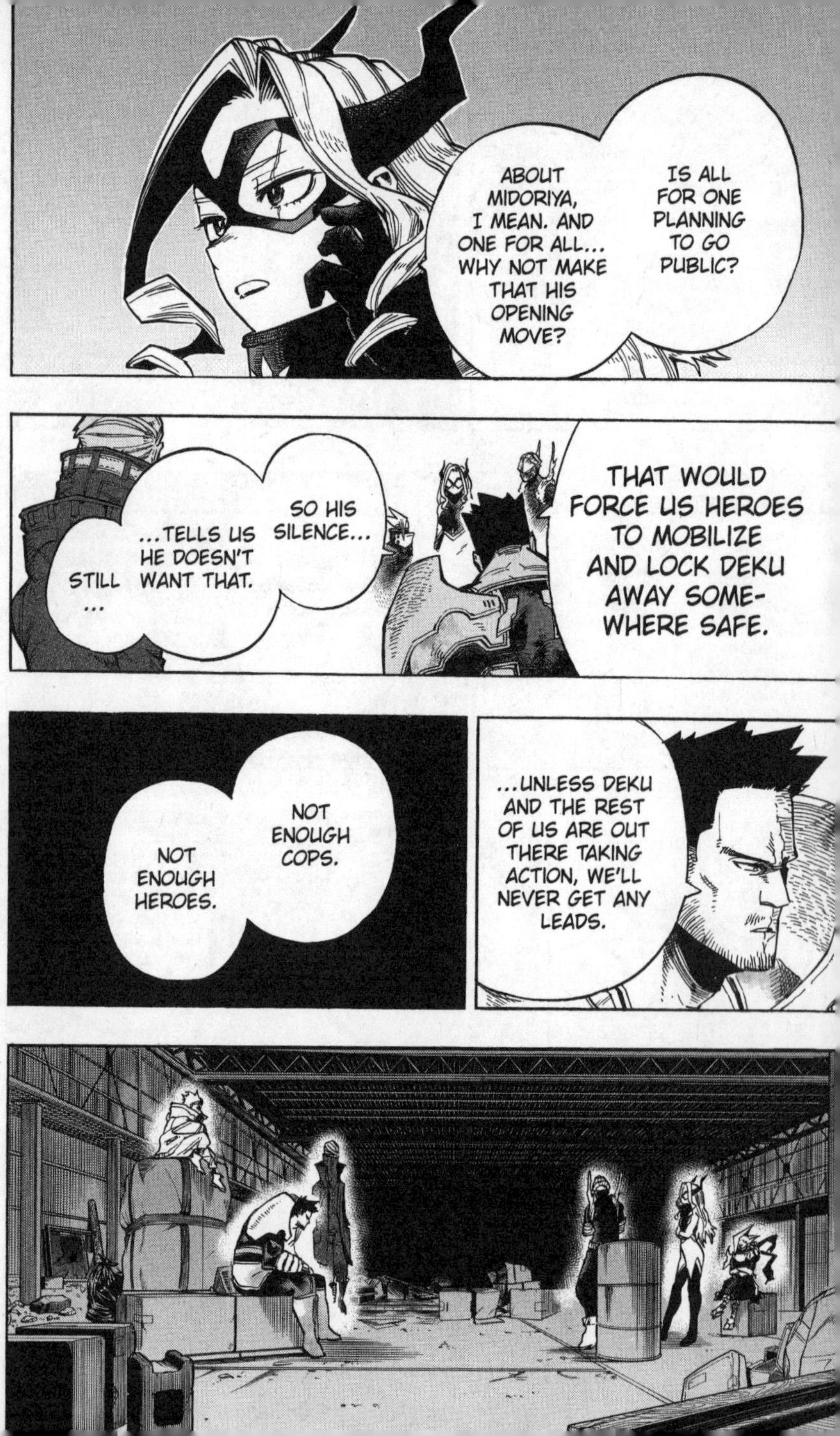
IS ALL FOR ONE PLANNING TO GO PUBLIC?
ABOUT MIDORIYA, I MEAN. AND ONE FOR ALL... WHY NOT MAKE THAT HIS OPENING MOVE?
THAT WOULD FORCE US HEROES TO MOBILIZE AND LOCK DEKU AWAY SOME-WHERE SAFE.
SO HIS SILENCE...
...TELLS US HE DOESN'T WANT THAT.
STILL ...
...UNLESS DEKU AND THE REST OF US ARE OUT THERE TAKING ACTION, WE'LL NEVER GET ANY LEADS.
NOT ENOUGH COPS.
NOT ENOUGH HEROES.

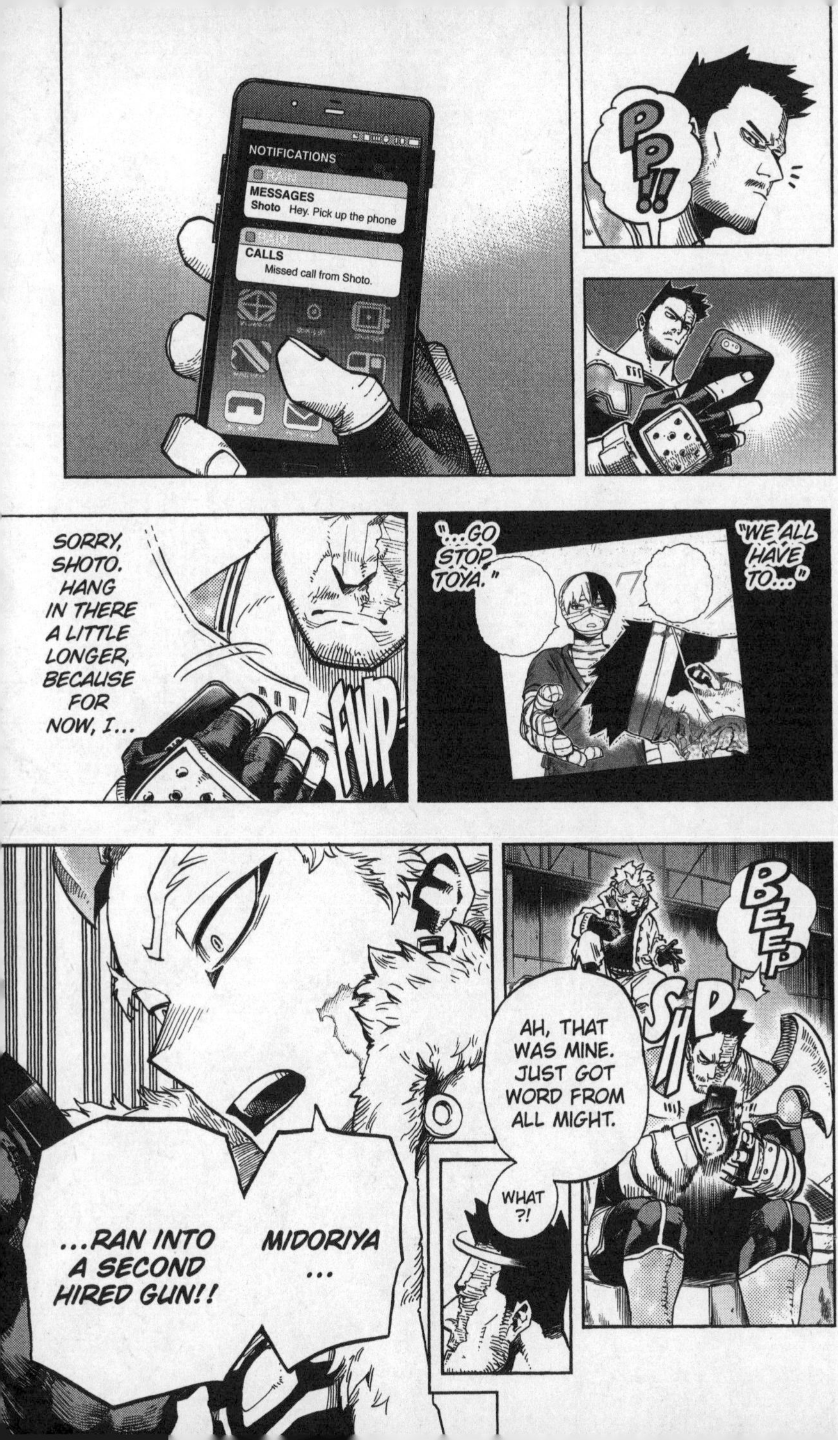
PP!!
NOTIFICATIONS
MESSAGES
Shoto Hey. Pick up the phone
CALLS
Missed call from Shoto.
"WE ALL HAVE TO..."
"...GO STOP TOYA."
SORRY, SHOTO. HANG IN THERE A LITTLE LONGER, BECAUSE FOR NOW, I...
FWP
BEEP
SHP
AH, THAT WAS MINE. JUST GOT WORD FROM ALL MIGHT.
WHAT?!
MIDORIYA...
...RAN INTO A SECOND HIRED GUN!!

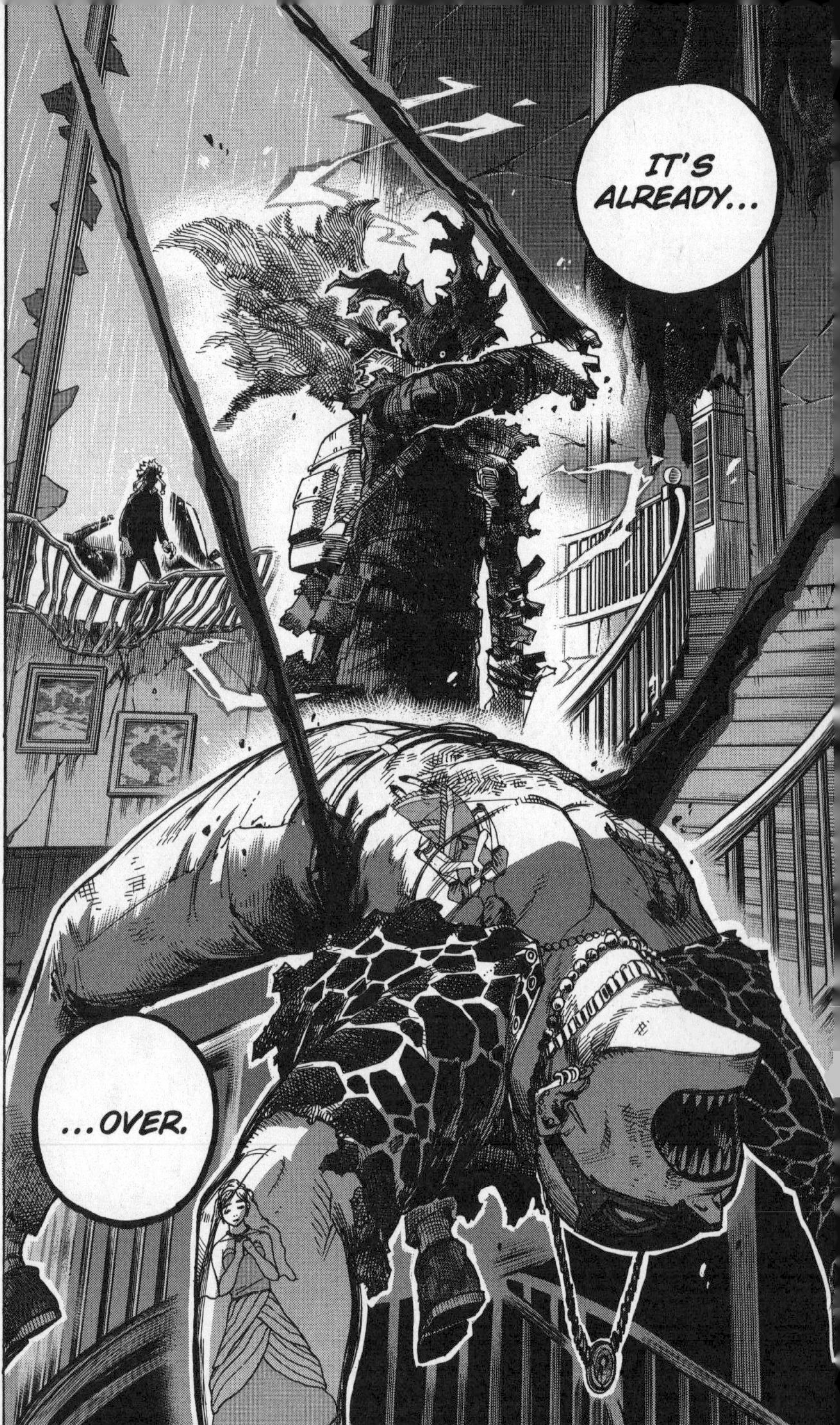
IT'S ALREADY...
...OVER.

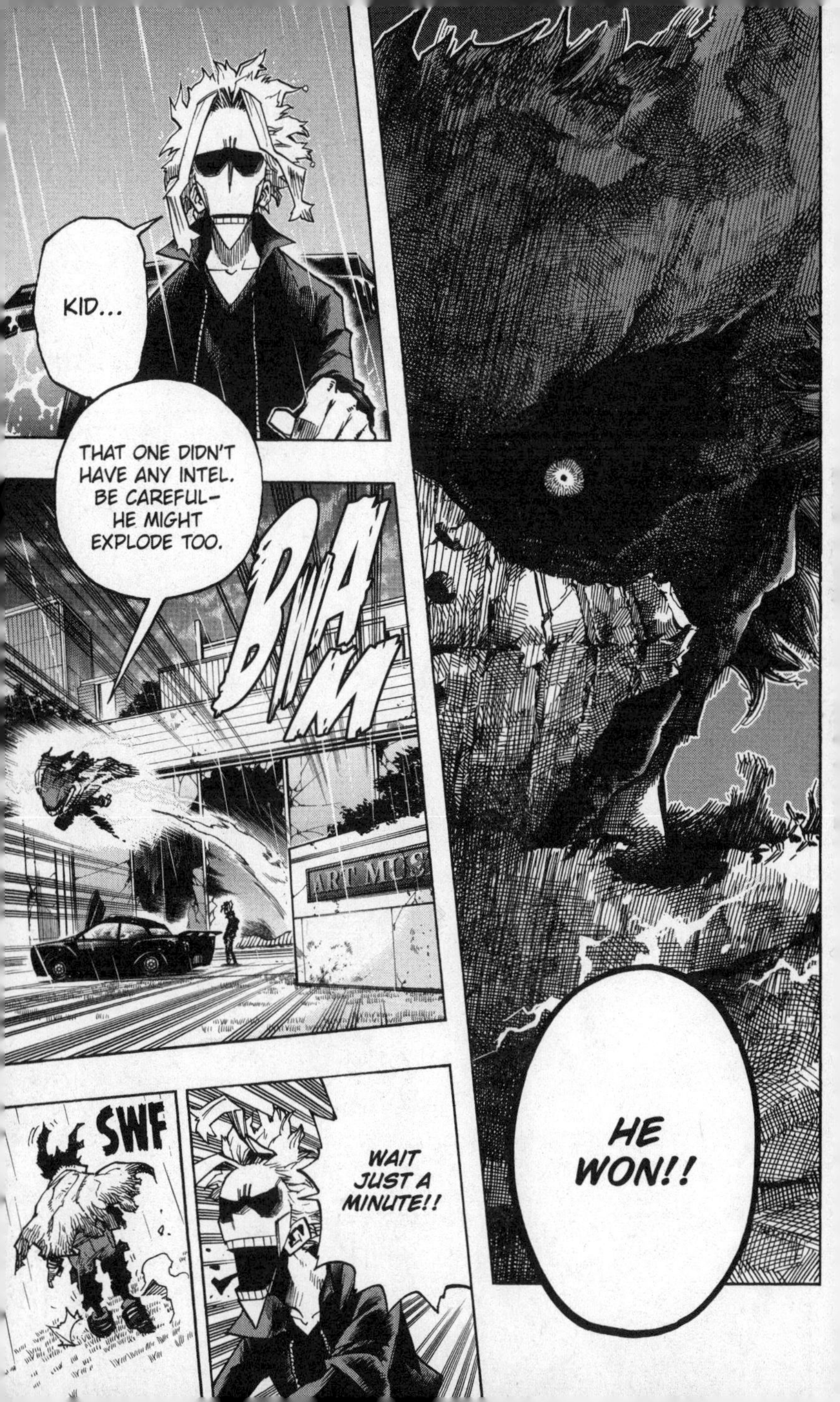
HE WON!!
KID...
THAT ONE DIDN'T HAVE ANY INTEL. BE CAREFUL— HE MIGHT EXPLODE TOO.
BLAM
ART MUS
WAIT JUST A MINUTE!!
SWF

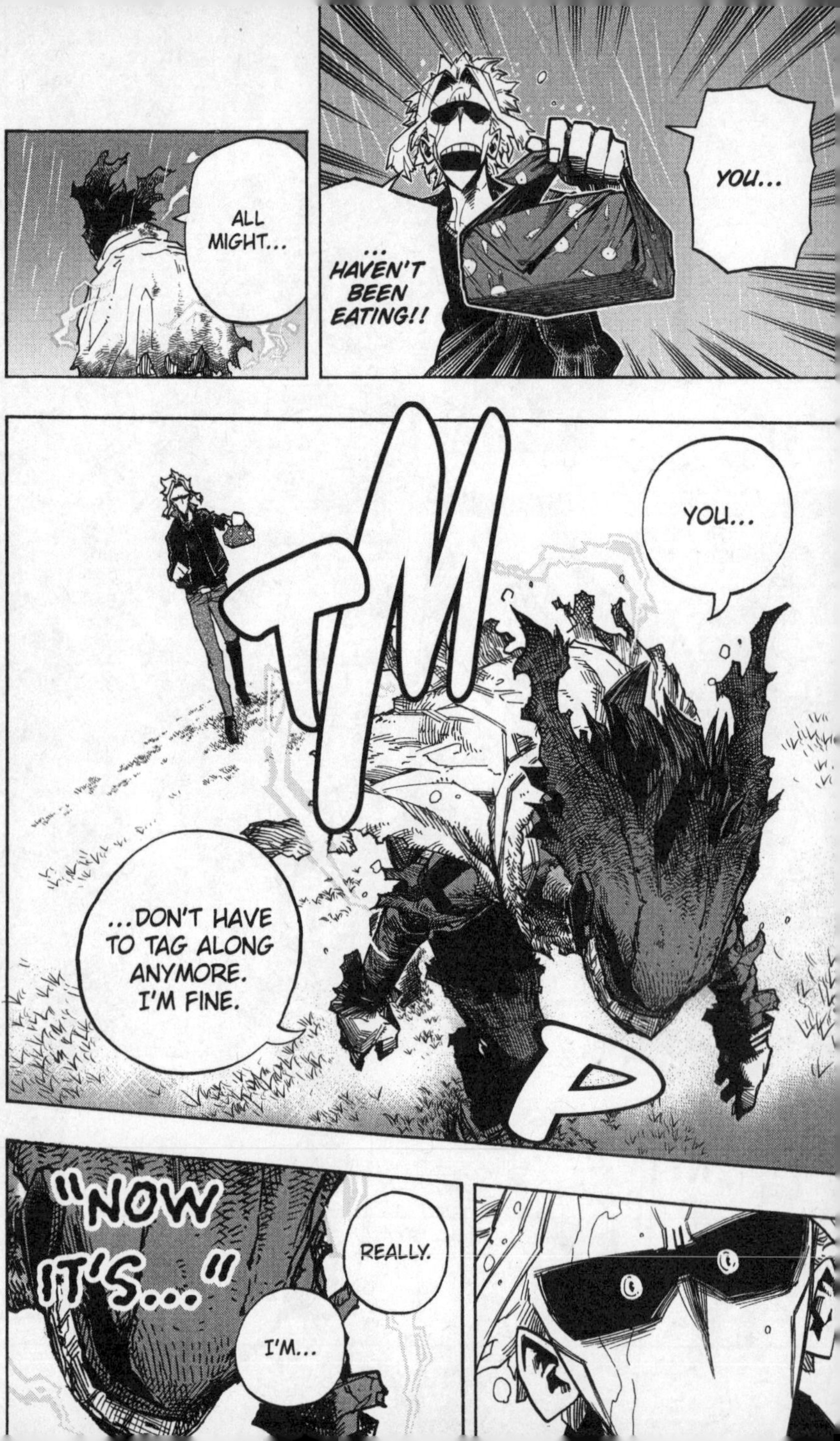
YOU...
...HAVEN'T BEEN EATING!!
ALL MIGHT...
YOU...
TM
...DON'T HAVE TO TAG ALONG ANYMORE. I'M FINE.
P
REALLY.
I'M...
"NOW IT'S..."

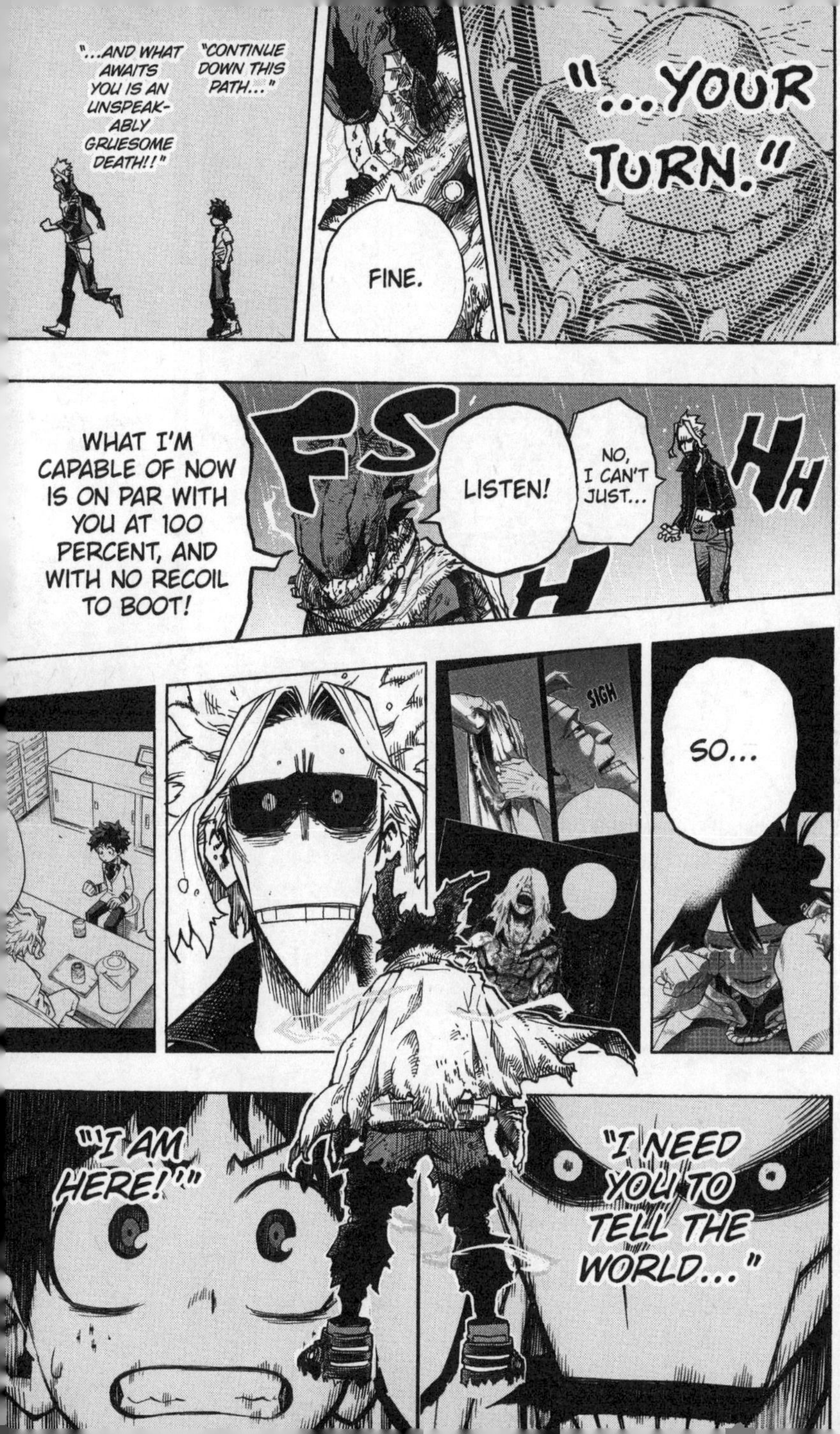
"...YOUR TURN."
FINE.
"CONTINUE DOWN THIS PATH..."
"...AND WHAT AWAITS YOU IS AN UNSPEAKABLY GRUESOME DEATH!!"
FSHHH
NO, I CAN'T JUST...
LISTEN!
WHAT I'M CAPABLE OF NOW IS ON PAR WITH YOU AT 100 PERCENT, AND WITH NO RECOIL TO BOOT!
SO...
SIGH
"I NEED YOU TO TELL THE WORLD..."
"I AM HERE!"

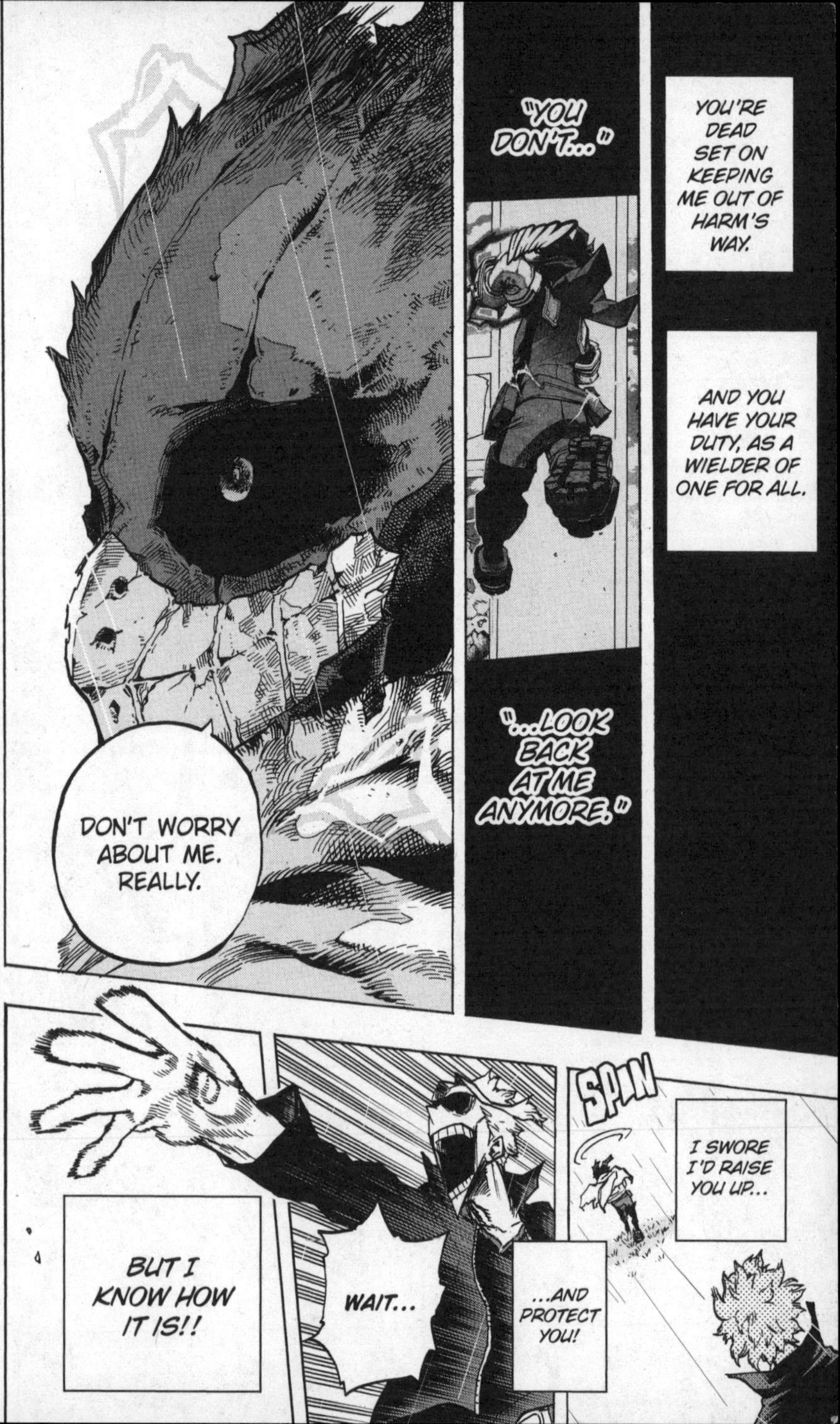
YOU'RE DEAD SET ON KEEPING ME OUT OF HARM'S WAY.
AND YOU HAVE YOUR DUTY, AS A WIELDER OF ONE FOR ALL.
"YOU DON'T..."
"...LOOK BACK AT ME ANYMORE."
DON'T WORRY ABOUT ME. REALLY.
SPIN
I SWORE I'D RAISE YOU UP...
...AND PROTECT YOU!
WAIT...
BUT I KNOW HOW IT IS!!

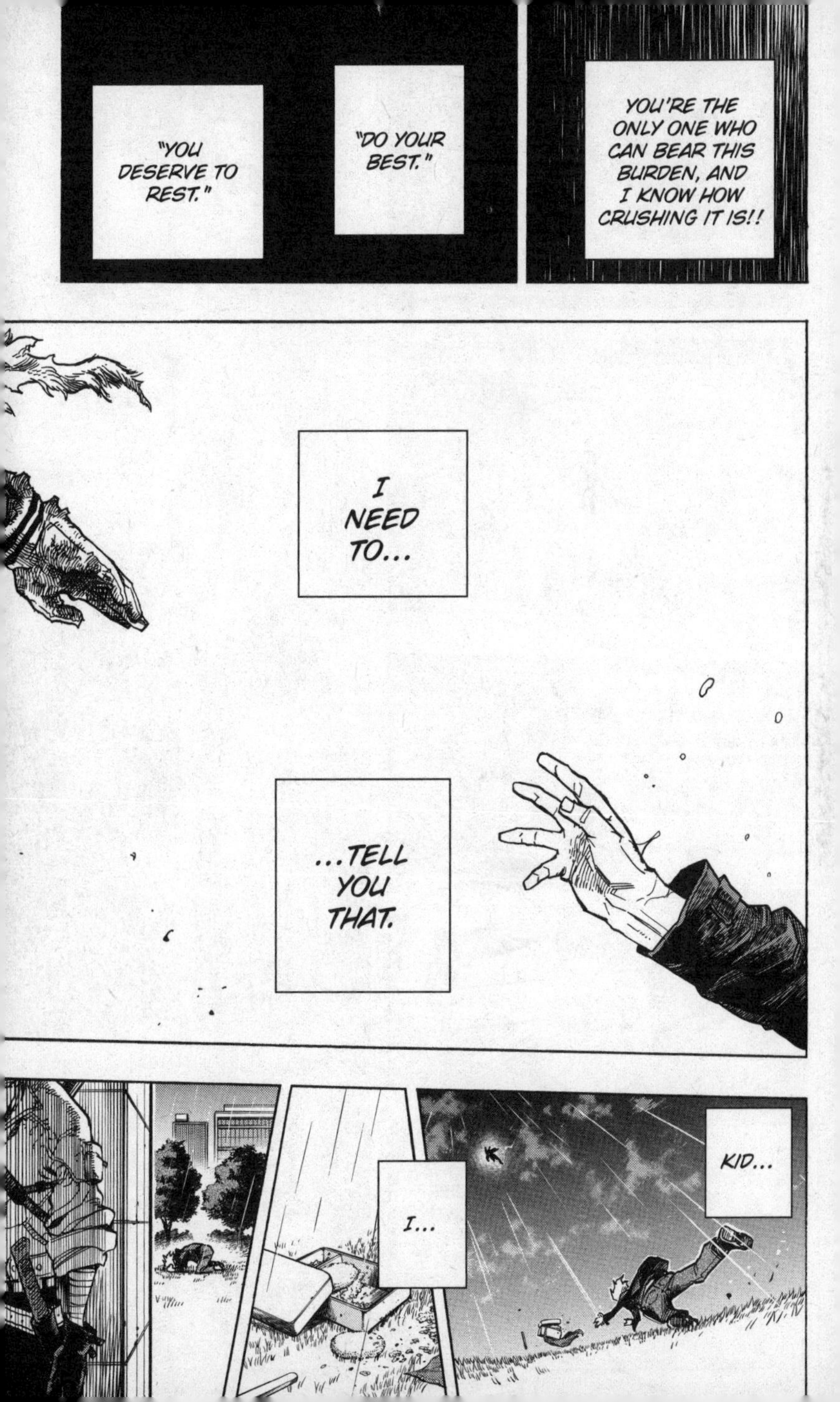
YOU'RE THE ONLY ONE WHO CAN BEAR THIS BURDEN, AND I KNOW HOW CRUSHING IT IS!!
"DO YOUR BEST."
"YOU DESERVE TO REST."
I NEED TO...
...TELL YOU THAT.
KID...
I...

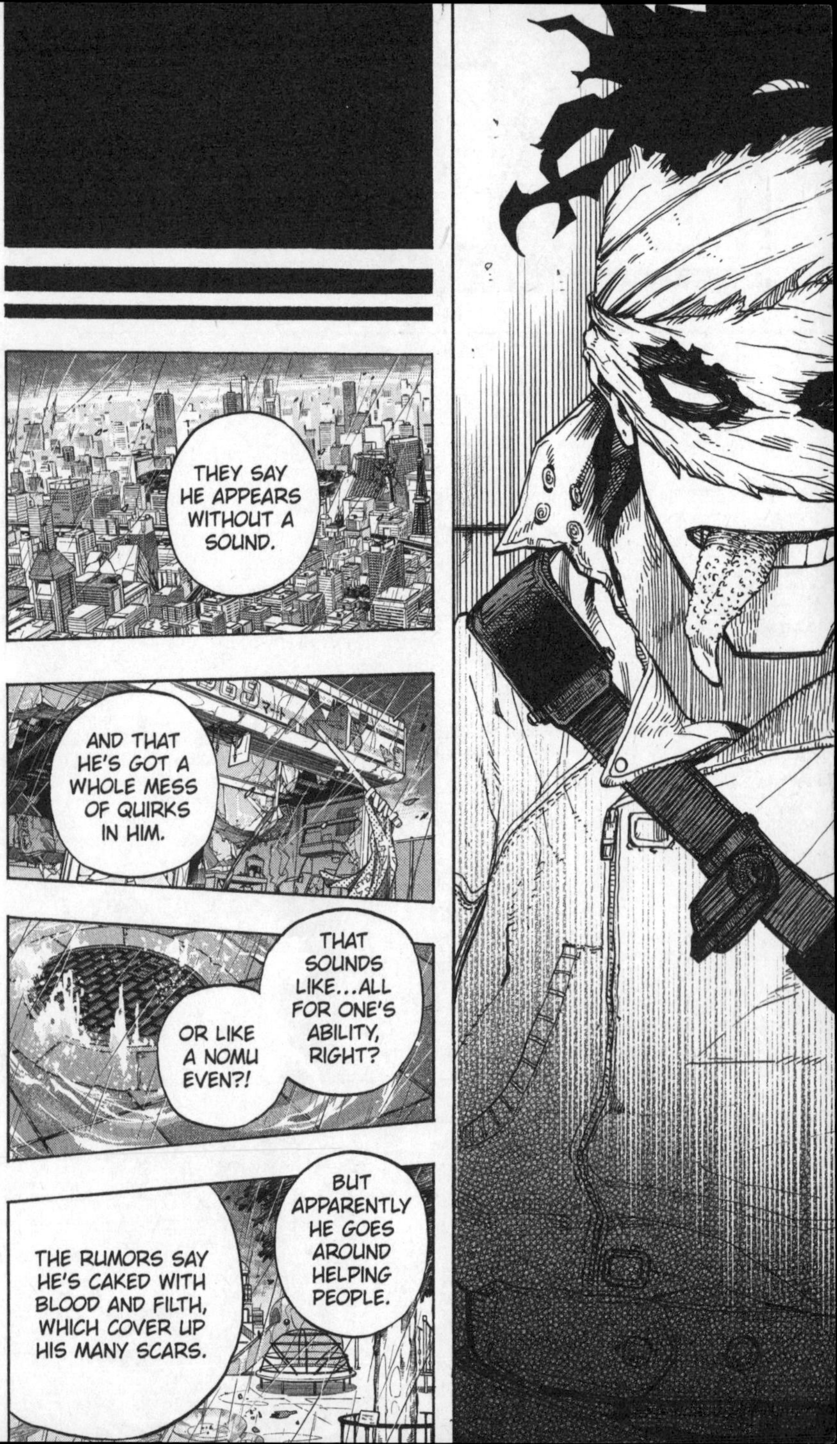
THEY SAY HE APPEARS WITHOUT A SOUND.
AND THAT HE'S GOT A WHOLE MESS OF QUIRKS IN HIM.
THAT SOUNDS LIKE...ALL FOR ONE'S ABILITY, RIGHT?
OR LIKE A NOMU EVEN?!
BUT APPARENTLY HE GOES AROUND HELPING PEOPLE.
THE RUMORS SAY HE'S CAKED WITH BLOOD AND FILTH, WHICH COVER UP HIS MANY SCARS.

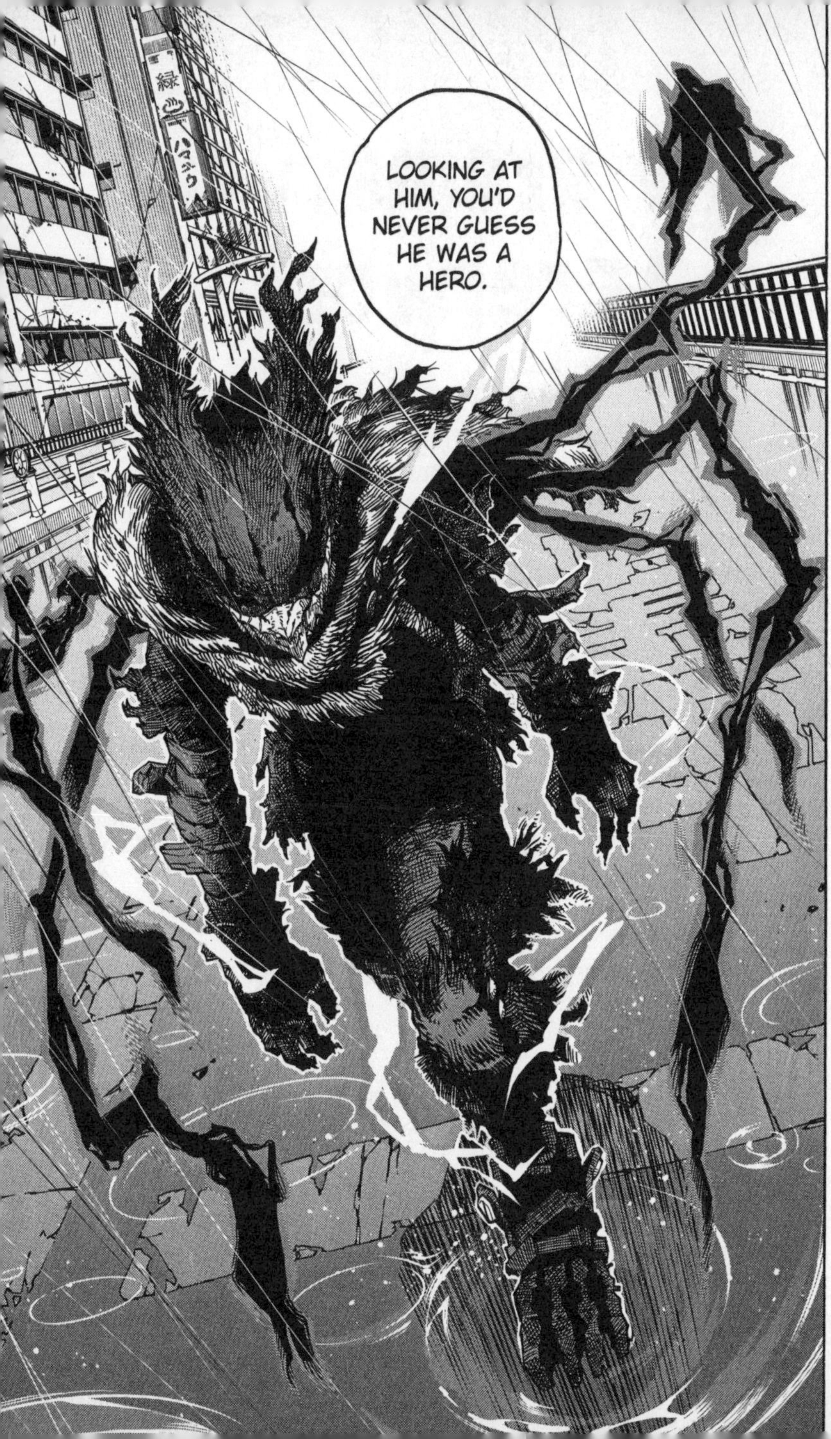
LOOKING AT HIM, YOU'D NEVER GUESS HE WAS A HERO.

THe Premature Afterword

Deku's in a pretty sorry state, huh. It's hard on me too, because those extra detailed drawings take extra time. Deku (version: sorry state). He's got Blackwhip activated all the time now so he can be ready to leap into battle at any moment.

The final act.

I thought the final act might last about five volumes, but now I'm not so sure anymore. So many questions left to answer. Like, what will become of Deku? What does it mean to be the greatest hero? Will Iris Vision ever appear in the actual story? There's sure to be a lot of excitement, and I hope it infects all of you who've come along on the journey and read this far.

See you in the next volume!

PLUS ULTRA!

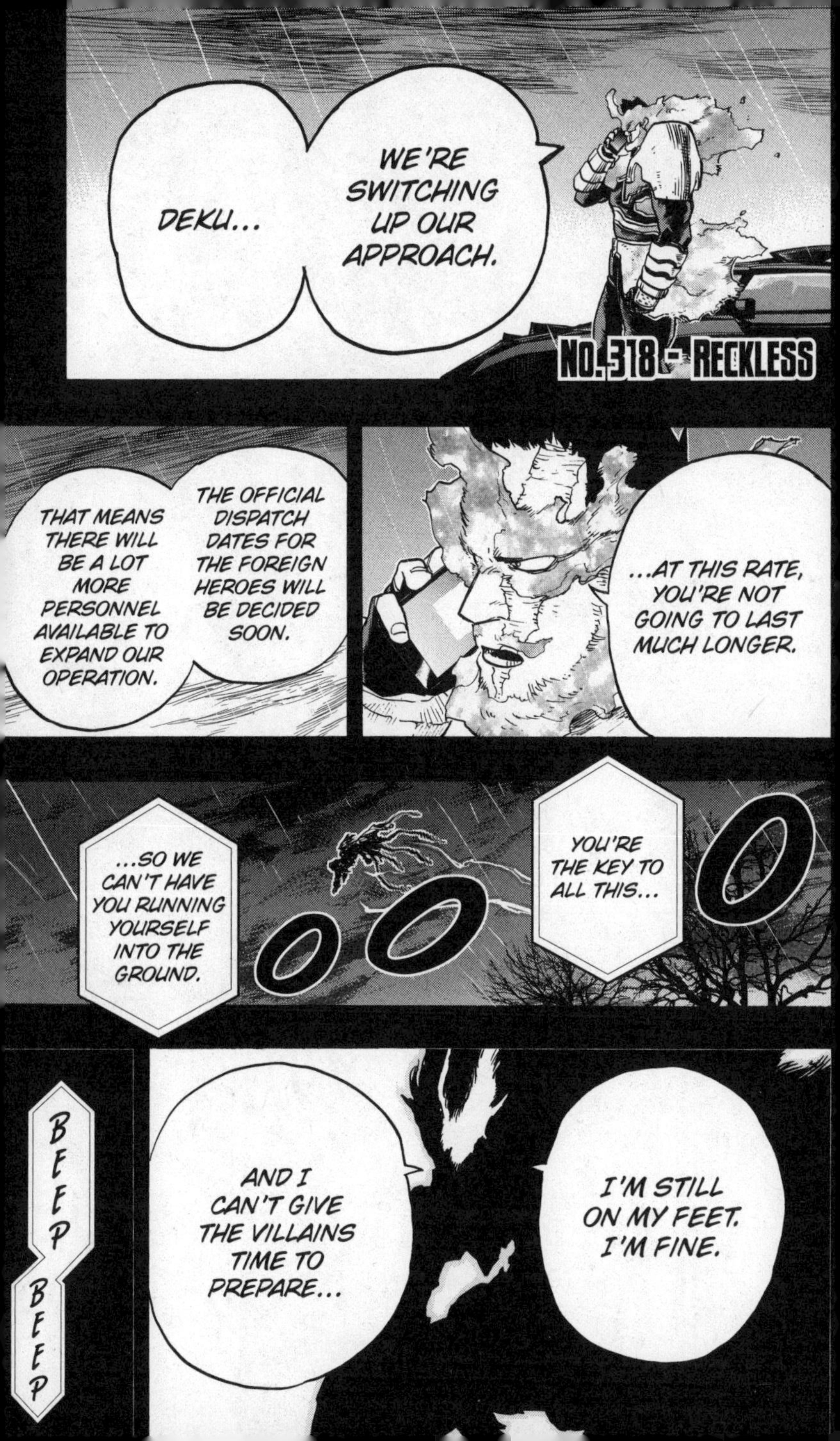
DEKU... WE'RE SWITCHING UP OUR APPROACH.
NO. 318 - RECKLESS
...AT THIS RATE, YOU'RE NOT GOING TO LAST MUCH LONGER.
THE OFFICIAL DISPATCH DATES FOR THE FOREIGN HEROES WILL BE DECIDED SOON.
THAT MEANS THERE WILL BE A LOT MORE PERSONNEL AVAILABLE TO EXPAND OUR OPERATION.
YOU'RE THE KEY TO ALL THIS...
...SO WE CAN'T HAVE YOU RUNNING YOURSELF INTO THE GROUND.
I'M STILL ON MY FEET. I'M FINE.
AND I CAN'T GIVE THE VILLAINS TIME TO PREPARE...
BEEP
BEEP

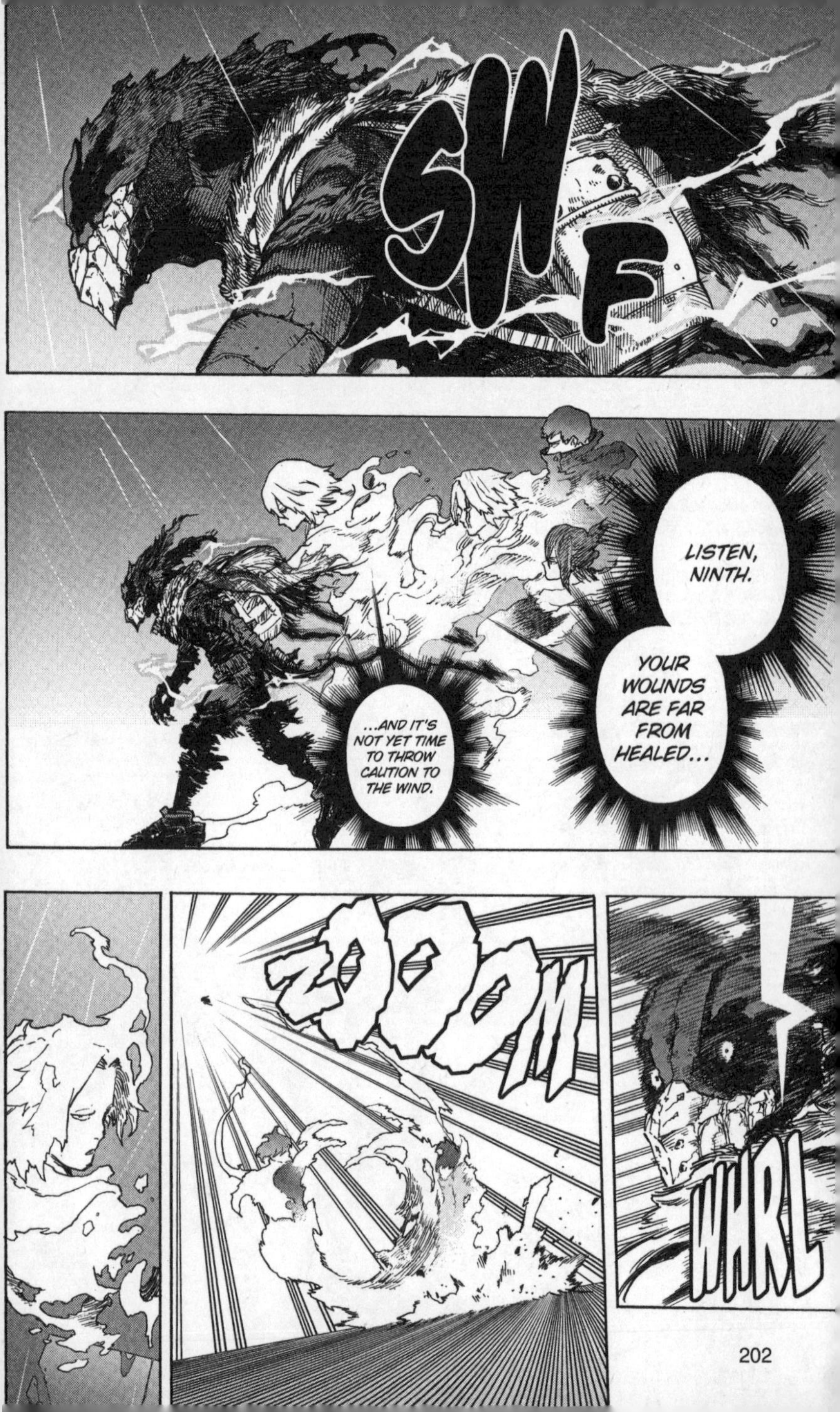
SWF
LISTEN, NINTH.
YOUR WOUNDS ARE FAR FROM HEALED...
...AND IT'S NOT YET TIME TO THROW CAUTION TO THE WIND.
WHRL
ZOOOM

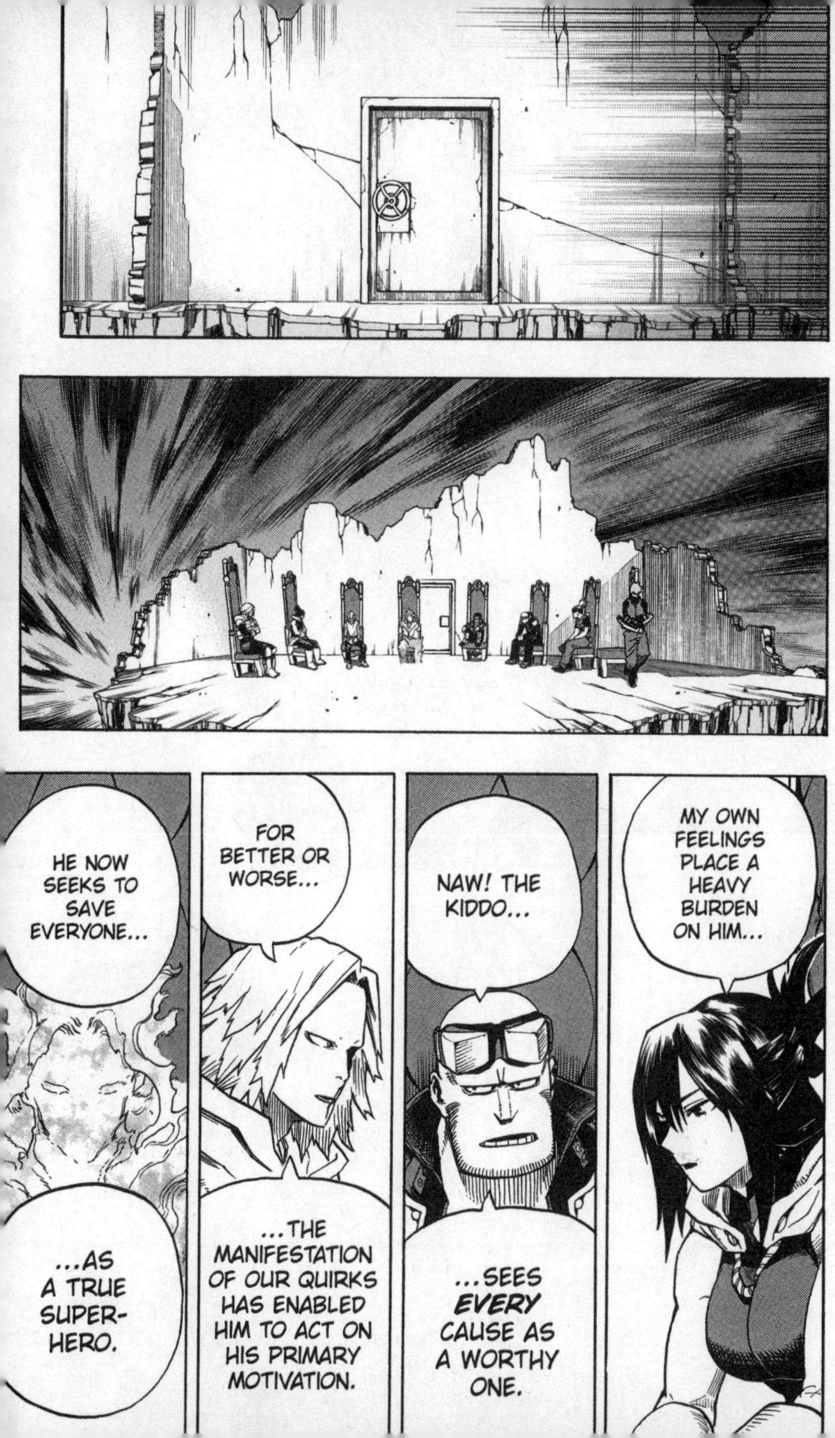
MY OWN FEELINGS PLACE A HEAVY BURDEN ON HIM...
NAW! THE KIDDO...
...SEES *EVERY* CAUSE AS A WORTHY ONE.
FOR BETTER OR WORSE...
...THE MANIFESTATION OF OUR QUIRKS HAS ENABLED HIM TO ACT ON HIS PRIMARY MOTIVATION.
HE NOW SEEKS TO SAVE EVERYONE...
...AS A TRUE SUPER-HERO.

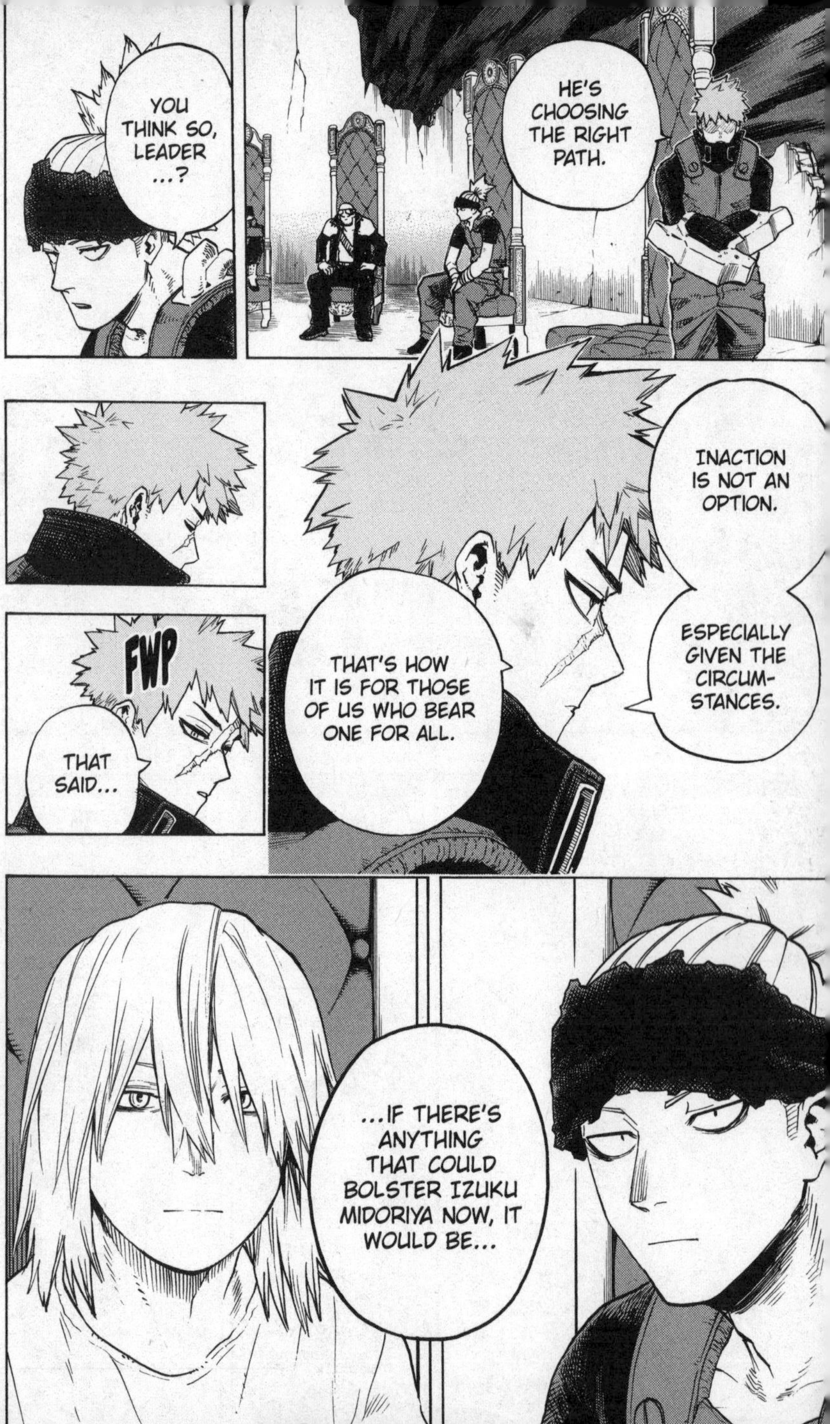
HE'S CHOOSING THE RIGHT PATH.
YOU THINK SO, LEADER ...?
INACTION IS NOT AN OPTION.
ESPECIALLY GIVEN THE CIRCUM-STANCES.
THAT'S HOW IT IS FOR THOSE OF US WHO BEAR ONE FOR ALL.
FWP
THAT SAID...
...IF THERE'S ANYTHING THAT COULD BOLSTER IZUKU MIDORIYA NOW, IT WOULD BE...

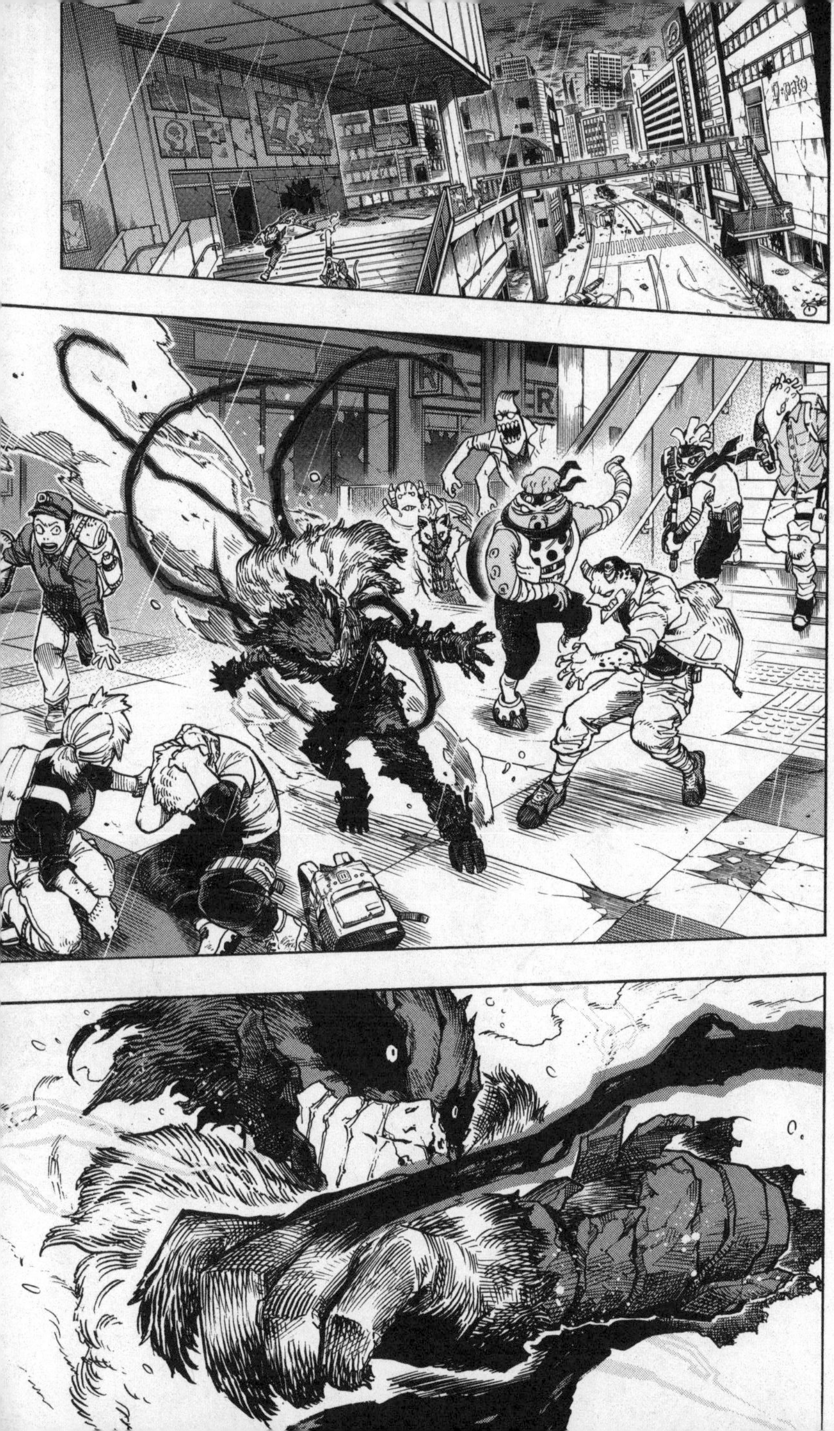

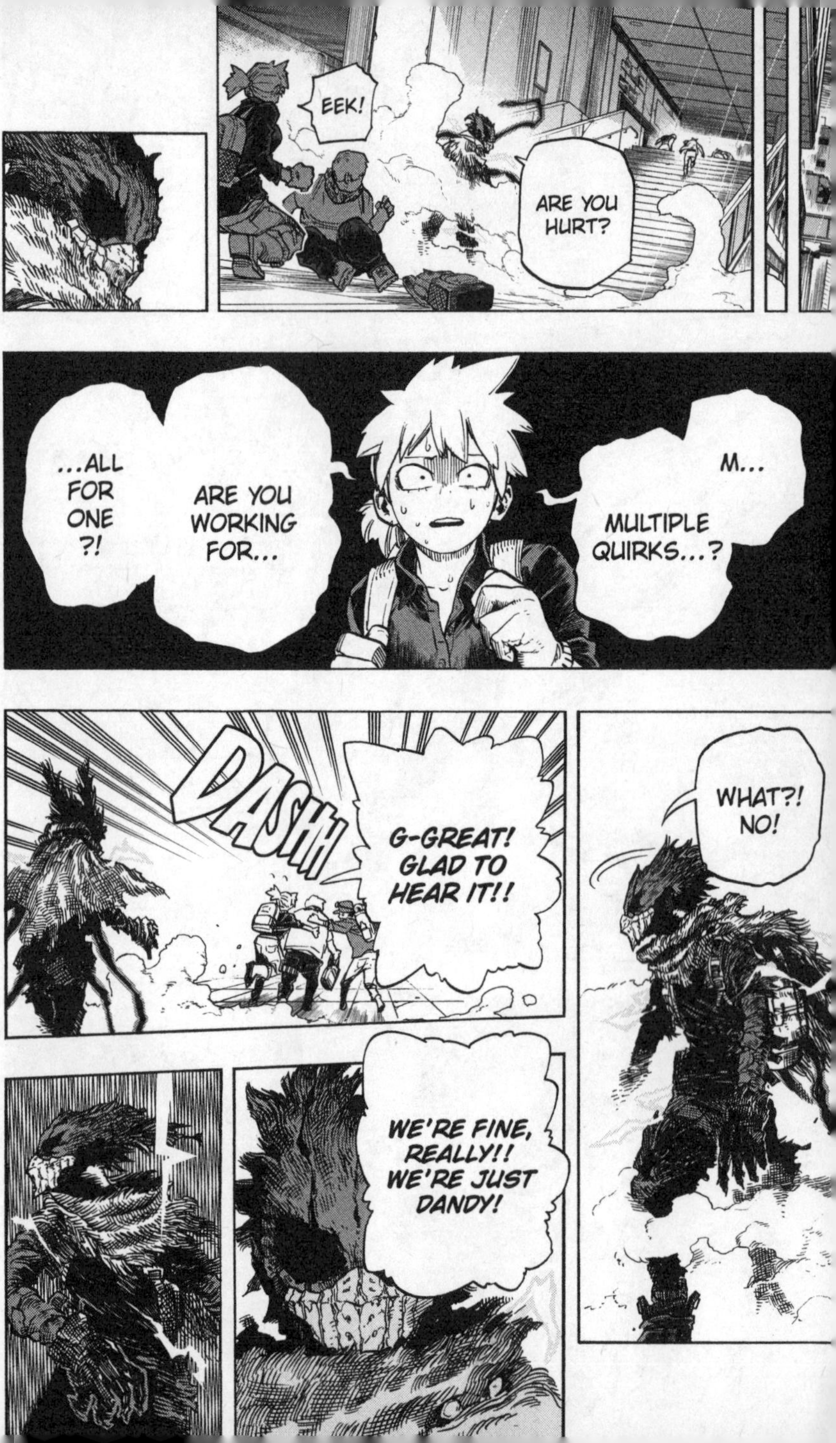
EEK!
ARE YOU HURT?
M...
MULTIPLE QUIRKS...?
ARE YOU WORKING FOR...
...ALL FOR ONE ?!
WHAT?! NO!
DASHH
G-GREAT! GLAD TO HEAR IT!!
WE'RE FINE, REALLY!! WE'RE JUST DANDY!

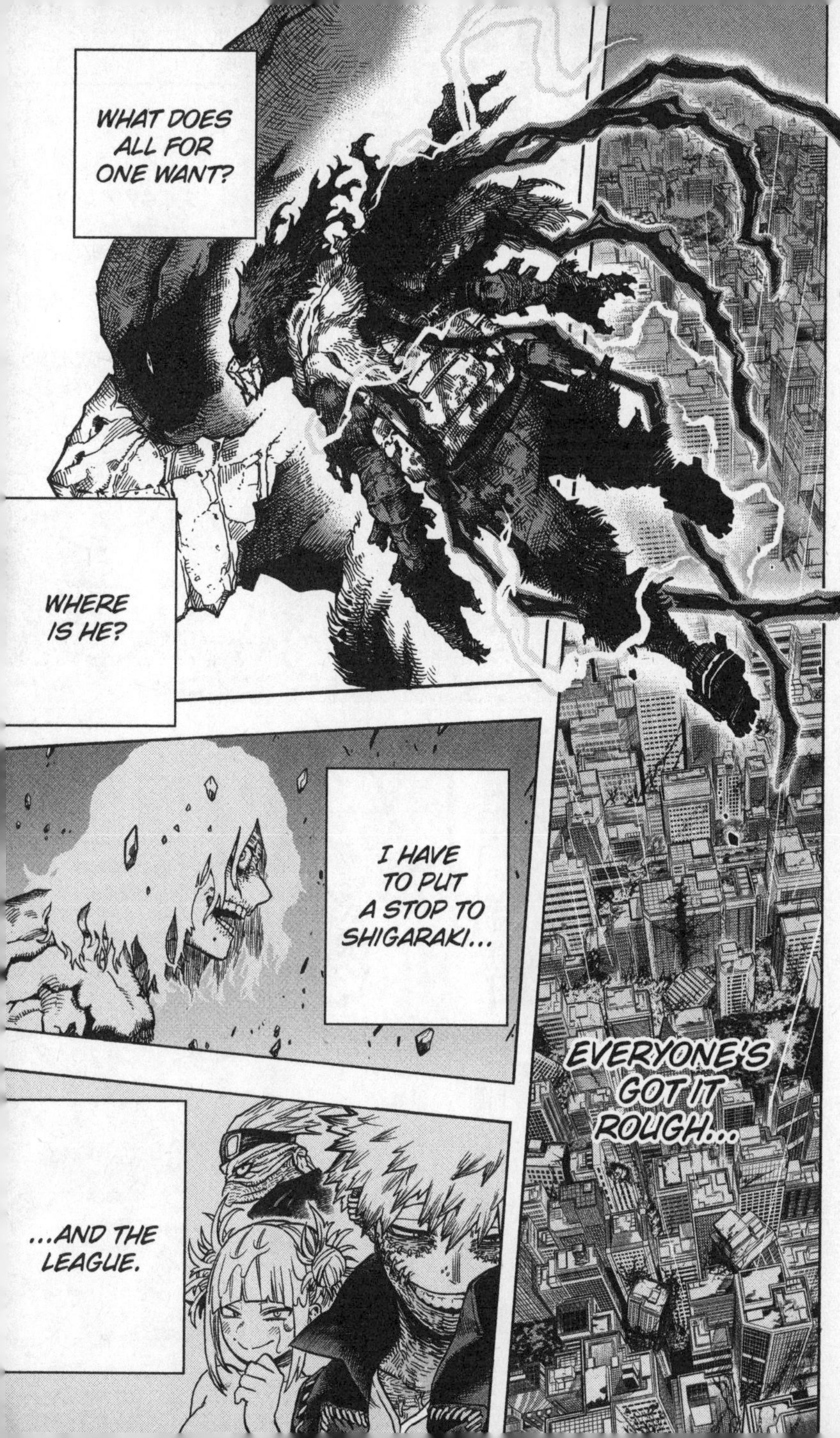

WHAT DOES ALL FOR ONE WANT?
WHERE IS HE?
I HAVE TO PUT A STOP TO SHIGARAKI...
...AND THE LEAGUE.
EVERYONE'S GOT IT ROUGH...

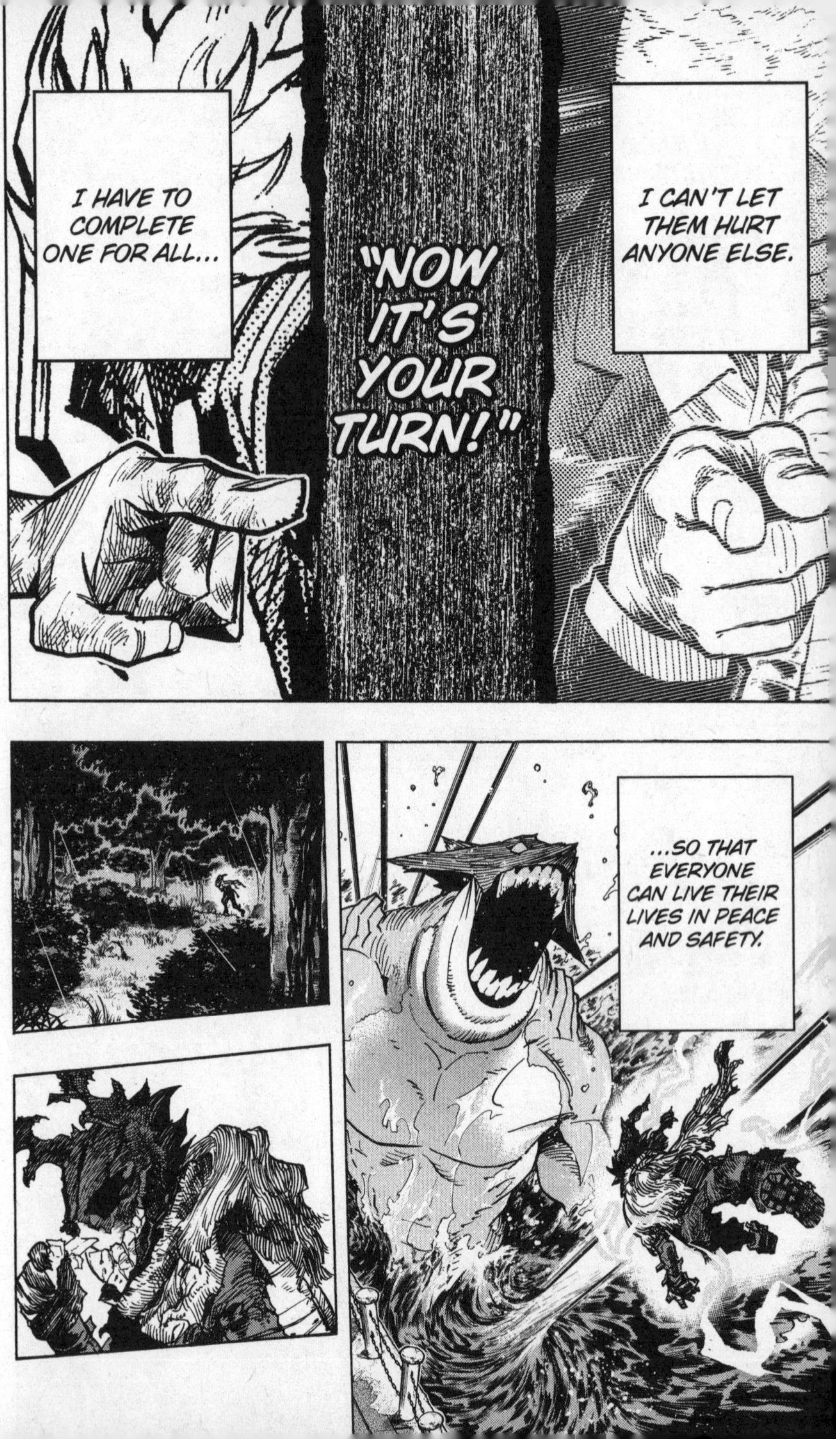
I CAN'T LET THEM HURT ANYONE ELSE.
"NOW IT'S YOUR TURN!"
I HAVE TO COMPLETE ONE FOR ALL...
...SO THAT EVERYONE CAN LIVE THEIR LIVES IN PEACE AND SAFETY.

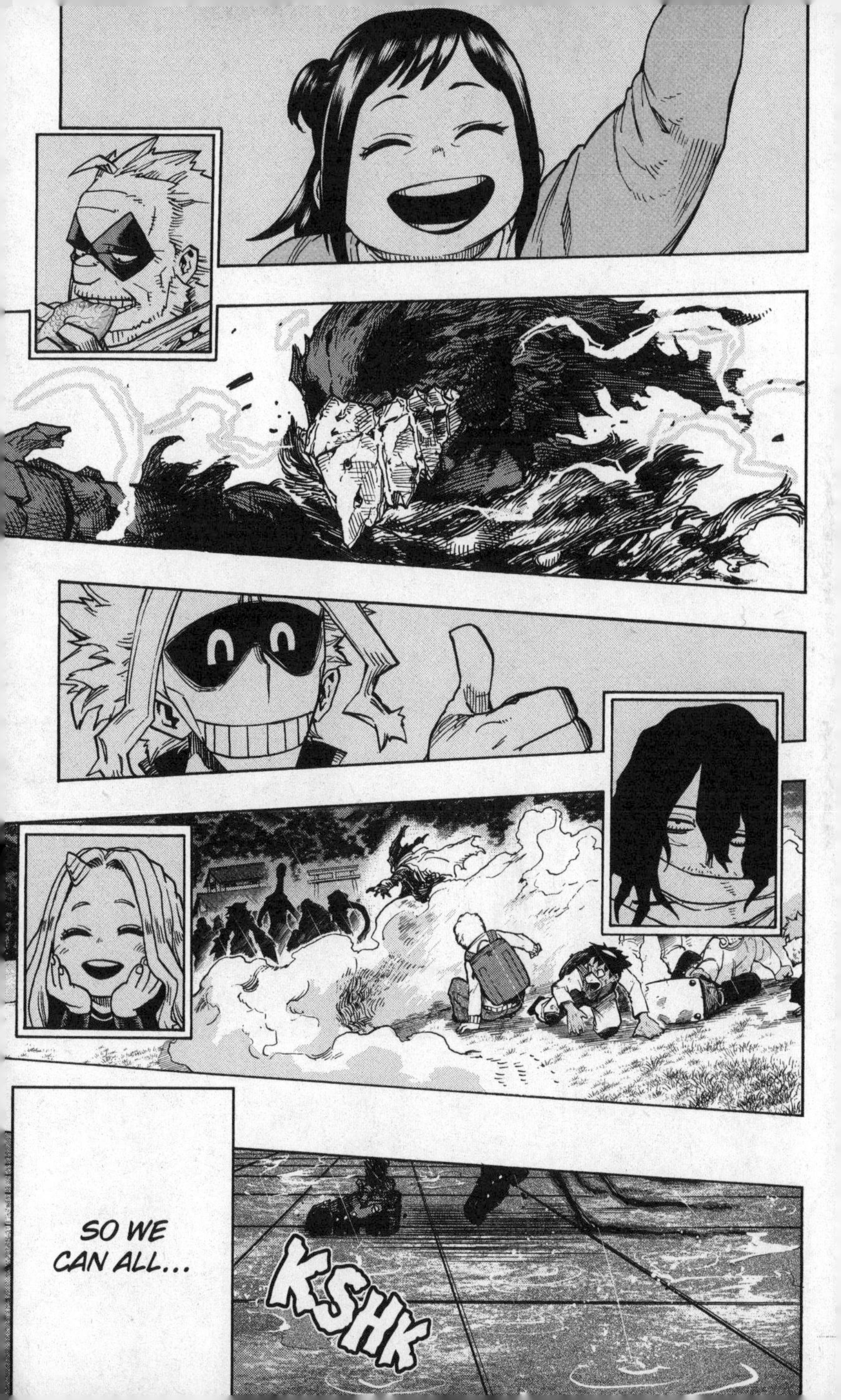
SO WE
CAN ALL...
KSHK

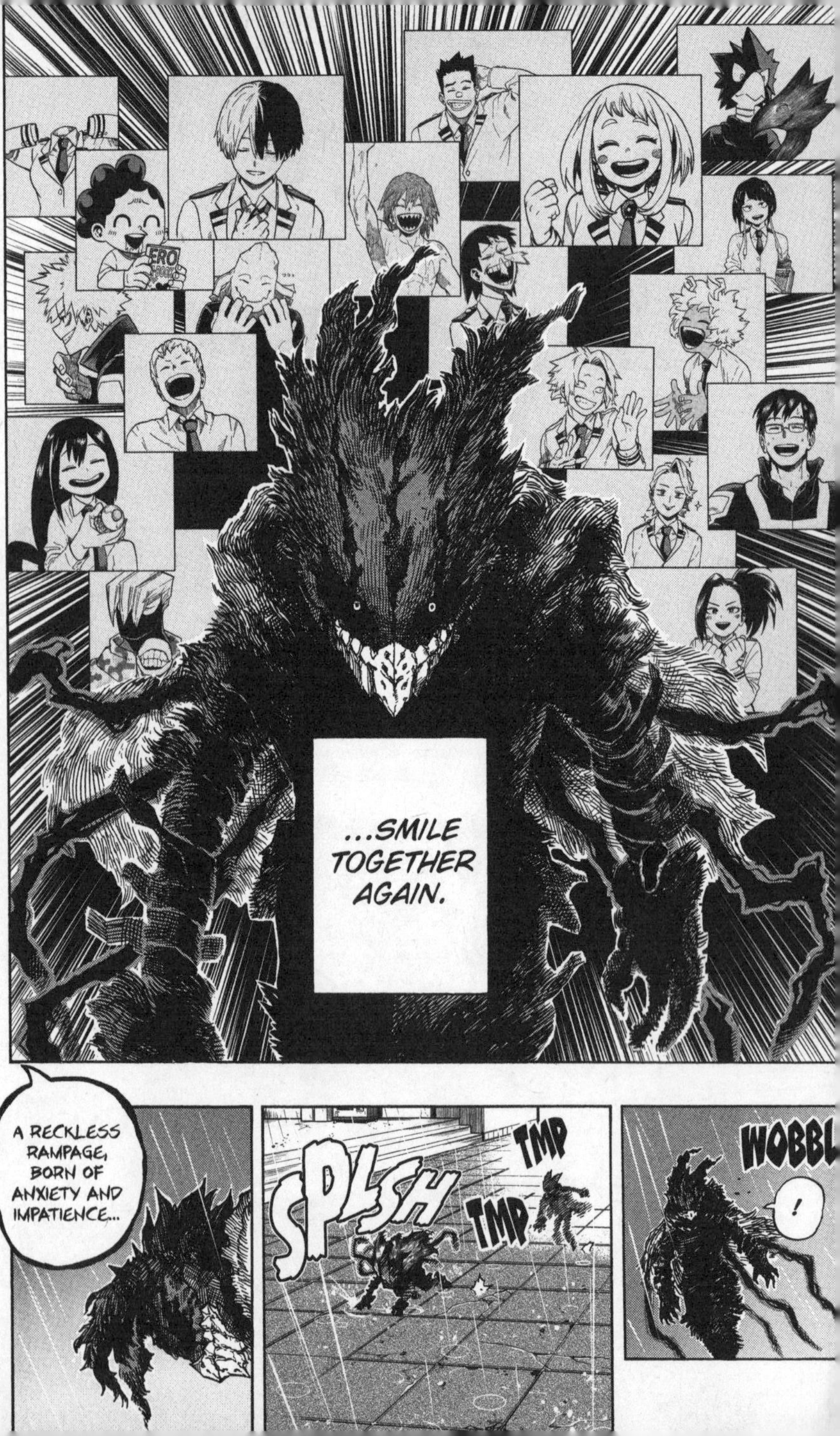
...SMILE TOGETHER AGAIN.
WOBBL
!
TMP
TMP
SPLSH
A RECKLESS RAMPAGE, BORN OF ANXIETY AND IMPATIENCE...

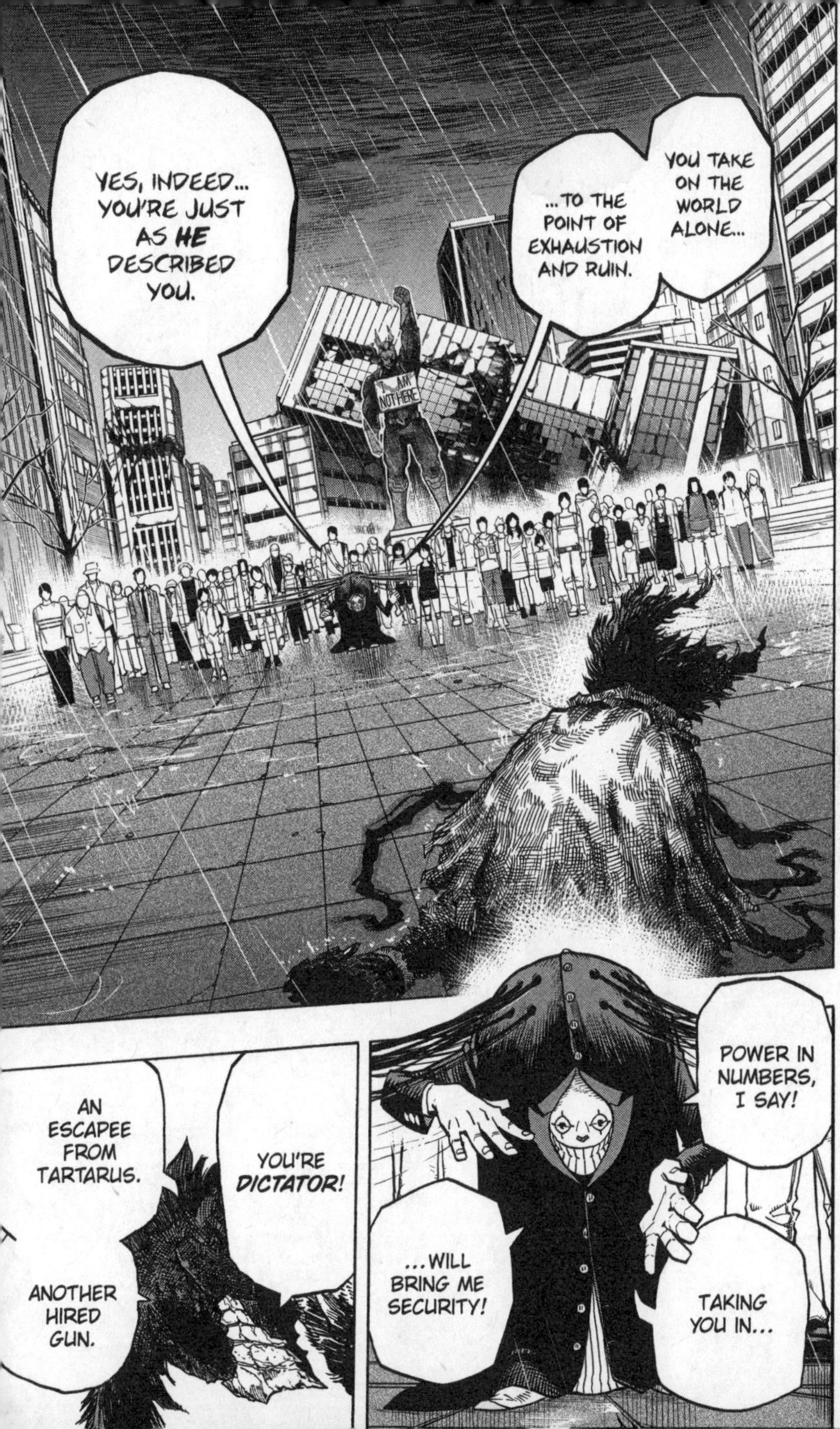
YOU TAKE ON THE WORLD ALONE...
...TO THE POINT OF EXHAUSTION AND RUIN.
YES, INDEED... YOU'RE JUST AS **HE** DESCRIBED YOU.
POWER IN NUMBERS, I SAY!
TAKING YOU IN...
...WILL BRING ME SECURITY!
YOU'RE *DICTATOR*!
AN ESCAPEE FROM TARTARUS.
ANOTHER HIRED GUN.

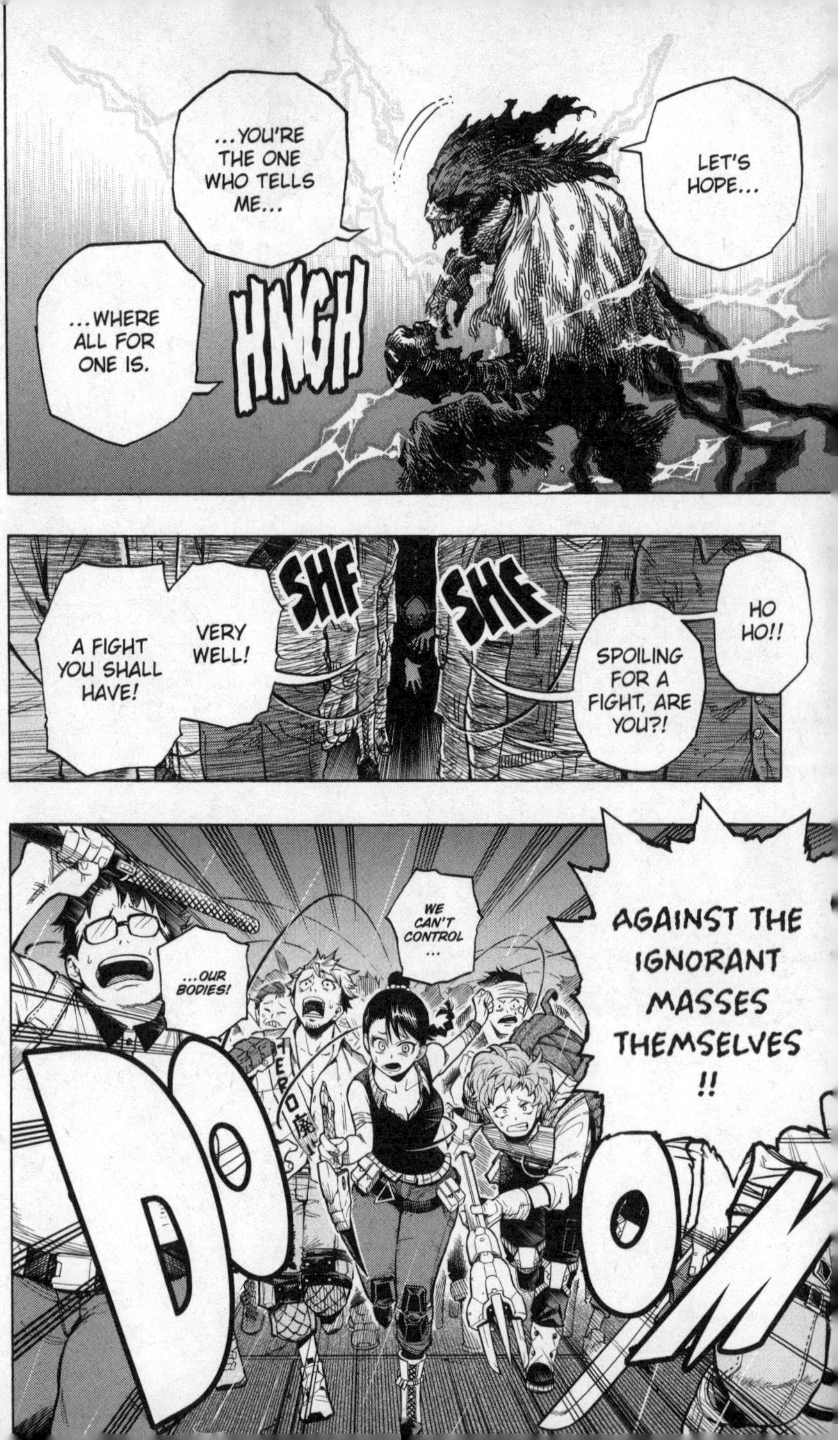
LET'S HOPE...
...YOU'RE THE ONE WHO TELLS ME...
HNGH
...WHERE ALL FOR ONE IS.
HO HO!!
SPOILING FOR A FIGHT, ARE YOU?!
SHF
SHF
VERY WELL!
A FIGHT YOU SHALL HAVE!
AGAINST THE IGNORANT MASSES THEMSELVES !!
WE CAN'T CONTROL ...
...OUR BODIES!
DOOM

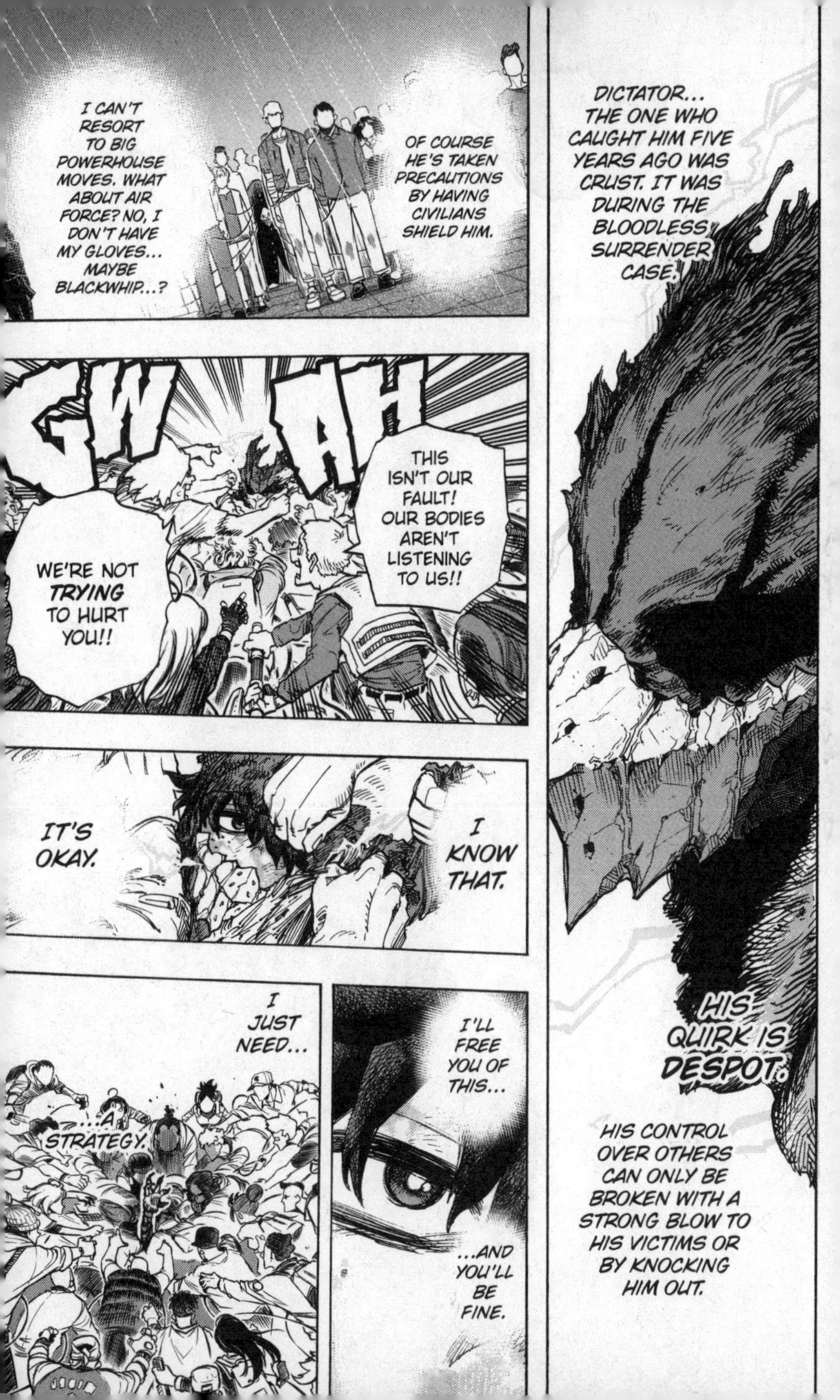
DICTATOR... THE ONE WHO CAUGHT HIM FIVE YEARS AGO WAS CRUST. IT WAS DURING THE BLOODLESS SURRENDER CASE.
HIS QUIRK IS DESPOT.
HIS CONTROL OVER OTHERS CAN ONLY BE BROKEN WITH A STRONG BLOW TO HIS VICTIMS OR BY KNOCKING HIM OUT.
OF COURSE HE'S TAKEN PRECAUTIONS BY HAVING CIVILIANS SHIELD HIM.
I CAN'T RESORT TO BIG POWERHOUSE MOVES. WHAT ABOUT AIR FORCE? NO, I DON'T HAVE MY GLOVES... MAYBE BLACKWHIP...?
GWAAH
THIS ISN'T OUR FAULT! OUR BODIES AREN'T LISTENING TO US!!
WE'RE NOT *TRYING* TO HURT YOU!!
I KNOW THAT.
IT'S OKAY.
I'LL FREE YOU OF THIS...
...AND YOU'LL BE FINE.
I JUST NEED...
...A STRATEGY.

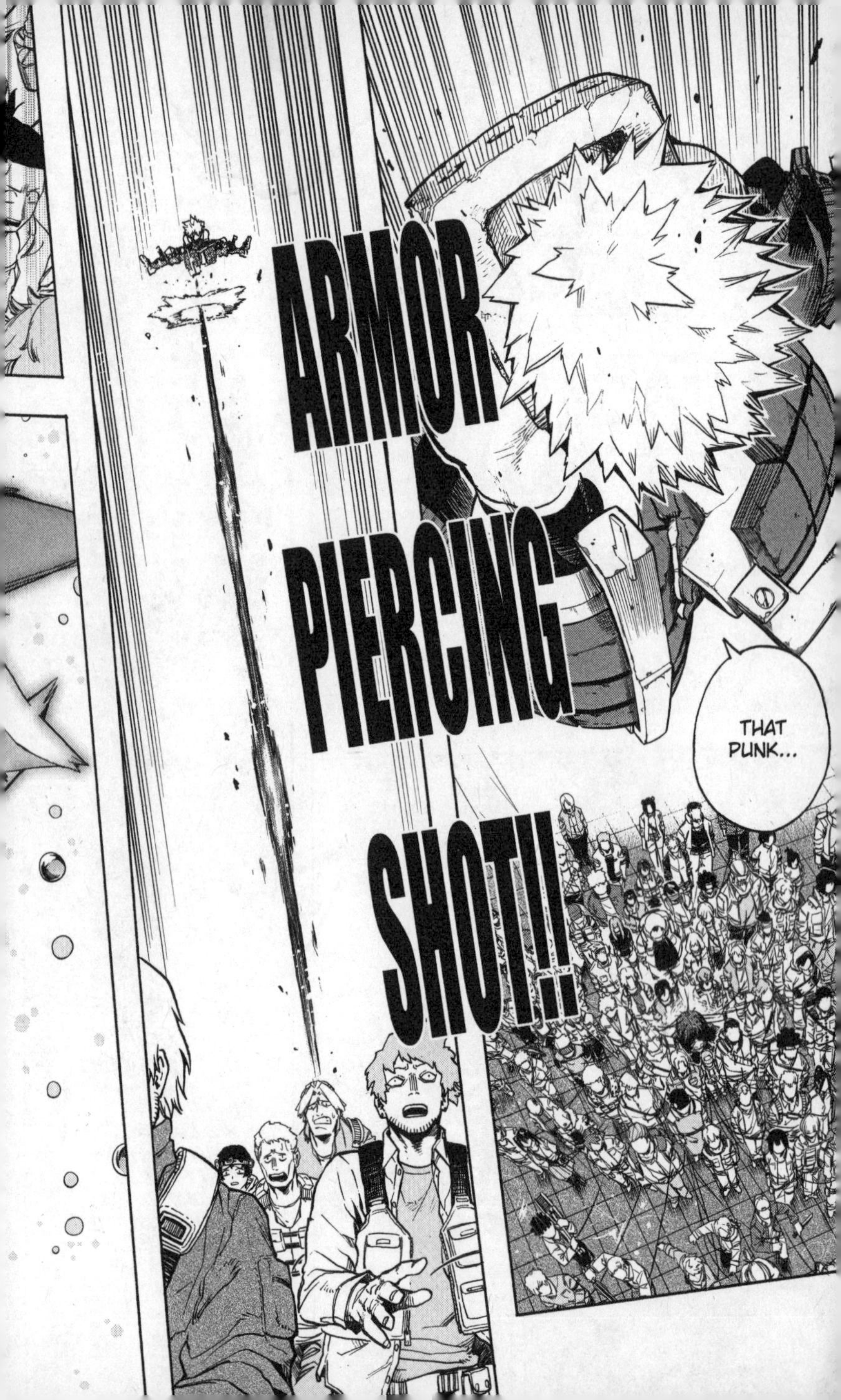
ARMOR PIERCING SHOT!!
THAT PUNK...

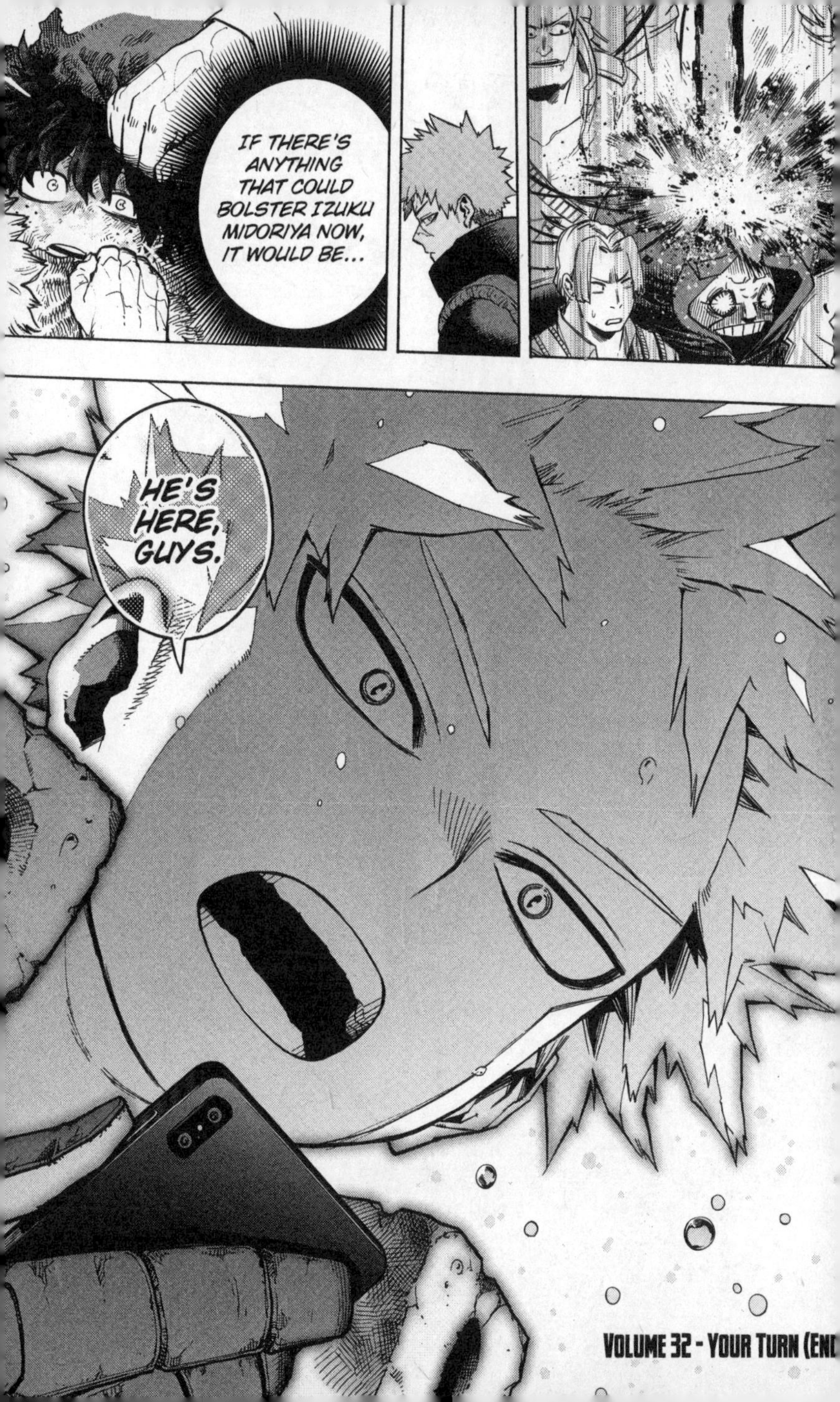
IF THERE'S ANYTHING THAT COULD BOLSTER IZUKU MIDORIYA NOW, IT WOULD BE...
HE'S HERE, GUYS.
VOLUME 32 - YOUR TURN (END

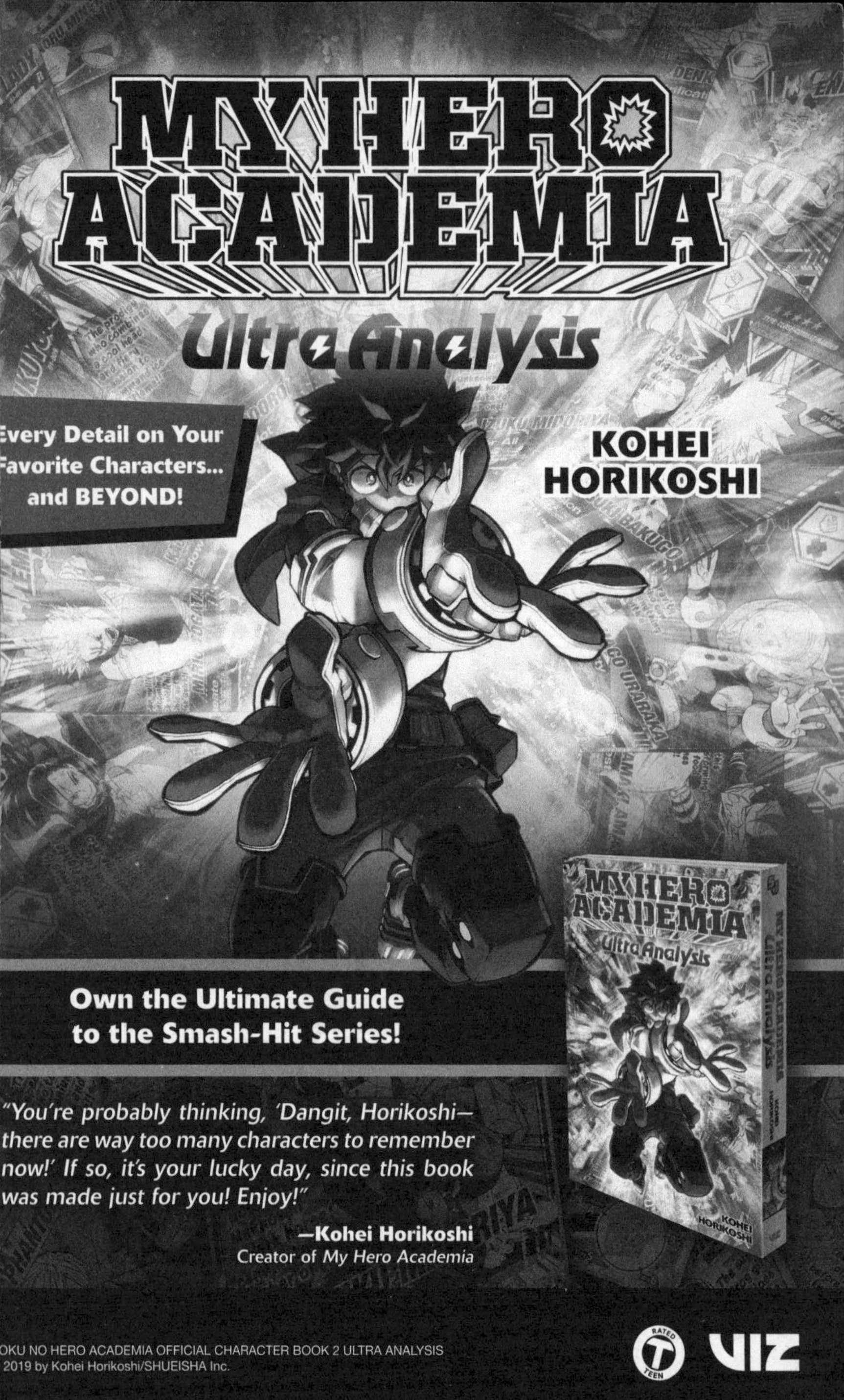
MY HERO ACADEMIA
Ultra Analysis
Every Detail on Your Favorite Characters... and BEYOND!
KOHEI HORIKOSHI
MY HERO ACADEMIA
Ultra Analysis
KOHEI HORIKOSHI
Own the Ultimate Guide to the Smash-Hit Series!
"You're probably thinking, 'Dangit, Horikoshi—there are way too many characters to remember now!' If so, it's your lucky day, since this book was made just for you! Enjoy!"
—Kohei Horikoshi
Creator of My Hero Academia
OKU NO HERO ACADEMIA OFFICIAL CHARACTER BOOK 2 ULTRA ANALYSIS
2019 by Kohei Horikoshi/SHUEISHA Inc.
RATED T TEEN
VIZ

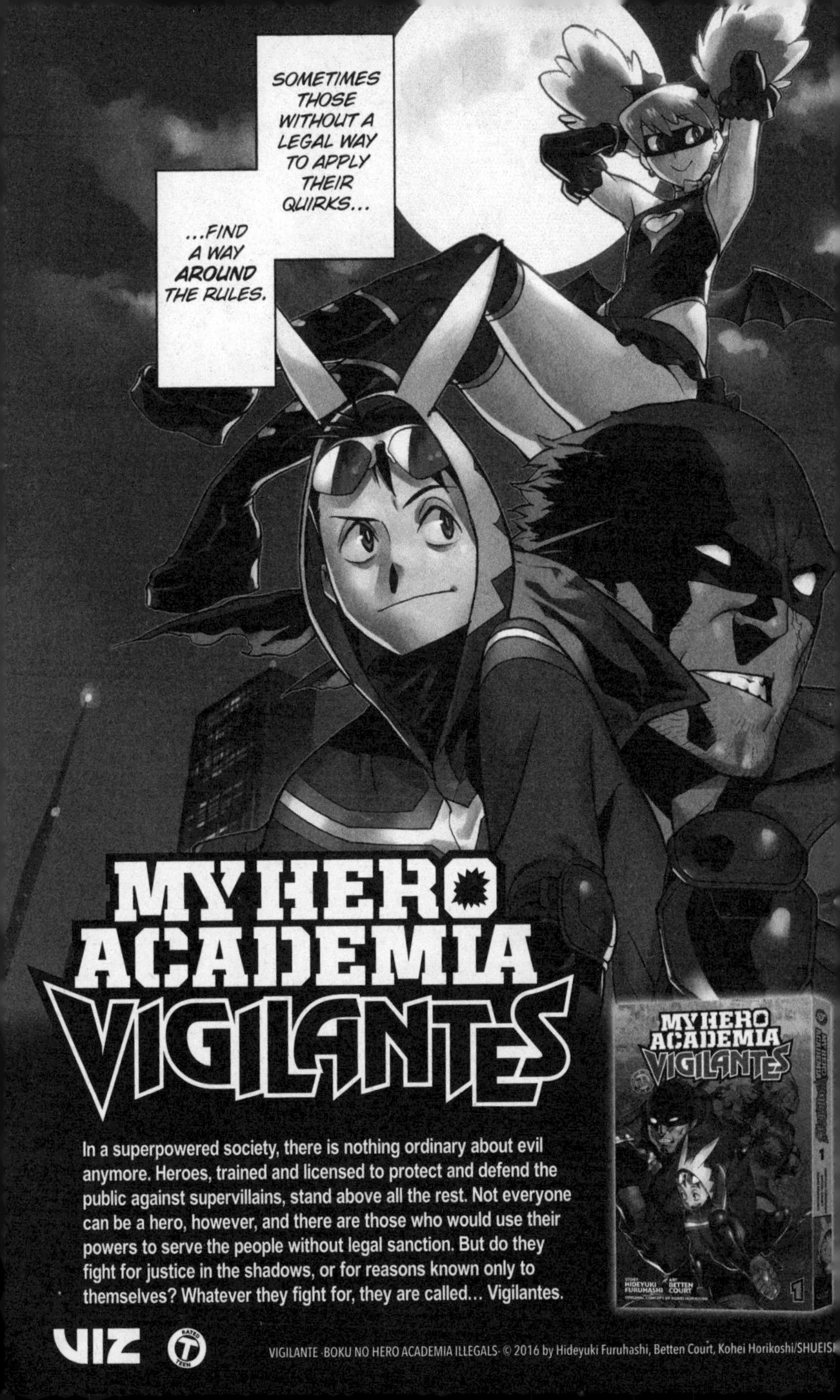

SOMETIMES THOSE WITHOUT A LEGAL WAY TO APPLY THEIR QUIRKS...
...FIND A WAY AROUND THE RULES.
MY HERO ACADEMIA VIGILANTES
In a superpowered society, there is nothing ordinary about evil anymore. Heroes, trained and licensed to protect and defend the public against supervillains, stand above all the rest. Not everyone can be a hero, however, and there are those who would use their powers to serve the people without legal sanction. But do they fight for justice in the shadows, or for reasons known only to themselves? Whatever they fight for, they are called... Vigilantes.
VIZ
VIGILANTE -BOKU NO HERO ACADEMIA ILLEGALS- © 2016 by Hideyuki Furuhashi, Betten Court, Kohei Horikoshi/SHUEIS

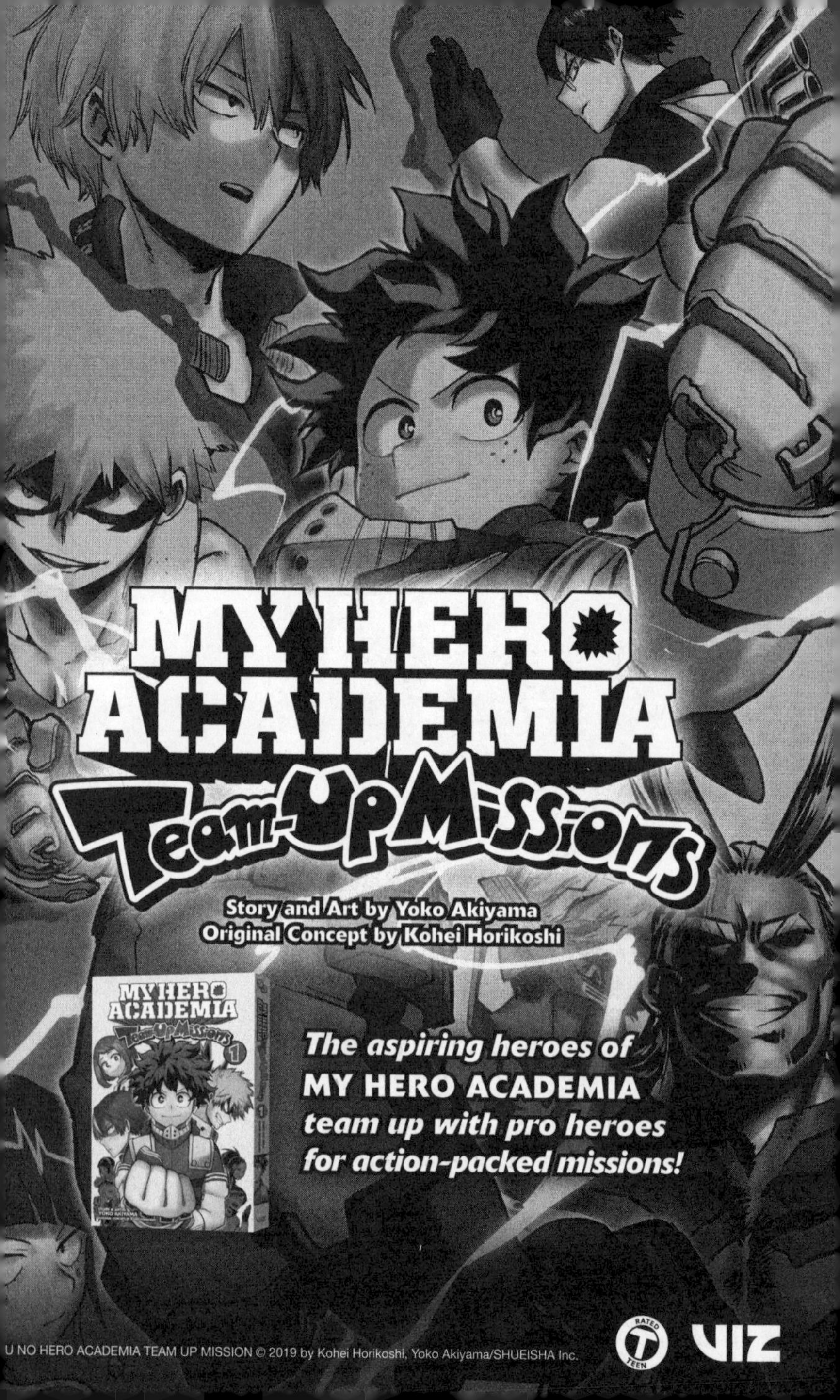
MY HERO ACADEMIA
Team-Up Missions
Story and Art by Yoko Akiyama
Original Concept by Kohei Horikoshi
MY HERO ACADEMIA Team-Up Missions 1
The aspiring heroes of
MY HERO ACADEMIA
team up with pro heroes
for action-packed missions!
RATED T TEEN
VIZ
U NO HERO ACADEMIA TEAM UP MISSION © 2019 by Kohei Horikoshi, Yoko Akiyama/SHUEISHA Inc.

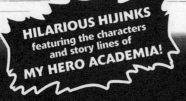

Dr. STONE

STORY BY
RIICHIRO INAGAKI

ART BY
BOICHI

...e fateful day, all of humanity turned to stone. Many millennia
...er, Taiju frees himself from petrification and finds himself
...rrounded by statues. The situation looks grim—until he runs
...o his science-loving friend Senku! Together they plan to restart
...ilization with the power of science!

Kafka wants to
clean up kaiju, but not
literally! Will a sudden
metamorphosis stand in
the way of his dream?

KAIJU NO. 8

STORY AND ART BY **NAOYA MATSUMOTO**

Kafka Hibino, a kaiju-corpse cleanup man, has always
dreamed of joining the Japan Defense Force, a military
organization tasked with the neutralization of kaiju. But
when he gets another shot at achieving his childhood dream,
he undergoes an unexpected transformation. How can he
fight kaiju now that he's become one himself?!

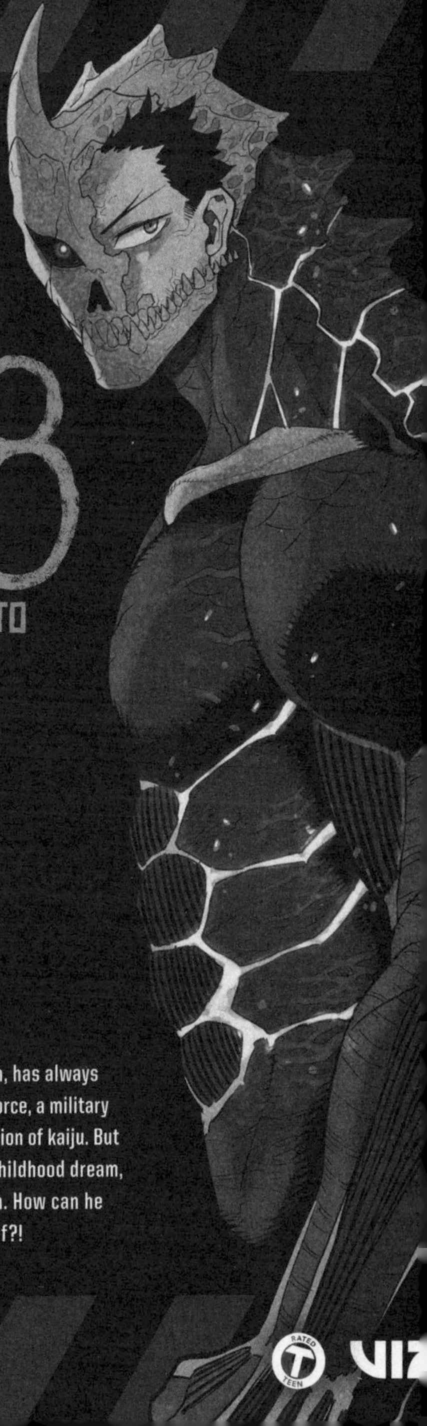

RATED **T** TEEN

VIZ

THE COMPLETE SAGA OF *DEMON SLAYER* ALL IN ONE EPIC BOX SET!

COMPLETE BOX SET

THIS BOX SET CONTAINS ALL 23 VOLUMES OF THE GLOBAL HIT *DEMON SLAYER* AS WELL AS A DOUBLE-SIDED POSTER AND AN EXCLUSIVE DATA BOOKLET WITH CHARACTER BIOS, GLOSSARY, AND STORYBOARDS.

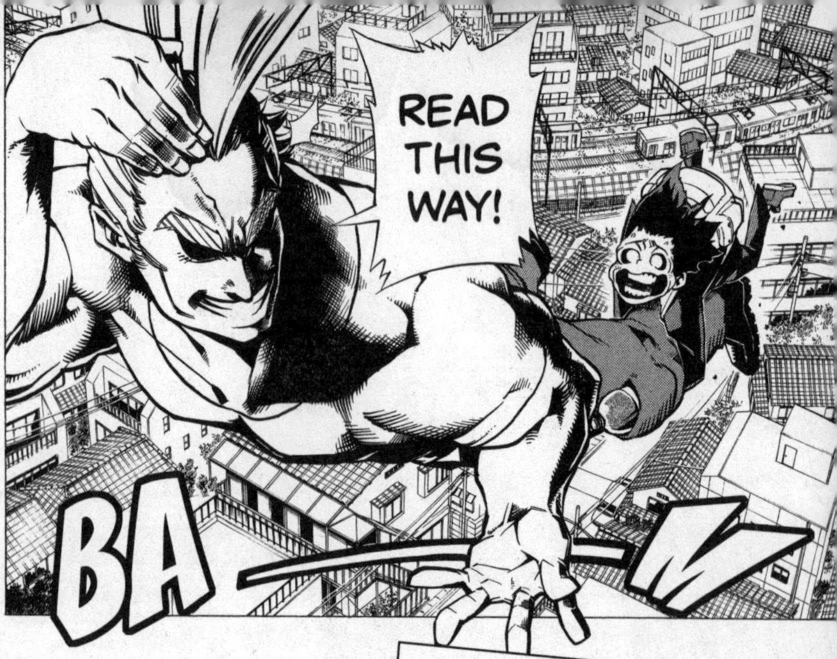
READ THIS WAY!
BA-M

MY HERO ACADEMIA

reads from right to left, starting in the upper-right corner. Japanese is read from right to left, meaning that action, sound effects, and word-balloon order are completely reversed from English order.

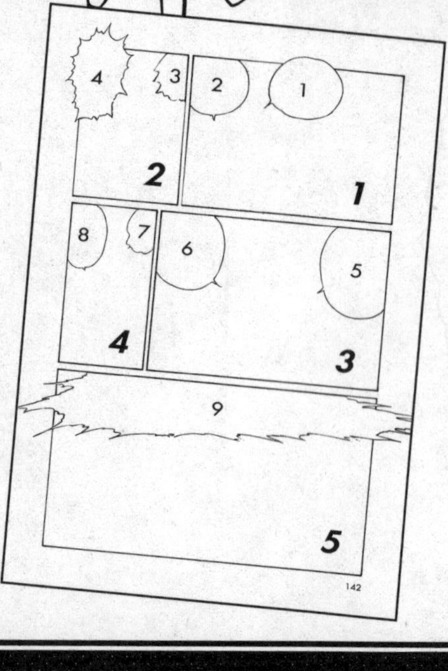